WEB DEVELOPER.COM®
GUIDE TO
STREAMING MULTIMEDIA

José Alvear

WILEY COMPUTER PUBLISHING

John Wiley & Sons, Inc.
New York • Chichester • Weinheim • Brisbane • Singapore • Toronto

Para mi Mamá y Papá, Marina and Julio.

Library of Congress Cataloging-in-Publication Data:

Alvear, José, 1968–
   Web developer.com guide to streaming multimedia / José Alvear.
       p.   cm
     "Wiley Computer Publishing."
     ISBN 0-471-24822-3 (pbk. / CD-ROM : alk. paper)
     1. Interactive media 2. Web sites--Design.
     I. Title.
   QA76.76.I59A44   1998
   006.7--dc21   97-48761
                                                                         CIP

Printed in the United States of America
10 9 8 7 6 5 4 3 2 1

CONTENTS

INTRODUCTION:
Defining Streaming Multimedia

Multimedia is all around us. It is on TV screens, theater screens and, of course, computer screens. You experience it every day, whether you listen to a radio broadcast, watch a television program, play a computer game, or surf the web. Computers, in particular, are great at multimedia; you can experience dazzling life-like graphics and CD-quality music.

Multimedia has flourished with the development of the Internet. Previously, multimedia was a private experience where you load a CD-ROM or wait to download a clip off the Internet. Today, you can log on to the Internet and listen to live radio programs from places half-way around the world. You can watch news clips whenever you please, or view the latest music video from your favorite rock group. All this with just a 28.8Kbps modem, Internet connection, and a multimedia computer.

Before we go any further, let's define Internet multimedia.

 Multimedia is one-way communication containing a mix of media elements, which can include any of the following: text, graphics, sound, video, and animation.

To put it another way, multimedia is somewhat like TV or radio broadcasting. You can view it, listen to it, and interact with it, but you can't talk back to it (well, you can, but it won't talk back). You use your remote control (or mouse) and choose to hear and see anything you want, and the data is sent to you automatically. If you're thinking of two-way interpersonal communications, then you're thinking of the telephone and its computer cousins, Internet telephony and videoconferencing. This book doesn't cover these topics.

This book specifically covers *streaming multimedia*, which allows for on-the-fly playing of audio, video, and animation files. First, it helps to know how Internet multimedia was experienced in the old days. A few years ago, you had to find a file, download it to your hard drive, and then play it. These files were usually very large, so downloading could take anywhere from 10 minutes to 1 hour. In 1995, "streaming" multimedia changed this forever.

Streaming multimedia means that data is being sent to a user's computer and displayed as it is being sent. Using a browser plug-in, you can now watch video-on-demand programs and even live images and sounds. Long download times are a thing of the past.

The impact of streaming multimedia isn't very apparent today, but will forever change the way you see the Internet. There will be hundreds if not thousands of streaming audio and video sites showing countless programs. You'll probably need a Web *TV Guide* to know the times and locations of your favorite programs. As streaming multimedia evolves, we'll someday see computers, multimedia, Internet, radio, and television combined into one multipurpose home appliance.

How This Book Is Organized

The book is organized into three sections:

1. An introduction to multimedia, streaming, and implementation.
2. In-depth guides to using the streaming software and how to make it work on your site.
3. A look to the future.

It is recommended that you read the book from beginning to end, especially if you are new to streaming multimedia. If you've used streaming programs before, you can go straight to Part 2, "The Programs: Learn What's Best for Your Site," which features the hands-on, solution-oriented chapters.

Part 1: Introducing Streaming Multimedia

This section begins by introducing you to multimedia over the Internet. It focuses on teaching you about the differences between traditional, downloadable multimedia and the growing world of streaming audio, video, and animation. You will learn how these programs work and how they differ from each other. You will also learn about client/server programs and server-less streaming programs.

Chapter 1, "The Basics of Multimedia on the Internet," introduces you to a wide range of streaming multimedia programs. If all you want to do is learn more about these programs and the different technologies available, you can review this chapter in depth. If you've already used streaming programs like RealAudio, you can skip this chapter.

In preparation for learning about implementing streaming multimedia on your website, Chapter 3, "Server Strategies: Choosing and Implementing the Right Streaming Multimedia System," describes the components you will use and helps you decide what system best suits your purposes. It shows you everything you need to know about the server side. You'll learn the difference between server and server-less technology.

Part 2: The Programs: Learn What's Best for Your Site

This section is the real meat-and-potatoes section. It is the largest section and is broken down into chapters that are devoted to certain topics, strategies, and individual programs. For example, if you have a small site and only want to put streaming audio on your site, you can check the Table of Contents to jump directly to that section.

Part 2 is further broken down into seven different sections:

Streaming Audio. This includes three popular streaming audio-only formats: LiquidAudio, TrueSpeech, and Audioactive.

The "Big Five" Streaming Video Programs. The "Big Five," as I've come to call them, are the biggest and most popular streaming video programs on the Internet. They are VivoActive, VDOLive, NetShow, RealVideo, and StreamWorks.

Other Streaming Video. The rest of the streaming video programs are presented here, including TrueStream, CVideoNow, GTS, Emblaze, and a chapter devoted to intranet applications.

Streaming VRML and 3-D. This chapter deals with streaming 3-D programs.

Streaming Email. Although not a big area yet, this chapter covers streaming email and some nonstreaming programs, too.

Streaming Animation. Animation is multimedia. In these two chapters, I introduce you to many streaming and almost-streaming animation programs.

Pseudo-streaming. This is for those times when you don't want to use expensive, proprietary systems. Pseudo-streaming doesn't stream in the traditional sense, but gives you shorter downloads and previews.

Be aware that if you are serious about streaming multimedia, you might want to read as many of these chapters as possible so you know what the programs are capable of doing. Who knows, you may actually be able to use a more complicated program, or something you never thought of using before. That's the fun part—discovering new programs, seeing how they work, and finding new streaming applications.

Part 3: Future Directions

This forward-looking section covers emerging technologies and issues that will affect streaming multimedia in the future. It focuses on the 10 most important developments that will change streaming multimedia and other important advances to the Internet. It also covers related topics like interactive TV, video-conferencing, bandwidth issues, and much more. It can help you decide which vendors are likely to stick around in the future. There is a guide to choosing a good streaming multimedia program.

Who Should Read This Book

This book is written for anyone who wants to put streaming audio, video, or multimedia on his or her Internet website or company intranet. It offers practical applications and easy-to-follow instructions to make your site a streaming multimedia site. The ideal reader can be a professional web developer at a Fortune 500 company, a web hobbyist with a personal homepage, and everyone in between.

Don't make the mistake of thinking that streaming multimedia isn't powerful because just about anyone can use it. It's just the opposite. Streaming multimedia is uncomplicated because there are so many approaches and solutions to a given problem. For example, do you need just web audio? Live video? On-demand multimedia for training? There are multiple solutions and multiple programs you should consider. One of your biggest problems will be deciding which program to use on your site. Do you want a simple and quick way to add streaming multimedia, or do you need the control and administration capabilities of a more complicated program? Find your answer by learning about what's available.

What should you know before reading this book? You should be familiar with the Internet and computer multimedia in general. It also helps if you're familiar with setting up and administering a web server, especially on a Windows NT or UNIX workstation. Finally, a working knowledge of HTML and web page creation is important.

If you've already used streaming multimedia, then you're a step ahead.

Tools You Will Need

This book focuses on using Windows95 and Windows NT systems, but the same concepts apply to Macintosh computers. Practically all of the streaming multimedia programs support Windows95, so if you don't have it, get it. Macintosh is supported by many of the programs, but it doesn't have the wide support that Windows95 does. On the server side, most programs require Windows NT Server 4.0, so if you're planning on using high-end systems, you'll need to be familiar with it. Also supported are UNIX and operating systems like Linux, Silicon Graphics' IRIX, and Sun Solaris.

First and foremost, you'll need a powerful, multimedia computer. You should already have software to watch movies or listen to audio. On the hardware end, Windows95 computers should have at least a Pentium 90MHz processor with about 16MB RAM and around 2GB of hard disk space. You can use older computers, but your results will vary. Naturally, a top-of-the-line Pentium II system is much better; streaming video can be very processor intensive. Of particular importance is hard drive space, because some movies can be very large—easily over 15MB. If you can, use SCSI drives because they are faster than IDE drives. Macintosh users should use a multimedia-ready Mac like a PowerPC with System 7.x (or higher), with at least 16MB of RAM and lots of hard drive space. Of course, you'll also need an Internet connection. If you using a modem, get the fastest you can, like the new 56Kbps modems.

In order to transfer movies from your VCR or camcorder to your computer, you'll need a video capture card and audio and video editing software. The software package used by most video professionals is Adobe Premiere. If you don't have a capture card to make your own audio or video, you can use multimedia files you already have on your computer. Also, the CD-ROM included with this book has sample audio and video files. Chapter 4, "Desktop Video: Capturing and Editing Computer Video," has more on creating, capturing, and editing audio and video.

What's on the CD-ROM

The CD-ROM will probably be your most valuable resource. It is jam-packed with lots of goodies. Included in the CD-ROM are:

- Demonstration versions of some of the popular streaming programs available. You'll be able to easily set up and run the client programs to get a feel for them. Just connect to the Internet and start viewing some streaming media. We won't include all the client programs because they change so often and new versions are being released all the time. We've added links to the vendors' websites so you can find the latest software available. Some companies also include server software so you can test their systems quickly.
- A glossary of terms used in streaming multimedia.
- Full manufacturers' contact information, including hyperlinks to their websites.
- As a companion to Chapter 4, there is a list and descriptions of video capture board makers, video camera manufacturers, video kits, and software like audio and video editing programs.
- There are also many tools, like audio editors, video editors, and other multimedia creation programs. Use these programs to fine-tune your files and make them ready for broadcast over the Internet.
- As mentioned earlier, some sample audio and video clips are included. Much of the work with streaming programs is in converting and compressing files, so you'll need a good supply of clips with which to practice. Don't forget, you can use the same clips on different programs to see how they compress and encode files. This is important because you'll be able to compare the original file with the converted file and see which one works best.

Overview of the Book

The purpose of this book is to show you which streaming multimedia systems are available and to help you decide which one you should use. Most chapters have step-by-step instructions on how to use a particular system. Other chapters with lots to cover simply show you what's available and how they work together.

When writing a book like this, it isn't possible to cover every nuance of a particular program. That's why you should try these programs first hand. Also, these programs tend to change often, so by the time you read this, some features will have disappeared while other features may have been added—the life cycle of

Internet software is usually very short. Always visit the vendor's website for more information or for updated software.

As you read this book, keep in mind that streaming multimedia shouldn't be viewed as a replacement for traditional radio or TV—use these programs as a supplement. The much talked-about convergence of PC and TV is coming, but it won't reach mainstream audiences for quite a while. This book gives you a sneak peek into the future. You have the opportunity to use this powerful technology today and even help shape its future.

I hope you read this book and use it to create entertaining and enthralling audio and video. Hopefully, you can attract hundreds, thousands, or even millions of visitors to your new streaming multimedia site.

May your hit counts be high. See you on the Web.

Acknowledgments

I've learned so much writing this book and it has been a great (though exhausting) experience. Thanks to everyone at Wiley for making this all possible, especially Carol Long for signing me on to this project. Special thanks to my editor Pam Sobotka for keeping me honest and staying on top of everything. (I don't know how you do it!) Thanks for being in constant communications with me and for helping with every facet of this book.

This book wouldn't be complete without the assistance of the many companies mentioned in this book. I'd like to thank the many PR people, agencies, and company representatives I've talked to and that have helped me with technical assistance and questions. I don't want to mention any names for fear of forgetting people, but you all know who you are.

I'd also like to thank my friends who understood why I was so busy while writing and was always unavailable for doing all the cool stuff. Sorry for all those unreturned messages and emails while I was in near-hibernation. I'll get back to everyone someday! A very special thanks to Kimberly for being a great friend and for always being so supportive. Finally, thanks to my family, especially mom and dad, who sometimes saw me once a day even though I was just in the next room. This wouldn't have been possible without them. Last but not least, thanks to my bro, sister-in-law, and especially my niece Stephanie who always reminds me what's really important in this life.

PART ONE

INTRODUCING STREAMING MULTIMEDIA

THE BASICS OF
Multimedia on the Internet

The history of multimedia on the Internet can be traced back to the very early personal computers—Apple and IBM computers. Early IBM computers, for example, had primitive multimedia; graphics were monochrome and sound was just a series of beeps. Watching a movie on your computer was just a dream. As computers migrated from office use to home use, everything changed. Home computers became multimedia enhanced, and CD-ROM drives arrived, making multimedia much more accessible. The arrival of CD-ROMs helped bring about the massive revolution in games and computer graphics, because they allowed huge amounts of storage. Today, many multimedia computers come standard with high-resolution monitors, speedy CD-ROM drives, microphones, speakers, and 3-D graphics cards. Computers can now display millions of colors at the same time, so you can watch a full-screen movie with crystal-clear, CD-quality, stereo sound.

As personal computers advanced, so did the Internet. When the Web was first invented in 1989, it was just a bunch of text, and you could surf the Web using a text-only browser—things were pretty drab. The beginning of web multimedia can be attributed to the invention of the graphical web browser. In February 1993, a small group at the University of Illinois at Champaign-Urbana developed a graphical interface to the World Wide Web called Mosaic. Mosaic displayed graphics and text on the same web page and made the Web as easy to use as using your mouse to point and click to your next destination. Later, Mosaic technology was used on many operating systems, eventually leading to today's advanced browsers like Netscape's Navigator and Microsoft's Internet Explorer.

Mosaic and its predecessors gave rise to web multimedia. Whereas watching a movie from your computer CD-ROM was simple and quick, viewing a movie over the Internet posed a big problem. Sure, you could download a movie to your hard drive, but files were often too large, sometimes reaching up to 2MB in length. Downloading a 2MB movie could take hours using a 14.4Kbps modem. Another problem was getting and installing the right multimedia player for every type of file. By the time you downloaded the movie clip and installed the player, you probably forgot why you downloaded the file in the first place. Clearly, something had to be done. There needed to be a better way.

Streaming Multimedia

The solution was *streaming*. Progressive Networks released the Internet's first streaming player, RealAudio, in April 1995, which allowed users to listen to audio files as they were being downloaded. This streaming technology revolutionized web multimedia—instant audio was now just a click away. Granted, the quality of RealAudio transmissions wasn't as good as downloadable audio, but at least you didn't have to wait forever. RealAudio was an instant success, and in a matter of days, numerous radio stations from all around the country began using RealAudio to broadcast live radio feeds all over the Internet. Radio broadcasting no longer served just a narrow market; with RealAudio, it could transmit its signal all around the world (see Figure 1.1).

Figure 1.1 This is the RealPlayer, which can play live and prerecorded audio and video.

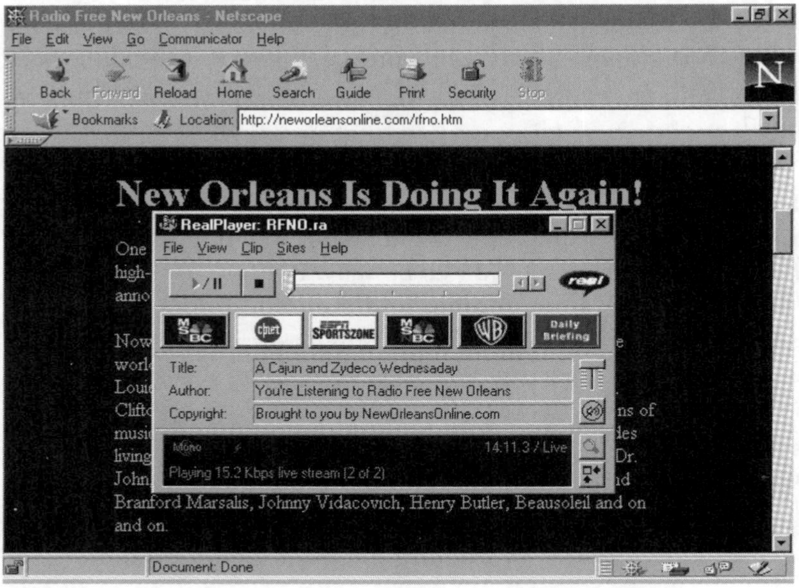

While audio broadcasting bloomed, video was pretty much ignored. The first Internet streaming video player was Xing Technology's StreamWorks, released in August 1995 (see Figure 1.2). It was a remarkable achievement, but its poor video quality and small video windows didn't impress many people. Many StreamWorks movies resembled slide shows with unsynchronized audio and video tracks; however, much of the problem with video quality had to do with the limited bandwidth, especially 14.4Kbps modems.

In late 1995, a new streaming audio and video system called VDOLive was introduced by VDOnet Corp., which greatly improved video quality. By mid 1996, more and more websites started showing prerecorded and live streaming audio and video. Perhaps the most anticipated introduction was in early 1997, when Progressive Networks (now called RealNetworks) released RealVideo along with a new, all-in-one audio/video player called the RealPlayer. In no time flat, dozens of websites like Virgin Records, MSNBC, C-Span, and ABC immediately jumped to the RealVideo format to transmit live events and prerecorded video. Eventually, more and more companies jumped onto the audio/video streaming bandwagon. Streaming audio and video are now very common on websites as well as on company intranets.

Figure 1.2 Xing's StreamWorks was the first Internet streaming video player.

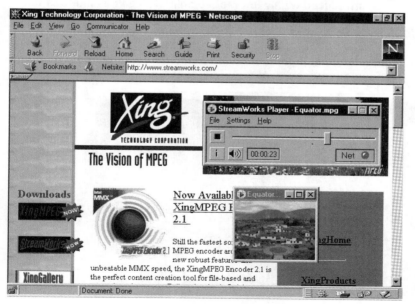

Another early entry to web multimedia was Shockwave, introduced in late 1995 by Macromedia. With the Shockwave player plug-in installed, you could experience interactive, CD-ROM-quality graphics, animation, and sound on the Web. Although Shockwave didn't provide audio or video, it allowed something new—interactivity. Users could click and play games or view animated graphics (see Figure 1.3).

Unfortunately, Shockwave files had to be loaded completely before being played, and downloading could take from 5 to 10 minutes. This changed in early 1997, when Shockwave added audio and streaming capability. Today, there are a handful of vendors who have released competing streaming and nonstreaming web animation programs. Many feature animations, sound, and graphics just like Shockwave. Even Java, the popular cross-platform programming language, can be used to create rich and interactive websites.

Meanwhile, other areas of multimedia were also flourishing. In 1994, 3-D on the Web through VRML (Virtual Reality Modeling Language) was introduced. VRML is the industry standard for 3-D over the Internet, and is comparable to HTML in that it is the language used to interpret 3-D images. With VRML, you can see computer graphic models of objects or even entire 3-D scenes or worlds. The worlds are similar to the 3-D, first-person games like Doom; you can move around

Figure 1.3 Shockwave introduced highly interactive animated games like this one.

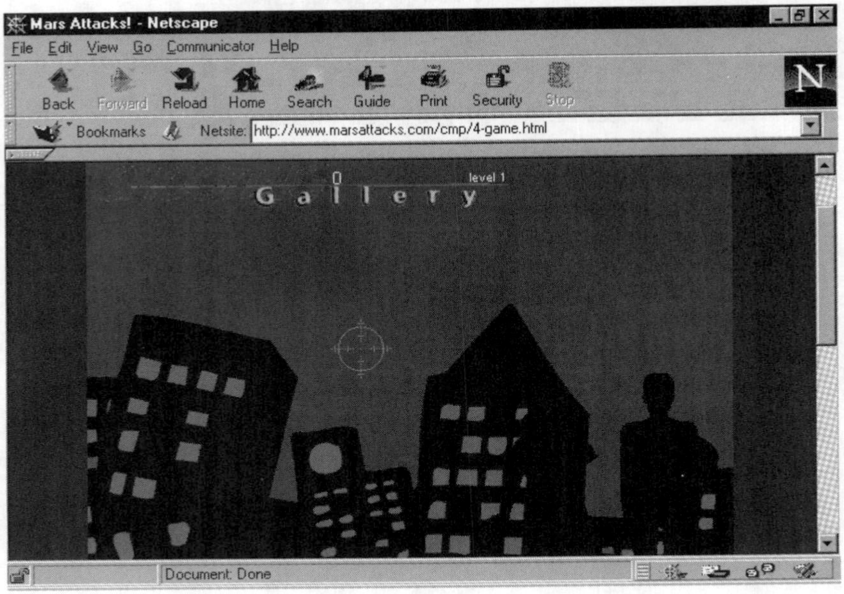

or walk in these worlds (see Figure 1.4). You can also rotate or move objects in any direction to see them from all angles.

VRML has since advanced so you can hear sounds, jump to websites, or watch animations of characters moving around or speaking. You can also visit multiuser VRML worlds where you can meet and talk to other people in real time. In the beginning, VRML files had to be completely downloaded before viewing them, but now there are some players that can handle streaming VRML files. It won't be long before all VRML players will be able to stream.

The smallest segment of streaming multimedia is *streaming email*. Just one vendor makes a streaming email program that can truly stream audio and video. In many ways, this can be seen as audio- or video-conferencing by email, because people can send video or audio images back and forth to each other. So far, streaming email hasn't been very popular, but it is good for when you need to exchange audio and video with other users.

The Latest Buzz

So what's new with streaming multimedia? Interactivity seems to be leading the way. RealVideo added *video hotlinks* so that clicking on a certain part of the screen loads a

Figure 1.4 You can move around in VRML worlds, much like you can in 3-D games like Duke Nukem 3D and Quake.

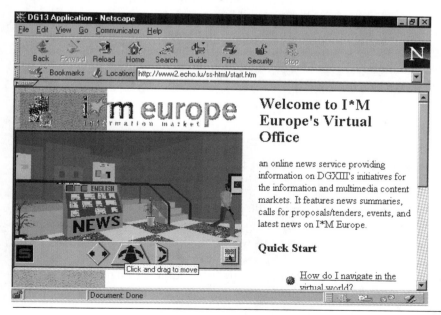

new video or sound clip, takes you to a new web page, or performs other tasks. Another promising program is called Liquid Audio. This music-only streaming player lets you listen to a song and then, if you like it, purchase it and download a CD-quality version to your hard drive. Another new type of multimedia is 360-degree panoramic images. Apple released QuickTime VR, a program that allows you to see a 360-degree view of a photographic image. You can zoom in and out, or pan left or right to see the entire area. Depending on the file, you can also look up and down to see tall objects or look at the ground. Panoramic images usually use photographs stitched together to form a complete view.

As you can see, streaming multimedia is more than just audio and video. There are interactive, cartoon-like animations, 3-D worlds, and panoramic images that all use streaming. Without a doubt, the age of downloading multimedia has come to an end, and the age of streaming multimedia has begun.

Downloading Traditional Multimedia

Before we enter the world of streaming multimedia, we must understand the world of traditional downloadable multimedia. Fortunately, downloading multimedia has become very simple—just choose the file, save it to your hard disk, and then *wait*. You'll have to wait for a very long time until it has finished downloading, and then play the file.

Most files that you find on the Web are MIME-typed. MIME (Multiple Internet Mail Extension) originally was used for transmitting images and files via email, but it has since been used by browsers to allow transferring of a large number of file types. Some of the most common MIME types are HTML pages, plain-text files, images, movies, and audio files. When your browser encounters a MIME type that it does not display itself, it does one of the following:

- It begins transmitting the file and opens it with a corresponding application that you previously selected.
- It allows you to save the file to disk.
- It asks you which application you want to open the file type with.
- It allows you to cancel the transfer.

In effect, your browser can then handle practically any file transfer, even those that it would normally not display, by using an external (or helper) application or a plug-in. Plug-ins and helper applications were first introduced with version 2.0 of Netscape Navigator, and they allowed browsers to view and access external files like audio files, movies, Microsoft Word, or any other application.

Plug-ins are small programs installed in your browser that allow you to load new MIME types. They are not complete applications, just tiny applications that load inside a web page to expand the use of your browser. (See the next section for more on plug-ins.) For example, one of the most popular plug-ins is Shockwave. Shockwave isn't an external program; rather, it's a plug-in that enhances the browser. With the Shockwave plug-in installed, you can watch many interactive and entertaining websites. In fact, many of the client programs in this book are browser plug-ins.

Helper applications are external programs, like Adobe Acrobat Reader or Microsoft Word, that load when you click on a PDF or DOC file. For example, you can set up your browser to automatically load Microsoft Word whenever it encounters a DOC file, or you can just save the file to your disk and open it later with Microsoft Word or any other word processing software.

Your browser can handle many MIME types, and you can install or uninstall plug-ins at any time. To see what MIME types your Netscape Navigator 4.0 browser understands, choose Edit/Preferences and then open the Navigator tree and select Applications. You can view all your helper applications and plug-ins there and even associate new file types with an application.

Plug-Ins, ActiveX Controls, and More

Plug-ins have become an industry in themselves, and there are literally hundreds available.

The reliance on plug-ins or using external applications is what keeps many users from accessing streaming multimedia. Many times, people are too busy to keep up with the latest plug-ins or don't even know they exist. Thankfully, new advances in plug-in technology make it easier to find plug-ins. Netscape, for example, can detect when a plug-in is not installed and can send you to the appropriate web page to download it. Once you download and install a plug-in, you must restart your browser and then access the page again.

Managing plug-ins can be difficult, especially with so many different ones available. If you download two programs that can read QuickTime movies, for example, there may be conflicts. Microsoft's Internet Explorer uses plug-ins as well, but it mostly uses something called *ActiveX controls*. ActiveX controls are nothing more than Microsoft's answer to Netscape's plug-ins since they perform the same functions. The good thing about ActiveX controls is that they can download and install themselves automatically. Once that is done, the page continues downloading, and you can see the whole web page.

Another way of viewing streaming multimedia is with *Java*. Java is an object-oriented programming language invented by Sun Microsystems in 1995. Programmers can create tiny Java applications or *applets* that can be executed by both Navigator and Internet Explorer while browsing a web page. Java effectively eliminates the need for plug-ins, external applications, or ActiveX controls. Instead, the applet will load so you can view a movie or listen to an audio file. As long as you use a Java-enabled browser, you can use any computer, such as Windows, Mac, or UNIX machines. That means that one Java applet can theoretically run on all operating systems. The future of third-party applications may well lie with Java but so far, not too many streaming multimedia vendors use Java for playback. Perhaps one day, Java can replace the need for all plug-ins and ActiveX controls.

Multimedia File Formats

Plug-ins are used to view multimedia files, and you need to download and install them in order to download and see audio, video, animation, and other file formats. This section is an introduction to the popular downloadable multimedia file formats. It is separated into two sections: audio and video. More information on digital audio and video can be found in Chapter 4, "Desktop Audio and Video: Capturing, Editing, and Compression."

All about Audio

First on the scene was audio, simply because it was easier than video and required less bandwidth. The main audio formats being used on the Internet today are AU, AIFF, WAV, MPEG, and MIDI files. The three most popular are AU, AIFF, and WAV, which are natively supported by UNIX, Mac, and Windows computers, respectively. Although these three seem different, they really don't differ very much at all—they all play very good quality audio, from simple speech to CD-quality music. They exist simply because each computer vendor wanted its own audio format for its operating system. Thanks to the expansion of the Internet, these once proprietary files are now rather universal, and with the right players, you can play all of these files on any UNIX, Mac, or Windows computer.

MPEG and MIDI files, on the other hand, don't belong to any computer. They are cross-platform file types that have been invented by various organizations to standardize audio on a wide range of computers. These five audio types are discussed next in more detail.

AU

For a long time, the most popular audio format on the Internet was the AU sound file. It started out as a UNIX (Sun and NeXT) file type because the Internet was a UNIX world back then. Now AU files aren't as popular, but there are still many sites that use them—usually educational sites or older sites that still use UNIX.

AIFF

The AIFF (Audio IFF) file was developed by Apple and is also quite popular on many other platforms besides the Macintosh. Any computer with the proper player can play AIFF files. AIFF files have a .AIF extension.

WAV

On Windows computers, the standard is Wave files, which use a .WAV extension. If you're using a Windows computer, you already know WAV files, the Windows standard, developed by Microsoft and IBM as an answer to Apple's AIFF files. Because of the popularity of the Web and Windows computers, WAV files are very commonplace, perhaps now eclipsing the AU format. Windows95 comes with its own built-in player and recorder, so you can create WAV files very easily if you have a microphone.

MPEG Audio

The newest audio file type is MPEG (pronounced M-peg), which stands for Moving Pictures Experts Group. MPEG is an organization that generates standards for digital video and audio compression. Its compression is very good: MPEG can shrink an audio file to 1/96th of its original size (a 96:1 compression ratio). MPEG audio files have the extension .MP2 or .MP3. To play them, you need an MPEG audio player like WinAmp or Xaudio. You can find free or shareware players that can play MPEG audio files for a variety of operating systems.

MIDI

MIDI (Musical Instrument Digital Interface) is different from the formats just discussed. It is a multiplatform file type for music only. Musicians can create MIDI songs on a MIDI-compatible synthesizer that can connect to a computer for further editing and creation. Many computers can now play MIDI files. You've probably heard some MIDI music; it is essentially instrumental (meaning no voice), synthesized music consisting of multiple tracks like drums, guitars, horns, and so forth. Many games use it to add music. There is no actual sound content in a MIDI file; instead, it stores information about what musical notes to play in order to recreate the music. Think of MIDI as sheet music. When you play a MIDI file, it sends instructions to the MIDI sound card or player to reproduce the music. Some MIDI files won't sound exactly the same on different computers; reproduction depends on the type of player or sound card you are using.

Because MIDI files contain no audio data, they are very small files. Typical files can be just about 20–40KB long. By comparison, WAV and AIFF files are very large because they store the actual sounds themselves, not just the notes. Although it is a downloadable format, MIDI can mimic streaming because of the small file sizes. Navigator and Internet Explorer can automatically play MIDI files that are embedded into a web page with hardly any download time. MIDI files have a .MID extension.

All about Video

Video files come in three varieties: QuickTime, Video for Windows, and MPEG. You've probably encountered one or all of these movie files. Typical file sizes range from 1MB to 3MB for short, 30- to 60-second movies. To keep sizes small, multi-media authors sometimes capture lower frame rates or don't use an audio track. Unless you have a screaming-fast computer, you won't see full-screen video—to conserve bandwidth, movies usually have very small windows. Some video windows are the size of a large postage stamp, but more common are sizes ranging from 160 × 120 to 320 × 40 pixels (about the size of a square Post-It note). This is fine for casual viewing, but when you're used to watching full-screen TV, it can be a little disappointing. Next are some details on these three video formats.

QuickTime

QuickTime is the jewel of the Mac and is what makes Macs so popular with artists and developers (see Figure 1.5). Its sophisticated, time-based engine makes it easy to create and edit. Apple makes a QuickTime for Windows player so Windows users can view QuickTime movies as well. QuickTime movies have a .QT or .MOV file extension. More information and QuickTime drivers and players are available for download at quicktime.apple.com.

QuickTimeVR (QTVR) is Apple's panoramic extension to QuickTime. It doesn't play a movie like ordinary QuickTime files—it is basically one large, static panoramic scene. QTVR works this way: A series of photographic images are stitched together to create a panoramic, 360-degree view. Once you click on a QTVR image, you must wait for it to download before you can see the panoramic scene. You can zoom in and out, move around, or even click on objects to identify them. You can download the free QTVR player for Macs and Windows at quicktimevr.apple.com.

Figure 1.5 QuickTime is the standard video format for Macs.

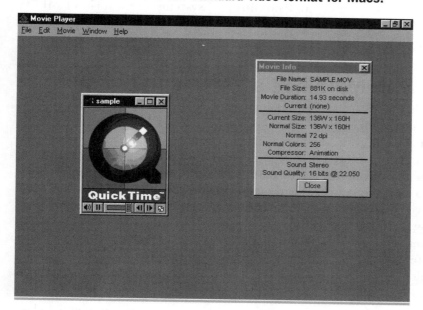

Video for Windows

Microsoft invented its own video file type for the Windows operating system called, appropriately enough, Video for Windows. These files have a .AVI extension. (AVI stands for Audio Video Interleave.) Although AVI movies do have compression, they tend to be the biggest of all video formats; therefore, they take the longest time to download. You can find many AVI files on the Web because more and more people are using Windows 3.1 or 95.

MPEG

The third major file type is MPEG, which uses a rather powerful but lossy (meaning it loses a good deal of quality) video compression scheme. As with MPEG audio, video MPEG compresses files into very small files. Unfortunately, MPEG ranks third in popularity among webmasters and users. MPEG movies have the extension .MPG.

To watch MPEG files, you need an appropriate viewer or an MPEG video add-on card. Using an MPEG video card will give you super-fast and smooth video, even a full-screen view, because the card handles all the compression and decompression. For those who don't want a video card, you can just use software to handle the decompression; an MPEG player handles it all, but you will need a powerful processor.

MPEG has industry-wide support, including the support of many noncomputer industries. So far, DVD, cable, and satellite TV systems use a form of MPEG compression. For more information on MPEG audio and video, visit the semi-official MPEG site at www.mpeg.org.

Working with Multimedia Players

Keep in mind that there are many more audio and video types, but the ones covered here are the most popular. Most state-of-the-art browsers like Internet Explorer and Navigator have built-in audio players that can play many audio file types. Watching video can be more difficult because you usually have to download the newest players and drivers for the format you want to see. Internet Explorer 3.0 for Windows95 can install a very good media player called ActiveMovie—it plays all sound and video files mentioned here. ActiveMovie can even "pseudo-stream" movies by allowing you to play a file as it is being downloaded. QuickTime (along with some other vendors) uses pseudo-streaming to make *fast-start* movies. These play the first few seconds as a preview to see if you want to download the whole file. The problem is that not every player recognizes movies that are optimized as fast-start.

Where can you find audio and video players? There are many commercial players available, like InterVU, Duplexx Software's Net Toob, and Xing's MPEG Player. There are also countless free and shareware programs available. For the very latest players, visit sites that have shareware collections like TUCOWS (www.tucows.com), CWSApps List (cws.internet.com/), Filez (www.filez.com), and Shareware.com (www.shareware.com).

If you encounter an unknown file type or just want to convert one type of file to another, you can use a converter program. Search the file repositories just mentioned to find a good converter.

 For Mac users who want to play and convert audio files, use Syntrillium's CoolEdit (www.syntrillium.com). SoundApp is a good freeware Mac converter. Windows users can listen to many audio formats with GoldWave (www.goldwave.com) or with ActiveMovie.

Streaming versus Downloading

Both streaming and downloadable media have their pluses and minuses. Despite the focus of this book, there are some good things about downloading files. For example, with downloadable media you can download and save files to your hard drive so you can listen to them at your leisure or send them to others. Streaming files usually can't be saved for later listening—they are meant to be disposable. You're meant to use them now and forget about them.

A big plus is that downloadable files are standards based. Practically any computer can read and play any format with the right player. Open standards allow sharing of files on various types of computers and configurations. Proprietary file types like those that typically make up streaming media make sharing files difficult. For example, many streaming programs and players don't have players or plug-ins available for UNIX or Mac platforms. Practically all the streaming players mentioned in this book work on Windows95 machines. Ignoring a platform or operating system is a big mistake since it will limit your audience.

Downloadable audio and video has much better quality than streaming media. You can usually expect much clearer movies with faster frame rates and richer audio. If you've ever experienced streaming multimedia, you will have noticed the lower audio and video quality.

Last, from a webmaster's point of view, there are no restrictive or expensive bandwidth requirements. If you want to show good quality streaming media to a large number of people, you'll need lots of bandwidth. A bigger connection allows you to have more simultaneous visitors, and it also helps you transmit nonstreaming media from your regular web server. Essentially, streaming multimedia puts the burden of the bandwidth on the web developer's side. With downloadable media, the bandwidth burden is on the user—web developers simply upload multimedia files to the web server and let the visitors worry about downloading them.

Streaming multimedia takes much more resources and time to set up than downloadable media. You'll need to know about web servers, bandwidth availability, and networking, as well as editing and compression. Don't forget about price. Streaming multimedia can be very expensive, but worth every penny for certain applications.

Despite all these points, you'll realize that streaming is the best way to add multimedia to your site. Downloading files is just no fun and takes too much time. With streaming, you can broadcast long, feature-length videos or short, one-minute clips. File size doesn't matter because there is no time lost downloading. Perhaps more importantly, streaming multimedia opens the world to live broadcasting. Anyone with a good streaming program can transmit live audio and video all around the world to friends, family, or strangers. It's like having your own personal radio and television studio right in your computer.

Is Streaming Ready for Prime Time?

Streaming multimedia has been with us since 1995. Is it really ready for mainstream use? I'd say a very definite "yes." In the beginning, sound quality was rather fuzzy, and RealAudio was not well suited for music—it often sounded like an AM radio station. Audio quality is now very good, even when used over 28.8Kbps dial-up lines. Some newer programs can deliver CD-quality audio needing just a 128Kbps connection. Still, there are naysayers who claim that streaming multimedia over the Internet is not ready for prime time.

Perhaps the most maligned of all is streaming video. This is somewhat unfair because streaming video over the Internet is relatively new; it just hasn't reached the same level of sophistication as streaming audio. More importantly, use and acceptance of streaming video have not had support from webmasters and users alike. The problems, which are discussed next, are lack of bandwidth, quality, and cost.

Bandwidth and Quality

Bandwidth is directly related to the problem of low quality. Unfortunately, the Internet's popularity is causing its problems. As more and more users connect to the Web, there are more busy signals and bigger bottlenecks. These bottlenecks most often occur at peak usage times, such as noon to 3 PM Eastern Standard Time (EST).

The real bottleneck, however, is probably your own modem and computer. If you're using a 28.8Kbps modem to connect to the Internet, you're just not getting enough data to see a high-quality, streaming video image. At 28.8Kbps, herky-jerky video, some fuzziness, and even skipping audio are quite common. Also, the sound and video may be unsynchronized, so movies may resemble cheaply dubbed foreign films. You'll see a definite improvement with the new 56Kbps modems, but it still won't be very clear or completely in sync. Nor will you be able to see full-screen video.

The best way to get really good, TV-quality video is to use fast Internet access like a cable modem, T1 line, or even ISDN. Although you may hit some slow streaming servers, you can watch TV-quality video and receive CD-quality audio with some of the programs mentioned in this book.

Yet another way to get high-quality audio and video is on an intranet. Most company intranets use 10BaseT Ethernet, which has network speeds of 10Mbps. Others have already moved to Fast Ethernet (100BaseT), where bandwidth is 100Mbps. Newer technologies like Gigabyte Ethernet and ATM promise to offer multiple megabytes, or gigabytes, of bandwidth, and at these speeds, you'll see the true power of streaming multimedia. You'll have no problem receiving full-screen, full-motion, TV-quality video along with CD-quality audio.

For most of us still using 28.8Kbps, 33.6Kbps, or 56Kbps dial-up Internet access, we'll have to continue suffering with scratchy audio and fuzzy video until high-bandwidth lines reach more homes.

Cost

The second consideration is cost. Setting up a website with streaming audio or video is a costly and somewhat complex project. Besides recording and editing the audio and video files, you must also have the proper hardware and software. It requires constant testing and retesting to make sure everything is working properly. Setting up live broadcasts is even more costly and time-consuming. You need to be familiar with audio and video principles, broadcasting, networking, computers, and streaming software to do live broadcasting.

Cost is a consideration because many streaming vendors charge by the stream or by the number of users. Client/server solutions are much more expensive because they allow you to scale the system to your needs—the more streams you need, the more it costs. Prices for streaming systems range from completely free to as high as $13,000 for a high-end, customizable, streaming video network. Server-less systems are considerably cheaper, usually ranging from free to a few hundred dollars.

What Can You Do with Streaming Audio and Video?

Now that you know what streaming multimedia is all about and know the problems associated with it, why would you still want to use it on your site? There are plenty of reasons. Here are some common uses for streaming multimedia. Can you imagine these uses on your site? Can you imagine other uses?

Want to buy a CD? Go to CDNow (www.cdnow.com) and search for your favorite artists. Chances are there will be streaming audio samples so you can preview that new CD.

Want to hear the latest news? You can listen to broadcasts from ABC News, C|Net, MSNBC, or just about any other organization. Most news stories are updated numerous times a day. Alternately, you can listen to news as it happens by tuning in to actual police scanner transmissions from major U.S. cities at www.policescanner.com.

Want some local content from your hometown? Tune into AudioNet (www.audionet.com) and browse through listings of live radio broadcasts—including some Internet-only broadcasts (see Figure 1.6). Just choose your city, state, or country and listen to news from all around the world.

Did you miss going to that computer conference on the opposite coast? Some conferences like Comdex and Mecklermedia's Internet World broadcast live or "tape-delayed" shows of key speeches and presentations over the Internet. Now you can just stay at work and save hotel costs and airfare. Other conferences keep their movies archived so you can access them at any time, even when you're at home.

Can't make it to the arena to watch the Knicks? Tune into ESPNSportZone (espn.sportszone.com) and hear the live audio broadcasts of every single NBA game.

Want to view a movie preview? Go to Metro Goldwyn Mayer's homepage (www.mgm.com) or Film.com (www.film.com) and watch sneak

Figure 1.6 AudioNet is the place to go to tune into audio broadcasts. Browse through hundreds of radio stations or listen to an Internet-only broadcast.

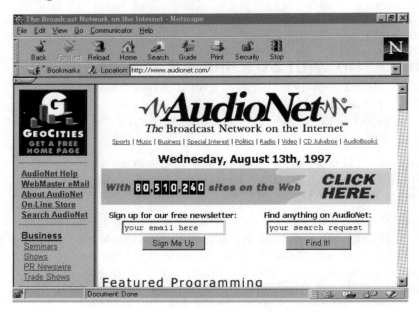

previews of upcoming movies. Then listen to some exclusive interviews with the cast and crew.

Want to see a classic Bugs Bunny cartoon? Just visit the Warner Bros. site (www.warnerbros.com) and view the cartoon of the day.

Summary

As you can see, streaming multimedia has many uses—both fun and practical. There are so many other applications, it's just too lengthy to list them all. RealAudio and RealVideo are currently the *de facto* standards over the Internet, but there are other alternative solutions that are easier to implement and less costly. Because there are so many companies creating competing streaming multimedia applications, you have many more choices. The market is really booming for intranet video systems, and many companies are seeing the benefits of adding live and on-demand audio and video to their intranets.

The next chapter introduces you to the streaming multimedia players so you can see what else is available, and look at them from the user's point of view. Later, once your appetite has been whetted, you'll learn more about the server side, or how to begin implementing the systems on your site.

Streaming multimedia is an industry that is still in its infancy but is ready to break out into the mainstream. The real breakthrough will come when everyone has high-speed access to the Internet. 28.8Kbps or 56Kbps modems are just not fast enough. We have not yet begun to imagine all of the possibilities of streaming multimedia. We've come a long way from the chintzy, monochrome computer displays of yesteryear. If you think of how much the industry has grown in the last few years, you can see why the future looks so bright. It's hard to predict how computers and multimedia will change in the future, but it seems practically limitless.

THE CLIENT SIDE:
Introducing the Programs

Knowing about streaming multimedia software, especially trying to figure out what to use on your site, requires that you know all about a specific program. This chapter helps you familiarize yourself with all the major audio, video, multimedia, 3-D, and other streaming players. Not every single streaming multimedia player is listed here—just some of the more popular players along with some promising newcomers.

Concentrating on the popular programs is important if your defined user base is Internet users. You'll have a much wider audience, since more users are apt to have the right player already installed or may have at least heard of the program. If you're designing an intranet with streaming multimedia, you have a much wider choice. Not only won't you be limited by bandwidth, but you can also use less popular or newer programs that accomplish tasks better or at less cost.

This chapter doesn't have much on the server side; it is just for client-side programs. However, using these players will give you a good idea about what each program can and cannot do. This discovery process is very important, so test these programs thoroughly and try to use as many as you can.

The goal of this chapter is to show you what's available and to help you decide what you want to use on your site.

Downloading and Installation

Most of the client programs are available for download as Netscape plug-ins, but there are also some ActiveX controls and external helper applications. For best results, use the newest browsers available, like Microsoft Internet Explorer 4.0 and Netscape Navigator 4.0.

Also, make sure you're using powerful computers. Although hardware requirements vary from program to program, the better the system, the better your performance. For optimal Windows95 performance, use a Pentium 90mHz or better, with 16MB of RAM and, of course, speakers and sound card. Macintosh users have it easier: just a PowerPC Mac with System 7.x (or higher), with 16MB RAM and plenty of hard drive space. You can still use the programs in this chapter on low-end systems, but performance (especially streaming video) will be drastically affected.

General Tips

Since you'll be installing and using lots of plug-ins, the following tips should help, whether you're using Navigator, Internet Explorer, or any other plug-in-enabled Mosaic browser:

- BrowserWatch (browserwatch.internet.com) keeps you up to date on the latest browsers and plug-ins. It contains an ActiveX Arena and a Plug-In Plaza to download the latest browser additions. Another good source of information is www.browsers.com, part of the C|Net family of websites. They too keep tabs on plug-ins, ActiveX controls, and anything else related to browsers.

- Both Navigator and Internet Explorer already come bundled with a good number of plug-ins, like Shockwave or the RealPlayer. Always check to see which version you have. It's best to visit the vendor's website to download the most recent plug-ins available.

- If running on a slow computer, don't run any other applications while using streaming programs. Also, don't download files or otherwise take up precious bandwidth. Avoid starting or quitting applications when playing files because it can cause skipping.

- If you don't like a particular plug-in and are running Windows95, just uninstall it. True Windows95 applications have an uninstall program that can delete all traces of the program from your computer. If a program doesn't have an uninstaller, it may have a README file that tells you what files were installed. You can also un-install by pushing Start, Settings/Control Panel, then click on Add/Remove Programs. Select the plug-in from the list. Only as a last resort should you manually delete the files, directories, and shortcuts yourself. There are also some utility programs you can buy (like Quarterdeck's CleanSweep) that keep track of what you installed and can fully delete them from your computer. If you'll be using lots of plug-ins, these may be a good investment.

- If you are running both Netscape Navigator and Internet Explorer on your computer, don't forget to install the plug-in or helper application for both browsers. You'll want to see what they look like on both. Sometimes this requires two files and two downloads; other times, one program handles both. Some installation programs can automatically find all browsers on your hard drive and install to each of them.

- Avoid connecting to streaming video sites during the Internet's busiest times, meaning anywhere after 12 P.M. to 3 P.M. EST. Most streaming players can show you statistics on the speed of your connection or whether you are losing too much data. If the quality is totally unacceptable, stop playback and try connecting at another time.

- If you've installed beta versions of some of these programs, they sometimes time-out after 30 days. If you find that a plug-in no longer works, just download a new copy from the vendor's website.

Netscape Navigator Tips

Plug-ins were introduced with Netscape Navigator 2.0, and were intended to be used as an extension to the browser to allow it to handle many file types. Since then, every version of Navigator can handle plug-ins, but it is best to use the latest version available, like Navigator 4.0. When installing plug-ins, be sure to check whether they are compatible with Navigator 4.0 or with the upcoming 5.0, since vendors don't always update their plug-ins for these newer versions. Also, if you're using Windows, make sure that you're using the right one, either the 16-bit or 32-bit version.

The following are some other tips for Netscape Navigator users:

- If you use more than one copy of Navigator on your hard disk, make sure you install the plug-in to each version. Both have their own subdirectories for plug-ins.

- If you're upgrading to a new version of Navigator, plug-ins are not always automatically transferred to the new version. In some cases, you can just copy the .DLL files from your old Plug-in directory to the new one and then restart Navigator. The plug-ins should work; if they don't, you'll have to reinstall them.

- To see what plug-ins you have installed, select Help/About Plug-ins (in Windows) or About Plug-ins (in Mac). You will see a list of all plug-ins currently installed and which ones are enabled. Also handy is a link to Netscape's plug-in download page, home.netscape.com/comprod/products/navigator/version_2.0/plugins/index.html.

- Navigator can detect if you are missing a plug-in and can take you to the correct download site. A message box will appear saying: "Plug-in not loaded: This page contains information of type XXX that can only be viewed with the appropriate Plug-in. What do you want to do? Get the Plug-in or Cancel." Click on Get the Plug-in to be taken to Netscape's Plug-in finder page.

- Before installing any plug-ins, you should close down Navigator. If you forget and leave it open while installing, it's okay, but just remember to close and restart Navigator so the plug-ins can be recognized.

Microsoft Internet Explorer Tips

Microsoft Internet Explorer uses ActiveX controls as well as plug-ins. ActiveX controls were invented by Microsoft as an alternate method of extending the capabilities of its browser. Like plug-ins, ActiveX controls can do many things and can handle many file types. They can be used to view movies, unzip files, load programs, and more. The main difference is that ActiveX controls can do things automatically, like download and install themselves on the fly. Here are some other tips and tricks when using Internet Explorer:

- Only Internet Explorer's final release 3.0 can use ActiveX controls. It is always best to use the latest browser, like Internet Explorer 4.0, to get the most out of your Web experience.

- Internet Explorer downloads, installs, and loads ActiveX controls automatically. For example, when you reach a site that does not have an ActiveX component installed, the page stops loading and Internet Explorer asks you if you want to load the incoming application. If you say yes, it will then download the ActiveX control by itself and even run the installation programs without prompting. Once it's installed, you can instantly use the ActiveX component and the web page should load as normal.

- To download some other cool controls, visit C|Net's ActiveX site at www.activex.com.

- If you are concerned about security or downloading viruses, you can turn off ActiveX controls, plug-ins, or JavaScript. Select View/Options and then click on the Security tab, then check or uncheck each security option.

- Although Internet Explorer has its multimedia controls turned on by default, you can turn them off whenever you wish. Go to View/Options and then select the General tab. When all the multimedia options are checked, you can hear background WAV files and watch video files.

Playing Streaming Audio

Audio applications vary. There are programs that cater to speech-only transmissions, or high-quality, prerecorded music, or just general-purpose audio. RealAudio, of course, is the most well-known and most versatile, handling all types of audio with very good sound. If you're looking for alternatives, look no further: This section introduces you to a wide range of streaming audio players that you can install and try out for yourself. Unfortunately, not all platforms are supported. You should check the vendor's website for any updates or new platforms that may be supported by the time you read this.

RealAudio

Company: RealNetworks
Website: www.real.com
Platforms: Macintosh, UNIX, and Windows 3.x/95/NT
Price: Free, but a commercial version is available for $29.99
Type: Plug-in, ActiveX, and external application

RealAudio is the leader and pioneer of streaming audio. Because of that, it is the most mature program available. To play RealAudio files (.RA, .RM, .RAM), you should use the RealPlayer 5.0, which plays both RealAudio and RealVideo files. Most RealAudio files that you will encounter on the Web should tell you what bandwidth they are optimized for. Many default to 28.8Kbps, but sometimes there are files designed for bigger bandwidth connections like 128Kbps.

 If your company uses a firewall to access the Internet, you may need to modify the firewall to allow RealMedia files. For more help on configuring firewalls, see www.real.com/help/firewall.

RealPlayer looks and feels just like a CD player. You can play, stop, forward, rewind, and pause. There is also a sliding Seek bar where you can drag the pointer forward or backward to a new location in the file. There is also built-in volume control and a Mute button. An onscreen display shows you the elapsed time of the clip, as well as the total time. (If you're listening to live audio, the display will read "Live.") It also displays information on the file, like artist name, title, and copyright information. RealPlayer can also check for upgrades. Select Help/Check for Upgrade to log on to Progressive Networks' website to see if there are new versions available for download.

RealAudio is highly customizable. For example, you can program a whole group of prerecorded audio files to play consecutively. These clips can be set up at

Timecast (www.timecast.com). Once you're ready to start listening, the RealPlayer will have all the "clips" queued up and ready to play. To move to the next clip, just select Clip/Previous Clip or Next Clip from the menu bar.

You can also program preset channel buttons, much like a car radio. By simply clicking on a Destination button, you can automatically start to play the selected RealMedia file. To set up your Destination buttons, go to www.real.com/destinations/.

For those who are serious about RealAudio, you can purchase the RealPlayer Plus (for $29.99), which includes features like scan, more preprogrammed buttons, and the ability to save RealMedia files to your hard drive for later listening.

StreamWorks

Company: Xing Technology
Website: www.streamworks.com
Platforms: Windows 3.1/95/NT, Mac, and UNIX
Price: Free
Type: Plug-in, Helper application

Like RealAudio, StreamWorks pulls double duty as both an audio and video player. Since it began life as an audio player, and many sites still use audio-only Stream-Works files, I've included it in this section.

The StreamWorks player is rather small and utilitarian, because it only has Play/Pause and Stop buttons. There are no Fast Forward or Rewind buttons, just a sliding Seek bar. A display shows you the elapsed time, and pressing the I button will show you more information about a file. For the more technically capable, there are many options: You can select your transmission speed, switch to stereo or mono sound, or set up your firewall information. You can also choose between Optimize Audio Quality or Optimize Video Quality. For the best results, leave this option as Mixed. To monitor bandwidth and performance, a tiny light on the lower-right side indicates what's going on: A green light means that sound is playing and that everything is all right. If the light turns red, it means there is heavy network congestion or an overburdened server that is drastically affecting playback quality.

To watch StreamWorks movies, connect to the Xing Gallery (www.stream-works.com/content/).

Liquid Audio

Company: Liquid Audio, Inc.
Website: www.liquidaudio.com
Platforms: Windows95 and Mac

Price: Free

Type: Helper application

For commerce applications, no streaming player compares to Liquid Audio. Instead of being an all-in-one player like RealAudio, Liquid Audio carved its own niche as a music-only player with killer commerce capabilities.

Using the Liquid MusicPlayer, you can listen to high-quality, prerecorded streaming music with Dolby stereo sound. If you really like a song, you can even buy and download a CD-quality song or purchase the whole album. To complete your purchase, Liquid MusicPlayer will connect you to the artist's website or an online music store. If you have a CD recorder, it can even burn your own musical compact discs. Bootleggers beware: Liquid Audio uses a digital watermark to identify the origin of the file. Artists and record companies can breathe easily.

The Liquid MusicPlayer is like any other player with Stop, Play, and Seek commands. What's different is that Liquid Audio also displays lyrics, recording information, cover art, notes, promotional text, and credits (see Figure 2.1).

Also unique are the Buy CD or Buy Download buttons. Perhaps the biggest downside to downloading CDs is that it can take hours on a 28.8Kbps connection.

Figure 2.1 For music and commerce applications, Liquid Audio has no competition.

For the impatient, you can have the CD mailed to you. Liquid Audio is in partnership with a number of online retailers like Music Boulevard (www.musicblvd.com), the online CD store. Once this catches on, this could be a very hot program.

AudioActive

Company: Telos Systems
Website: www.audioactive.com
Platforms: Windows 3.x/95/NT, and Mac
Price: Free
Type: Helper application

AudioActive is one of the newest players on the Internet. It is for radio broadcasters who want to become web broadcasters, so practically all the content is comprised of radio stations. AudioActive uses a mix of hardware and software to help radio stations set up shop on the Web. Its biggest competitor is RealAudio, which also has a large following with radio broadcasters.

The AudioActive player is rather compact: You can play, pause, stop, rewind, and fast forward, but there are no volume controls. The display resembles a CD player; it shows elapsed time and the current track number (see Figure 2.2). You can also view information on the file, like title, artist, and author, by clicking on the I button. AudioActive can also stream prerecorded MPEG Layer 3 audio files (with a .MP3 extension).

For a complete list of AudioActivated radio stations on the Web, visit AudioActive at www.audioactive.com.

TrueSpeech

Company: DSP Group
Website: www.dspg.com
Platforms: Windows 3.x/95.NT, and Mac
Price: Free
Type: Helper application

As its name implies, TrueSpeech is a streaming audio format specializing in speech-only transmissions. (Some sites also use TrueSpeech to stream music with varied results.) Although popular at one time, it is difficult to find many websites with TrueSpeech files. It's best to visit the TrueSpeech website to see where to go. The TrueSpeech Internet Player looks Spartan. There are play controls like a CD player, but no volume controls. A status bar is just a long, horizontal bar that travels with the audio as it plays. You can click anywhere along the bar to quickly seek to a new location in the current file, or you can click and drag. One nice feature is the ability

Figure 2.2 AudioActive is a new program that specializes in radio broadcasts.

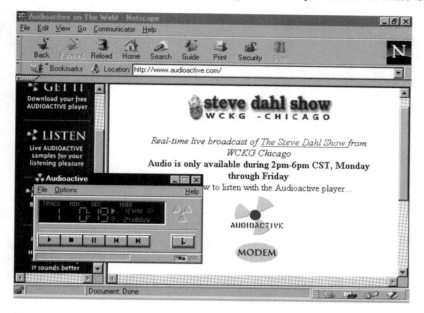

to bookmark files that are on the Web or on your hard disk. You can change the sampling rate and the buffer size, but otherwise, there are not many user controls.

TrueSpeech streams any TrueSpeech-encoded WAV file for listening on the fly. It can also play WAV files locally on your hard drive. The TrueSpeech compression algorithm is built into Windows 3.1 and 95, so they can use and create TSP files very easily. Internet Explorer has TrueSpeech built in and plays TrueSpeech files automatically with the Media Player.

Internet Wave

Company: Vocaltec
Website: www.vocaltec.com/iwave.htm
Platforms: Windows 3.1/95/NT
Price: Free
Type: Helper application

Internet Wave is very old school and hasn't changed much since being released in 1995. The strangest thing about the player is its look and interface, which looks nothing like a CD player (see Figure 2.3). Instead, it has a rounded dial that shows

Figure 2.3 Its unorthodox look makes the Internet Wave player stand out from the crowd.

you the elapsed time, along with a Pause and Play button in the middle. There is also a blue line that circles the entire interface to indicate playback time. To seek to another part of the file, just drag your mouse pointer to a new location along the round dial or click anywhere on it. It also has a volume control, plus displays that show you the network connection, buffer level, and the bandwidth level.

Also unique to Internet Wave is its close integration with a Web telephony program called Internet Phone (also by Vocaltec), which you can load with just the click of a button.

LiveAudio

Company: Netscape Communications
Website: home.netscape.com/eng/media
Platforms: Windows 3.x/95/NT, UNIX, and Mac
Price: Free, included with Navigator or can be downloaded separately
Type: Plug-in

LiveAudio can play live or on-demand streaming audio. It is not an external player; rather, the sound controls are embedded onto a web page. Audio can be integrated and synchronized with HTML, Java applets, or other multimedia.

Netscape's LiveAudio hasn't been widely used on the Internet but it hopes to be a major player in the growing video enterprise market. Netscape invented the LiveMedia Architecture (LMA) as an alternate to RealMedia and Microsoft's formats. So far, development has gone slowly for Netscape, since it doesn't have video capability yet.

Playing Streaming Video

Streaming video players have multiplied in recent months. Whereas there were just three or four players on the market early on, now there are over a dozen streaming video programs available. This is not necessarily a good thing, especially over the Internet. Some websites will require you to have a certain plug-in installed, while another site will require you to download another plug-in. That means that you'll have to do plenty of downloading and installing in order to see some content.

The newest generation of streaming multimedia programs doesn't have a client program at all, so no client downloads are needed. A tiny Java player is sent with the file and begins to play within a few seconds. Essentially, those using a Java-enabled browser can experience streaming audio and video without dealing with the hassle of downloading and installing plug-ins. This opens up your market to a much larger audience base. However, most programs still use browser plug-ins, but more and more programs should be using Java over time.

As with the audio players, make sure you're using the most recent version of the player by downloading it from the vendor's website. Updates and new programs are released almost daily, so check for new ones often.

Following are what I like to call the "Big Five" of the Internet streaming video players. These five systems are the most popular and ones you may already be familiar with.

RealVideo

Company: RealNetworks
Website: www.real.com
Platforms: Windows 95/NT, Mac
Price: Free, and a commercial product for $29.99
Type: Plug-in, ActiveX control, and Helper application

Although just introduced in early 1997, RealVideo is already one of the more popular streaming programs on the Internet, because it is the leader in streaming audio. As described in the previous section, you must use the RealPlayer 4.0 or above to play RealVideo files.

When RealPlayer encounters a live or prerecorded RealMedia file, it automatically starts the player and begins buffering the video image. After just a few seconds of buffering, the video begins to play. All the controls and options are the same as when using RealAudio files. You can even set video files as your preset Destination buttons. The main difference is the video window that opens when you watch video. You can increase the video window size by zooming in and out with a left mouse button click. At 28.8Kbps, RealVideo can play files at around eight to ten frames per second (30 frames per second is TV quality) (see Figure 2.4.).

One big difference is the invention of video hotlinks that enable users to click on certain parts of the video window to perform an action. Users can be taken to a new web page, a new RealVideo file, or any other option. To find updated audio or video content, go to Timecast at (www.timecast.com).

StreamWorks

Company: Xing Technology
Website: www.xingtech.com
Platforms: Windows 3.1/95/NT, Mac, and UNIX
Price: Free
Type: Plug-in, Helper application

StreamWorks video files work similarly to audio files. StreamWorks' player automatically knows what type of file it is playing and will open up a separate video window to display the movie (see Figure 2.5). The size of the video window varies depending on what is being displayed, but it is roughly half the size of a standard business card.

For more information on the StreamWorks player, see the section, "Playing Streaming Audio," earlier in the chapter.

Figure 2.4 The RealPlayer opens up a video window when playing RealVideo files.

Figure 2.5 StreamWorks plays video files in a separate window.

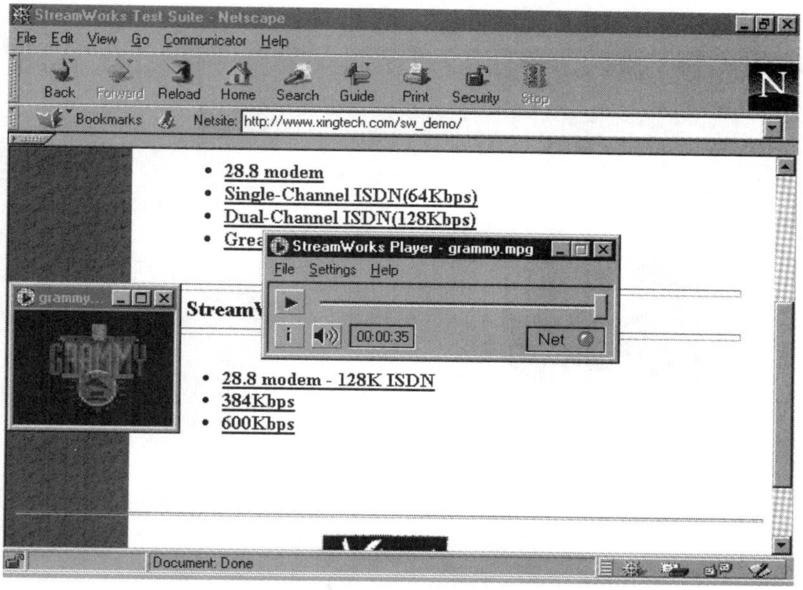

VivoActive

Company: Vivo Software, Inc.

Website: www.vivo.com

Platforms: Windows 3.1/95/NT, and Mac

Price: Free, and an advanced version available for $12.95

Type: Plug-in and ActiveX

Unlike other client programs, VivoActive does not have an external player but shows videos embedded inside a web page. Whenever your browser encounters a file with a .VIV or .VIVO extension, it begins to play the file as the web page opens. This is good if you hate having yet another external program open up, but can be inconvenient when you're Web surfing and want to visit other websites.

VivoActive doesn't have many player controls; there is no Seek bar or Fast-forward button. Vivo just has a semitransparent Play/Stop button shown unobtrusively in the lower right-hand corner of the video window (see Figure 2.6). There is also a commercial version called VivoActive PowerPlayer available for $12.95.

Window size of the video tends to be small, and the quality is dependent on the network traffic since it uses HTTP for data transmission—the same as all other

Figure 2.6 The VivoActive window appears inside a web page and doesn't have many controls.

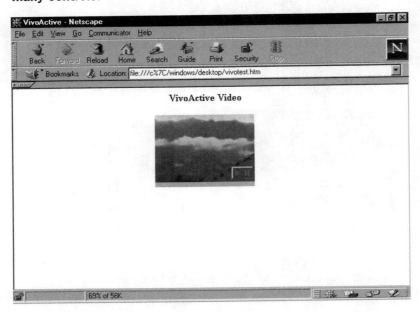

Web traffic. HTTP is good for those viewing Vivo movies behind a corporate firewall. Unfortunately, VivoActive cannot transmit live broadcasts; movies must be prerecorded as in a "tape-delayed" broadcast.

Because it is inexpensive, easy to create files with, and simple to broadcast, VivoActive sites are plentiful. Even novice computer hobbyists can put up Vivo movies on their personal homepage or small website.

VDOLive

Company: VDOnet Corp.
Website: www.vdo.net
Platforms: Windows 3.1/95/NT, and Mac
Price: Free
Type: Plug-in and ActiveX, Helper application

Among the most popular formats is VDOLive. First released in late 1995, VDOLive promises very good quality, even on low-bandwidth connections. It broadcasts prerecorded and live video.

The VDOLive Video Player resembles a small television set (see Figure 2.7). There is a slide volume control, but no Seek methods—just Stop and Play buttons. A status bar on top of the video window tells you what's going on, or if the player is waiting, playing, or is stopped. Although the screen size depends on the actual video, the default size is about 320×240 pixels. VDOLive has one of the best traffic-monitoring options: You can see the percentage of data not getting to you. Alternatively, you can use the Network Diagnostic Meters to see how network traffic is affecting your playback.

VDOLive works as an ActiveX control for MSIE, and if set up properly, it can be viewed from inside a web page with Navigator without loading the external program. If you're not using Navigator, the external player will automatically pop up and play the file.

NetShow

Company: Microsoft Corp.
Website: www.microsoft.com/netshow/
Platforms: Windows 95/NT, Mac, UNIX

Figure 2.7 VDOLive is yet another popular format for streaming live and pre-recorded movies on the Web.

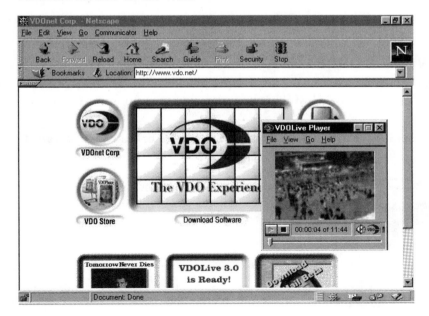

Price: Free

Type: ActiveX, Plug-in

Microsoft released NetShow so it wouldn't be left off of the streaming media bandwagon. NetShow is tightly integrated with other Microsoft products like Internet Explorer and Windows NT Server software.

NetShow supports both *unicast* and *multicast* delivery methods. Unicast means that the server sends a stream each time it is requested so users can control playback—like using fast-forward, rewind, stop, and play. Multicast means that the server sends one copy of the stream for many computers to receive. However, you lose the ability to fast-forward and rewind. When you click on a NetShow file, the NetShow player will load and play. It can also play video inside a web page (see Figure 2.8).

Microsoft uses the Advanced Streaming Format (ASF) as its file types, which is a more open file format than the other four systems. In August 1997, Microsoft acquired VXtreme, a company that made a streaming video program called WebTheater. It also entered into strategic partnerships with other streaming vendors like VDOnet, Progressive Networks, and Vivo Software. This consolidation of the leading streaming video companies is sure to make NetShow very popular. Microsoft is aiming to take a lead in the streaming multimedia market and is trying to consolidate streaming to make ASF the default streaming system on the Internet.

To see some NetShow content, visit AudioNet's NetShow page at www.audionet .com/netshow.

Playing Web Animation

Animation on the Internet has been around since the introduction of Shockwave by Macromedia. It brought CD-ROM-style animation and interactivity to web

Figure 2.8 The NetShow player can play inside a web page or load as an external player.

pages. Shockwave movies have many uses, like interactive games, advertisements, or just jazzing up a professional website with animation. The problem was that Shockwave movies were very large and they needed to be downloaded completely before beginning to play. Recently, Macromedia released a version of Shockwave that can stream and use Java to play files. This means that you no longer need to download and install plug-ins; just a Java-enabled browser like Navigator or Internet Explorer.

Shockwave

Company: Macromedia
Website: www.macromedia.com
Platforms: Windows 3.x/95/NT, Mac, or any Java-enabled browser
Price: Free
Type: ActiveX and Plug-in, Java player

Shockwave animations are created with Director, a powerful and popular graphics and animation package that's the standard for creating CD-ROM software and animation. When you have the Shockwave plug-in installed on your browser, it automatically loads a Director movie. Load times depend on whether you're using the latest version of Shockwave, which can now stream.

Flash

The newest addition to web animation is Flash. These movies are much smaller than regular Shockwave files because they merely send the instructions to draw and recreate images. Flash is best used to animate toolbars and menus, respond to mouse clicks or "mouse overs," or even add small snippets of video or sound. New versions of Shockwave and Flash will have the ability to play using Java so that no plug-ins are needed; only a Java-enabled browser like Navigator and Internet Explorer.

Enliven

Company: Narrative Communications Corp.
Website: www.narrative.com
Platforms: Windows 95/NT
Price: Free
Type: Plug-in, Java player

Enliven is another animation viewer that can stream Director movies. To watch Enliven movies, you can install a plug-in, or just use Java to play files. Enliven can play fancy, dancing graphics just like Shockwave. The difference is that Enliven has moved almost exclusively to the banner advertising market to deliver streaming, interactive, and graphical ads. These ads are animated, eye-catching, and look more like games than banner ads. The newest version of Enliven has added ad tracking abilities.

Since these aren't technically movies, you can't play or stop them, but there is plenty of interactivity.

Playing VRML and Panoramic Files

The smallest market for streaming multimedia is 3-D programs, but that's only because it is so new. Virtual reality can usually be experienced with browsers or plug-ins that display files. The current 3-D standard is VRML, or Virtual Reality Modeling Language, files. VRML is the industry standard format for making 3-D movies and pictures and is the language that authors use to describe 3-D objects for the Internet. It can be used to construct sites or worlds with nearly infinite space and depth. Objects in these worlds can do many things, including link to other locations or play animation, audio, and video files. Depending on what the author designed, you can usually interact with different objects and zoom in and out while moving around in this 3-D environment.

As you might have guessed, these files originally had to be downloaded to your computer before beginning to play. Newer programs can stream 3-D files, so you can begin to interact with the worlds while they are downloading. Often, this means that the picture isn't even completely downloaded. Within a short period of time, we can expect that many vendors will switch to the streaming concept in order to deliver interactive, 3-D images in the fastest way possible.

Panoramic files also need to be downloaded completely, but there are some programs that can stream or quickly play these files. One popular panoramic viewer is discussed next.

Cosmo Player

Company: Cosmo Software, Div. of Silicon Graphics
Website: cosmo.sgi.com
Platforms: Windows 95/NT, UNIX
Price: Free
Type: Plug-in

The Cosmo Player is one of the Web's most popular VRML browsers. It is bundled with Netscape Communicator 4.x or can be downloaded separately from Cosmo's website. (Microsoft Internet Explorer 4.x also has its own VRML browser that you can download separately.)

Cosmo can stream to some extent, because you can use it while it is still downloading the whole file. VRML files can be large, depending on their complexity, so streaming is a very welcome concept. When you visit a VRML world, Cosmo will open the picture and display it inside your browser (see Figure 2.9).

You can walk around in the VRML world by using your mouse or the arrow keys. You can also rotate objects, click on items, watch animation, listen to audio, jump to another VRML world, and much more. It all depends on what the VRML author programmed the world to do.

To view some VRML files, you can visit Silicon Graphics' website at vrml.sgi.com.

LivePicture

Company: Live Picture, Inc.
Website: www.livepicture.com
Platforms: Any with Java browser
Price: Free
Type: Java browser needed

Figure 2.9 Use Cosmo to view 3-D VRML worlds.

LivePicture delivers photorealistic images of 360-degree panoramic scenes. Live-Picture now uses Java to display these scenes so you don't need a plug-in at all.

Generally, you can do things like zoom in and out, pan left or right, even look up and down to see a very large area. Just use your mouse or keyboard to move in any direction (see Figure 2.10).

When you zoom in, however, you just see large colored pixels, and you don't get the detail you might expect. You can click on some areas of the images to be taken to another location or bring up descriptions of the objects.

Working with Email

Although the Web is the first place people turn to for multimedia, not everyone has the time and patience to go out and look for files. Enter streaming email. These allow you to send audio, video, and animation over email. Essentially, these programs convert existing multimedia into streaming files that can be viewed on the fly. When you send files, the recipient just needs to open the link and the streaming file begins to play. It doesn't download anything to the hard drive.

Figure 2.10 LivePicture can let you see a 360-degree view of panoramic scenes like this cityscape.

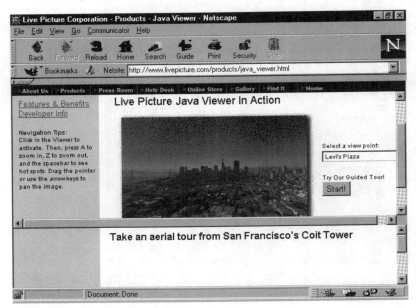

Perhaps the biggest downside to streaming email programs is that they are not always compatible with many different platforms. Generally, users must be using the same operating system to see transferred files. Also, there aren't many true streaming email programs available.

Will the market for streaming email grow? It's hard to say. What may be more popular is the ability to send highly compressed multimedia files for later viewing. A few vendors have already tried this approach by making multimedia files executable and self-playing, so there is no need for players. This can be very handy for those users who don't have the proper players installed. For now, the market for streaming email programs is very tiny and not well developed.

Video Express Mail

Company: Imagemind Software, Inc.
Website: www.imagemind.com
Platforms: Windows 95/NT
Price: Free player, but the creation tool costs $59.95 and monthly subscriptions are required

Video Express Mail is the only true system for sending streaming email multimedia files. There are no file attachments to download and no waiting for files to download. Instead, you receive a normal email message that contains a link to a Video Express Mail file. Just click on the link to begin streaming the media file. The recipient doesn't need to own Video Express Mail to receive messages because the player can be sent along with the file. You can record your own audio or video messages or import existing WAV, MOV, or AVI files. You can also import Microsoft PowerPoint presentations.

Pseudo-Streaming

Another way to view streaming multimedia is to use a client-only solution, sometimes called *pseudo-streaming*. That means that a software package you install does all the streaming, while the website does nothing but provide the files. The files themselves are sometimes modified to be *fast-start* files or have a proprietary compression scheme. Fast-start movies begin to play when only a certain percentage of the file has been transferred—anywhere from 10 to 30 percent of a file. That means that you can often see the first frame immediately and then see the first few seconds after a few minutes of download time. Client-side and fast-start movies are not as fast as regular streaming, but they are helpful when you're not sure if you want to download the whole file and want to see a preview.

These plug-ins are rather territorial and will begin to play every downloadable multimedia type available. They may even conflict with one another. To bypass any plug-in and just download files to your hard drive, hold down the Shift key while clicking on a file. (In Windows, you can also right-click with your mouse to save it.) Once it's downloaded, you can then access the file with any multimedia player you want.

Some pseudo-streaming programs are discussed next.

CineWeb

Company: Digigami
Website: www.digigami.com
Price: Free for 30 days, $29.95 after trial period
File formats: AVI, MOV, MPG, FLI, WAV, MID
Platforms: Windows 3.x/95/NT

CineWeb is a complete viewer that can play almost any type of multimedia file, including WAV, AU, MOV, AVI, and MPEG. It installs as a plug-in and acts as the default viewer for many file types. CineWeb streams QuickTime files that are optimized as fast-start movies with its MovieScreamer technology. It plays files while they are still downloading inside the browser window; it is not an external player. After a certain percentage of the file has been transferred, you can begin to view the file. Of course, you won't see the whole movie, but it is an improvement over not seeing anything at all. Even if the fast-start option isn't active, you can still use CineWeb to load and play files after they have completely downloaded.

The worst problem is that CineWeb plays so many multimedia files; it is the most territorial program described here. This is especially annoying if you already have a good multimedia player or want to choose which program to view files with. Since Microsoft's ActiveMovie also plays (and streams) many of the same multimedia types, CineWeb may seem redundant to some Windows95 users.

QuickTime

Company: Apple Computer
Website: quicktime.apple.com
Price: Free
Platforms: Windows 3.1/95/NT, and Mac
File formats: MOV and MPEG

Like CineWeb, the QuickTime player can also play fast-start optimized MOV files. Users can begin viewing movies with only a small fraction of the file downloaded.

It may only be a matter of time when Apple develops its own true streaming multimedia solution with QuickTime. Apple tested a Mac program called QuickTime TV (QTTV) that allowed broadcasts of live video over the Internet. QTTV development was later stopped, but it did show the promise of streaming QuickTime.

Summary: What Should I Use on My Site?

As you can see, there are many types of streaming multimedia programs, and they handle a wide range of multimedia files. Which one is best? Which should you use? Those are the big questions. Part II will help you answer these questions by showing you the different solutions and methods that programs use. Perhaps more important is the next chapter, where you will find out more about the server or administration side of these streaming programs.

Now that you know about the many types of streaming players that are available, you can begin to get an idea of what system might be best for you.

SERVER STRATEGIES:
Choosing and Implementing the Right Streaming Multimedia System

Now that you've seen and used many of the most popular streaming programs, it is time to think about implementing them on your website. This chapter helps you decide what streaming multimedia system to use by asking you a series of questions. This self-discovery process is important because you don't want to rush into a streaming solution only to find that the program you've chosen does not fit your needs. It's best to find a solution that is good for your strategy today, but one that can grow and help you realize your goals for tomorrow as well.

Some of the questions you will answer in this chapter are:

- Do you want to use a client/server system or a server-less system? Do you have the time and resources to implement a more complex client/server architecture, or will a simpler server-less system suffice?

- Will you use Windows NT or UNIX? Which type of hardware will you choose for your server and which operating system?

- Do you need more bandwidth? Will you use IP multicasting? Will you need to upgrade your network?

- Where will you use streaming multimedia, on your intranet or on the Internet?

- Do you just want to use streaming audio? Do you need streaming video, animation, or VRML?

- Will you use live audio and video, prerecorded multimedia, or both?

- How much are you willing to spend on buying and developing a streaming multimedia site? Do you want a free system? Is price no object? What costs should you consider?

- Do you need customer support? Do you need extra help?

These are just a few of the questions that will guide you into making a decision. Once you have an idea of what you need, what you have now, and what you will need in the future, then you'll be ready to learn about specifics.

You'll also find out about the software components you'll be using with streaming systems, and get a sneak peek at how they work together to create a streaming site.

The Steps to Implementing a Successful Streaming Solution

The key to a successful launch of a streaming system is to research and then test the system exhaustively.

Here are some of steps most users take when implementing streaming multimedia:

Research. That is what you are doing now by reading this book. Learn about companies and what solutions they provide. Some programs will handle one task better than others, so make sure you choose a solution that is flexible. Keep up with the trade magazines to learn about any new developments in the industry and see what recommendations they have made. Finally, revisit a vendor's website for any new announcements and new versions.

Experiment. Get down and dirty by using the programs you have determined to be the most useful for your applications. As discussed in Chapter 2, "The Client Side: Introducing the Programs," this makes it easy to know what the programs can do and may even show you a new way of doing something. This book and CD-ROM will help guide you to certain vendors and solutions.

Choose. Once you've learned about certain streaming multimedia programs, you can narrow your options to just a few. Try them out! Again, use the enclosed CD-ROM to experiment with software and media files to see what results you get. Also, download any tools like new encoders, software, and documentation from the vendor's website. Many companies give away trial versions of their products; others are completely free so you can play with them all you want.

Test, test, and test. Don't skimp on this. Take notes, get friends to help you, and make sure everything is hunky dory. If you're going to use streaming multimedia over the Internet, make sure you test files there. Something might look good on your computer but may look different in a live situation. Try to emulate a typical user's experience. Try different browsers to see how they handle your files, then connect at different bandwidths to see the differences. On an intranet, try to test your system on a small private network or just on your desktop computer. Don't use it on your intranet server's computer. The last thing you want to do is have to take your intranet server down in case of a crash or for maintenance. This is also a good time to check your network's bandwidth requirement—if you find you need more bandwidth, get more. Once you've narrowed your options further, you can begin testing that one system fully so you understand it inside and out.

Implement. Before implementing, test it again and again. Once you're sure everything is running as it should, hold your breath and release the system to a small number of friends and get their comments. If everything goes well, you can fully release it to everyone and bring it live. Don't be surprised to hear complaints, suggestions, questions, and problems within minutes of implementation, so leave your email address or a form so users can give you feedback. Check your server logs to see who is accessing your files and to see how your network is faring. Do you need more bandwidth? Is traffic flowing smoothly?

Create fresh content. The biggest part of the job may be continually creating fresh, new content so you can attract new and returning visitors. You need to create or capture some content before you implement everything, but also remember to keep your site updated. If your multimedia presence is more of a static nature, however, you may find that you won't have to create new content very often. Keep in mind that creating video and audio is easy, but high-quality audio and video should be left to the professionals. You may or may not already have some experience in capturing and creating multimedia. If you're planning extensive content, you should consider hiring video professionals or a service bureau so you won't have to worry about it yourself. If your company has the resources and equipment, you might be able to save some money by doing it all in house.

Reevaluate. Once everything is set up and things are running smoothly, your job still isn't over. You should keep up to date on the ever-changing world of streaming multimedia. There are bound to be new programs from other vendors and even updated software from your own company.

Is it time to upgrade to a completely new system? You might have to start this process all over again.

Streaming Audio and Video—How Does It Work?

Now that you know a bit about the process, let's get down to the nitty gritty. You should understand how streaming multimedia works. First, here's a primer on how the Internet works.

Behind the Scenes on the Internet

When you access a website, a few things happen. When you type in a web page address, your browser sends that command to a server where it looks up the address's true location, or its IP address. After contacting the web server, it sends data back to the web browser and begins to display the data. In the case of a normal web page, it sends back the HTML file. For every HTML, JPEG, or GIF file, your browser sends a new request to the server until the page finishes displaying. This means that any graphics files will load separately.

The Internet uses a TCP/IP-based network to exchange data. TCP/IP stands for Transmission Control Protocol/Internet Protocol and is really a family of data delivery protocols. All web traffic travels on these "roads" or protocols, but there are many layers and many protocols being used on the Internet. For example, web pages travel via HTTP (HyperText Transfer Protocol), email travels along SMTP (Simple Mail Transfer Protocol), while file transfers via FTP use the File Transfer Protocol.

Because of their greater dependence on speed, many streaming multimedia programs use a faster protocol called UDP (User Datagram Protocol) to travel the Internet and get to their destination. UDP is faster because it doesn't have error checking like TCP/IP, but there are no guarantees that it will get to the destination. Conversely, TCP/IP is slower because it *does* have guaranteed delivery—it resends lost data until it gets to its destination. By default, many streaming programs use UDP to send data, although others use TCP/IP or more accurately, HTTP, the Web protocol.

UDP has disadvantages because you may lose a lot of data and because configuring UDP on a network can be a hassle. Many intranets have firewalls that restrict or prohibit the use of UDP, so those users trying to view a streaming movie may be blocked from doing so. That means that you'll have to reconfigure your firewall to accept some UDP data. Another option is to use HTTP streaming. More and more streaming programs are beginning to use both UDP and HTTP to send data. HTTP is good because it bypasses firewalls completely. The problem is that HTTP streaming is very slow—you won't get very good audio or video quality. Smart streaming systems can sometimes sense which protocol is best to use and change protocols on the fly without you having to do much.

New Internet Protocols

Since streaming is still very new, there aren't very many standards. Some new Internet protocols are being discussed and developed to make streaming media programs work better.

Some of the newer protocols for streaming multimedia include:

RSVP—Resource Reservation Protocol. This is a standard for reserving bandwidth so that the data gets to its destination quickly and accurately.

SMRP—Simple Multicast Routing Protocol. A protocol that supports conferencing by multiplying the data to a select group of recipients, like IP Multicast.

RTSP—Real-Time Streaming Protocol. This is used specifically by streaming multimedia programs for controlled delivery of real-time data.

RTP—Real Time Transport Protocol. An emerging standard for sending real-time multimedia data, RTP is already being used by some routers and supported by some streaming media systems.

RTCP—Real-Time Control Protocol. This is a Quality of Service (QoS) protocol for providing end-to-end guarantee of quality.

These new protocols are better for streaming high-bandwidth files like audio or video. They can also be used in programs like videoconferencing to guarantee bandwidth and delivery of data. Only RTP is an international standard so far; the rest are still in the discussion stage or are close to being ratified as standards.

Three Components: Client, Server, and Encoder

Streaming multimedia systems usually come with three programs with which you should become familiar, since we'll be using them throughout the book. The three software components are the *client* or player, the *server*, and the *encoder* or producer.

Working with the Client

The *client* is the player, or the program (either a browser plug-in or helper application) that the user must download and install before being able to play streaming media. Generally, client programs are free and available for downloading from a vendor's website. Practically all of the streaming client programs in this book are available for Windows95. Other platforms like Windows 3.x, Macintosh, or UNIX may be supported as well, but Windows95 has almost universal support.

Working with the Server

The *server* is exactly what it is to a regular website—it handles and oversees the distribution and access of the streaming files. Oftentimes, it even has administrative duties such as keeping track of who is accessing the system or allowing more bandwidth. The server is nothing more than a program that must be installed alongside a regular web server. It runs in the background and allows access to all streaming files. Server programs help you manage streams and users and are made to serve large numbers of simultaneous users, usually in the hundreds or even thousands. (The actual number of simultaneous users depends on the program, your network bandwidth, and other attributes of the file.) Most vendors sells stream licenses so only a certain number of streams can be sent at a time. The server software can also give detailed logs on what is happening and help you manage network bandwidth. Usually, server programs run on Windows NT or UNIX workstations because they need high security and close integration with web servers in order to run properly.

Working with the Encoder

The *encoder* (sometimes called a *converter* or *producer*) is a program that converts file types from regular downloadable multimedia (AVI, QuickTime, or MPEG) to the vendor's own file format that will make it stream capable. This essentially means that you will be encoding or compressing a regular file into a much smaller file for transmission over your network. You'll be doing a lot of compressing so we'll go into that in Chapter 4. Once you convert an audio or video file, copy the file to the server computer so users can access the file. Producer programs mostly run on Windows 95/NT or Macintosh computers and come bundled with the whole client/server system.

Three Classifications: Client/Server, Server-Less, and Client-Less

Streaming multimedia programs can be divided into three major classifications. First is the *client/server* architecture, which includes all three components (client, server, and encoder). It is the most popular and most flexible model, but is also the most complex to implement. The second type is the *server-less* model, which doesn't use server software—it works solely on HTTP streaming. This is much easier and works more like a "create and forget" system. The last system is the *no-client*, or *client-less*, model. It is named no-client, but should more accurately be called a no-plug-in system since it uses Java to play files. No-client systems may or may not use a server program. Following are more details.

Client/Server

Client/server is the most scaleable solution and the most popular with larger web-sites. It comes with three programs: client, server, and encoder. The server software is installed onto your web server to manage and distribute the requested data. There are compatibility issues including installation and setup difficulties, so this model is the most complex and most difficult to implement. As you might suspect, it is also the most expensive. On the plus side, client/server gives web administrators the most control over who is watching and what is being sent, especially over an intranet. If you're planning a high-traffic video network, you should probably use this system.

Server-Less

A server-less system (also called *HTTP streaming systems*) doesn't use a dedicated streaming server program; it only comes with a client player and the encoder soft-ware for creating files. You simply encode a file to its appropriate format (using its producer software), then place it on a web server where you normally put other HTML pages and web images. When a user requests a streaming file, it is sent via HTTP like any other web data. The bad part about the server-less method is that you can't control your bandwidth or usage like you can with the client/server system. Server-less streaming is limited by your network capacity. It can only handle a few dozen simultaneous streams even when using a T1 line (1.5Mbps), but this is the easiest and fastest way of putting streaming media on your site.

Client-Less

The client-less solution works much like the server-less model. The big difference is that there is no client program to download or install. Instead, the video is pushed along to the user with a built-in player, usually written in Java. Once the player is loaded and the movie is buffered into memory, the Java player plays the file. With this method, the barriers to streaming multimedia are now lowered so that anyone with a Java-enabled browser can use it with no downloading or installation worries. Currently, just a few vendors use this model, but it seems to be a very good way to get a wider audience base. Other vendors will likely support this no-client method in the future. These no-client systems may or may not use a server, but they should always include an encoder.

As should be evident, using a client/server system is best for high-end applications. You can have hundreds, or even thousands of people requesting files at any one time. The capacity is limited by your network or the number of streams that you purchase from the vendor. Client/server systems are good choices for those that already have a Windows NT or UNIX web server on a network. HTTP, or server-less streaming, is better suited for smaller websites or for those who use virtual web hosting. Finally, the no-client system makes sense for anyone that doesn't want to use client plug-ins. Always remember, however, to find out if the no-client system needs a server or not.

Basically, your first main decision should be whether you want to use a server or a no-server approach, but don't decide just yet. First, let's learn more about encoding and compression.

Encoding and Compressing Files

You probably noticed that the only software component that you always need (no matter what system) is the *encoder* software. Encoding or converting files is a very important part of using streaming multimedia. The encoder converts files from standard formats like AVI, QuickTime, and MPEG, and makes them into stream-ready formats.

Each multimedia system will have its own encoder, so you can't use one encoder with another system. They have different and proprietary compression algorithms, making one streaming program better than another. You can convert files into almost any size you want, so they are optimized for users with different connection speeds. If your users are Internet users, you may want to limit your files so they can be viewed over 28.8Kbps. You can also have high-quality files for users who have a lot of bandwidth, like T1 users or those with cable modems. Thus, a movie converted for intranet users will have much better quality than a clip converted for 28.8Kbps modem users. Naturally, the better the compression, the smaller the file, and the worse it looks and sounds. Thus, T1-optimized files will be much larger but can approach TV-quality video with CD-quality audio. That's about all we'll get into compression in this chapter. Chapter 4 will have more on capturing, recording, and compressing audio and video files.

Bringing It All Together—Using the Server, Encoder, and Client Programs

Practically all audio and video streaming systems work the same way. The implementation process follows a series of steps that will be repeated often in

---

this book. Next are details on how you'll be using the three software components of a client/server system. Use them as a reference for when you need to be reminded of what you need to do.

1. Install the server, encoder, and client programs. If you're using HTTP streaming, you can ignore the server part.

2. Run the server program and make sure it is active.

3. Capture, create, and edit your multimedia files (AVI, QuickTime, WAV, or other sound files).

4. Use the encoder program to convert those files into streaming format.

5. Create a text pointer file. Practically all the systems in this book use a pointer file that points to the actual streaming file. It usually consists of just a single line of text with the URL of the actual file. Without this pointer file, your streaming audio or video player won't be able to stream; it will just be downloaded. This file can be created by any ASCII text editor.

6. Create or update your web page to create the hotlink. You need to link to the ASCII pointer file, not to the actual encoded streaming file. You can use the A HREF link, although some can use the EMBED tag.

7. Add or change MIME types on your web server. Each streaming system will have its own MIME type and associated file that you need to add. Your web server needs to be told about this new MIME type and associated file(s). If you don't add the MIME type, browsers won't recognize your new streaming type. Since all web servers work differently, you'll have to check your server's documentation on how to change or add server MIME types.

8. Upload or copy the streaming file to the server computer and proper sub-directory. If using HTTP streaming, just copy the file to the web server.

9. Upload or copy the text pointer file and the updated HTML page to the web server.

10. Test it by clicking on the link. The client program should launch and begin to play the file. After a few seconds of buffer time, you should see or hear your file.

That's it! Make a mental note of steps 5 and 7, since they are things that you have to do on your own. You'll be hearing a lot about pointer files because so many programs use them, and changing MIME types should be something you do often if you are a webmaster. If you don't have local access to your server, ask your web-master to change it for you.

For broadcasting live audio or video, the steps will be slightly different. Instead of step 4, you'll simply have to use another program to capture the live audio or video and send it to the server. Once it reaches the server, it is ready for use. You can follow the other steps to create a pointer file, change MIME types, and upload the files to the web server.

What Do You Want to Use on Your Site?

This section helps you learn more about the server and administration side of streaming multimedia. It leads you by asking you a series of questions that will help you select one solution. By the end of this chapter, you should have some idea of what you want to use on your site.

Client/Server or Server-Less Streaming?

Thinking of using client/server programs? Almost all streaming programs use file formats and client/server software that are proprietary and incompatible with other programs from other vendors. In other words, a StreamWorks server cannot be used with RealAudio to stream files. One exception is Microsoft's NetShow, which can play its own file format, Active Streaming Format (ASF), as well as RealMedia files. As the industry consolidates, you'll find many more vendors with interoperable soft-ware, but for now, the problem of interoperability is a big issue. There are so many streaming audio/video systems that it doesn't make any sense for them to work independently of each other. Will industry consolidation ever happen? So far, the situation doesn't appear to be improving much, but if streaming multimedia is to grow, it will need some type of interoperability.

Once you choose one system you will be locked into it until you replace it. Do you still want to use a client/server system? If you already operate a website or an intranet, you are already familiar with the client/server architecture and how pow-erful it can be. The streaming server software works alongside your regular web server, and its job is to handle all the file requests for the streaming files. It also keeps tracks of users and data requests so you can manage your network better by seeing what is going on with all your data. Most vendors in this book have server software available for either Windows NT or some flavors of UNIX only. (See the next section for more on hardware and operating system options.) If you already run Windows NT or UNIX, then you don't have to buy any hardware—just get the streaming server software and install it. The server simply runs in the background.

And yes, you can run multiple servers from different streaming vendors, but make sure to read all the documentation to see if there are any port conflicts.

What if you don't already run a website or intranet? What if you use a web hosting service to host your website? What if you don't want to use a client/server approach? The only other option is the server-less system where you don't need a separate streaming web server—your regular web server software handles the streaming files. You simply need to convert, upload, or copy the files to your web server. It handles everything for you. The server-less system is great for those who want low-maintenance, create-and-forget streaming multimedia. It also is more affordable.

Still undecided? Your choice may be easier because some vendors now support both client/server and server-less (HTTP) streaming. You can now have the best of both worlds.

Choosing Server Hardware: UNIX or Windows NT?

One of the biggest debates in the Web world is what hardware to use as your web server. There is the classic and ever-raging Mac versus Windows debate. More recent is the rivalry between UNIX and Windows NT servers. This section won't delve deeply into these great debates. With so many similarities between these systems, sometimes the deciding factor can be a matter of personal taste.

Should you use one of the many flavors of UNIX or go the desktop route with Windows/Intel (Wintel) computers? UNIX hardware can be very expensive, costing in the tens of thousands of dollars. Wintel systems are less expensive and somewhat easier for the beginner to use. Much of the answer depends on what you're already using on your network or if you're starting a network from scratch; in which case, you'll have lots of room to choose and explore.

UNIX computers and operating systems are very popular on the Internet mostly because UNIX computers ran the Internet in the early days. Today, many websites still use UNIX web servers—it's usually more well-suited for Internet tasks. If you're already familiar with UNIX, you should have no problem sticking with it as your main server. There's no real compelling reason to switch to Windows NT, because most streaming vendors have server software for both. With so many flavors of UNIX (like IRIX, Xenix, Solaris, Ultrix, GNU, and the freeware Linux), choosing the right UNIX operating system is important. Most vendors tend to release software for the popular versions of UNIX. You can't go wrong by choosing Sun Microsystems' SPARC server running its Solaris 2.6 operating system. Another popular choice is Silicon Graphics' server with its version of UNIX, IRIX 6.2.

Wintel systems have been crossing over into the enterprise sector and are very good alternatives to UNIX workhorses. Windows NT 4.0, the most popular operating system for high-end applications and web server solutions, is not just an operating system but also a networking environment. Windows NT Server 4.0 comes with its own web server software, Internet Information Server (IIS), and HTML authoring software, so setting up an intranet or Internet site can be very simple. Windows NT even has native support for its own streaming solution, NetShow. Clearly, Microsoft wants you to use its proprietary products and software.

Windows NT is a good solution, especially if you're a complete Windows enterprise. Perhaps the biggest benefit to using Windows NT is that a growing number of vendors are writing server software for NT systems. In fact, almost every single server program mentioned in this book can be used on NT. Those that don't yet have NT server software will probably release them in the near future, perhaps by the time you read this.

This book uses Windows NT as a server computer, not because it is necessarily better than UNIX, but because it is much more accessible to the average user.

Bandwidth: Do You Need More?

To a webmaster, bandwidth is more precious than any jewel. With the arrival of push technology, groupware, and other multimedia products, bandwidth can quickly be eaten up on a typical 10BaseT Ethernet intranet. Even the Internet has had occasional regional brown-outs and network outages. For developers implementing streaming multimedia, the problem can be even more acute because of the huge amounts of data being consumed.

For those using an intranet, it is very easy to upgrade an existing LAN and add more bandwidth. New technologies like Fast Ethernet, Frame Relay, and Asynchronous Transfer Mode (ATM) enable transfer speeds many times faster than typical Ethernet connections of 10Mbps. ATM, for instance, promises speeds of around 2.5Mbps to 2.4Gbps. For a good quickie upgrade, you can easily upgrade your 10Mbps intranet into a 100Mbps monster with minimal investment of new equipment—other, faster technologies will take much more know-how and money. When you've done all the upgrading you can handle, you need something that dramatically lowers your bandwidth, like *IP multicasting* (see next section).

If you plan on using an HTTP system, bandwidth is even more important because there is no software controlling and managing your streaming data; requests for the files are automatically handled by your web server. As long as your network can handle it, data will be sent to whomever asks for it. The data is sent along with any other usual web data like GIF, JPEG, and HTML files, so your whole network can slow down under heavy usage.

With a client/server system, managing network bandwidth is an integral part of that architecture. You can usually tell your streaming server to slow down and not handle as many requests or raise the maximum number of streams that it can handle. Also important is that client/server systems allow you to change the protocol and port that you are using. Instead of using HTTP to send data, you can open up UDP ports, which allow for much faster transmission of data.

For those setting up shop on the Internet, you can do your part by getting the biggest and fattest pipes for your website. Try getting a connection that is closest to the Internet backbone so there won't be many reasons for delays or interruptions. T1, T2, and T3 lines are all available but for a big price. Are they worth it? You bet. If you're planning on running a high-traffic website with lots of streaming content, be prepared to get multiple lines and multiple servers to keep up with heavy demand.

The Benefits of IP Multicast

Everyone wants more bandwidth, and when you get more it's never enough. Implementing a streaming multimedia system on your network can be a big drain on your bandwidth. What is the solution to an overloaded network? The most obvious solution is to just add newer network hardware, increase the pipes, and get more bandwidth. The other is to use *IP multicasting*. IP multicasting is a bandwidth-conservation technology that enables multiple PCs to tap into a single stream of data. That single stream is sent out over the network but is multiplied and redistributed to a large number of recipients via network routers.

Ordinarily, data is sent one-on-one in a system called *unicasting*. In this model, every recipient is sent his or her own stream of data. As more data is sent to more people, bandwidth is rapidly depleted. For example, a 500MB stream sent to 40 users can quickly saturate a typical intranet. Another method of transferring data is the *broadcasting* model, which consists of sending one data stream for everyone to receive. It is up to the recipient to accept or decline the broadcast. Again, this model takes up unnecessary bandwidth. Multicasting solves these problems by sending a single data stream, which is then multiplied and distributed to a select group of users who have registered or subscribed to that particular transmission (see Figure 3.1).

As you can see, multicasting offers huge bandwidth savings over unicasting or broadcasting. It is especially good for bandwidth wasters like videoconferencing, streaming video, live broadcasts, software updates, and push. This frees up your network for regular net data like web and email, which are not well-suited for multicasting.

Implementing IP Multicasting

How can you implement IP multicasting? There aren't many barriers so there's almost no reason to upgrade if you have large bandwidth demands on your network. To implement it on your network, the server, clients, network switches, and routers must all be able to support multicasting. The biggest job is handled by the routers, which take one stream and multiply it. If your routers are new, they should be multicast-capable already. If they are older, they just need to be upgraded with more memory. (Check the manufacturer of your router or your supplier.) You also need to add new protocols to your network like Real Time Protocol (RTP) or Real-Time Streaming Protocol (RTSP), which conserve bandwidth for real-time applications. One more thing you need is some sort of scheduling software, so users can subscribe to certain multicast sessions whenever you schedule them. At the

---

Figure 3.1 Unicasting wastes plenty of bandwidth by sending the same data to recipients. IP multicasting sends just one data stream, splits it, and directs it to a large number of users.

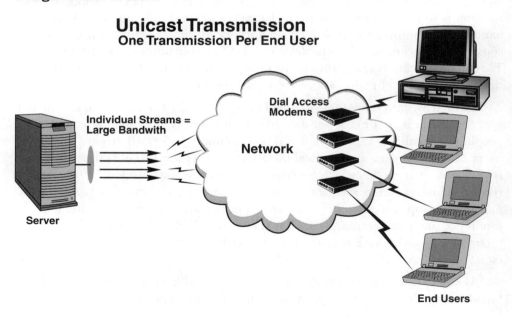

scheduled time, the user just needs to open up the client player to tune in to the multicast transmission.

IP multicasting is possible over the Internet, but it may take some time before Internet Service Providers (ISPs) decide to use it extensively, mostly because of costly hardware upgrades. In 1996, the IP Multicast Initiative (www.ipmulticast .com) was founded to help implement multicasting, especially over the Internet. Already, over 60 companies have joined from industries including software, networking, and ISPs. Some companies like General Motors and Smith Barney have already implemented multicasting on their intranets to transmit data like software upgrades, inventory reports, and even live video. Companies with multicast-capable software include IP/TV, StarCast and RealVideo (streaming multimedia), ProShare and CU-SeeMe (videoconferencing), and StarBurst (software transmissions and updates).

For more help on IP multicasting, check out the IP Multicast Initiative's website or visit networking companies like Cisco (www.cisco.com), Bay Networks, (www.baynetworks.com), or 3Com (www.3com.com).

Figure 3.1 *Continued*

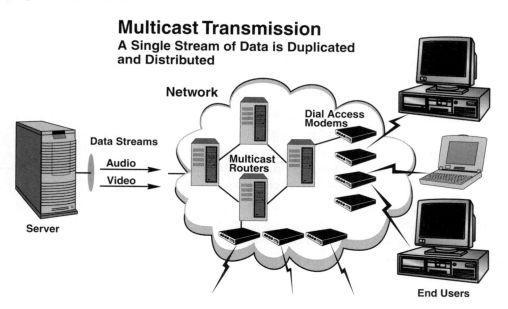

Multicast Transmission
A Single Stream of Data is Duplicated and Distributed

Intranet or Internet: Which Is for You?

Will your streaming multimedia system be used over the Internet? If so, then you have a whole new set of issues to consider. Individuals on the Internet can be a problem since there are so many different platforms, browsers, and operating systems being used. Some users may not bother with downloading a certain plug-in or might have an older version that no longer works. Since you have no control of the network or the users' software, much of your audience will be determined by market share. In other words, only the most popular streaming software should be considered for use over the Internet. Using newer or experimental software is a quick way to befuddle Internet users. As you can probably guess, the no-client system is great for use over an intranet or the Internet. Clients don't need plug-ins to watch your content, just a Java-enabled browser. This is the best solution, since you can have a virtually unlimited audience.

For those implementing streaming media on an intranet, things are more in your control; you set the operating system, client software, plug-ins, network bandwidth, and more. With only one standardized player and solution on your intranet, you won't have incompatibility. Also, since you can install the plug-in or player on each client, everyone will have equal access.

Implementing an intranet streaming model is a great way to see what these programs can do under high-bandwidth conditions. You'll be able to have very high-quality audio and video. If you're running an existing intranet, however, make sure you test your system on an isolated part of the network so you won't affect overall performance. Once you've completed testing, you can roll out the system on the whole network.

What can you do on an intranet? You can deliver live speeches and market news to every desktop. You can have video instructions so that the answer to a specific question can be queued up and shown by just selecting the specific question. You can allow for presentations, training, customer support, and many other applications that can be broadcast to a large number of users.

You can, of course, implement both systems—intranet and the Internet. Just make sure to have a firewall that prevents any data on your intranet from leaving your network. Likewise, you can keep unwanted visitors from using your streaming content with the same firewall.

Should Your Multimedia Be Live or On-Demand?

Depending on what you want to do, the answer to this question is rather simple: Using on-demand, or prerecorded, multimedia is the easiest setup. Files can be recorded, stored on a hard disk, and accessed by anyone at any time. Of course, most client/server systems can do both live and on-demand multimedia, so check with the vendor first if this will be a major consideration for you.

Live setup is more demanding and definitely more expensive. Some client/server systems use hardware encoders to capture and compress an incoming analog audio or video stream. The system then passes the stream along to the streaming server. If you have a great deal of live content, you may even want to devote an entire computer as your live broadcast station so it won't slow down your regular web server. Usually, the data is sent directly to the server so there's no need for disk access that can seriously slow a transmission. You can also choose to save your live broadcasts to disk for later rebroadcasts or on-demand use. Live broadcasting takes up plenty of bandwidth and lots of processor power, so make sure you have a very powerful and capable machine handling the live broadcasting.

Another solution is to use "tape delay," or *almost live*, transmission. This way, files can quickly be captured and compressed without the need for expensive hardware additions or dedicated lines. You can put up the taped event within a few minutes or hours of a live event. You can even use a less-expensive server-less system for tape-delayed or on-demand files.

Should You Use Audio or Video?

What type of multimedia do you want to use—just audio, or do you want some video, too? First, you must ensure that you have a compelling need for audio and video on your site. You should not use multimedia simply because everyone else is, or because you want to increase traffic. You should implement streaming multimedia because it somehow helps people who visit your site or somehow enhances your message. Once you've decided on your message, you can begin asking yourself whether you want audio or video on your site. Perhaps you want a mix of both audio/video and streaming animation.

Many streaming programs specialize in one type of application or another. One program specializes in streaming speech but can't be used with music. Other programs are better at displaying clear, steady video at low frame rates, while others handle frame rates better so you get a smoother picture. Carefully evaluate what type you need.

Whether you choose audio or video also depends on what your company does. Are you an entertainment company that wants to deliver streaming videos, news, movie previews, high-quality music, or celebrity interviews? Maybe you're a business that wants to send speeches, training materials, presentations, or video aids to clients or employees over an intranet or extranet. Perhaps you just want to jazz up your website with compelling multimedia, like product demonstrations, customer testimonials, and animated logos.

Whatever your purpose for wanting streaming multimedia, you must ask yourself how much audio and video content you will need. You may just want streaming audio, but perhaps a few months down the line you may want to incorporate video, too. Can the system you initially chose provide you with everything you need not just now but in the future? If you're on the Internet, it is a good idea to mix both audio and video especially if you have a large, varied audience. That includes having some downloadable audio and video for those who don't have the streaming plug-ins installed. Also, having downloadable media is good for those who simply wish to view movies later after they have disconnected from the Internet.

Another good idea is to have perhaps two major streaming formats on your website. Some websites use a mix of RealMedia and VivoActive content, for example, or RealAudio and StreamWorks, so that more people can access these files. That does not mean that you should use every single major streaming format on your website. Just try to have a good mix of streaming systems, perhaps a server-less and client/server approach on your site.

Having a wide range of media options makes it much easier to get your message across by giving users the option of choosing the file formats they want to view. Not everyone has installed the popular streaming player plug-ins, and it may prevent them from watching your movies and staying at your website. After all, the last thing you want to do is alienate your audience and have them go somewhere else, like your competitor's website.

Cost of Ownership

Some streaming media systems with licensing fees and extra software can cost thousands or up to tens of thousands of dollars. Although very important, don't let the high cost of many of these systems scare you. These initial costs may seem high, but if the program does the job well, the investment will be worth it. You should first find the right solution for your job, and then worry about costs. On the other hand, there are many free to low-cost solutions available. Keep this in mind, especially if cost is a major factor.

Either way, there will be other hidden, long-run costs. Yes, there will be up-front costs, but in the long run, you will need money to keep creating and updating your multimedia files. Buying recording equipment and new hardware is something else to consider. Don't forget, creating and editing multimedia files is a time-consuming process that takes up precious manpower. You may even want to outsource audio or video recording to an outside agency that handles audio/video recording and post-production. In other words, don't be caught short-handed when it comes to content creation.

Finally, keep in mind that streaming multimedia is a very new industry that has not yet established open standards. Chances are you will have to upgrade to a new system when standards are set within a few months or in the next few years. At the very least, you will have to upgrade your existing system because vendors update their software and release new versions very often. You should reevaluate your and your audience's needs regularly to see what new technologies or advances have cropped up since you last implemented your system. Also consider hardware and networking costs if you need to upgrade your network or Internet connections.

Customer Support

Once you've decided on a system, don't forget to look at its customer support. If you use a client/server system, you may need some help in configuring options for your web server. Make sure you know the company's customer support offering and see whether it has a premium service in case you want extra technical support.

Another option is to get support from other users. Most companies have web discussion groups, newsgroups, or mailing lists that cater to their programs. Take advantage of these offerings when you buy their products, so you can see what problems or issues other customers are talking about.

What about the Future?

As it stands now, the streaming multimedia market is not a perfect one. There are many complex parts and many things you must know before you even begin implementation. You must be a network guru, web administrator, and even have a hand in the creative process by capturing and converting data formats. You must know about bandwidth, incompatible file formats, and streaming protocols, and arm yourself with the knowledge that things may change drastically within a few months or years.

In order for things to improve, the industry must consolidate. Already, there are close to two dozen proprietary streaming video formats available. Practically all of them work independently, so they cannot be used with others' programs. There is the RealMedia architecture, Microsoft's Active Streaming Format, and many more formats striving for market dominance. In order to bring more order to the market, vendors should strive to make an open standard that is used by the whole industry. Having proprietary formats only hinders industry growth, and growth can came through dialog or with mergers and acquisitions.

Either way, something must be done, since there is no real market leader. The first company to make any gains in this area may well be the leader in the future. So far, the 500-pound computing gorilla, Microsoft, is making some efforts to consolidate the industry. It wants its own Active Streaming Format (ASF) to be the file of the future. It has taken the lead in the industry by buying stakes in a few major competitors and forming alliances with many other vendors. Only time will tell who will come out on top.

For more things to consider and computer technologies to watch, read Chapter 22.

Summary

The promise of streaming multimedia is very appealing. Once the bandwidth is in place and a file format is standardized, there is no telling what can be accomplished with these technologies. Practically anyone can set up and broadcast his or her own Internet show and have a wide audience. Interactive TV? Movies on demand? Although traditional television and broadcasting still have not realized those dreams on a wide scale, the Internet is already bringing interactive and compelling live and on-demand movies to millions of users every day.

The next chapter is about creating and capturing audio and video on your computer.

DESKTOP AUDIO AND VIDEO:
Capturing, Editing, and Compression

This book would not be complete without discussing how to get your audio and video files to your computer. At first, you will probably want to experiment using existing multimedia files, but eventually you will need to use your own audio and video files. Getting video to your computer has become easier in recent years with the great advances in graphics and multimedia hardware and software. There are a number of ways of putting video on your site, from using regular camcorders connected to a video capture board, to using video cameras tethered to your computer, to the newest invention: a tapeless MPEG video camera.

This chapter concentrates on video and how to capture it to your computer. There is also a list of manufacturers and hardware devices. We won't spend much time on audio, since capturing sound on your computer is as easy as talking into a microphone nowadays. The remainder of this chapter describes video and audio editing software.

Desktop Audio and Video

Desktop video capturing and editing used be something that only video professionals did; now it's accessible to anyone with a good computer and the right hardware/ software. Before starting down the road to capturing, creating, and compressing audio and video, you should ask yourself what you hope to accomplish. You shouldn't use audio and video just for the heck of it; there should be a clear purpose behind your use of multimedia.

Why use audio and video? You need to think about the message you are trying to convey, whether you need video or perhaps a slide show presentation with audio, and whether you need speech, music, or a combination of both. What input device will you use? You can connect a camcorder, VCR, digital camera, Digital Audio Tape, or any other source.

Will you broadcast live? If so, what quality do you want? If you're looking for high quality, you need professional equipment, mixers, and more—maybe a professional audio person should help. Video broadcasting is even more difficult. Will you need an outside production agency? Can you handle it all yourself? Does your company already have professional audio and video equipment? Will you need to rent equipment?

Are you using prerecorded media? If you're planning on a lot of video capture, you might want a dedicated computer, or you may want to outsource it to a bureau (like www.encoding.com) that specializes in video capture and encoding.

Who is your audience? Know your audience so you know what they would benefit from. Don't be overly simplistic or go over their heads.

How will you deliver the audio or video? What size bandwidth should you create for? If you're creating for Internet streaming, you might want to use less motion and less action. For bigger bandwidth, you can use higher-quality audio or video.

If you're capturing third-party multimedia, do you need copyright clearance? Using copyrighted video or audio can put you in a legal quagmire. Always ask or get permission if you're in doubt.

You don't need a Hollywood budget to get good video; just one person can handle the whole video capture and editing process. Don't be afraid to seek professional assistance to get professional results.

Digital Audio Basics

Before starting out on capturing and editing audio and video, you need to know some basics of digital multimedia, because we'll use these terms often. Let's start with audio first. When recording audio on your computer, it is usually saved as a raw audio file that has certain properties. There are three parameters of digital audio files:

1. Sampling rate (can range from 8kHz to 48kHz).

2. Number of bits per sample (8 or 16).

3. Number of channels (Mono or Stereo).

The higher the sample rate, the better the sound is, and the same rule applies to the bit rate. Therefore, a file that is 48kHz, 16-bit stereo will sound much better than an 8kHz, 8-bit mono file. As you might suspect, the 48kHz file will be much larger, so keep that in mind if you're making it available on the Internet. To help you understand these attributes, see the following chart:

Audio	Sample Rate	Bits	Channels	Data Rate
Telephone quality	11kHz	8	Mono	662KB/Min.
CD quality	44.1kHz	16	Stereo	10.6MB/Min.

Those are the two most commonly used audio types, but, of course, you can use a mix of attributes for any audio file. Many audio programs like Windows Sound Recorder allow you to convert files from one sample rate to another or change bits from 8 to 16. You can't, however, convert a mono file into a stereo file. It will send the monaural signal to both channels, but it won't be true stereo. It is always easier to downsample, so you should always work from high-quality files, then change them to whatever parameters you want. When you reduce the sample rate or number of bits, you also greatly reduce the size of the file. So choose wisely: You can either make a good-quality file that's large or make a lower-quality file that's small. For more on reducing the size of a file, see the section, "The Compression Solution," later in the chapter.

Working with Audio

Recording audio is much easier than capturing video. It is as easy as using a microphone connected to a multimedia computer. Video cards that also capture audio (not all do) are best, especially for synchronizing sound with video. If your video capture card doesn't support audio, you will just have to use your regular sound card. Both Windows and Mac users can record off a microphone without much of a hassle.

Windows users can record speech using Sound Recorder, the standard Windows audio player and recorder. Just connect your microphone, hit the Record button, and talk. Recording music from a CD is easy, too. You just have to change your input device so that it accepts your CD-ROM, and then hit Record.

Recording and Editing Audio

Like video, editing sound usually means cutting and changing the sound so it's just right. Although you can edit sound with some video editors, your best bet is to stick with audio-only editing software.

Besides editing, you can also record audio with many of these programs. Sound editors give you more options and better control of your recording sessions. You can record from a wide variety of sources: from your microphone, your CD-ROM, or from your audio card. Just connect any analog audio device into your computer's audio "in" plug and connect it to any source like a VCR, Digital Audio Tape player, cassette player, or camcorder. You should always capture audio at the highest quality available (44.1kHz, 16-bit stereo). You can later convert the file to a smaller sample rate or remove a track to make it mono.

> **TIP** Want better-quality audio recordings? First, use good-quality microphones. Those inexpensive ones may be a bargain, but the sound you get won't be very good. If you want stereo, make sure you get a stereo microphone. Second, it's important to keep your background noise down. Work in a quiet place. Third, check your recording level. Keep it low enough to avoid clipping or audio breakup. If the level reaches the red zone, you're in the danger zone. Last, if you need more help or want a professional product, use an audio professional.

What audio program should you use? They should all be able to do the basics like cutting and pasting, raising the volume, removing pauses, and changing the properties of the audio file. Any good audio editor should have sound effects that you can control like echo, distortion, doppler, reverse, reverb, and delay. Others even support MIDI control, so you can synchronize all your sounds. A very good program will also be able to convert files into streaming format.

Audio Editing Software

There aren't many sound editors available, but the ones there are *are* very good. Here are some Mac and Windows programs:

SoundEdit 16. Macromedia (www.macromedia.com) makes this powerful Mac sound editor. It has multitrack editing, many codecs, its file formats are supported, and it comes with a free trial period. It costs about $419.

Sound Forge. Sound Forge by Sonic Foundry (www.sfoundry.com) is a sound editor for Windows 32-bit computers. It also makes an editor that is well suited for Internet and streaming, Sound Forge XP. This version allows you to record and edit many types of audio including RealAudio, NetShow, and TrueSpeech files. The regular program retails for $495, while the XP version is $149.

GoldWave. GoldWave (www.goldwave.com) proves that not all good programs are commercially released by big companies. GoldWave is a shareware program available for Windows 3.x, Windows95, and NT. It is a full-fledged, multitrack, audio editing program that can play and convert many different audio formats (see Figure 4.1). Registering costs just $30.

CoolEdit. CoolEdit by Syntrillium (www.syntrillium.com) is a shareware program that acts like a full-fledged professional program for Windows 3.1, Windows95, and NT. If you like CoolEdit, you can register it for $25 to get just basic functions, or for $50 you can get the whole program, allowing you to do more advanced functions and effects. There is also an advanced program called CoolEdit Pro.

Digital Video Basics

Before we go any further with video, some definitions are needed. *Video* is nothing more than a series of pictures displayed quickly to give the illusion of motion. There are three worldwide video broadcasting standards: SECAM, PAL, and NTSC. In the United States, we use NTSC (National Television Standards Committee) for analog broadcasts. This is defined as a picture having 525 lines per frame of video displayed

Figure 4.1 GoldWave is a shareware program that has features similar to the high-cost audio editors.

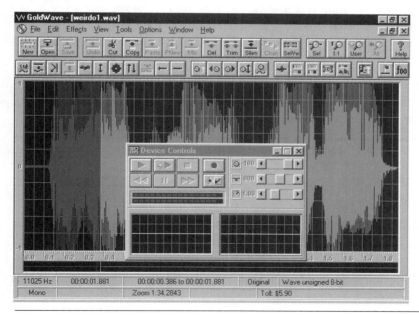

at around 30 frames per second (fps). At 30 fps, our eyes can see fluid motion—anything below 25 fps or so, we see jerkiness that is very distracting.

For computer and digital video, there are newer definitions and terms that we use to define a video file. Picture resolution, color depth, and frame rate are the three most important variables:

Picture resolution. This is simply the measurement of the number of pixels in a video frame. Pixels are beams of light that make up your video image. Picture resolution is usually expressed as width multiplied by height. Most computers and monitors can display a wide range of screen sizes (800×600 and 1024×768 are two common display sizes). Full-screen video is defined as just 640×480 pixels. Two other common video sizes that you might come across are CIF (Common Intermediate Format), which is 352×288, and QCIF (Quarter Common Intermediate Format), which is 176×144.

Color depth. This expresses the number of colors used in a video file. Common descriptions are 8-, 16-, and 24-bit color depths. Eight-bit files can only produce 256 colors, while 24-bit files can display 16 million colors. Of course, the more colors that are used, the larger the file.

Frame rate. This is the rate at which frames are shown on the screen represented in frames per second. Normal television and movies are shown at 30 fps, but not all computers and video cards are capable of capturing a frame rate this high. Fast processors are necessary to handle this big load. Many AVI or QuickTime movies are at 15 fps and look reasonably good.

As you may know already, video files take up a lot space on your hard drive. Why is this? It is just the sheer amount of data that must be squeezed into a typical file. Even a modest file like a medium-sized window (320×240) at 24-bit and 15 fps is about 207MB for one minute. See the following table for more specifics:

Window Size	FPS	Bits	Data Rate
640×480	30	24	27.65MB/Sec
320×240	15	24	3.46MB/Sec
160×120	15	24	865KB/Sec

Even a five-minute video can be extremely large. Can you see how quickly you'd run out of disk space? Can you also see how difficult it is to send video over the tight 28.8Kbps pipes of a modem? The solution is *compression*.

The Compression Solution

Compression can be defined as taking large files and making them smaller, and it works by eliminating redundant information. Compression is also known as *codec*, an abbreviation for COmpression/DECompression. Codecs can shrink a 30MB video to one as small as 80KB.

There are two kinds of codecs: *hardware* and *software*. Hardware codecs mean that you install a board, usually an MPEG board, to handle compression and decompression. Software codecs work the same, except that hardware codecs work faster since they relieve your processor of some of the burden. Software codecs are very popular because they are usually free and easy to obtain and install.

Your computer comes with its own codecs, but there may be free, third-party codecs that you can install. You may also get a new codec when you add new multimedia hardware or when you install a new program like some of the encoders mentioned in this book. When you record an analog signal (your voice, for example), and record it digitally, it uses the PCM (Pulse Code Modulation) by default. This is a simple but popular format that is used on Windows and Mac computers.

If you're using Windows95, you can see all your audio and video codecs by clicking the Start button and then choosing the Settings/Control Panel. Next, choose Multimedia and click on the Advanced tab. Then open up the options labeled Audio Compression Codecs and Video Compression Codecs to see all of your loaded compression schemes (see Figure 4.2). You'll notice that many have rather strange and cryptic names. Don't worry if you don't know what they are or how they work. You'll basically be using the codecs that come with the encoder programs for each vendor in this book. There's also a short chart later in the chapter on some of the more popular codecs.

Essentially, you can compress a file with two types of compression:

Lossy. This eliminates data in order to compress it tightly. Usually it deletes the repetitive or redundant data, so the output file is not an exact copy. This results in lower-quality movies, but is great for Internet transmittal (like streaming) or storage. MPEG, with a 200:1 compression ratio, is a good example of lossy compression.

Lossless. This preserves all data so you get the very same file. There is essentially no loss of data, just compacting. PKZIP is lossless; it keeps the same data yet compacts the file.

Figure 4.2 You can see all your audio and video compression schemes that your computer understands by clicking on the Multimedia icon in the Control Panel.

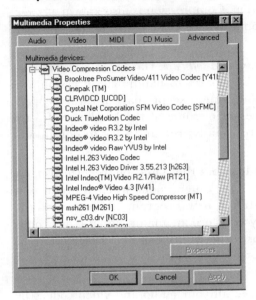

 TIP Remember, good compression is when you don't notice its presence. Try to make it so that you achieve as small a file as possible without noticeably losing quality.

There are many kinds of codecs and they all have their strengths and weaknesses. Here is a list of some popular codecs that may be installed on your computer:

Audio

Voxware	Used for compressing speech and for use at low bit rates.
G.723	Good all-purpose codec.
MPEG Layer 3	Scaleable for low or high-quality, but best when used with music.
Groupe Special Mobile (GSM)	For higher bit rates only.
TrueSpeech	For speech applications. Low bit rates only.
Lernout and Hauspie (CELP)	Good for speech at low bit rates.
PCM	Uncompressed format. Good for low- or high-quality audio.

Video

VDOWave	Used by VDOnet for streaming. For low bit rates only.
Indeo Video Raw YVU9C	Excellent quality. Can be used in place of uncompressed video.
MPEG-4	Soon to be standard. Good for high and low quality.
TrueMotion (Duck)	For high bit rates. Provides excellent quality.
H.263	Very popular telephony standard. For low bit rates.
ClearVideo	For use over Internet to compress AVI files.
Cinepak	Good high quality. For high bandwidth.

There are many more codecs, but they can't all be covered here. For example, MPEG-1 is very popular. Many vendors in this book use this compression to stream video. MPEG-1 is a hardware compression method, so you'll need an MPEG hardware encoder. It can capture 30 fps video at a size of 352 × 480, but it depends on your card.

> **TIP** Don't want to bother with compression or even capturing video yourself? You can probably use your ad agency to do it for you or choose a specialized video production company. There are also some compression service bureaus that handle compression and other video-related duties. For those who really don't want to do any work, there are full-fledged video production companies that can do everything for you.

Much more can be discussed about various compression and decompression algorithms and how to create the best files possible, but you'll get lots of practice in this book. You don't need to know how they work; just use them and see the results.

Video Capture

Now that you know about digital video, you need to know how to get your analog source to your computer. Generally, you need a video capture device usually in the form of a PCI or ISA card. There is also a new option—external devices. Let's take a look at both external and internal methods.

The external devices connect to your computer's parallel port. The parallel port uses a very slow connection to your computer, so it is not good for high-end video or professionals. Generally, these devices use the MPEG-1 codec for capturing video to your computer. Most of these kits are priced around $200 to $500.

These are geared for home users, novices, and hobbyists who want budget systems along with good software bundles.

Internal capture cards are for those who are serious about video. They are more expensive solutions—they start at about $200 and go as high as $1,000. Internal cards usually come with professional-quality software like Adobe Premiere. Another low-end option is a TV tuner card that is made for watching TV or accepting VCR inputs so you can watch video on your computer.

There are other options, however. You can also use videoconferencing kits. They come with a video capture card, digital video camera (that connects to the board), software, and sometimes even a high-speed modem. These kits are popping up everywhere now that video and videoconferencing have finally become very popular and inexpensive. The good thing about videoconferencing kits is that they come with their own camera, albeit attached to your computer. Otherwise you must supply your own input device like a VCR, TV, camcorder, or other analog signal. For low-end video, you can also use digital video cameras that connect to your parallel port and don't require a capture device. These cameras tend to cost between $99 and $200. Keep in mind that using a capture device gives you a much better picture since the card handles the input instead of your processor. If you're serious about video, you shouldn't use these parallel devices.

Mac users have it the easiest when it comes to capture devices. Most Macs already have audio and video capability built into the computer. Although there are some video cards available for Macs with no audio/visual capability, PowerMacs really don't need them since they can already accept incoming video. At best, PowerMac users can install MPEG cards that allow them to capture higher frame rates with higher resolutions. Windows users have a more daunting task. They must choose a capture device, install it, and then choose and buy video editing and capturing software. Another option is to purchase video capture kits, which come complete with hardware, software, and cables.

In general, the external kits are more suited to home users or novices who don't want to open up their computers and install new hardware. The more experienced tend to like the freedom of choosing a video card that best fits their specific needs.

Capturing, Editing, and Storing Video

It is helpful to break down video capture into three distinct parts:

Video capture. This deals with actually getting video into your computer. You can choose from external video kits and capture boards.

This section will also talk about cameras and the newest digital camcorders.

Video editing and effects. Once the movie is captured, you can begin editing. That can mean cutting scenes, adding titles and audio effects, or other special effects.

Storage. This deals with how you choose to save a file (resolution, color depth, and data rate). It is crucial to making a good streaming file.

Step 1. Capturing Your Video

The actual capturing process is very easy; the hard part is installing your capture device. Once it is installed, plug in the audio and video input cables to the card and connect the output cables to the source (TV, VCR, Camcorder, etc.). Then turn on your computer and make sure your computer recognizes the device. You might need to load a driver or video capture program first. When that's done, just start the capture program. You'll see a blank screen. Just hit Play on your source or turn on your camera to watch a preview (see Figure 4.3). Then record at any time by following the directions on the capture program that you have. That's it!

Figure 4.3 Here is a sample of my capture program called Asymetrix DVP Capture.

Capturing video is a time-consuming process, so don't make it take longer than it should. Always use a computer with a fast processor. Windows users should use Pentium 133 or faster computers. Also, capturing data requires lots of disk space—you should set aside at least 2GB for video capturing. It helps to use a high-capacity SCSI drive since they are faster than IDE drives. Lastly, you should defragment your hard drives regularly. When you capture video, the software usually saves it to temporary space on your hard disk, so defragmenting it can really improve your video capture rate.

Much of the video capturing process is dependent on the video capture card or device that you are using. Using an internal video capture card instead of an external parallel device generally works better and faster, thereby giving you much better quality video. Also, don't forget that some cards work better than others. The goal of video capture is to get the best video possible with the fewest number of lost or dropped frames. Dropped frames are always a problem, no matter what program or capture board you are using. Once your video is captured, your program should tell you how many frames were captured and how many were dropped.

 Always capture video at full motion, 30 fps. You can always lower or compress your file, but you can't ever increase the frame rate of a file. The window size you capture should be appropriate for your content. Full-screen 640 × 480 won't always be good, especially for use over the Internet. Choose something like 320 × 240 instead.

The number of video capture cards and kits has multiplied in the last year. Because there are so many, we've just included a few of the more popular vendors in the next section. Use it as a guide to see some of the features you can expect when you shop for a video capture board or kit.

Video Capture Kits

Capture kits are a newer invention, spurred by the multimedia revolution and the growing speed and power of personal computers. They are also becoming very popular, specifically with the Windows95 platform. They frequently come bundled with either an external capture device or an internal capture card and lots of video editing software. The external versions try to match the look and feel of the Snappy by Play Inc., which was an exceptionally popular and easy-to-use external device that captured still video frames and pictures from any input source. Kits such as QuickVideo Transport, Dazzle and Snazzi, AVerMedia MPEG Wizard, Python, and Buz Multimedia Producer tend to have everything that you need to capture, edit, and compress your movies. Some even come with higher-end internal versions for better video capture. Go to the enclosed CD-ROM for additional information on each program.

Working with Video Capture Cards

There are plenty of video capture cards, so covering them all is next to impossible. Video capture cards vary widely in features and quality, so you should look out for a few things when shopping for one.

There are essentially two types of capture cards. The most basic and least expensive is the *input only* card. This card simply captures data into your computer, but does not have any output capability. These are best for most users. The second type has input *and* output lines. This is for users who want to capture video, edit the movie, and then send the movie back out to analog form, like a VCR. The input/output cards are for more serious users or video professionals who want to do desktop editing. For the purposes of this book, you just need the input-only type of capture card. Even an inexpensive one is good, since we'll be using it to stream at low bit rates.

Since manufacturers offer a variety of video capture kit options, look carefully for the features most important to you. If they cost more, make sure you get your money's worth; see if you can try them out before buying. Although some cards may look similar, they may not perform as well. Do your research and learn about the cards available. Buying a video capture device should be a serious decision.

Some things to look for:

- Make sure the card can handle the input you need. S-Video or RCA-style plugs are the two most popular connections. Also, do you need an output to send video back out to analog form?

- Ensure that you have the right card. NTSC and PAL are popular. NTSC cards are used in the United States, and PAL is used in the United Kingdom and in Europe.

- Read the vendor's feature list to see their capture rate, number of codecs they support, and maximum resolution.

- Color depth is very important. Make sure you're getting true-color cards.

- For powerhouse, high-end, full-screen video capture, make sure that you can at least get 640 × 480 pictures at 30 fps.

- Check to see if the card comes with any video editing software.

- Since products tend to come and go quickly, check the vendor's website for current information before you go shopping. Once you purchase a card, check back to their site often to look for new codecs or drivers.

- Find out if the card is a PCI or ISA card and if it's compatible with Macs or Windows. ISA is somewhat slower than the newer PCI cards.

What follows is a list of the bigger names and most popular cards. Go to the CD for a description of each.

Broadway PC Video Maker	www.b-way.com
Osprey Video Cards	www.osprey.mmac.com
Bravado 2000 & Targa	www.truevision.com
WinTV	www.hauppauge.com
Videum Capture Card	www.winnov.com
Computer Eyes 1024	www.digvis.com
All-in-Wonder 3D	www.atitech.ca
Smart Video Recorder III	www.intel.com
Supra VideoKit	www.diamondmm.com
miroMotion DC20	www.miro.com or www.pinnaclesys.com
VideoBlaster SE100	www.creaf.com
DigiSuite	www.matrox.com
VideoVision & MotoDV	www.radius.com
STB TV PCI Television Tuner	www.stb.com
AVer TV-Phone	www.aver.com
Matrox Rainbow Runner	www.matrox.com
VideoMotion	www.genoasys.com
Fast F60 & Screen Machine II	www.fastmultimedia.com
AzeenaVision 500	www.azeena.com

Working with Video Cameras

Selecting a capture card is only half the job. The other half is deciding what type of input you're going to use, usually a camcorder, VCR, TV, or cable connection. Another option is to use a digital video camera that connects to your computer, like those used for videoconferencing. We won't go into analog stuff like VCRs; this section concentrates on digital cameras. It also discusses the new MPEG camera and the arrival of digital video camcorders.

Digital video cameras are cameras that are tethered to a computer. They usually look like small golf balls or even come with stretchable necks. Low-end models just connect to your computer's parallel port, while higher-end cameras connect to video capture cards. As you might expect, cameras that use video cards capture much better video than parallel units. These cameras were primarily used for video-conferencing programs, but they can also be used to capture video and stills.

Of course, you're greatly limited by the length of your camera's cord, but you can still make some pretty good videos this way. Some good applications for recorded video might be video greetings and e-mail, video business cards, and product demonstrations. They are also good for quickie jobs when you need something recorded right away—near your computer, of course. Laptop cameras are now available, so travelers can record movies while on the road and not be hampered by cord length.

More computer vendors are beginning to bundle digital video cameras along with new computer systems. As videoconferencing and video applications become more popular, cameras will probably become standard equipment. In the not-too-distant future, it is possible that all desktop computers will have them preinstalled.

Some popular digital video cameras are discussed next.

Parallel Port-Based Video Cameras

These cameras connect to the parallel port on Windows or to the serial port on Macs. Priced around $150 to about $299, these cameras are not for good quality video capture but do an adequate job for streaming purposes. For example, these typically won't be able to capture full-screen video at 30 fps. They can usually capture about 15fps per second at around 352 × 240. Most cameras are color cameras, but you can still find some older black and white cameras for about $100.

Creative Labs' Video Blaster WebCam	www.creativelabs.com
Connectix Corp.'s Color QuickCam	www.connectix.com
ACS Innovations' Compro D Cam	www.acscompro.com
Best Data Products' SmartOne	www.bestdata.com
Corel Corp.'s CorelCam	www.corel.ca

Videoconferencing Kits with Capture Boards

Since digital cameras are mostly used for videoconferencing, they are sometimes sold as videoconferencing kits. The kits may include cameras, capture boards, software suites, and even modems. Some systems come with headsets or microphones since the cameras don't usually have microphones. Videoconferencing kits are perfectly capable of capturing good video, too. Unless the kits come with a capture board, however, don't expect to get great quality. If you do get a capture board kit, don't forget that you can connect any other source to that input jack, like a VCR, camcorder, or TV. You aren't limited to just the videoconferencing camera.

Winnovs' VideumConf Pro	www.winnov.com
Diamond Multimedia's Supra Video Phone Kit	www.diamondmm.com
Panasonic's EggCam	www.panasonic.com/alive
US Robotics' Big Picture Kit	www.3com.com
AVER Media's Video Phone Kit	www.aver.com
Boca Research Inc.'s BocaPro Video Phone Elite	www.bocaresearch.com

MPEGCam

One of the newest gadgets is the completely tapeless, all-digital MPEG camera from Hitachi (www.mpegcam.net). This power toy is a video professional's dream. There are no tapes, no scanners, no capture board, and no capture software. It looks and works like any other camcorder (see Figure 4.4). It has an LCD video display, 6X zoom, and a 180-degree swivel lens. You just shoot your video and then download the movie into any computer. It also connects to any TV or VCR, so you can play it back anywhere.

The camera comes with a 260MB hard drive Type III PC Card, so you can move it from the camera to your computer that has a PC Card slot installed. It has an MPEG-1 codec chip that compresses video in real time. Unfortunately, it can only record 20 minutes of MPEG video at 352×240. This is good for quick jobs, but it spells trouble for any lengthy taping. Of course, you can always carry a laptop to download the video every 20 minutes, but that can be tedious. The MPEGCam can also be used to record about 3000 JPEG still pictures (704×480) or 1000 stills with accompanying 10-second audio clips.

This is clearly a multifunctional device that is the way of the future. After all, why bother with camcorder tapes and other analog devices? Just shoot and pop it into your computer. As storage space becomes cheaper and smaller, we can expect digital video cameras to hold much more audio and video.

Digital Video Camcorders

Sure you own a camcorder and you may even use it to capture your images. Chances are it's an 8mm or VHS-C camera that does an adequate job of taping regular day-to-day events. But don't you want the highest-quality digital recordings you can get?

Figure 4.4 Hitachi's MPEGCam is the world's first MPEG camera.

For the best quality recordings, nothing, not even the MPEGCam, beats the newest crop of digital video camcorders (DVC). These cameras, also sometimes known as DV cameras or just DV, are all the rage in professional video circles. Since the MPEGCam uses MPEG compression, it loses some data, making some pictures less than sharp. DV cameras, on the other hand, maintain their digital signals so the result is crystal-clear videos. All the major electronics companies like Sony, Panasonic, JVC, and Sharp make DV cameras.

 If you're new to video and camcorders, you should talk to video equipment suppliers or video production professionals for more on the best equipment to use, like cameras, lenses, lighting, and so forth.

Digital camcorders' main competition is the Hi-8 format, an analog tape system that is already in use by many video professionals. Hi-8 delivers very good video, but there many differences between the two that makes DV the clear winner.

For one, they have better resolution: 500 lines versus 400 lines (VHS is only 240 lines). Better resolution means that you can make many copies without degradation of the video as you can with normal tape, especially VHS. With VHS, after about four generations of copying, the copy will be almost unwatchable. DV cameras can record multiple generations suffering no degradation in quality. They also compress data as they record and play; while this can lead to some loss of signal, it is almost unnoticeable. Hi-8 systems have the advantage of price, however. Hi-8 systems cost around $1,000, while DV cameras can start at $1,500 and go up to $3,000.

Despite their high cost, DV cameras are the way of the future. While you may be hesitant to switch to a DV today, in a few years, the point will be moot since most high-end cameras will have switched to that format.

For a fast, pure-digital connection to your computer, DV camera owners should use a FireWire (or IEEE 1394) connection. FireWire is the newest and greatest thing to happen to digital video. It essentially is a way to connect devices to your computer and transfer data back and forth between the computer and a peripheral at very high speeds. FireWire can transmit data at 100MB per second and can reach speeds of about 1GB per second—all with no loss of quality. You just need to add the FireWire PCI card to your computer and hook everything up. A FireWire system costs around $1,000 to $4,000, but it is worth the money for fast and high-quality video transfers. Fast's DV Master, (www.fastmultimedia.com) costs $3,996 and comes with all the necessary equipment to get you started. Another manufacturer is Miro Video (www.miro.com), who makes the miroVIDEO DV 100 FireWire kit.

 Start slow—you probably don't need DV cameras or FireWire yet, but it is fun to play around with it now. It is especially good for those who have the money and can justify completely digitizing their video production equipment. It's a major task. In the meantime, stick with 8mm, VHS-C, or Hi-8.

Step 2: Editing Your Video

Now that you've captured your video, you need to start editing it.

Some video editing programs come with built-in capture ability, so you can capture and edit movies in one integrated package. Other editing programs are just for editing. If you choose to buy a kit with bundled software, you can get very good deals on video editing software and get a chance to use a variety of applications. Those bundles are more consumer-friendly programs that are aimed at home users. Professional versions come unbundled and tend to cost much more. Which one should you buy? It is up to you to gauge your current and future needs. You can usually do a lot with a low-end product, but you should know when it is time to move up to the bigger, more powerful programs.

Most video editors use nonlinear editing. *Nonlinear* simply means that you aren't editing every line sequentially. You can move around and jump backwards and forwards during the editing process (see Figure 4.5).

What should you look for in a good video editor? Cost isn't always a good gauge; many low cost programs are available that essentially mimic the big expensive programs. Even the most basic editing program can do a number of things like add titles, make transitions, edit frames, and compress files. What separates a good program from a professional program is the number of features, their flexibility, and the level of sophistication. Even the most basic programs can control start and stop capture times via frames or by time-code locations. You should look for the ability to handle plug-ins, since you'll be working with streaming media. Many high-end programs allow you to install components to create and edit streaming file formats. Also look for a program with a good audio editing feature; otherwise, you'll have to look for a separate audio editor, as discussed above.

Some other basic editing features are discussed next. You'll probably hear some terms that aren't familiar to you, but don't worry—you'll learn more about video editing the more you use multimedia.

Figure 4.5 Adobe Premiere is a popular editor with a timeline interface.

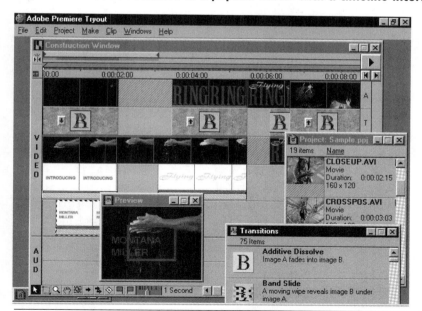

Editing

The first bit of editing you will probably do is post-capture editing, like clipping frames from the beginning or end of the video. Afterwards, you'll probably want to do more advanced edits like moving a clip to another location in the movie, adding titles and transitions, or doing other special effects. The advanced programs let you save and reuse titles or credit sequences that you use frequently.

Analog editing uses time codes in the form of hours:minutes:seconds:frames that are a standard in the industry. Most digital editing programs can use that format, but they can also use frame numbers. Most programs use a timeline approach that shows you a series of frames. This is best for adding multiple tracks and adding effects.

Transitions

Transitions are effects for combining two scenes. The most popular transition is a *cut*, so named because the next scene is cut in front of the previous one. Other transitions include wipes, blends, fades, and dissolves. In all, programs have around 10 to 20 types of transitions, and that is all you will probably need. Adobe Premiere 4.2 has about 70 transitions, and you can even tinker with them to create your own customized effects. Try not to overdo it with the fancy transitions—it's the sign of a true amateur who has just discovered his or her video editing program. Remember, the best transitions are those that go unnoticed.

Special Effects

Anything that changes the sound and texture of audio or video can be called a *special effect*. That includes color correction, tint, brightness, fading to black, as well as warping. Most programs can do all of these and much more.

Titles/Chromakey

Most basic editors do a capable job of adding titles and graphics. For more complex jobs, Adobe Premiere is more flexible.

Chromakey is used to add titles and other special effects. Chromakey is also the technique used to make Superman fly. For example, you record a scene where Superman is lying down in front of a (usually) blue screen. Later, that blue screen is erased and combined with another scene, the city backdrop. The finished effect is very good. It is a particularly fun effect, because it makes you feel like a big Hollywood director.

Go to the CD for a list and description of some of the more popular video editing programs available.

Step 3: Storing Your Videos

Once you've edited the file all you can and added all the effects, you must save it. Saving means choosing between three formats: AVI, QuickTime, and MPEG. Not all software can save or export movies in all three formats. Most common is AVI, although Macs use QuickTime as their default format.

Saving a file also means choosing the frame rate and color depth of a file. You may want to create movies with different properties. For example, you may want to create a movie with a 15fps rate along with a 30fps for those users who want better quality. Before saving your file, experiment with different frame rates. Talking-head videos just need 8 to 15 fps, while high-action video needs 15 fps or more. Don't scrimp if you don't have to. Keep previewing your file until you get that right balance of frame rate and picture quality.

Don't forget about your audio track. You can always sample your audio at a lower rate—16kHz, mono is fine for general-purpose audio. The lower your audio sample rate, the smaller your file will be. You won't always need 44.1kHz, CD-quality audio. Of course, your movie doesn't have to include an audio track at all—not having one will greatly shrink your file size.

Fortunately, a few programs allow plug-ins to export them as different files. Other programs already support many streaming file formats, too, like NetShow ASF file, or a RealVideo file. This saves you a step from having to use the vendor's producer or encoder program.

Summary

You've done the hard part: You learned about actually converting those analog signals into digital 1s and 0s. Now you can take your time and play around with video and audio editing programs. Have fun with them; desktop video editing doesn't have to be all work. You can capture all your home movies and edit them so you won't bore your relatives.

You're probably thinking one thing: Why is capturing and editing multimedia so hard? Sure, it seems that capturing video and audio could be much easier, but things have really improved in the last few years. Many companies are targeting the home user now. Desktop video editing was once the province of a professional videographer, but now almost anyone with a good multimedia computer and basic video equipment can be a budding Steven Spielberg. Powerful editing programs are everywhere, so there's no reason not to believe you can make the next Hollywood blockbuster (or at least the next Internet blockbuster).

Your next step is to learn more about the streaming multimedia programs and put those newly captured and edited movies to good use. We're on to Part II, which gives you the hands-on work. Those chapters are broken down by the following categories of streaming multimedia:

- Audio
- Video: The "Big Five" Internet systems
- Other streaming video: intranet video, smaller systems
- Streaming e-mail
- Streaming animation
- VRML, 3-D, and panoramic
- Pseudo-streaming

PART TWO

THE PROGRAMS: LEARN WHAT'S BEST FOR YOUR SITE

LIQUID AUDIO:
Music Publishing and Commerce

Liquid Audio is unique among streaming multimedia programs because it is the first music publishing and commerce application designed for the Internet. Aside from listening to streaming music, consumers can also download demos, purchase songs, or even burn their own CDs if they have a recordable CD-ROM drive.

Liquid Audio was built from the ground up as an answer to the music industry's concerns about copyright infringements and pirating. It uses a digital watermark that identifies the artist and purchaser, so if someone *does* make a copy of the song, it can be tracked down easily. Liquid Audio also tracks artists' royalties, and because the distributor is left out of the equation, more money goes directly to the artist.

Liquid Audio uses a proprietary codec to stream high-quality, Dolby-encoded music. You can even download high-quality samples to your hard drive. If you really like what you're previewing, you can purchase the song and receive a CD-quality downloaded file. You can also purchase the whole CD via download (yes, it will take many hours) or be taken to the artist's homepage or an online music store to finish the transaction.

Liquid Audio is a client/server system comprised of three parts:

Liquifier Pro. The Liquifier Pro is the first step that music publishers take in preparing files for Liquid Audio delivery. It has advanced digital editing features and gives you the ability to change sample rates to get the best audio possible. The Liquifier also provides digital watermarking to authenticate copies of the song—it writes information on who bought the song and about the artist. It also allows you to combine text-like lyrics, song information, copyright credits, and even album artwork into one file called the *Liquid Track*. A Liquid Track contains three different file types: a *preview* file that is streamed, a better-quality *sample* file that can be downloaded, and a CD-quality *purchase* file for downloading. Developers can create a Liquid Track with sample files set at various levels of audio quality. Purchased copies of Liquid Tracks are password-encrypted, so they can't be illegally redistributed to others.

Liquid MusicServer. The MusicServer is what actually runs the whole system, and you keep the Liquid Tracks there so users can access them at any time. The server can track distribution, create reports with the help of outside databases, and ensure that users get the files without a hitch.

The Liquid MusicPlayer CD. This is the helper application that loads when it encounters a Liquid Audio file. It streams Dolby sound and can also download high-quality and CD-quality demo songs. While the quality of the streaming songs is very good, the downloaded files are of *excellent* quality. The MusicPlayer can also display album art, copyright information, lyrics, and other track information. Users are issued a Liquid Passport that allows them to download a Liquid Track to be played back on their computer only or to record it onto a recordable CD.

Using Liquifier Pro to Convert Clips

The Liquifier Pro 2.0 software records, edits, encodes, and prepares a song to be published on the MusicServer. It is an audio production tool for Windows that prepares the Liquid Track for distribution over the Internet. Liquifier also adds all the nice goodies: the lyrics, copyright information, album notes, and cover art. Since it uses Dolby digital encoding, sound quality is very good. Unfortunately, Liquifier must convert stereo files to mono, but the resulting file, the Liquid Track, is still better than most other streaming sound over the Internet.

The process for creating Liquid Tracks follows a logical progression. Everything can be done by clicking and dragging and choosing options, so making your own clips is as easy as using a sound editing program.

1. Open the music file you want to convert into a Liquid Track. You should always use the highest-quality recording available, preferably a digital recording. (The Liquifier can also perform batch conversion if you need to do multiple audio tracks.)

2. At the Preview screen, select a small clip (usually 30 seconds) to convert and use as the streaming preview clip. You can use handy preset buttons

to instantly encode the clip at standard speeds like 14.4Kbps, 28.8Kbps, or ISDN connection speeds (see Figure 5.1). You can sample songs as small as 8kHz or up to full-digital quality at 44.1kHz and 48kHz.

3. Preview the converted clip by pressing the Play button. At any point, you can listen and make changes to the Liquid Track. You can also listen to the original file and compare it to the one you've compressed.

4. The next screen is the Liquify screen. Here you can enable the commerce options so users can buy CDs and purchase downloadable songs. Type in the prices for the Buy Download and Buy CD options, and enter the corresponding URL where users can buy the song or CD (see Figure 5.2). This location can be your homepage or an online music store.

5. Insert graphics, type in copyright information, text-like lyrics, and other acknowledgments.

6. Next, choose your bandwidth. You can select as many different bandwidth types as you wish, and they will all fit inside the one Liquid Track.

Figure 5.1 Liquifier Pro is audio mastering software that readies Liquid Audio files to be used over the Internet. This is the Preview window where you encode your streaming preview clip.

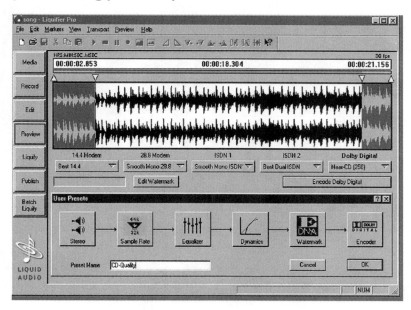

You can choose from 14.4Kbps all the way to digital-quality or LAN speeds. If you choose all the options, your Liquid Track file will be very large (reaching 50MB or more), but you will cater to many different speeds and users. Don't worry about such large files—the users don't stream the whole file, merely the portion of the file that corresponds to their connection speeds. In the end, you'll have one Liquid Track that has text, graphics, and sound all in one proprietary file format.

7. The encoding and watermarking is done automatically during the encoding process. The anti-piracy features are quite strong. The Liquifier embeds a digital watermark that is invisible to the consumer. It includes your name (who encoded the song), along with the time and date of the conversion.

8. To encode the file, push the Create Liquid Master button on the Liquify screen. Make sure you enter a new filename.

9. Click on the Publish button to see the Publish screen. Here you see the Liquid MusicServer in the right window pane. Simply drag the new Liquid Track from the Liquifier to the Liquid MusicServer. This is a

Figure 5.2 The Liquify screen is where you choose download data rates and enter the prices and URLs so users can buy your music.

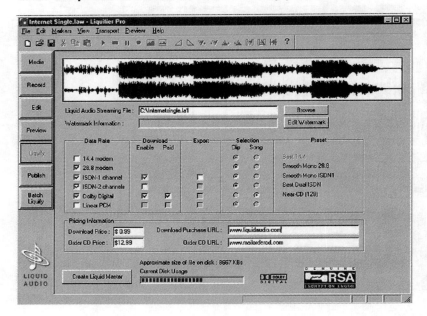

secure connection, so no one can track your transaction. Once it is copied to the server, it automatically generates a corresponding URL so you can listen to the file. You can cut and paste the URL to any email, or insert it on a web page so people can just click and listen to your music.

10. That's it! The song should be playing. You can test everything to see if the text, graphics, and links to your URL work correctly. If you selected the Buy CD or Buy Download options, you can test those as well.

 The Liquid MusicPlayer CD does not let you enter URLs to play files; you can only load files. To play newly created files, you must launch the player from a link. The best way is to quickly create an HTML page, save it, and launch it from your browser.

The Liquifier Pro also has some basic audio editing tools, like a fade in/fade out feature, cropping, cutting commands, and more. It has a 4-band equalizer that lets you fine tune the song just the way you want it. It can also record from analog and/or digital devices (like a CD-ROM), so you can work with pure digital files.

Liquifier Pro 2.0 is available as a Windows95 program ($995) or as a Mac plug-in for Digidesign's Pro Tools audio editing software.

Using the Liquid MusicServer

The Liquid MusicServer is what hosts and runs the whole system. It stores all your Liquid Tracks and sends them out over the network when requested by users. It logs all transactions and keeps a report for submission to rights agencies.

There is built-in security, so files that are dropped in the server are secure. The server can handle a large number of simultaneous streams—the actual number depends on your network bandwidth.

The Liquid MusicServer is available for UNIX now, but a Windows NT version should be available by the time you read this. Its cost is very high—$20,000 per server.

Using Liquid MusicPlayer CD

As mentioned previously, the Liquid MusicPlayer CD is a streaming player that allows you to listen to short music samples or even entire songs. It uses Dolby compression techniques that were modified by Liquid Audio to come up with a brand new codec. The player itself looks pretty much like a standard CD player (see Figure 5.3), but is different in that besides the player functions, you can also see other miscellaneous data. It can display artwork, credits, lyrics, and copyright

information. You can also access promotional materials, coupons, tour schedules, and other special offers from the promotion screen.

A few seconds after clicking on a Liquid Audio file, Liquid MusicPlayer buffers data into memory and then begins to play the song. For better quality and less skipping, you can increase the size of its buffer under the File/Preferences menu option; however, a larger buffer means it will take longer to open a file. From the Preferences screen, you should also select your correct bandwidth: 14.4Kbps, 28.8Kbps, ISDN, or T1 speeds. This is important because the Liquid MusicPlayer uses this information to select the correct file to stream to your computer. You can also select the transport protocol that you use, either UDP/RTP for faster playback or TCP for those users behind firewalls.

The most striking difference between Liquid MusicPlayer and other streaming players is the three buttons: Buy Download, Buy CD, and Free Sample. They allow you to buy CDs from websites and purchase downloadable songs for instant Internet delivery to your desktop. Before purchasing anything, you must request your Liquid Passport. (See the next section for more on the Passport.) Here's how the buttons work:

Buy Download. When this button is active, a price appears next to it. This is the price of a single track that you can purchase and download to your computer. Prices start at around 99 cents and reach no more than two dollars. Clicking the button will open a web page where you can buy the song. Just enter order and payment information (usually credit card) and once the transaction is approved, a new web page appears where you can begin the download. The web page will only be available for 24 hours. Bookmark this page in case you get interrupted while downloading, or want to download some other time, because you need to come back to this page to download the song. If you change your mind and don't want the song, abort the download; you aren't charged until you download the entire song. Remember that downloading times vary widely, so it can take anywhere from 10 to 15 minutes to get one song, depending on your connection and the length of the song. The downloaded file is saved to your hard drive and is password-protected so it can only be played with *your* copy of the Liquid MusicPlayer.

NOTE	When you are downloading samples or songs, you won't be able to use the Liquid MusicPlayer until it finishes downloading, and download times can be very long on slow connections. You can't even listen to new songs or access any player functions. What's worse is that there is no time display to let you know precisely *when* you might be finished downloading. You are only shown a progress bar that gives you a very rough idea of when you *might* be finished. If you really must use the player, just stop the download, but remember that you have only 24 hours to return and download it.

Free Sample. If you select this button, you can download high-quality sound samples of the song you were just listening to. Sometimes you are given a choice between lower-quality and high-quality downloads. The size of the file is also provided so you can gauge the time it will take to download it. Free samples are almost always small—usually around 30-seconds long. Nevertheless, they are a good alternative when you want to listen to a higher-quality song than the streaming version.

Buy CD. This button allows you to purchase the entire CD from the artist. Next to the button is the price of the CD. You will be taken either to the artist's homepage or to an online music store where you can

sh the purchase and receive the CD by snail mail. So far, no artists
ompanies are selling entire downloadable CDs, but this may change
he future.

<blockquote>
NOTE   Keep in mind that your Liquid MusicPlayer isn't involved in the commerce aspect at all. It does not collect or ask you for payment information; all purchases are handled via a secure connection between your web browser and the online merchant. If you haven't shopped online recently, you shouldn't be concerned about security; web encryption has evolved so that shopping online is very secure.
</blockquote>

All three of the buttons must first be activated by the person authoring the tracks; otherwise, they will be grayed out and inaccessible. Sometimes you may find that only one or two buttons are available.

If you've downloaded any free samples or complete songs, you can create your own playlist so you can play the files back whenever you want, even off line. Use the Tracks/Create/Edit Track List to add files to your list. It shows you the songs you've downloaded (either free or purchased) and you can edit the list at any time. You can create multiple tracks with different songs. Use the Track List Manager under the Tracks menu option to keep track of all your playlists (see Figure 5.4). You can then select and create your own customized tracks for later playback. If you have a recordable CD drive, you can record these Track Lists by choosing Tracks/Make CD or pressing the Make CD button on the Track List Manager screen. To prevent piracy, you are only allowed to record a track once to a CD. These custom-created CDs can be played on your computer or with any regular CD player. With recordable CD drives now priced at around $200 to $400, more people will certainly be buying and using them.

The Liquid MusicPlayer is available free for Mac and Windows 95/NT users and can be downloaded at the Liquid Audio website: www.liquidaudio.com.

Liquid Passport

The Liquid Passport is what enables the Player to buy and download Liquid Tracks. You don't need it if you just want to stream files or want to download demo songs. To get a Passport, you must choose File/Request Passport. You must then enter your personal information, including a credit card number. Liquid Audio says that the credit card information you enter won't ever be charged; it's simply used to verify your identity.

Figure 5.4 The Track List Manager is for organizing your Track Lists. You can include either free or purchased songs in a Track List. If you have a recordable CD drive, just press the Make CD button to begin recording.

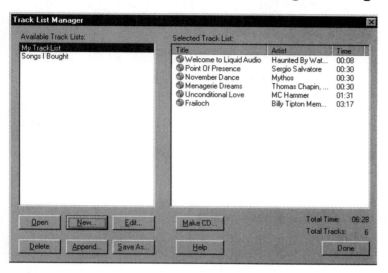

Once you submit the required information and it is verified, Liquid Audio sends you the Liquid Passport. You may get a message from your browser asking you to save the file or open it with Liquid Audio Player. Select Open to allow the Passport to be installed on your computer, and then type in a password that will keep your Passport secure on your hard drive. The Passport and your personal and credit card information are always secured by your password—only you can enter and see it. This is necessary because Liquid Audio only allows you to play songs from one Player. Once your Liquid Passport is installed, you can begin purchasing songs online.

 The credit card information is Liquid Audio's way of ensuring that you don't make illegal copies of your Liquid Passport and distribute them. Since your name, address, and credit card information is always attached to your Player, you probably won't want to let others use it or make a copy of it. This is a slight problem when you have more than one computer or laptop that you use with Liquid Audio. In that case, simply copy the whole Liquid Audio directory to your other computer's drive. That way, all your Liquid

Audio tracks, Liquid Passport, songs, and credit card information go wherever you go.

If you ever lose your Passport, you won't be able to listen to music that you've purchased. Contact Liquid Audio tech support so they can restore it for you. You'll first need to provide proof of identity. It's important to safeguard your Passport file named passport.dat. You may want to make a back-up copy of it.

Your Passport file is now encrypted and saved in the Liquid Audio directory. You can view it from within the Liquid MusicPlayer by choosing File/View Passport (see Figure 5.5). Only your name and email address are displayed. If you want to see your address and credit card information, you must enter your Passport password first.

Liquid Audio Hosting Services

The Liquid MusicServer is very expensive ($20,000), so only the most dedicated music sites will even consider using it. For those who don't plan to have extensive Liquid Audio content, or who need to test it out before implementing it fully, there are Liquid Audio Hosting Services available.

Contact Liquid Audio for more information on their pricing plans.

Figure 5.5 Your Passport displays your name and email address. Notice that the credit card information is left blank because the password was not entered.

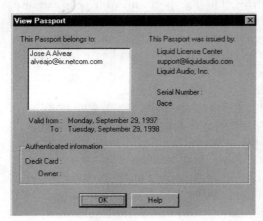

Should You Use Liquid Audio?

Liquid Audio is not for everyone, just for those serious about making the transition to online musical commerce. For those who need speech, video, or other multimedia, Liquid Audio is probably not the best choice. Liquid Audio is made for professional musicians, recording companies, online music stores, and others who want music delivery and commerce.

Artists who want to release music directly to fans should take advantage of this software. Likewise, musicians who want to share their music with a small community of people can create and post Liquid Audio tracks anywhere and let people listen to a song as soon as it is created. Record companies can directly release preview CD singles for sale or for free. Capital Records (www.hollywoodandvine) has already started to sell songs online with Liquid Audio. The buzz about Liquid Audio is really starting; more artists, recording companies, and online merchants (even a radio station) are now using Liquid Audio.

Online music stores can feature teaser clips for download and then offer to sell the whole CD via regular mail delivery. One online CD store, Music Boulevard, is selling Liquid Audio singles for 99 cents per song.

Pros and Cons

Liquid Audio has sound quality that beats almost any other streaming music available. It beats RealAudio sound hands down, and it approaches the quality of MPEG Layer 3 encoded files. At speeds of 28.8Kbps, you get good, FM-quality sound.

Liquid Audio is great for digital delivery of music and musical commerce. There is nothing else like it on the market. However, it is very single-tracked—it is specifically for music and ignores the speech and live audio markets. This severely limits its potential audience.

One thing that Liquid Audio can't help or overcome is the long download times you'll encounter when downloading your purchased or free songs. If you're serious about Liquid Audio and downloading music, invest in bigger pipes—perhaps a new 56Kbps modem.

Another sign that Liquid Audio is for the serious musician or music lover is its support for burning your own CDs. Making your own personalized CDs sounds like an audiophile's dream come true: digital sound, customized tracks, and taking your CDs anywhere you want. True, only a tiny percentage of hard-core computer users have recordable CD drives, but prices are dropping. Liquid Audio no doubt realized that recording CDs would eventually become popular and that prices would drop. Soon, recordable CD drives will be as affordable and as common as CD-ROM drives.

The Future of Online Music Commerce

Liquid Audio and its strategic partners have essentially invented a brand new method of delivering and purchasing music. They call this music delivery system *emod*, or *encoded music online delivery*. It even has its own website, at www.emod.com. This electronic method of delivering music can very well be the future of musical commerce.

> **NOTE** Liquid Audio was not the first company to introduce musical commerce and online musical delivery to the Internet. It is, however, the first and only company to combine streaming and music commerce into one system. Eurodat (www.eurodat.com), a French company, offers music delivery with strong anti-piracy features. As this book was being written, Eurodat was going through a trial period for French users connected to cable modems. It is not known if the system will continue after the trials. A second company, Cerberus (www.cdj.co.uk), a U.K. company, also offers Internet music delivery but no streaming options. Payments are made directly to the Player, and songs are downloaded when the transaction has cleared. Keep an eye on these two vendors to see what develops.

The demand for online music is very high. In 1996, over 300,000 people downloaded an original David Bowie song released on the Internet, despite the large file size. Many people enjoy surfing and reading about their favorite bands—it is one of the most popular activities on the Internet. Also, with the creation of online music stores, more and more people are purchasing CDs over the Internet. People obviously enjoy the convenience of searching for music and shopping online, and sales of music products on the Web have increased dramatically. Having online delivery of music seems like the next logical step. Liquid Audio is tapping into this wide market by allowing users to preview, listen to, download, and buy music online. Liquid Audio's anti-pirating measures are also very reassuring to the artists and record label executives.

Introducing this pay-per-song strategy is also a breakthrough. It is so inexpensive that many will probably buy songs impulsively or just because they're so darn cheap. After all, haven't you ever wanted to buy just one song from an album instead of the whole thing? With Liquid Audio, you can purchase only the tracks you want. Plus, with a recordable CD drive, you can record them to make your own customized CDs.

Online music commerce is extremely beneficial to artists. After all, having samples of your songs available to anyone online is a great way to market your name. Artists can release individual songs instead of whole albums, or even release experimental music to see how audiences respond. Some artists are using Liquid Audio to premiere their music on the Internet before releasing it to the public at large.

Eventually, major artists may choose to have their music available *only* via the Internet. With Liquid Audio, artists and companies can leave out the middlemen (the distributors and stores) and sell directly to consumers. Companies can save on retailer, distribution, and CD mastering fees, while artists can pocket more of the money themselves. Theoretically, artists can sell their music directly and bypass the record companies completely!

On the downside, with current bandwidth, online delivery of songs, especially CDs, takes way too long to be practical. Downloading just a 5-minute song can take 15 to 20 minutes with a 28.8Kbps modem. If you ever decide to buy an entire album online, you may be downloading the file for over 5 hours. Also, those who can't make and record their own CDs must keep the songs on their hard drives to listen to them; Liquid Audio is not very portable.

Serving the Needs of a Growing Market

The market for online music delivery isn't very large now, but it should grow as more people come online and as people use Liquid Audio. Despite that, it will be hard to change a consumer's habit of purchasing CDs at a Tower Records or even on the Internet. Purchasing music online may be too scary for some people, so converting users to this new online music delivery may take time and good experience.

Nevertheless, Liquid Audio is a very promising new medium and method for delivering music; however, it cannot survive on its own. It needs the support of artists, consumers, record companies, and music stores to make it a winner. Perhaps part of the problem is converting artists and record companies to Liquid Audio. There needs to be more content before Liquid Audio really becomes widespread. Is Liquid Audio just a cool way of listening to good-quality music, or will it eventually become a new way of doing business? Will record companies and artists use it? Is this just a fad, or is electronic delivery of music here to stay?

So far, the signs are very promising. Large music companies like BMG Entertainment and Capitol Records have started using Liquid Audio. Also, America Online's music site, The Hub, has started offering music. Even Microsoft has shown interest in Liquid Audio. Clearly, this market is growing.

About Liquid Audio, Inc.

Liquid Audio, Inc., was formed in 1996 to create a new platform for delivering and distributing music over the Internet, and in March 1997, the first version of Liquid Audio was released.

Liquid Audio now has many partnerships and sites using the player and music commerce system. Website maker N2K, the creator of Music Boulevard (www.musicblvd.com), a leading online music store, is a lead partner. Not only can you purchase regular CDs and tapes at Music Boulevard, but it also offers songs for sale with the Liquid Audio player. Its introductory offer was a song for just 99 cents. Also, the Internet Underground Music Archive (www.iuma.com) plans on converting all of its files to Liquid Audio format and beginning to sell music. BMG Entertainment has signed on as well. It will offer Liquid Audio at its music-genre sites: Peeps Republic (www.peeps.com), BugJuice (www.bugjuice.com), and TwangThis! (www.twangthis.com). Expect more companies to use Liquid Audio in the near future.

Microsoft is perhaps Liquid Audio's most important partner. Liquid Audio and Microsoft announced plans on a strategic relationship to jointly market each other's products. Future versions of the Liquid MusicServer will be available on Windows NT Server. Liquid Audio will also support NetShow products and the Active Streaming Format (ASF). This will certainly help Liquid Audio build a better-sounding future.

Liquid Audio, Inc.
2421 Broadway, 2nd Floor
Redwood City, CA 94063
Tel: (415) 562-0880
info@liquidaudio.com
www.liquidaudio.com

TRUESPEECH:
Streaming Speech

TrueSpeech by DSP Group, Inc., is a player optimized for playing streaming speech files. TrueSpeech is a server-less system, so files just need to be converted from WAV format to the TrueSpeech format before being placed on your webserver.

Speech files are like any other audio files, except they just contain speech. Anything that is not music falls into this category, for example, interviews, speeches, meetings, transcripts, logs, or even educational materials. TrueSpeech's audio compression scheme is optimized for just speech; it does a very poor job of compressing music or sound effects.

TrueSpeech's audio compression scheme is also called TrueSpeech and it is licensed to many computer vendors. In fact, it is licensed to Microsoft, so it is included in Windows95 and NT operating systems. TrueSpeech is also used by many other computer telephony companies for use in their web telephone and videoconferencing applications.

There are two parts to the TrueSpeech system:

TrueSpeech Internet Player. This is a helper application that plays streaming audio and speech files. It plays TrueSpeech-encoded WAV files as they are being downloaded and can also play standard WAV files. One of the benefits of the TrueSpeech Player is that it has a bookmarking capability so you can listen to files without launching your browser. The Player is available for Windows 3.1, 95/NT, and Macs.

TrueSpeech Internet Encoder. This encoder simply converts standard WAV files into TrueSpeech-encoded, streamable files at a compression rate of 40:1. It is available for Windows 3.1 and Mac users only. There is also a DOS version that can handle multiple encoding. Windows 95/NT users don't need to use this program since they already have TrueSpeech built in; they can just use Windows' Sound Recorder to easily record and encode WAV files into TrueSpeech format.

TrueSpeech is a completely free system and it is available for download on the DSP Group's website at www.dspg.com.

The TrueSpeech Player

The TrueSpeech Player is a standalone application that plays streaming speech over TCP/IP networks. It can also play standard WAV files and TrueSpeech-encoded WAV files from your hard drive. The Player looks very plain, although it has standard Play controls and Seek functions (see Figure 6.1).

Also of note is its unique bookmarking capability, so you can instantly return to your favorite TrueSpeech files (see Figure 6.2).

Because TrueSpeech files are sent along with standard Web traffic, you may experience some delays and skipping audio during high-traffic Internet hours. Unfortunately, there isn't much you can do about these interruptions, since you cannot control network traffic.

 TIP If you're getting too much line noise and playback is stuttering, just let it play through the whole file one time. Then the file will be saved in the cache. When you play the file again, it should play flawlessly. You can also save the file to your hard drive for later playback.

Figure 6.1 The TrueSpeech player streams WAV files. Here you can see the amount downloaded and how much remains to be downloaded.

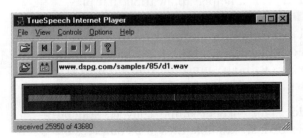

Figure 6.2 This is TrueSpeech's Bookmarks window.

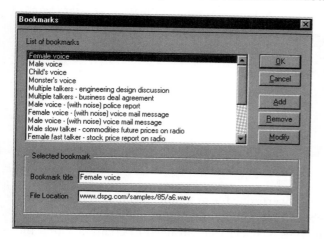

TrueSpeech Internet Encoder

As mentioned earlier, the TrueSpeech Encoder is just for those people using Windows 3.x or Macs (see Figure 6.3). The TrueSpeech Converter only supports conversion of WAV files sampled at 8kHz/16-bit PCM format. There is no support for native Mac AIFF sound-file types or even AU files.

Converting a file is as simple as choosing File/Open and selecting the WAV file you want to convert. Then press the Convert button. After that, name the file and the conversion will be completed.

TrueSpeech DOS Batch Conversion Utility

The DOS Batch Conversion is yet another way to encode files. You can convert one file at a time, or many files at once.

 Files should be saved as 8kHz, 16-bit PCM format before attempting to use the Batch Converter. If they are not, the program will give you an error message and will not convert the file.

The parameters for the program are:

```
batchcnv <input filename> <output filename>
```

The input filename should be your 8kHz, 16-bit PCM WAV file and your output filename can be named anything you want.

Figure 6.3 Windows 3.x and Mac users must use this rather bland TrueSpeech Converter to convert files.

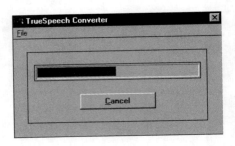

Because Sound Recorder only converts one file at a time, it can be very slow when you have a large number of TrueSpeech conversions to perform. The Batch Converter is best for this. To convert many files at once, you will need to create a Batch file. Simply create a new document with any text editor (for example, Notepad) and name it with a .BAT extension. Then type in the Batch Converter command line for each file you want to convert. A sample .BAT file looks like the following:

```
batchcnv file1.wav tsfile1.wav
batchcnv file2.wav tsfile2.wav
batchcnv file3.wav tsfile3.wav
```

When you're finished, simply save the .BAT file and then execute it. The file conversions should be finished in a short while. The DOS Batch Converter does not notify you when it is done or when files have been created; just check your current directory to find the newly created files. The best way to use this program is to specify a drive and directory for your output files.

Encoding TrueSpeech Files with Windows' Sound Recorder

The easiest way to create TrueSpeech files is to use the Sound Recorder available in Windows95 and NT. You can simply record and create a file from scratch, or encode a previously recorded WAV file into TrueSpeech.

 For best results, the WAV file should be mono and have an 8Khz sampling rate with 16-bit resolution. If the file does not match these requirements, you can convert it with Sound Recorder. You can use PCM files with other sampling rates and resolutions, but quality will suffer somewhat.

To convert WAV to TrueSpeech, follow these steps:

1. Under Windows95, load Windows' Sound Recorder, usually located in the Accessories/Multimedia folder.

2. Select Open from the File menu and choose the WAV file you want to convert. (To record a new file, you can simply record a new WAV file as usual.)

3. Select Save As and click on the Change button to bring up the Sound Selection window.

4. Open the Format dropdown list box and select DSP Group TrueSpeech, then click OK.

5. Change the filename, if desired, but keep the WAV extension. Press OK and a progress bar will begin showing the conversion process (see Figure 6.4). After a few seconds, the file should be finished. The file is now encoded in TrueSpeech format and is ready to be streamed.

Putting It All Together: Using the TrueSpeech System

Now that you know how to encode files in a variety of ways, we can put the whole system together and see how it works. Follow these steps:

Step 1: Encode the File

Use any method mentioned previously to encode the file to TrueSpeech format: the TrueSpeech Internet Encoder, the DOS batch converter, or Sound Recorder.

Step 2: Create a Text Pointer File

Using a text editor (for example, Notepad), create a file and give it a .TSP extension. You can name this text file anything you want, for example, TEST.TSP. This file is necessary for the browser to properly launch the TrueSpeech Player when a

---

Figure 6.4 This progress bar pops up during the conversion process.

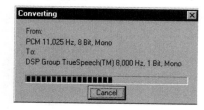

TrueSpeech-encoded WAV file is selected. The TSP file should contain the following (case-sensitive) HTML line:

```
TSIP>>URL/*.wav
```

For example, for a TrueSpeech-encoded file named SPEECH.WAV located in the directory www.homepage.com/speech, the one-line TSP text file should read:

```
TSIP>>www.homepage.com/speech/speech.wav
```

Next, create the HTML links and make other changes to the web page. Make the link point to the TEST.TSP pointer file.

 Do not include the "HTTP" before the URL. Also make sure TSIP is in all caps. If your website is "virtually hosted" and is not on a single dedicated server, then you must type in the actual web address. Because your site is hosted and being shared with other users, you must specify the precise domain name and directory. For example, I must use the actual address, www.webcom.com/ alvear/sound/speech.wav, and not the URL I normally type: www .alvear.com/sound/speech.wav.

Step 3: Copy Files to the Server

Copy all three files (the TrueSpeech-encoded WAV file, the text TSP file, and your modified web page) to your web server. Make sure to put them in the proper directories or TrueSpeech won't be able to play the file.

Step 4: Configure the Server

The final step is to make your web server understand the TrueSpeech MIME type. You must edit the server's configuration so it can recognize the following MIME type:

```
application/dsptype tsp
```

Check the documentation that came with your server if you're not sure about how to add or change MIME types. Every web server on the market uses a different format, so it is impossible to list them all here. If your website is located on a remote web server, contact your service provider and have him or her make the appropriate changes.

Playing TrueSpeech Files

There are four ways to play TrueSpeech files:

Streaming with TrueSpeech Internet Player. The most common method is to use the TSP text file to point to the TrueSpeech-encoded file as shown earlier. When your browser finds the file, it automatically loads and plays the file with the TrueSpeech Internet Player.

Streaming with ActiveMovie Player. Windows 95/NT users can also stream files with ActiveMovie, which comes with Internet Explorer 3.0. It can also be downloaded separately at www.microsoft.com. To stream with ActiveMovie, simply link to the actual TrueSpeech WAV file. (Do not use this method with the TSP text file.) ActiveMovie recognizes it as a TrueSpeech file and begins to download, buffer, and play it (see Figure. 6.5).

Auto Loading TrueSpeech Internet Player. You can make the browser automatically launch the TrueSpeech Internet Player as the page is loading. Insert the following HTML code at the beginning of your page:

```
<META HTTP-EQUIV=REFRESH CONTENT="0; URL=filename.tsp">
```

Simply replace filename.tsp with the filename of your TSP file. If you replace filename.tsp with the TrueSpeech WAV file, like true.wav, for example, your browser will launch whatever application is associated with WAV files.

Playing Nonstreaming Background TrueSpeech Files. The last option is to make a TrueSpeech file play without launching any player. Instead, the file plays in the background when it is completely downloaded and as the Web data is being received. Important: This method does not stream TrueSpeech files, so only use it with small files that can be loaded quickly.

Unfortunately, Internet Explorer and Navigator handle background sounds differently. For Internet Explorer, add the following HTML code at the beginning of your web page:

```
<BGSOUND src="filename.wav" loop="Infinite">
```

Figure 6.5 When you click on a TrueSpeech-encoded file, ActiveMovie opens and begins to stream it. Notice the progress bar, which tells you how much of the entire file has been downloaded.

When using the "Infinite" loop, the sound plays continuously. To stop playback, press the ESC key or click on the Stop button. You can also leave out the LOOP command to play the file just once.

Netscape Navigator developers must use the following code:

```
<EMBED src="filename.wav" hidden=true>
```

 If you're creating background sounds for both Netscape and Internet Explorer users, you can input both of the HTML lines just shown into the same web page. Both browsers ignore HTML commands that they don't recognize and will see their correct corresponding code.

Should You Use TrueSpeech?

Is TrueSpeech right for you? In many ways, it is very primitive. Fortune 500 companies may not want to bother with something that does not have high-quality sound, cross-platform support, or scaleable streaming ability. It can't handle music or other sounds very well; therefore, its appeal is limited. TrueSpeech is best for small websites or personal web pages that just use speech and WAV files. It is a great way to create quick-and-easy streaming speech files; just don't use it for music files because sound quality deteriorates drastically. If you do decide to try it out, you will have some very unflattering music files. In the end, it's the classic multimedia dilemma: streaming poor-quality small files (TrueSpeech) versus downloading good-quality large files (WAV).

Another negative is that not many developers use TrueSpeech, so there isn't much content available. If your audience is comprised of Windows users, however, you can encode all your WAV files as TrueSpeech files so they can all be streamed, and the compression scheme decreases file size appreciably.

The following questions can help you in selecting TrueSpeech for your site. If you answer Yes to any of them, you should consider using TrueSpeech, perhaps even on a limited level:

- Do you want low-cost, low-maintenance, streaming speech?
- Do you just want prerecorded speech on your site and no music?
- Can you accept a smaller installed user base and therefore a smaller audience?
- Do you usually work with speech and voice files?

- Do you have no need for streaming video?
- Do you work mostly with WAV files?

Pros and Cons

Although TrueSpeech is good for beginners and Web hobbyists, it is not a good, general-purpose audio streaming solution. That's because the compression scheme works best only for speech applications and does not handle music or other sounds very well. This naturally limits its usefulness and will similarly limit the number of users. Trying to make TrueStream play *live* speech is possible with software from the vendor, but there are better and easier solutions.

TrueSpeech has limited support for UNIX computers or even Mac audio file types. Make no mistake, TrueSpeech is best used in the Windows environment. Users of Windows 95/NT, especially those using Internet Explorer 3.0 and above, will see the most benefits from TrueSpeech.

Perhaps the best thing about TrueSpeech is that it is very easy to use and requires little knowledge of servers, streaming technology, or computer audio. You can just convert a file, drop it on a web server, and forget about it; and all the software is free, so you can create hundreds of streaming files on your website.

About DSP Group, Inc.

Aside from licensing its computer compression technologies, DSP Group is also active in the digital signal processing (DSP) field for wireless communications and is a market leader in supplying processor chips used in telephony and digital telephone answering devices. Its TrueSpeech compression is widely known and widely used. A version of TrueSpeech is used in the audio compression standard G.723 set by the International Telecommunications Union (ITU). This standard, called H.324, is now used for videoconferencing over regular telephone lines.

Over 200 websites are currently using the TrueSpeech codec, mostly in other computer telephony and multimedia products. Its compression scheme has been licensed by many vendors including Microsoft, Lucent Technologies, Vivo Software, Intel, VDOnet, and AT&T.

DSP Group, Inc.,
3120 Scott Boulevard
Santa Clara, CA 95054
(408) 986-4300
www.dspg.com

AUDIOACTIVE:
Streaming Audio and Online Radio Stations

7

When it came to streaming audio over the Internet, RealAudio was the only game in town. Other programs slowly surfaced, but they were mostly low-end solutions that catered to HTTP streaming only. RealAudio was the only program that handled live, real-time audio. When it first became available, scores of traditional radio stations jumped at the chance to become Internet radio stations.

Today there are more audio solutions, but RealAudio still garners a very large share of the market. Audioactive by Telos Systems is a new product that cuts right into RealAudio's live broadcast market. Audioactive is a streaming system that broadcasts on-demand and real-time audio over networks. It is very radio friendly, because it has a hardware encoder and server that make it easy to connect radio stations to the Internet.

The Audioactive Experience

Audioactive differs from other streaming audio programs because it uses industry-standard codecs and file types, MPEG Layer 3 (MPEG-3). As described in Chapter 4, "Desktop Audio and Video," MPEG-3 (MP3) is a highly scaleable compression algorithm that offers excellent audio quality even at low bit rates. At ISDN speed, (128Kbps), MP3 audio matches CD-quality audio. Since we will be dealing with MP3 audio, we will have to learn a bit more about how this compression works.

Audioactive is both a server-less and server/client system. For on-demand files, you can just put files on ordinary web servers for HTTP streaming. You only need two programs:

Audioactive Player. This is the client program that is used for listening to Audioactive files. It is a helper application available for Windows 32-bit computers and Macs, but plans for other systems are in the works. Upon installation, it is easily configured to be used with both Internet Explorer and Navigator.

MPEG-3 Producer. This is Audioactive's converter program. It converts WAV files into MP3 files that Audioactive can stream. This encoder is used for on-demand, stored audio content only and is available for Windows95 and NT systems. Since MP3 is an standard compression system and file type, you can actually use other shareware or free programs; but for now, we will focus on Audioactive's MPEG-3 Producer program.

Live broadcasts require a server/client system and a hardware encoder. The hardware encoder accepts input from any audio source and sends it to your server computer—you can use Audioactive's own UNIX-based server or NetShow's server for Windows NT systems. The client/server solution is best for professional use, especially radio stations that want to broadcast their signal over the Internet.

About MPEG Layer 3

Before we start on Audioactive, it helps to know more about MPEG Layer 3 compression. First, MPEG (Motion Picture Experts Group) is the name of the organizational body that approves standards for audio and video. This international organization approved the MPEG audio and video compression that is used by many systems worldwide in a variety of applications, from satellite systems to computers. MPEG Layer 3 is just one type of compression layer; there are also MPEG Layers 1 and 2. MPEG-3, however, is the most advanced and offers the best compression with hardly any loss in quality. MPEG-3 was invented in Germany by the Fraunhofer Gesellschaft Laboratory (www.iis.fhg.de/departs/amm/layer3/), an audio research center. In fact, MPEG-3 is sometimes referred to as FhG.

MPEG-3 compression works so well because it eliminates perceptual data, which is audio that humans cannot hear or perceive. It works best when used for encoding music, especially CD-quality music. In fact, the compression is so good that you won't hear a difference between the original CD file and a compressed MP3 file, yet the MP3 file will be 1/12th the size of the raw original CD file (a 12:1 compression ratio). For example, a typical raw, CD-quality, 16-bit WAV file recorded at 44.1Mhz stereo takes up over 10MB per minute, so a 4-minute song at this rate takes over 40MB. You can imagine how quickly CD-quality WAV files can fill up your hard drive. MPEG Layer 3 compression shrinks the same 40MB file to just under 4MB with no perceptible loss of quality.

Even better, MP3 is scaleable, so if you don't need CD-quality audio, you can have highly compressed files. At its highest compression, you can compress files down to around 96:1, which gives you a mono, 2.5kHz file suitable for voice-only applications. The lowest compression offers the highest-quality MP3 files—they are compressed at a ratio of 12:1 as mentioned earlier. As you can see, MP3 is a great compression method. In fact, MP3 files have become so popular that they have spawned an underground music pirate trading community on the Internet.

Although the 12:1 compression ratio is often used when discussing MPEG-3's CD-quality compression, your results may vary depending on your encoding

MPEG-3, Piracy, and the RIAA

MPEG-3 compression is so good that it means bad news to the recording industry. MP3 can compress files to a fraction of their original size and keep their CD-quality sound; therefore, it has become very popular with pirates. These pirates copy or "rip" songs from CDs and distribute them for free or trade them for others. Distribution points are usually websites or FTP locations but can also be places like Usenet groups, IRC chatrooms, and email. No money changes hands; this is just the Internet community helping each other.

The reason that MP3 copying and trading is so rampant is because everything is free, from the music to the tools needed. Oftentimes, it is college students using college computers that set up FTP or websites for trading, and because many colleges have high-speed Internet lines, a 4 or 5MB MP3 file can be transmitted in a matter of seconds. Also, it is easy; practically anyone with a CD-ROM-equipped computer can rip songs. There are numerous shareware or freeware MP3 players and ripper programs available. Some players look very similar to CD player interfaces and have features like Track Lists, 5-band equalizers, and advanced Play controls.

MP3 files themselves have become somewhat harder to find in recent months. Although there are quite a number of MP3 master link sites and search engines available, they disappear very quickly. MP3 sites usually have a very short life—some not even lasting one day.

MPEG-3, Piracy, and the RIAA (Continued)

The main reason that so many sites are shutting down is because of the RIAA (Recording Industry Association of America), which believes that when people copy and trade MP3 files, they will not purchase the legitimate recordings, thereby costing companies and artists lots of money. Although there hasn't been an official study to estimate the number of royalties and earnings lost to MP3 trading, it is thought to be very high. To combat MP3 trading and pirating, the RIAA has a team of surfers hunting down MP3 sites and trying to close them down. Threatening letters and emails are enough to scare most universities, Web-hosting companies, and Internet Service Providers, who in turn close down rouge sites. Sometimes, users close down their own websites for fear of being the next RIAA target. Whenever a site closes, however, a new one opens up somewhere else.

This cat-and-mouse game cannot go on forever. Although there are no hard numbers available on how many MP3 sites there are, it is believed that there might be hundreds or even thousands. No one really knows how many songs or CDs have been ripped. One problem for the RIAA is that its grasp doesn't reach off the shores of the United States. How can the RIAA stop pirates in other countries from copying and distributing MP3 files? What is the solution?

One way to combat MP3 piracy is to use some kind of copy protection or watermarking. That way, illegal copies can be controlled or at least tracked back to the original ripper. Another solution is Liquid Audio's music delivery and commerce system (see Chapter 5, "Liquid Audio: Music Publishing and Commerce"). Liquid Audio allows users to download CD-quality, copy-protected files from the Internet for about 99 cents a song. But why would someone pay 99 cents for a song when he or she can get the MP3 version elsewhere for free?

Some form of copy protection is one solution, but it will be virtually impossible for the RIAA to completely eliminate all illegal MP3 encoding and distribution from the Internet. You'll probably be hearing a lot about MPEG-3 and pirating for a long time to come.

method. If you use an old shareware program, for example, you may get just a 10:1 ratio. Some software encoders use older algorithms and don't use the newest advances in MP3 coding yet. Audioactive's MP3 Producer was the first commercial MP3 encoder available on the Internet. There are many free encoders available as well, so it makes sense to try out a few different ones to see how well and how quickly they work.

 Software encoding can be a very processor-intensive process, so make sure your computer can handle it. Pentium and MMX computers are good choices. Also use batch encoding, so you encode multiple files at once.

Audioactive, Microsoft's NetShow, and Macromedia's Shockwave are all using MPEG-3 audio in their products. Better yet, the next generation of MPEG-3, to be called MPEG-4 perhaps, is just a few months away. MPEG-4 promises even better compression. In the future, you can bet more companies will use this impressive and scaleable compression method.

Using Audioactive for HTTP Streaming

Audioactive makes server-less or HTTP streaming very easy. Here are the steps for using Audioactive for on-demand broadcasts.

1. Make sure to install the MP3 Producer and Audioactive Player on your computer. Always use the most recent version of the programs, so check Audioactive's website frequently.

2. Next, you need to use the MP3 Producer to convert WAV files into MP3 format. Remember to always work with CD-quality WAV files. Choose your settings and bit rates and begin converting (see Figure 7.1). The first time you use MPEG-3 compression, try to compress files at a number of different settings so you can hear what they sound like. Compression time varies depending on the level of compression and the number of files you choose, so it helps to use batch compression.

3. You need to create M3U pointer or playlist text files. These text files point to the location of the MP3 file and can be created with any text editor. They also serve as playlists for when you play MP3 files locally.

4. Configure MIME types for your web server so it can handle MP3 and M3U files. (Check your server's documentation for more on this.)

5. Create links to the M3U files on your web page.

6. Upload or copy the M3U, MP3, and updated web pages to the web server.

7. Play the MP3 file. If you did everything correctly, the stream should play after a few seconds of buffering.

Setting Up a Live Audioactive Broadcast

Those who tend to use Audioactive for live broadcasts are usually radio stations that want to mirror their signal over the Internet. Audioactive offers everything you may need: UNIX server software, a speedy hardware MPEG encoder called the Internet Encoder, and even a digital signal processor to fine-tune your sound. For those users who do not want to have their own UNIX server, Audioactive also offers server hosting services. That way, the signal flows from your location over ISDN lines to Audioactive's server, and then out to the users.

You can use the Internet Encoder with Microsoft's NetShow Server. This option is great for those who have Microsoft NT 4.0 Server or are already using Microsoft servers. The advantage to using NetShow's server is that you can send out multicast streams instead of just unicast streams. This saves you tons of bandwidth. For more on NetShow, see Chapter 10.

Here are the steps you take when setting up a live broadcast with Audioactive:

Figure 7.1 Convert files from WAV to MP3 format with the MP3 Producer.

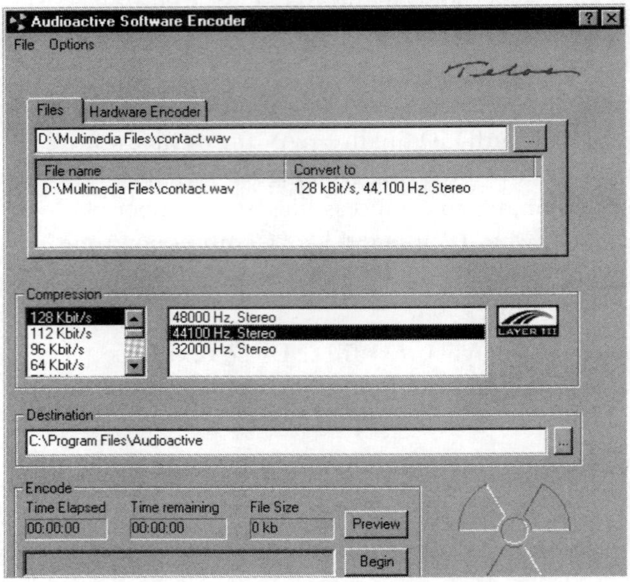

1. Connect your Internet Encoder to your signal using XLR-type inputs.

2. Connect the Encoder to the server. This can be done with a simple serial cable if the server is next to the Encoder. Alternately, you can use high-speed wires (ISDN or 10BaseT) to connect to a remote server.

3. Create a playlist M3U file. It only needs to point to your server including the port number (for example: www.audioactive.com:2023/).

4. Create a link to the M3U file and upload the M3U file and the HTML page to your web site. Anyone who clicks on the link will be able to tune in to the broadcast.

5. Your server takes over and sends out the signal to users who request it. If you're using the NetShow Server, users will need the NetShow Player. If you decided to use Audioactive's server, the client computer needs to have the Audioactive Player installed.

That's it in a nutshell. For more on using Audioactive's server, see the documentation that comes with the software.

Creating Playlist or M3U Files

The pointer files for Audioactive have M3U extensions. They are simple text files that point to the real location of the MP3 files. M3U files are also called *playlist files* since they can contain multiple URLs or local paths. Simply type each location on its own line.

For HTTP streaming, a typical M3U file may look like the following:

```
www.audioactive.com/jazz.mp3
www.audioactive.com/rock.mp3
```

Name the M3U file anything you want and place it on your web page. When you click on the M3U link, the browser opens up the Audioactive Player and begins to play the file. If you use multiple URLs as in the previous example, you can skip back and forth between files somewhat like a CD player moves between tracks.

Playlist files can also contain links to play local MP3 files. This is good for when you want to create your own tracks from songs saved on your hard drive. You can rearrange files in any order you wish. A typical M3U file looks like the following:

```
c:\test.mp3
c:\audio\jazz.mp3
```

Just double-clicking on an M3U file will launch the Audioactive Player, which will begin playing files. The playlist allows you to skip forward or back to other songs; the track number on the Player will change as it plays each file.

The last type of M3U file is for live broadcasts. Since there is no file created, you just need to point to your server and port number. For example:

```
www.audioactive.com/intro.mp3
streamer.audioactive.com:2002/
```

In the preceding example, an intro file will play before the actual live broadcast. This is good for introducing your radio station or adding a commercial or plug for your web site. As you can see, the URL for the server is just the server name along with the port number.

The Audioactive Player

The Audioactive Player lets you listen to MP3 files either streaming over the Internet or playing locally from your hard drive. The Player isn't great, but because it was still in beta as of this writing, it is hoped that it will be improved before it is released. It has a digital display that shows the amount of time elapsed and the track number (see Figure 7.2). It also displays the sample rate (in kHz) and bit rate (in Kbps) of the current file. It has regular buttons like Play, Pause, and Stop, but it lacks Fast Forward and Rewind buttons. It can only go forward or backward to different tracks, not within a song. A sliding Seek bar would also be a very good addition.

Another feature lacking in the Audioactive Player is that it does not display the name of the file (or stream) that is playing. It would be great to have the song title, artist, or filename displayed somewhere on the main Player window. You can press the I button, but the only information that appears on that page is the filename. The author, artist, title, and composer fields are never filled in.

You can open local files or streams from within the Player. Just select File/Play File or File/Play Location and type in the filename or URL. In addition, you can add a proxy address or choose the settings for the incoming file, like changing the resolution, frequency, or mode (stereo or downmix). One neat feature: You can

Figure 7.2 The Audioactive Player can stream MP3 files or play them locally from your hard drive.

select Options/URL Play Settings and change play modes from Play Only to Play and Save or Save Only (see Figure 7.3). That way, you can save incoming files to your hard disk and listen to them later.

 TIP If your sound is coming in broken and intermittent, stop playback and increase the buffer. Go to Options/URL Play Settings, increase the buffer time to 10 seconds or so, and then try playing the file again. If you're still getting audio breakup, try connecting at another time when Internet traffic isn't so heavy.

In the future, the Audioactive Player will be able to play MP3 files, NetShow audio, and WAV files. Support for playing CDs is also planned. The Audioactive Player is free and is available for Windows 3.1, 95, NT, and Power Macintosh. A UNIX player should be available by the time you read this.

Using the MP3 Producer

For those just starting out in streaming audio or MP3 encoding, software encoding is a very good solution. Audioactive's MP3 Producer is completely software-based and is available on Windows95 and NT. The MP3 Producer converts WAV files into MP3 files. It works like any other encoder program—specify an input file, set your compression settings, then press Encode to create files.

To use the MP3 Producer, you will need to know your way around compression and what the files sound like. If you're unfamiliar with MP3, that's okay; just try to convert sample files and hear what they sound like when you stream them. You

Figure 7.3 Use the URL Options screen to save MP3 files or change other options.

have to play around with compression settings because MPEG-3 is *so good*. It can handle many different bit rates from 8Kbps all the way to 128Kbps. That means that you can really cater your file to a specific audience. Chances are you'll use the 8Kbps and 16Kbps bit rates the most for use with 28.8Kbps modem users. At those speeds, sound quality resembles mono radio transmissions. At 128Kbps, sound quality comes through as full-stereo, 16-bit, CD-quality sound. This beats everything on the market; no other program can stream CD-quality music at 128Kbps. Switching to one channel (mono) will take you down to just 56Kbps; music will still sound very good. As mentioned earlier, compression ratios range from 96:1 to 12:1, so you can get just the sound quality you need.

MP3 Producer has a Batch Mode for converting multiple files at once so you can have unattended sessions. You can save files as normal MP3 files, compressed WAV, or Shockwave audio (SWA). The MP3 Producer can also be used with Audioactive's hardware encoder. Just choose the port where the encoder is connected, choose your compression, and then start encoding. The hardware encoder is super-fast, so encoding happens in real time (see Figure 7.4).

Yes, there are many shareware and free MP3 encoders on the market. Why use (and pay for) the MP3 Producer? For one reason, it is the only commercial MP3

Figure 7.4 If you have the Audioactive Internet Encoder hooked up, you can use this screen to change your settings.

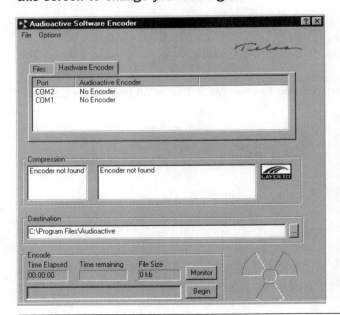

encoder available. That means that if you ever have problems, you can always get support from Audioactive. They also claim that it is one of the fastest encoders available. Many shareware or freeware encoders take a very long time to encode files, so perhaps the time you save may be worth the price you pay for the Producer.

Audioactive Pro

For live unicasts, Audioactive uses a more sophisticated client/server system. You can't use the software encoder, but rather a hardware encoder called the Audioactive Internet Encoder. The Encoder is placed at your audio source and can connect to any streaming server. You can use Audioactive's Linux server for unicast transmissions or Microsoft's NetShow Server to handle your multicast needs. Because Audioactive just has Linux streaming server software, it may not suit some companies. The NetShow Server is compatible with Windows 4.0 NT Server only. For more on working with the NetShow Server software, see Chapter 10.

A typical live broadcast requires a series of connections from the audio source, to hardware encoder, to streaming server software, to a client's computer (see Figure 7.5 for a rough sketch of a connection).

Figure 7.5 This picture from Audioactive's website depicts a typical connection for live broadcasting.

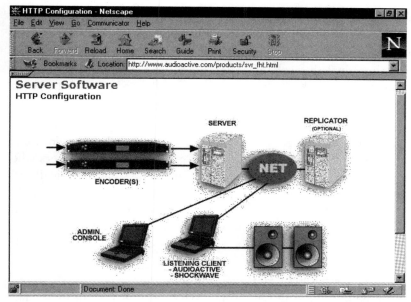

Audioactive Internet Encoder

The Internet Encoder takes the job of encoding files away from your computer, so it can do other tasks. The encoder accepts audio input from any source (digital or analog) and outputs it as an MPEG Layer 3 stream. The converter has an LCD display, LED input meters, and a control that lets you quickly and easily change output bit rates and sample rates. The Encoder connects to the computer via a standard RS-232 port for audio bit rates up to 64Kbps; for higher rates, you should use a serial card, which plugs into a PC slot. The hardware encoder can be used with NetShow, Shockwave, Audioactive, and other MPEG Layer 3 products.

One encoder makes a stream at a single bit rate. If you want to broadcast multiple bit rates, you need to use multiple Encoders. It's usually a good idea to use two Encoders so you can support 28.8Kbps users and ISDN users. A connection like this will allow you roughly 200 simultaneous streams depending on your hardware and bandwidth. Audioactive also sells Replicator Software that mirrors your streams, so you can increase the number of streams that you can deliver.

For live broadcasts, you can put the hardware encoder near the audio source and place your server anywhere. Then connect them both via a high-speed network, direct cable, or the Internet. That way, you can adjust settings with your browser or through a telnet session. Usually, however, once you set your Encoder's bit rates, you won't have many reasons for changing them.

Should You Use Audioactive?

Audioactive is very versatile. It can be used by audio professionals for radio cybercasting or by novices who want to use streaming on-demand MP3 files. Because of the impressive compression, dual-channel ISDN users can hear streaming CD-quality stereo music. Nothing on the market today beats that. Even 28.8Kbps users get good-quality audio.

Audioactive is perfect for radio stations that want to increase their audience to the global Internet. Audioactive's solution may cost more than RealAudio's, but you get significantly better audio. It is even good for those do-it-yourselfers who want to put up their own Internet-only radio station or online show. Practically all the tools you need are available free or at shareware prices. Likewise, since MP3 files are gaining in popularity every day, more people will have players that can handle that file format. It's just too bad that MP3 doesn't work on video, too.

Pros and Cons

Audioactive is in a peculiar position. Having made an agreement with Microsoft, Audioactive will soon handle the ASF file format. What does this mean for Audioactive? Will it continue supporting its own products and the MP3 file format? Also, its site has a lot of NetShow and Shockwave content because of its hardware solution that can use almost any streaming server. Nevertheless, Audioactive's main market, online radio stations, is growing. Audioactive excels because of its high-quality sound, especially when using the hardware Internet encoder and digital signal processors.

One big strike against the hardware solution is price. The hardware encoder is very expensive, so just professional sites are likely to use this solution. Another big problem is that Audioactive lacks multicast support. This is significant because high-quality MP3 files can be very large. Fortunately, the hardware encoder can be used with NetShow in order to take advantage of multicasting.

For HTTP streaming and everyday stored audio, Audioactive works very well and is practically free. You don't need to purchase Audioactive's MP3 Producer to create MP3 files; there are plenty of shareware or freeware converters available. The Audioactive Player is completely free, so theoretically you can be up and running rather quickly.

So far, MP3 files aren't as popular as other file formats. That may certainly change, but there needs to be better awareness so the masses can identify MP3 files and get the Audioactive Player. Chances are you won't run into many sites using MP3 files, much less trying to stream them.

Last, the Audioactive Player is not as advanced as other MP3 players. It has a lackluster interface and offers few player controls. This can be fixed, however, in future versions of Audioactive.

About Telos Systems

Telos Systems is known to radio broadcast engineers for its Zephyr ISDN components for transmitting audio, which are in use by many broadcasters like NPR and the BBC. Telos also makes networking and telephone interface products for talk-show programming, remote broadcasts, and call-in radio shows. Audioactive is its newest product and its first product for use on the Internet.

Like many other streaming vendors, Telos has also partnered itself with Microsoft and has gotten behind NetShow and ASF. Future versions of Audioactive will support the ASF file format.

Telos Systems
2101 Superior Avenue
Cleveland, OH 44114 USA
(216) 241-7225
info@zephyr.com
www.audioactive.com

VIVOACTIVE:
The Easiest Way To Stream

By far, the easiest and most inexpensive way to stream a file is the serverless or HTTP streaming method because you don't need to buy expensive hardware or bother with time-consuming administration. VivoActive by Vivo Software, Inc. uses HTTP streaming to simplify the cumbersome task of putting streaming video on your site.

VivoActive has two parts:

The VivoActive Player. This is a plug-in or ActiveX control that you must install to see Vivo movies. Movies appear inside the browser window; there is no external application. It is available for Windows 95/NT and Macintosh.

The VivoActive Producer. This is the encoder that converts files from standard formats (like AVI, MOV, WAV, AIFF) to stream-ready formats (either VIV/VIVO files or NetShow ASF files). It is available for Windows 95/NT and Macintosh.

Vivo also sells a starter producer called the VivoActive VideoNow, a low-cost version that doesn't have the high-end features of the full-blown Producer.

This chapter focuses on the Producer and how to create streaming Vivo files that are perfect for your site.

The VivoActive Player

The player is a browser plug-in. After installing the plug-in, you just select a movie and wait a few seconds for it to begin playing. The movie appears inline, inside your web browser window (see Figure 8.1). It only has one player button, a semi-transparent Play/Stop button that's displayed in the video window.

The player doesn't have many options at all. You can right-click on the window and choose About This Movie to bring up information on the movie. It will show you the length of the file, the author, title, copyright, and more (see Figure 8.2).

VivoActive Player 2.0 is free and compatible with Internet Explorer and Navigator. If you're using Internet Explorer and don't have Vivo installed, Internet Explorer can automatically download and install the ActiveX Vivo player so you can quickly view the movie. Netscape users need the plug-in. It is available for Windows 3.1, 95/NT, and for the Macintosh.

A new advanced player called the VivoActive PowerPlayer was released while this book was in development. It has many advanced features like a volume control, a Rewind button, and the ability to zoom video to twice its size. It can also save Vivo files. The VivoActive PowerPlayer costs $12.95 and is available for Windows 95/NT and Macs. It can be purchased and downloaded from Vivo's website at www.vivo.com.

Figure 8.1 The VivoActive player is not an external program. It is a plug-in, so movies are shown inside the browser window.

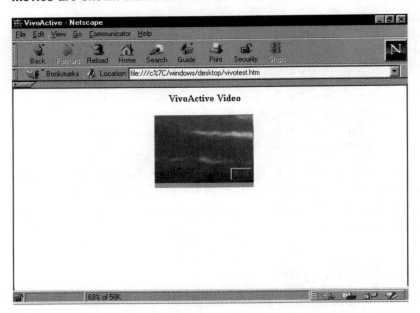

Figure 8.2 For more information on a movie, right-click and choose About This Movie.

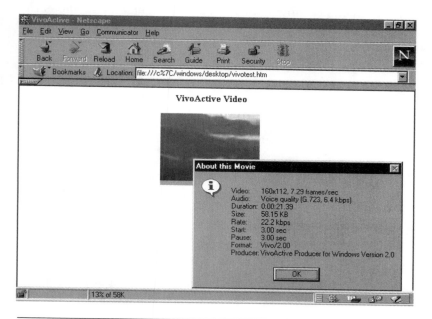

How to Use VivoActive Producer

VivoActive Producer is essentially a file converter that converts standard down-loadable multimedia files into streaming files. Using its proprietary compression algorithm, Vivo can shrink files at a 200:1 ratio. Astonishingly, a 30MB AVI file can be compressed to just under 100KB. Although compression is very good, the video quality does suffer. A movie recorded at 30 frames per second (fps) will drop to only 8 fps, and the video picture will look blurry and grainy. Audio quality, however, won't suffer as much—at its best setting, Vivo delivers FM-quality sound, even at 28.8Kbps.

Creating VivoActive files with the Producer is easy and requires the following three steps:

1. Convert a multimedia file to Vivo format.

2. Add the appropriate HTML lines to embed the movie on your web page.

3. Copy the files to your web server.

Once you've done all that, your Vivo movie is ready to play.

Step 1: Converting a File

When you load the Producer, the main video window consists of two video windows. The window on the left shows the input video, while the right window shows the output file. The bottom portion of the window shows you a list of files that you are converting. You can convert one file at a time or many files at once.

To convert a file, select an AVI or MOV file from your hard drive by selecting File/Add Movie or clicking the Add Movie button. The first frame of the movie will be displayed in the left window, and the file name will be listed on the bottom panel (see Figure 8.3).

Next, click on Movie Info to enter copyright information, the title of the movie, and the author's name.

Once you've added the movie to the list, you can choose from over 20 pre-defined settings. Push the Settings button to see a list of the available settings (see Figure 8.4). The typical setting to use is "28.8 Modem FM," because it creates a Vivo file that is optimized for a 28.8Kbps user and has good, FM-quality audio.

Figure 8.3 Once you select your input movie, the first frame appears and you are ready to continue converting the file. You can also preview the input video by pressing the Play button.

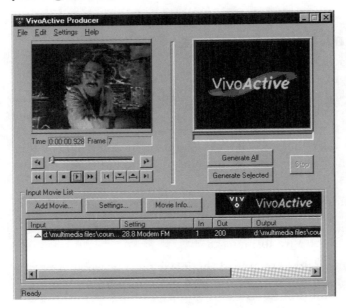

Figure 8.4 Convert your file by choosing from among 20 predefined settings.

From there, you can just click on Generate All or Generate Selected. VivoActive will then begin converting the file (or files) using the default settings. You'll see both windows (the original and Vivo video) displaying the movie as it is being generated (see Figure 8.5).

The file(s) in the Batch List will now have checkmarks next to them to indicate that they have been converted.

 If you plan on converting multiple files, you can continue to add movies to the Batch List and use your favorite predefined setting. Batch conversions are good for hands-off, unattended use, especially when working with lengthy movies.

The Producer can also convert WAV files; simply use the instructions just given for WAV audio files. Since there's no video, the VivoActive logo will appear in the window frame during playback.

Figure 8.5 The VivoActive Producer displays the input and output windows so you can see the conversion process.

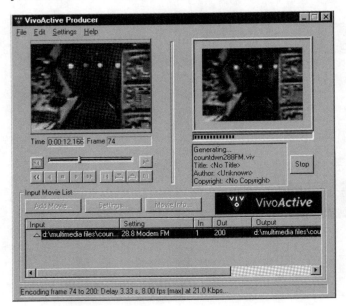

Advanced Settings

As you saw previously, the Settings button comes with predefined settings that work well in most situations. You can choose from a limited number of criteria, including data transfer rate, audio quality, and even screen size. Data transfer rate options are: 28.8, ISDN, T1, and LAN. Audio options are more limited: for low quality, choose Voice; for better audio, choose FM. You can also convert files to ASF format for streaming with Microsoft NetShow.

Although we used "28.8 Modem FM" in the previous example, the setting you use should correspond to your audience. You can also choose "28.8 Modem Voice Clearer Picture" to make the video display a sharper image. Another popular choice is "28.8 Modem Voice Smoother Motion," which displays smoother video but doesn't look very clear. If you'll be using Vivo movies over an intranet, you can use the higher-quality selections like ISDN, T1, and LAN since you'll have plenty of bandwidth. Internet users, however, should limit themselves to the 28.8 or ISDN options.

Advanced users may want to tinker with the advanced options. Fortunately, VivoActive Producer allows you to create your own settings and save them for later use. To create your own setting, click on the Movie Info button and then choose the Advanced tab (see Figure 8.6). In this screen, you can choose the Client's Connection Type (28.8Kbps, ISDN, etc.), the maximum frame rate (anywhere from 1 to 30 fps), the output size of the video (from 65 × 49 to 352 × 264), and much more.

 TIP If you have an audience with varying bandwidth connections, you can choose the All Bit Rates option to create every single type of file. It is also helpful when experimenting with Producer, so you can see for yourself how a low-quality, 28.8Kbps file differs from a high-quality, LAN file, for example.

Once you've made all the adjustments you want, just click on Save As to create a brand new setting. Don't forget to type in a new description so you can easily remember what changes you made. In the screen shown in Figure 8.6, I've saved as "My Settings," so I know that this is my style. Once it is saved, you can find your new setting when you push the Settings button.

Figure 8.6 The Advanced screen lets you adjust settings and save them as new settings so you can use them later.

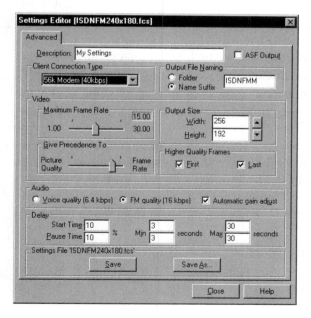

Step 2: Updating Your Web Page

After you've finished converting files with the Producer, you must add the video to a web page. Remember that Vivo videos are displayed inside a web page and no external player will load.

 You can only display one VivoActive movie at a time, so create a new page for each movie.

Insert the following HTML code into the page that will contain your video:

```
<object classid="clsid:02466323-75ed-11cf-a267-0020af2546ea"
codebase="http://www.vivo.com/dldv2/vvweb.cab#Version=2,0,0,0" align="baseline"
border="0" width="XXX" height="YYY">
<param name="URL" value="YOURFILE.viv">
<param name="VIDEOCONTROLS" value="ON">
<param name="AUTOSTART" value="TRUE">
<embed src="YOURFILE.viv" align="baseline" border="0" width="XXX" height="YYY"
autostart="TRUE"></object>
```

Insert the Vivo filename for YOURFILE.viv and the width and height of the video for XXX and YYY. Netscape will ignore everything but the EMBED line, but Internet Explorer uses the other lines to search your Windows95 computer and checks to see if the VivoActive Player has been installed. If the player is not found, Internet Explorer will automatically download the ActiveX control and install the player. Once installation is done, it displays the movie.

 By default, the movie is left-justified, but you can change the position of a VivoActive movie by embedding it into a table, by using the align command on a paragraph tag, or using JavaScript to create a tiny popup browser window.

Now, you'll probably want to test the output. The easiest way to view a Vivo file is to use Netscape Navigator. Simply load the file using Netscape (with the Vivo player already installed), and it will automatically begin playing the video (see Figure 8.7). Note that Internet Explorer does not automatically display Vivo files this way; you must create a brand new web page with the HTML code for it to play.

Don't forget to add new MIME types for Vivo files on your web server; otherwise, you may have trouble playing them on your website. See www.vivo.com/help/servers for a list of commands and instructions for the different server

Figure 8.7 Use Netscape Navigator with the VivoActive plug-in installed to view your recently converted file.

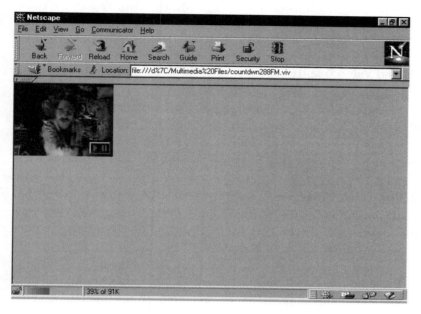

types. The MIME type should be associated with files containing .viv and .vivo extensions.

Step 3: Copy Files to the Web Server

VivoActive works with any web server, including Microsoft IIS, WebStar, Netscape Enterprise Server, NCSA, Apache, and O'Reilly's Web Site. Putting Vivo files on your website is as easy as copying them to your regular web server directory. If you're working on a remote server, just use your FTP program to upload the files.

Once someone requests a page with the Vivopage embedded in it, the video starts to play within a few seconds. That's it! Don't forget to put a link where you can download the VivoActive plug-in.

Bandwidth and Simultaneous Streams

Unlike other vendors, Vivo doesn't sell stream licenses to restrict the number of users who can watch videos; and since it doesn't use a server, you can't control users either. The number of simultaneous video streams that you can broadcast is only limited by your bandwidth capacity, so the bigger your bandwidth, the larger your audience. For example, if you're connected to the Internet via a T-1 line, approximately 40 to 50 people can simultaneously view a 28.8Kbps video. This doesn't take into account other factors, like the amount of normal Web traffic or the size of your video clip.

Improving Audio and Video Quality

For audio, you have two choices: Voice Quality (which takes up 6.4Kbps) and FM Quality (16Kbps). Voice Quality is a good choice for standard movies and low-bandwidth applications. The sound tends to be a bit muffled, and many of the lows and highs will be missing. Since Voice Quality only takes up 6.4Kbps of the data stream, the rest of a 28.8Kbps stream (22.4Kbps) will be devoted to the video.

For music applications, or any other time you want very good sound quality, choose FM Quality, which works well even with a 28.8Kbps modem. Since FM Quality devotes 16Kbps to audio, you will have less bandwidth available for video. As a result you'll have a bad picture with very good sound. To improve picture quality, you can shrink the video size to about 176 × 144.

 The Producer comes with a Movie Analyzer (under Movie Info/Show Analysis), which compares the source file to your settings. It makes recommendations (like changing screen size or reducing the sample rate) to help you create the highest-quality video possible.

In many cases, there won't be lip synchronization—movies viewed over a slow connection tend to look like badly dubbed films. This is directly related to the number of frames per second that you chose when you created the Vivo file. To get better lip synch, you should increase the number of frames per second. Using the slide bar, give precedence to Frame Rate rather than Picture Quality. Also make sure that your original file was captured with at least 10 frames per second. Of course, you'll be able to add more frames for movies created for ISDN or LAN connections rather than modem connections.

Yet another way of improving quality is to have higher-resolution videos. Keep in mind that having high-resolution movies takes up considerable bandwidth, so it is not for slow connections, like modems. When you create Vivo videos, you can shrink or increase the size of a movie.

You may not be able to produce great-looking Vivo movies the first time you try, but with some fine-tuning you can get the best quality for the bandwidth for which you're creating. Remember that having interrupted audio is much more distracting then losing a few frames and having less-than-perfect video. Also keep in mind that Vivo movies won't be like the perfect 30 frames-per-second movies on TV. Nevertheless, you can make very watchable videos with good-quality, uninterrupted audio.

 One way to shrink file size is to shorten your video clip. Instead of altering your original video, you can use VivoActive Producer to choose a beginning and an end point. (The controls are next to the play controls.) You can then convert only that small section instead of the whole video.

VivoActive Producer Requirements

The encoder, VivoActive Producer 2.0, is also available from Vivo's website. You can buy it for $495. To use VivoActive Producer, you need a Windows95 or NT with 16MB RAM and about 3MB of disk space. You can also use a PowerMac. You can download a free trial version of the Producer, but it adds an onscreen watermark into your Vivo movie. Otherwise, it works exactly like the commercial version.

There is also a "lite" version of the Producer called VivoActive VideoNow 2.0 that is designed for first-time Web developers and those new to streaming video. It costs just $119, and it doesn't include any of the advanced settings that Producer has. It is perfect for those who just want to create streaming Internet videos and don't need many options.

Vivo also makes the VivoActive Producer for NetShow ($695). It is an alternative to using Microsoft's free encoder tools. This program just encodes ASF files, it doesn't work with Vivo files.

Should You Use VivoActive?

VivoActive is best for Internet use. Not many companies would want to deploy a server-less system on an intranet. It just doesn't give you any control over streams, and if you get too many streams at once, it can slow your server and your network.

Choosing VivoActive for your Internet site boils down to a few issues. If you answer "yes" to most of the following statements, then VivoActive is probably a good idea for you:

- Do you want a quick, no-hassle way of producing streaming video on your site?

- Do you not need live video? (Tape-delay is possible, however.)

- Are you willing to sacrifice some audio and video quality?

- Do you want users to be able to watch video through firewalls, thereby reaching a wider audience than those who can't use UDP ports?

- Can you put up with the traffic on the Internet that can adversely affect a viewer's experience, especially during peak usage hours?

- Can you accept a smaller number of simultaneous video streams than you would get with server-based systems?

- Do you want an inexpensive way to stream multimedia and don't want to spend thousands of dollars on server software and dedicated hardware?

Pros and Cons

VivoActive movies travel over HTTP just like any other web page data. The advantages to HTTP is that it has guaranteed delivery. Other programs, like StreamWorks, use UDP to send packets. UDP is a faster protocol, but there is no guarantee that a packet will get there—many packets may get lost. With HTTP, the packets are guaranteed to arrive at their destination, but the data packets may arrive out of order or be delayed.

Another bonus is that HTTP can bypass intranet firewalls; the data simply comes in as any other web data. This translates into many more users who can see your video content. Unfortunately, VivoActive is susceptible to delays and lost packets, especially during heavy Internet usage times. Even if you have a fast connection to the Internet, the data may be getting bogged down by the thousands of other users on the Net. Or it could also be that the server computer is being overwhelmed by high demand. Also, HTTP streaming doesn't give you control over the number of simultaneous video streams.

About Vivo Software, Inc.

Vivo Software, Inc. was formed in 1993 and is one of the top producers of audio and video streaming technology. Over 3,000 sites use VivoActive Producer to put up streaming audio and video over the Internet. Some companies using VivoActive include Alfa Romeo, Hewlett-Packard, Intel, NCR, CNN, C|Net, MSNBC, CourTV, HBO, BBC, Intel, PictureTel, and ABC.

Vivo Software has partnered with two other heavyweights in the computer and streaming business: RealNetworks (formerly Progressive Networks) and Microsoft. Vivo files will soon be able to be streamed from NetShow and RealVideo servers. The Producer can already be used to create Microsoft's ASF files, plus Vivo makes a Producer program for Microsoft NetShow.

Vivo is a member of the IP Multicast Initiative (www.ipmulticast.com) and plans to support Real-Time Streaming Protocol (RTSP) in the future.

Vivo Software, Inc.
411 Waverley Oaks Road
Waltham, MA 02154-8414
(617) 899-8900
info@vivo.com
www.vivo.com

VDOLIVE:
Live and On-Demand Video

O ne of the first streaming video programs on the Internet was VDOLive by VDOnet Corp. It was released just after StreamWorks' video streaming player. Back then, streaming video wasn't very good—modems were slower, compression was poor, and video windows were the size of postage stamps. Nevertheless, VDOLive made it work. It was one of the better-quality streaming video programs on the market, and it remains so today. VDOnet has since improved VDOLive, and it is now on version 3.0 and branching out so it can be used over broadband networks.

VDOLive is a client/server solution that can also handle HTTP streaming. VDOLive consists of:

VDOLive Player. This is their client program for viewing VDOLive movies, available for Windows 3.1, Windows95, NT, and Macintosh. Over 5 million people have downloaded or have received the VDOLive Player.

VDOLive Tools. The tools are really two programs that handle the encoding duties. The first program, called VDO Capture, is a basic video capture program. The other, VDO Clip, compresses files with VDO's compression and outputs them ready for streaming. It is available for Window95, NT, and Macs.

VDOLive On-Demand. This is VDO's regular server used to handle on-demand video only. It is scaleable, so it can be used on many networks, from LANs to the Internet. The On-Demand server requires Windows NT or UNIX workstations.

VDOLive Broadcast. This is the live broadcast station. It accepts incoming video and connects to a server for distribution to clients. It can be used for sporting events, meetings, conventions, conferences, and more. It is available for Windows NT and UNIX.

Pricing for VDOLive is based on a per-stream basis. A 5-stream server starts at $199 and a 1000-stream version costs $55,000.

VDOLive Player

The VDOLive Player is the best place to start with the VDOLive system. It has a television-like appearance with a main playback video window plus controls on the bottom (see Figure 9.1). You see movies by clicking on a link on a web page that opens up the external VDOLive Player. The player is available as a plug-in, an external helper application, and an ActiveX control for Internet Explorer.

The Player doesn't have VCR-like controls like some other players; it only has two buttons, Stop and Play. Pressing the Play button will normally play a selected file, but if no video is loaded, it will prompt you to type in the address of a VDO clip. Most of the time, you'll have no idea what the real address of a clip is, so that's not very helpful. Instead, choose the What's Playing button to go to the VDOGuide. It will open your browser and take you the VDOGuide site so you can choose a VDO movie to watch.

 The VDOLive Player ranks among the more popular streaming video players. Nonetheless, it helps to have a place to go to test your player or find some cool videos. VDOnet's VDOGuide site (www.vdoguide.com) is just the place. There is a list of websites that are broadcasting with VDOLive, as well as special events. Unfortunately, it isn't always up to date, so you may find some sites have stopped broadcasting altogether or are using another streaming video system.

You can change the appearance of the player if you wish. Click on the Setup button and choose the Preferences tab. From there, you can show or hide the Session Statistics and Audio controls from the window (see Figure 9.2). The Audio controls give you a volume control bar, while the Statistics option lets you know what percentage of packets is getting lost and the speed of the incoming file. If you choose not to see the detailed statistics, you will just see a Reception bar telling you how well you are receiving data—100% means you're getting the best

Figure 9.1 The VDOLive Player opens whenever you click on a VDO movie link.

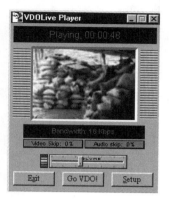

reception. The Setup button also lets you fine-tune your UDP protocol method and overall buffer size. You can also add a proxy firewall on that screen.

In the Setup window, select the User Details tab to enter your name, email, and company name. This data is automatically sent to the server for inclusion in the log, so make sure you want to include this information. If you want to protect your privacy or would rather not divulge this data, check the box at the bottom of the screen.

VDOLive Player has a status bar across the top of the screen that lets you know what is going on. It will read "Receiving," "Playing," or "Wait" during playback depending on what is occurring. During playback, you can right-click on the status bar to change the display so it shows the elapsed time, remaining time, frames, and frames per second of the current file.

Figure 9.2 You can change how the Player looks by hiding the Audio and Session Statistics. As shown here, this creates a more compact screen.

Figure 9.3 Zooming the video will make the video appear twice its normal size. You can toggle between the two views while a video is playing.

You can resize the window of the Player by right-clicking on the window area and choosing Zoom in/out from the menu (see Figure 9.3). When viewing a movie, the enlarged window will probably look a bit blocky. You can make it smoother by choosing Setup and then checking the box "Use Interlaced Double Display." It shouldn't appear choppy, but it may be a bit fuzzier. To zoom back to normal size, just right-click again and choose the Zoom in/out toggle.

> **TIP** For times when video is coming in very badly, you should choose Slide mode, which makes the video appear more like a slide show than like fluid motion. This is best for when you want better video quality and are willing to sacrifice motion. This saves bandwidth and makes your audio sound better, too. Choose the Setup button and click on the Preferences tab, then check the Slide Mode box.

The VDOLive Player is free and available for Windows 3.1, Windows 95/NT, and Macintosh users.

VDO Tools

The VDO Tools are really just two programs, VDO Capture and VDO Clip, that capture and compress files. Together, these two programs are everything you need to create videos and compress them to the proper format for streaming with VDOLive.

Capturing Video with VDO Capture

The VDO Capture program is a very basic capture program with a no-nonsense interface. When you load the program, the preview window will be open so you should be able to see your video source (see Figure 9.4). If the screen is blank, that means your input device isn't connected or is turned off. Your input source can be any video at all, from a VCR, camcorder, TV signal, or a digital video camera. If your video capture card supports it, you should choose Overlay Mode instead of Preview Mode. Select Options/Overlay from the menu. Overlay mode takes up less processor resources and shows you a better-quality image than Preview mode.

 VDO Capture is good for those who do not have a video capture program. If you already have a capture program or a video editing tool (like Adobe Premiere), it's probably best to use that instead.

1. The first step to capturing video is to select a name for the capture file. Select File/Set Capture File to give the file a name. It will be saved as an AVI file.

Figure 9.4 VDO Capture is a video capture program that creates AVI files that you can later compress to VDO format. The preview window, shown here, displays the incoming video.

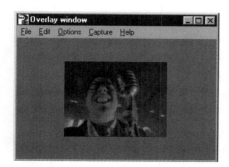

2. The next thing to consider is the window size. Go to Options/Video Format to change the size of the video window. The size primarily depends on your particular capture card and what resolution it can capture. Generally, try to keep the window size small for use over the Internet.

3. You should also check Options/Capture Settings to set your frame capture rate (15 frames per second is a good rate).

4. Once you're ready to capture the video, select Capture/Capture Video. Capture will start when you press the Enter key.

5. Record your video, then press ESC (or left-click) to stop capturing. Your new AVI file is now ready for use with the VDO Clip converter.

Converting Files with VDO Clip

VDO Clip is the conversion program that converts AVI files into VDO format. When you convert a file, it won't change extensions or file types; it will remain an AVI file. It will be compressed using VDOLive's compression called VDOWave. The VDOWave codec has become very popular and is now compatible with video editing programs like Adobe Premiere and Ulead's Media Studio Pro. If either is installed on your system, you may use that program instead of VDO Clip.

VDO Clip looks a bit like VDO Capture. (You can even open VDO Capture by selecting File/Capture.) When you open VDO Clip, you'll see a completely blank screen. To start the encoding process, choose File/Open to select an AVI or WAV file.

Once you've loaded the file, you will see the video on the main screen. VDO Clip displays the movie as a series of frames (see Figure 9.5). Chances are you'll see two or three frames at the same time, with the audio portion of your file directly below the video frames. The audio has a waveform display showing you the audio level. You can play the file by pressing CTRL-P or choosing Play/Play from the menu.

If you prefer to change your view, select Zoom from the menu. You can choose to have the video be normal size, half size, quarter size, or double and quadruple size. If you choose normal size (×1), you will only see one frame on the screen.

Now that you're familiar with the layout of the screen, you can edit the file. VDO Clip supports very basic video editing. You can cut, paste, delete, or otherwise edit the video and audio tracks.

Next, choose one of the four main compression options: Movie, Flip mode, Storybook, or Audio-only. Choose File/Drive Options to choose your compression mode:

Figure 9.5 VDO Clip shows the AVI movie as a series of video frames. You can drag the scroll bar left or right to see the rest of the frames.

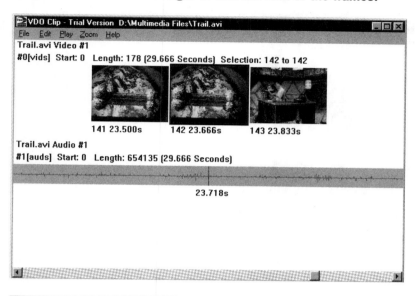

Movie mode. Use Movie mode for regular, high-quality, high-motion video. This is usually best for bandwidth connections higher than 28.8Kbps. You can actually select the movie's output rate by selecting the Playback tab and then using the slider bar or typing in the new Kbit/sec rate for the movie (see Figure 9.6).

Flip mode. This mode is best for when you want to make the quality of the video more important than the motion. Image quality will be good, but your frame rate will be no more than 2 frames per second.

Storybook mode. Storybook mode is just another word for slide show format. It does not contain motion, just a series of still images that may also include a synchronized audio track. You can use BMP, GIF, and JPEG pictures, and it is best to spread them out to appear every few seconds to give them time to be fully drawn.

Audio Program mode. The Audio mode is used when the file is audio only. You must include a still image at the beginning of the video. Import a picture like your company logo or something else relevant. VDO Clip includes the VDOnet logo as a BMP file that you can use.

Figure 9.6 The Playback Quality option is used to select the Kbit rate for the movie. This only works when your movie is in movie mode.

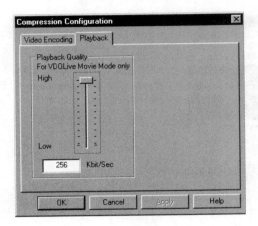

The final step is to actually start encoding the file. Choose File/VDO Encode to select the new filename and start encoding. The encoding time will depend on the length of the file and the speed of your processor. You'll see a percentage number increasing—this signifies the percentage of the file that has been compressed.

When it is finished, you can choose to view the VDO-compressed AVI file in an external player (called MCI Player) or use your own AVI video player to view it. The VDO-compressed movie is now ready to be placed on the VDOLive Server's computer for streaming.

 You can choose File/Merge to merge an audio track with a video track. To do this, first open a video-only track, choose Merge, then choose the audio file. The program will then show both the video and audio tracks in the window. You can then compress it as normal.

The VDO Tools programs are available for Windows95, Windows NT, and Mac OS.

VDOLive On-Demand Server

The VDOLive On-Demand Server is purely for prerecorded files. (For live video, use the VDOLive Broadcast system discussed in the next section). It serves the VDO-compressed AVI files to users who request the files. The same video file can be viewed and scaled by every connection type from 28.8Kbps to LAN speeds, because the files are scaleable. They can automatically adapt to the available bandwidth.

Using Token Files

Before you start using the Server, you need to learn something about Token Files. These are files created by VDOnet that contain the parameters of your Server: your server's expiration date, maximum playback time, maximum concurrent users, IP address, and your company name. The file is called VDOTOKEN and should be placed in the right directory for your operating system. (See the instructions that come with the Token File for more on where to place it. UNIX users just need to place it in the VDOLive Server directory.) You will need to replace the token file when you want to upgrade to more stream capacity or change any other of the parameters just mentioned.

Load the Server program and you'll see the opening screen. Depending on the version you're using, the interface may look different, but the idea will be the same. In Figure 9.7, you'll see the Windows95 trial version. The status bar will read "Ready," indicating that everything is running fine so far.

To start the server, simply press the Start button. After a few seconds, the status bar will report that the Server is active and will display "Server Running" (see Figure 9.8). It is now ready to stream files to clients. Depending on the version of the server you bought, your server will be limited in the number of streams that it can send simultaneously. Whenever you want to stop the server, just push the Stop button.

When you start the server, the "Open Channels" display will read zero, meaning zero connections, since you aren't serving files to any users yet. Once someone requests a file, that number will change accordingly.

Figure 9.7 The VDOLive On-Demand Server is available for many operating systems. This is the Start Up screen for the Windows95 trial version.

Figure 9.8 When the server is active, the status bar displays "Server Running." You can stop the server at any time by pressing the Stop button.

To change some options, select the Setup button. From there, you can change the port number, change the server log filename, and see the registration information. Press the Administrator button to see more options. In that screen, you can change the number of concurrent users you want to handle and change the maximum bandwidth allowed through a channel. As mentioned earlier, your server comes with a fixed number of maximum concurrent users, so you can't increase it past that maximum. You can, however, lower the number of users.

The server log for the Windows95 version is located by default at c:\windows\ system\vdostat_log.000 and contains all of the activity of the server. You may use any text editor or word processor to view the log. It contains information on when the server was started, who is watching videos, the names of the files being served, the time and date, file size, and much more (see Figure 9.9).

The VDOLive Server comes with the VDO Tools programs, so you can quickly start creating and compressing AVI files. It also comes with some user guides for using VDOLive and creating VDO pointer files. The pricing for the VDOLive Server is on a per-stream basis, starting at around $199. See VDO's website at www.vdo.net for current pricing. The VDOLive On-Demand Server is available for Windows NT and UNIX machines. Additionally, there is a fully functional, two-stream trial version of the software available for Windows95 users.

VDOLive Broadcast Server

The VDOLive Broadcast Server works just like the VDOLive On-Demand Server; the only difference is that the Broadcast Server is for transmitting live events. It comes with the VDOLive Broadcast Station, which is the program that captures

Figure 9.9 Here is a log file for the VDOLive trial server. Note that it can contain user information like name, email, and company information if the user inputs it into the VDOLive Player. The information can also be hidden by the user.

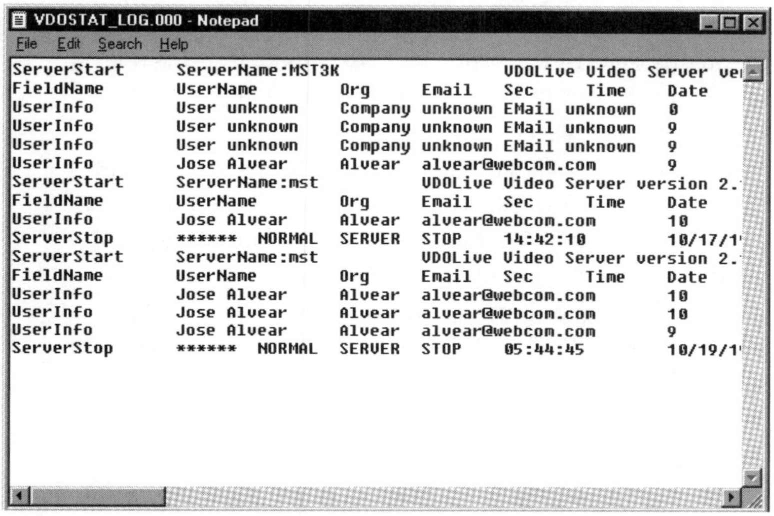

```
VDOSTAT_LOG.000 - Notepad
File  Edit  Search  Help
ServerStart      ServerName:MST3K              VDOLive Video Server ver
FieldName        UserName        Org     Email   Sec     Time    Date
UserInfo         User unknown    Company unknown EMail unknown   0
UserInfo         User unknown    Company unknown EMail unknown   9
UserInfo         User unknown    Company unknown EMail unknown   9
UserInfo         Jose Alvear     Alvear  alvear@webcom.com       9
ServerStart      ServerName:mst               VDOLive Video Server version 2.
FieldName        UserName        Org     Email   Sec     Time    Date
UserInfo         Jose Alvear     Alvear  alvear@webcom.com       10
ServerStop       ****** NORMAL   SERVER  STOP    14:42:10        10/17/1
ServerStart      ServerName:mst               VDOLive Video Server version 2.
FieldName        UserName        Org     Email   Sec     Time    Date
UserInfo         Jose Alvear     Alvear  alvear@webcom.com       10
UserInfo         Jose Alvear     Alvear  alvear@webcom.com       10
UserInfo         Jose Alvear     Alvear  alvear@webcom.com       9
ServerStop       ****** NORMAL   SERVER  STOP    05:44:45        10/19/1
```

the live video streams and sends them to the Server. You can install both programs on the same computer; in fact, that is the preferred method of communication.

The Broadcast Station is used for capturing live video from any input source. It compresses the file to VDO format and then sends it to the VDOLive Broadcast Server to distribute to users tuning into the live show. The Broadcast Station is available for Windows95 only. It requires a video capture card and audio board. The main screen of the Broadcast Station looks a bit like the VDOLive Player (see Figure 9.10). The video window displays the live, incoming video, or *self-view* window.

Here are the steps to use the VDOLive Broadcast Station:

1. Start the Broadcast Station, and you'll see the local video.

2. Switch to Overlay mode. Choose Setup, click the Devices tab, and check off the Overlay selection. Overlay mode is good because you will see a better picture, and it will also lessen the drain on your CPU's resources.

3. Next, change your video options. You can resize your window, choose your input source, and change color and other options. These options are determined by the video capture card you are using and will differ

between users. Check these options yourself to see that you are getting the best video and the right video window size. (Keep your window small for Internet broadcasts.)

4. Next, set the capture rate. This is the quality of video that you will capture. If you want better motion, change the capture rate to a higher selection. For better image quality, select low frame rates. To change it, press the Setup button, select the Devices tab, and then move the Video Capture Rate slider bar along the slide.

5. Check the TCP listening port. This is located in the Setup button and Settings tab. The port is where the server listens to the incoming stream from the Broadcast Station. You should leave it as the default (7001); otherwise, you will also have to change the port number in the server.

6. The same Settings tab also has the Rate Control option. This is the speed at which you will send data to the Server. It also sets the maximum bandwidth at which clients can receive the stream. You can use the slider bar or type in the rate. For 28.8Kbps broadcasts over the Internet, you should have a maximum of 30 to 40Kbps.

7. The connection between the Broadcast Station and the Server is initiated by the Server. (See the next section to continue the setup process.)

8. When finished with the live broadcast, click on the Hangup button.

VDOLive Broadcast Server

The server itself is pretty nondescript—it looks like the regular VDOLive On-Demand Server. It simply does the job of hosting the feed and sending it to users

Figure 9.10 The VDOLive Broadcast Station accepts input from any video source. The preview, or self-view window is shown here.

who are watching. You can hook up a number of Broadcast Servers to increase the number of live streams that you can send out.

To connect to a VDO Broadcast Station, you need to follow these steps:

1. Load the Broadcast Server.

2. Click on the Setup button, then click on Channels. This screen lets you set up the Channel Name and the VDO Broadcast Station to which it will connect.

3. Type in a Channel Name. This is the name of the file you will use in the VDO pointer file. Type in any name in the space provided.

4. Specify the location of the Broadcast Station. If it is on the same computer (as it should be), just choose the Broadcast Station selection from the drop-down menu (see Figure 9.11). Make sure the TCP port matches the port of the Broadcast Station. (Both default to the same port, so it should not be different unless you changed it.) If the Broadcast Server is connecting to another Broadcast Server instead, enter the IP address of the server.

Figure 9.11 The Channels screen is where you type in the name of the live broadcast and where you indicate the location and port of the corresponding Broadcast Station.

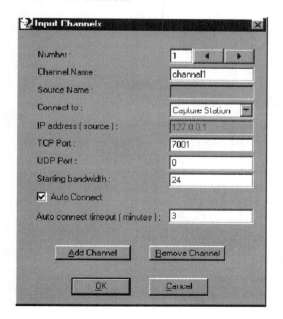

5. That's it! Start the server by pressing the Start button, and the whole system is ready for the live transmission.

6. Create the VDO pointer file (see the next section) and make sure to test the stream by going to another computer and viewing the broadcast.

For those not wanting to purchase the whole system for a one-time live broadcast, you can lease the server software from VDOnet. Cost starts at around $3,000 for up to four hours. VDOnet provides the VDOLive Broadcast Station software to transmit up to 300 concurrent streams. As always, check with VDOnet for more on pricing. The VDOLive Broadcast Server is available for Windows95 and NT 4.0 and Sun Solaris 2.5.

Creating VDO Pointer Files

When a user wants to play a VDO video, he or she is actually clicking on a VDO pointer file. The pointer file is a text file that you create that points to the server where the VDO file is located. As you've probably noticed, almost all streaming multimedia programs use pointer files. That's because clicking on the actual file won't stream it, it will just download it—and nobody wants that.

Create the file with any text editor, like Notepad, and name it with a VDO extension, like movie.vdo. The contents of the VDO pointer file are just the protocol, server host, and drive path of the AVI file. You can either put the IP address of the server, the computer name, or the DNS address. You also need the full drive and pathname of the AVI file. See the following example for serving a file on a Windows95 or NT computer:

```
vdo://server/c:\video\fun.avi
```

As you can see, the example is using the computer name, and full path of the file.

For those using UNIX servers, you just need to specify the path, relative to the virtual root. It should look like this:

```
vdo://255.132.255.0/video/fun.avi
```

For a live broadcast, the filename will be the Channel name you specified in the Broadcast Server. A live broadcast of a channel called "livefeed" will look like:

```
vdo://255.132.255.0/livefeed
```

After you've saved the VDO file, link it via an A HREF link on a web page. You can test it by loading the HTML page and clicking on the link. That should launch the external VDOLive Player.

Embedding a VDO Movie on a Web Page

Another way of displaying a movie is to embed it inside a web page using the VDOLive plug-in (see Figure 9.12). To do this, you need to use the EMBED tag. The easiest way to use the EMBED tag is shown here:

```
<embed src="http://www.server.com/video/movie.vdo" width=160 height=128
autostart="true">
```

There are other options you can add to the EMBED tag, but they can't all be covered here. To find out more, visit VDOnet's website or read the user guides that come with the server software.

Configuring MIME Types for Your Web Server

In order for your web server to recognize VDOLive movies and VDO pointer files, you need to add new MIME types to your web server.

MIME type   video

Sub type   vdo

File extension   vdo

Figure 9.12 This is a VDOLive movie displayed inside a browser window by using the EMBED tag.

There are many different types of web servers available, so check the documentation that came with your server to change your server's MIME types.

Putting VDOLive on Your Site

The entire process of using VDOLive is similar to other streaming multimedia systems. Here is the run-down of the entire process, specifically for using on-demand files:

1. Set up and install the VDO Live On-Demand Server, VDO Tools, and the VDOLive Player.

2. Create AVI files with the VDO Capture program. For stored AVI files, just use VDO Clip to compress the movies into the proper format using the VDOWave codec.

3. Post the compressed AVI files to the directory of your choice on the VDOLive Server's computer. (Unlike some systems, the file doesn't need to be in a specific directory, it can be anywhere on the server's computer.)

4. Create the text VDO pointer file that points to the AVI file on the server computer. Use the whole path to the drive and directory of the file.

5. Link the VDO file to an HTML page. Optionally, you can use the EMBED tag to show the VDOLive movie inside a web page.

6. Add the new VDO MIME types to your web server.

7. Copy the VDO and HTML files to the web server.

8. Open the VDOLive Server and make sure it is running.

9. Play the file. The server should send the movie and it should start playing within a few seconds.

That's it! For more on the live process, see the section on the VDOLive Broadcast Server.

Should You Use VDOLive?

The decision to use VDOLive over similar products like the RealSystem or NetShow will depend on the issues described in the next section. They are all very comparable; all handle live and on-demand audio and video and all work well on both intranets and the Internet.

You should also base your decision on whether you want to have a large installed Internet user base ready. RealPlayer is the number-one player right now and will be hard to topple. Also, take into consideration VDOLive's recent announcement that is was switching corporate strategy to deal with OEMs, major customers, and video compression and technology. What effect this will have on VDOLive remains to be seen.

Pros and Cons

VDOLive is one of the more sophisticated systems available. It has matured very well. The best thing about VDOLive is that you only need to create one file, not multiple files for different speeds. The one file can scale to any speed network, and that translates into a very good quality audio and video even at 28.8Kbps speeds. Its flip book and storybook formats are good for even slower speeds or high-action movies.

VDOLive can be compared to the likes of NetShow and the RealSystem. Both NetShow and RealSystem handle HTTP streaming like VDOLive. Compared to the RealSystem, VDOLive is not as feature-rich. The player doesn't have many VCR-like controls, nor can it play multiple clips, which are great for adding advertising.

In terms of price, NetShow beats them all. VDOLive's per-stream pricing structure is good news for casual users, but bad news for heavy users. VDOLive also doesn't have the level of interactivity that RealSystem or NetShow can provide, like video image maps. Finally, VDOLive would be much better if it had IP multi-cast support; so far, all streams are sent unicast.

The latest version, VDOLive 3.0, now supports HTTP streaming as well as client/server streaming. It promises more audio and video codecs as well as the ability to synchronize text, animations or scripts with VDOLive movies. It also includes a new redesigned player and a new Windows encoding tool called VDO Producer. These programs were just being released as this book was being developed, so look for them at VDO's web site.

VDOLive is a definitely a top contender and one to seriously consider for all your streaming needs.

About VDOnet Corp.

VDOnet has been at the forefront of Internet video technology since it was founded in 1995. Later that same year, it released a beta version of VDOLive and has been improving it ever since. VDOnet is also the maker of VDOPhone, a popular and easy-to-use videoconferencing software that ships with many modems and camera kits.

VDOnet has a very large clientele; there are scores of websites showing VDOLive videos. Some websites include CBS News Up-to-the-Minute, PBS,

Sportsline, MTV, and Preview Vacations. Another notable website is the American Film Institute (www.afionline.org.), which has classic films like Buster Keaton's *The Boat* and Charlie Chaplin's *The Rink*, available for on-demand viewing with VDOLive.

VDOnet is a privately held company. Major investors include Microsoft, Bell Atlantic (formerly NYNEX), and US West Media Group. Like other streaming multimedia companies, VDOnet is also a partner with Microsoft. Future versions of VDOLive will support Microsoft's NetShow ASF file format.

In September 1997, VDOnet announced it was refocusing its business strategy to cater to OEM products, video technology, and its support of major customers. It isn't yet known what effect this will have on the VDOLive line.

VDOnet Corporation
170 Knowles Drive
Suite 206
Los Gatos, CA 95030
(408) 871-3540
info@vdo.net
www.vdo.net

MICROSOFT NETSHOW:
The Future of Streaming Media

In mid-1997, Microsoft unveiled its new version of its streaming media system, NetShow 2.0. NetShow is a client/server system that streams live or on-demand audio, video, and illustrated audio. It can also be used as a server-less system to stream on-demand content. This newest version has taken advantage of new technologies like new codecs and multicasting. Best of all, NetShow and all of its related components are completely free.

NetShow is a client/server system comprised of three main parts:

NetShow Player. This is the client program that users must have to watch the streaming content. The player comes bundled with Internet Explorer 4.0 as an ActiveX component. There is also a plug-in available for Netscape Navigator users. It is available for Windows 3.1 and 95/NT, and UNIX, and will eventually support Macintosh as well. The player is free for download at Microsoft's NetShow site at www.microsoft.com/netshow.

NetShow Server. This is the server component that delivers and administers ASF files across a network. It can handle live and on-demand shows distributed through unicasting or multicasting. Like many other Microsoft products, it is limited to Windows platforms—it requires Windows NT Server 4.0. The server software is also free. It works in conjunction with Microsoft's Internet Information Server (IIS) and Site Server programs.

NetShow authoring tools. NetShow has a wide range of authoring tools, from command-line utilities to full programs like the Real-Time Encoder. They are used to convert standard files like QuickTime, AVI, and WAV into ASF format. The Real-Time Encoder is also used to capture live multimedia for delivery to the NetShow server for live cybercasts. In addition, there are many third-party programs that support ASF files.

Advanced Streaming Format (ASF) Files

Any introduction to NetShow should start with ASF (Advanced Streaming Format), Microsoft's new multimedia file format. Microsoft eventually intends to replace AVI and WAV files with ASF files, so it is best to learn more about this new format today.

ASF files are rather different from most vendors' streaming file formats. One advantage to ASF files is that they can contain audio-only, audio/video, or illustrated audio (what people call "slide shows"). They can also include scripting commands like JavaScript and VBScript, as well as "hot spots" or "video links" where users can click on certain parts of the video to launch new NetShow files, play sounds, go to a new URL, and much more. ASF files also have built-in error correction and error detection, something that Microsoft's competitors lack. Also, ASF files aren't just for streaming files, but can be used locally on your hard drive. They are rather versatile, too—ASF files can contain raw, uncompressed data or fully compressed data at a wide range of bit rates.

Another big difference between ASF files and other proprietary streaming file types is that they are codec-independent. You don't have to use one vendor's compression scheme; you have a choice of using almost any. NetShow comes bundled with 11 well-known audio and video codecs so you can choose the best ones that suit your purposes. This is a novel approach, since other vendors require that you use their native codecs. Perhaps the only problem with this independent approach is that you have too much liberty to use any codec loaded on your computer. For example, you may decide to use an obscure compression scheme, but the client who is playing the file might not have the corresponding decompression scheme. While this may not happen very often, it is something to consider. One way around this is to just use the codecs that come with NetShow or to include links to download the specific required codecs.

Another good feature is that ASF files can also be streamed via HTTP streaming for completely server-less streaming. Naturally, you pay the price for this easy streaming because HTTP streamed files cannot be multicast and do not have Seek and other advanced play features. For those features (and many more), you must use ASF files with the NetShow Server.

Compression

As mentioned earlier, ASF files are completely compression-independent, meaning that they don't use a single proprietary codec but can use many. Usually, you'll be using one codec for audio and another for video. Overall, you can create streaming files that are can take up only 4.8Kbps all the way to LAN speeds.

When you install NetShow, it comes with 11 different codecs, each with its own specialty and compression type. One of the most important codecs is MPEG-4, the newest and as yet unimplemented video compression standard. Another good codec is the MPEG Layer 3 (sometimes known as FhG IIS or Fraunhofer, Institut Integriente Shaltungen) audio codec, which is highly scaleable. It can send very good audio over 28.8Kbps modems or CD-quality sound over ISDN and faster connections.

The complete list of audio and video codecs that ship with NetShow, along with their bit rates and what applications they are best for, is in the next section. Use this as a guide when creating ASF files for certain bandwidth rates.

Using a combination of MPEG Layer 3 audio and MPEG-4 video compression, a 57MB AVI file was reduced to 150KB. This was optimized for 28.8Kbps transmission. Similarly, a raw, CD-quality 10MB WAV file was compressed to a 124KB file for 28.8Kbps pipes.

 When choosing codecs for your files, consider the total streaming bandwidth. An ASF file may contain many things like audio, video, scripts, and more. For 28.8Kbps connections, Microsoft recommends making the total stream no more than 22Kbps. When using video, try to compress your audio as much as possible without sacrificing too much quality. Whatever is left of the bandwidth automatically goes to the video portion. Obviously, if you have more bandwidth to work with, you can make higher-quality files. In any event, you may find that you will have to test many combinations of audio and video codecs for your particular bandwidth needs.

Audio Codecs

The audio codecs included with NetShow are very popular, so chances are you already have some of them installed on your computer.

Voxware Metavoice RT24. For low-quality, speech-only applications. Audio is compressed so it takes up only 2.4Kbps, so you have lots of room left for video.

Lernout & Hauspie CELP. Double the bandwidth of Metavoice so sound quality is better. L&H takes up only 4.8Kbps and it is good for live or stored audio.

Voxware MetaSound. For medium- to high-quality audio. Handles speech and music equally well and is good for a combination of both. Bit rates start at 8kHz and go to 22kHz mono sound.

MPEG Layer-3. This is a very good scaleable codec that is good for low- to high-quality speech and/or music. It can compress CD quality audio at a 12:1 rate with no noticeable loss of quality. You can compress sounds as low as 8Kbps to as high as 256Kbps. Definitely recommended for many applications.

Vivo G.723.1 and Vivo Siren. This is best for low bit-rate audio, mostly speech. The G.723.1 is an industry standard for audio compression.

Video Codecs

NetShow's video codecs range from good low-bit all the way to very good, full-motion codecs. As with the audio codecs, when first trying to compress files, it is best to try multiple codecs to see the results you get. Once you're more familiar with them, you'll have a better idea of which codec to use for a specific network or application. You'll also have favorites that you use more often.

Microsoft MPEG-4. Advanced compression of a new MPEG standard. This is an impressive video codec that gives you variable bit rates, from low to high quality. It works especially well over fast network connections. Even though MPEG-4 is not yet an international standard, chances are it will be implemented sometime in 1998.

VDOnet VDOWave. This is good for low- to mid-rate video with small window sizes. Usually good for general-purpose Internet delivery.

Duck TrueMotion. This should be used for high- or medium-quality applications, especially fast networks. Can do full-motion video.

Intel H.263 and Vivo H.263. Like VDOWave, this codec is good for low- to medium-rate video over 28.8Kbps connections. It is an Internet standard for video, so it is a very popular codec.

ClearVideo. This is popular with live video and low- to mid-quality video. It is a well-known codec that is being used by many vendors.

Steps for Using NetShow

Now that you know about ASF files and the types of compression that you can use, you can begin to learn how to implement them on your network.

Your first decision will be whether you want to use on-demand or live content; NetShow can handle both very well. If you're using on-demand content, you have a choice of using HTTP streaming or regular streaming with the NetShow Server. For live events, you must use the NetShow Server since it can best regulate transmissions and send out multicasts.

Once you've decided on your network and delivery options, follow the steps outlined here to set up a NetShow-enabled site:

1. *Install the NetShow Server and other programs.* (Even before this step, you should already know whether you will or won't use the NetShow Server.) For live transmissions, you must install it onto your Microsoft NT 4.0 Server computer. (For live audio or video, you must also use the Real-Time Encoder and skip to step 4.) Otherwise, you have the option of using the server-less or client/server system. Install the authoring tools and the NetShow player.

2. *Convert files to ASF format.* Whether you're using new or existing audio or video, you must convert AVI and WAV files to ASF format. Here you have the option of using a number of different tools. If you will be using illustrated audio, you must use a program called ASF Editor to create files. Your other choices are command-line programs or the Real-Time Encoder, which can convert files.

3. *Create ASX pointer files.* Pointer or redirector text files are necessary when using streaming files. These are text files that users must click on so that the NetShow Player starts and plays the file. You always need ASX text files if you are using HTTP or streaming from a NetShow Server.

4. *Make changes to your web page.* Add links to the ASX pointer files, either in a web page or anywhere else, like email or on your desktop. Selecting that file will automatically make NetShow play the file.

5. *Upload to the NetShow Server or web server.* If you are using HTTP streaming, just drop everything—ASX and ASF files—to your web server. If you are using the NetShow Server, the files must be sent to the server instead.

6. *Play the file.* Last but not least, everything should be ready so you can just sit back and play the file.

7. *Manage the NetShow Server.* If you're using the NetShow Server, you will be able to administer and manage your ASF files. You can see who has been playing files, get statistics, and manage multicast or unicast sessions.

Now that you know the entire process, we'll spend some time exploring each step. Of special importance is using the production and converter tools and making ASX files.

Step 1: Installing NetShow

Installing NetShow means installing three components: the player, the tools, and the NetShow Server. If you don't plan on using the Server, you can always skip that step.

More important are Microsoft's array of production and authoring tools. Microsoft created a rag-tag assembly of creation and converting tools, including:

ASF Editor. This program is used to create illustrated audio or other interactive ASF files. You can use JavaScript, VBScript, synchronized audio or text, still images, and URLs inside ASF files.

VidToAsf. A DOS command-line program that converts AVI and MOV movies into ASF files.

WavToAsf. A DOS command-line utility that converts WAV files into ASF files.

PowerPoint Publish to ASF. An add-on to Microsoft's PowerPoint that allows you to create ASF files from PowerPoint files.

ASF Real-Time Encoder. An encoder or converter program that is mainly used for live encoding of ASF files. It can also be used to create stored ASF files.

ASFChop. A command-line program that allows you to cut certain sections of ASF files.

Why Microsoft chose to use so many programs instead of one all-purpose program is unknown. It can be rather annoying to have to use command-line programs for converting files, then switch over to a graphical Windows programs like ASF Editor to create interactive slide shows. Another option is to use third-party authoring tools; these are covered later in this chapter.

Step 2: Creating ASF Files

Once everything is installed, you're ready to begin converting files. This step assumes that you are creating on-demand, multimedia files. For live broadcasts, skip ahead to the ASF Real-Time Encoder section.

First, you should know that there is no one unified or central program that you can use to convert files from AVI, MOV, and WAV to ASF format. You will probably have to use a number of programs, including some third-party programs.

The most important thing to consider when making ASF files is to know your audience's bandwidth. If you're using NetShow on the Internet, you will probably want to create video files that begin at 28.8Kbps and range as fast as 56 or 128Kbps. Whichever tool you use, you must remember that you set the bandwidth when you create an ASF file, so choose wisely or your audience may never get to see the file at all.

 Currently, there is no way to edit an existing ASF file. Make the conversion step your last step. First edit the file as you normally would and when you are completely satisfied, then use the tools to convert it. If you ever have to make a change to an ASF file, you will have to make the change to the original media file and then convert to ASF. Hopefully, there will be software available soon that allows editing of ASF files. So make sure to save your raw files in case you have to make a change.

There are so many ways of creating ASF files that we'll look at each program separately.

ASF Editor

Microsoft's ASF Editor is used to create interactive slide show or illustrated audio files. ASF Editor uses a timeline display so you can quickly see your project and edit it. You can drag and drop audio and still images anywhere along the timeline. Basically, it works much like a video editing program.

Let's make one thing clear: ASF Editor is *not* for creating or editing video. It is just for slide shows. You can, however, simulate animation by using a sequence of related still images. ASF Editor only accepts a few file formats: WAV, BMP, RLE, and JPG. You can add GIF images, but ASF Editor automatically converts them into JPEG format. For any other file formats, you must convert them yourself using third-party programs.

Making your first ASF slide show file is easy, especially since it comes with a small tutorial and sample multimedia files. You can use them to practice making your own files from scratch.

As seen in Figure 10.1, the screen is split in two. The top half is the timeline where colored blocks represent images and sound files. In the bottom half, you see the list of multimedia filenames that you will use to create the file. When you glide your mouse pointer over the colored blocks in the timeline or over the filename, you can see a preview of the still image in the far upper-left corner of the window. Unlike some popular video editing programs, you don't see the images in the timeline.

You work with ASF Editor project files, so saved projects have an AEP extension. It saves all your settings, conversions, and file locations so you just have to reload an AEP file for editing in the future. ASF Editor also comes with templates so you can quickly get started editing files instead of worrying about configuration options. One of the hardest things to do is to synchronize audio with the images. It will take some tinkering to finally get it right, especially if you are using voice-overs.

You can view your project at any point during the creation process. First you must build the file and then play it using Stream/Test or Stream/Play. Testing the

Figure 10.1 ASF Editor has a timeline interface and drag-and-drop capability to easily edit and create slide show files.

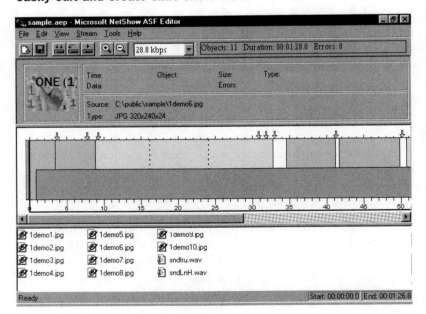

file brings up a small window where you can play the file. If you choose Play, the NetShow external player pops up instead.

Adding the interactive elements can be done at any time, but try not to include too many until you are sure of your final file. You can include URLs, scripts, EXE commands, images, HTML, and more. One of the most important things you will do is to choose a bit rate: 14.4Kbps, 28.8Kbps, or higher. The program comes with preset transfer rates but you can also create your own. Using codecs correctly is vital to having a file that is small yet presentable. See the earlier section on NetShow's codecs for more help on which you should choose.

VidToAsf

VidToAsf is a DOS utility for converting AVI or QuickTime movies into ASF files. Before using VidToAsf, make sure your file is edited, compressed, and ready for conversion. Conversion should always be your final step, when you are ready to publish the file and make it an ASF file. Remember, this does not handle any compression or editing, it just converts files. If you want to convert MPEG files, you must first convert them to QuickTime or AVI format.

First, type in "VidToAsf" to see a list of the format and commands that can be used. The basic format for VidToAsf is this:

```
vidtoasf -in move.avi -out movie.asf
```

Therefore, a sample file conversion with VidToAsf should look like this:

```
vidtoasf -in c:\windows\movie.avi -out c:\movie.asf
```

Remember to specify the input file's drive and directory. If you leave the destination field blank, the output file is saved in the same directory as the input file, and it just changes the filename to movie.asf.

The flags that you can use include changing the wavespan, changing leadtime (the time before playing), using error correction, making a seekable file, adding a script file, or using another audio in place of the existing audio file. Whenever you need help with these advanced commands, just type VidToAsf at any command prompt.

You may want to open the MS-DOS prompt and keep a window open instead of trying to launch the file by double-clicking on it. The conversion process doesn't take very long, even for large files. Also, converting a file doesn't change its file size.

 VidToAsf doesn't handle multiple or batch files, but you can write a batch file to handle multiple conversions. Unfortunately, it doesn't recognize wildcards, so you can't enter *.* for conversions. You must put each filename on its own line.

WavToASF

WavToAsf is a command-line utility for converting Windows WAV files to ASF format. It works just like the VidToAsf program with similar input and output file commands. Here is a typical command:

```
wavtoasf -in c:\windows\sound.wav -out c:\windows\desktop\sound.asf
```

Your options in WavToAsf include error correction, changing the wave span, designating a script file for a URL, and changing the leadtime. Remember, you can always see a list of flags and commands by typing "wavtoasf" at any DOS prompt.

ASFChop

The format for ASFChop is the same as the other two command-line programs. You must type "ASFChop" followed by the in and out files and then choose how you want to chop. You can do it by designating the start and end times or by choosing a beginning and overall length of the file. The only other option with ASFChop is the "–eccspan" flag, which turns error correction on or off.

PowerPoint Publish to Asf

Publish to ASF is an add-on to Microsoft PowerPoint that turns presentations into ASF format. Using it is as easy as choosing Publish to ASF from PowerPoint's Tools menu.

The actual process is simple, too. Microsoft suggests that you use PowerPoint to create a narration to the presentation, so that when you save it as an ASF file, your audio and the images will be perfectly in synch. So make sure you're using a good microphone. Follow these steps to use Publish to ASF in PowerPoint:

1. Open the PowerPoint presentation that you want to convert and switch to slide show mode.

2. Record narration so that the audio synchronizes with the presentation. Speak as you display the first slide, then when you are finished, press the space bar to go to the next slide. Record narration again for each slide and continue this until the presentation is completed.

3. When finished with the audio recording, select Tools/Publish to ASF to export all the slides. The program will ask for your target bandwidth; select either 28.8Kbps, intranet, or enter a custom speed.

4. Choose the name and directory of the file and press Enter to begin the conversion process.

5. When finished, PowerPoint brings up a Play button so you can watch the ASF presentation. It launches the NetShow player and plays the newly

created ASF file. (You'll notice that there are tick marks along the Seek bar. These represent each individual slide.)

Publish to ASF works only with Office 97 PowerPoint, so if you're using an earlier version, you should download and install the PowerPoint Internet Assistant (PPIA) from Microsoft's website. The PPIA converts presentation graphics to JPEG and HTML formats. Simply use the JPEG files with other creation tools (like ASF Editor) to create ASF files. Otherwise you'll have to upgrade to Office 97 to get the full benefits of Publish to ASF.

ASF Real-Time Encoder

The Real-Time Encoder is used primarily for broadcasting live events, but it can also be used to create stored audio and video. Like any other producer or encoder program, you must choose your original input file and an output destination. Your output can be a file stored on your hard disk or a transmission straight to the NetShow Server for live broadcasting.

Getting started with the Real-Time Encoder is easy because it guides you through a series of questions:

1. Will you use stored or live audio or video? If live, choose your input audio and/or source.

2. What is your network bandwidth? (There are options for 14.4Kbps, 28.8Kbps, ISDN, and intranet speeds.)

3. What compression will you use? (For more on what compression schemes are best for certain applications, see the Codec section earlier in this chapter.

4. Finally, name your output files if you're storing data; otherwise, choose the location of the NetShow Server. (Another option is to do both live transmission and store your output in case you want to save a live transmission for later rebroadcasting.)

Once you've answered all these questions, you are ready to start transmitting files wherever you want (see Figure 10.2).

This whole setup process is done to create a profile of your configuration options. These configuration files, or ASF Stream Descriptor files (ASD), have settings that the Encoder needs to send a stream. The Real-Time Encoder already comes with a wide range of ASD templates so you can choose one quickly. Choose File/Open to see the list of available ASD files (see Figure 10.3). You can also start a new ASF configuration by choosing File/New. You will then be guided through the setup process again. Afterwards, save your ASD file so your settings are saved for use at another time.

Figure 10.2 When you've selected all your configuration options, the Real-Time Encoder is ready to start capturing your live video source. Just press Start to begin transmitting to the NetShow Server.

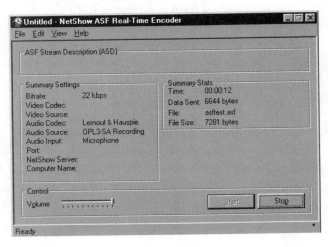

Figure 10.3 Choose File/Open to see all the preconfigured configuration files (called ASD files). You can also create new types and save them for later use.

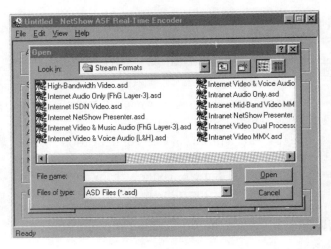

For live broadcasts, you will probably just send the stream to the NetShow Server. When starting the file, you are asked for the input audio and video sources and the location of the server. Once you've selected those, you must choose your audio and video codecs, as well as network connection speed (modem, ISDN, or LAN). When everything is selected and you are ready to transmit the audio and video, you simply press the Start button. All your configuration options are displayed on the screen and the Summary Stats tell you how long the stream has been playing. You can stop transmission at any time by pressing the Stop button. You can also save a live feed to a local disk for later NetShow transmission.

Because the Real-Time Encoder was created for live broadcasting, the file conversion process for stored media is a bit awkward. Unlike some encoder programs, Microsoft's encoder doesn't show you the conversion while it is taking place; it simply works in the background. Also, there is no batch conversion so you must convert each file individually. Nevertheless, the Real-Time Encoder is handy when you don't want to use the awkward and command-heavy WavToASF or VidToASF programs.

Encoding files is a very CPU-intensive process. You should use a fast computer to run the Real-Time Encoder. Microsoft even thinks that a multiprocessor computer is a good idea. If you can't do that, try to use a computer with MMX or one running Windows NT Workstation. If you're transmitting a live event, it is best to use a dedicated machine.

Step 3: Creating ASX Files

As we should know by now, we need to create a text file that actually points to the real ASF file so it can begin streaming. Microsoft calls its pointer files Active Stream redirector, or ASX, files. It tells the browser where to get the actual ASF file. Remember that if you make a link directly to an ASF file, it won't stream; your browser will download it instead.

A typical ASX file is simple. It can consist of one line, as shown here:

```
asf mms://server/content/movie.asf
```

In this example, the MMS stands for the NetShow Server protocol. Use this when streaming from a server. The server name can be entered as a regular IP address (if you know it), as the domain name, or as your machine name.

For HTTP server-less streaming, the ASX file should look like this:

```
asf http://www.yourserver.com/content/movie.asf
```

You can also include additional information in the ASX file in case you need to include another location for an ASF file or want to include descriptive information. The following text is an example of this optional information:

```
[Reference]
Ref1 = MMS://server/virtualdir/movie.asf
Ref2 = HTTP://server/virtualdir/movie.asf
Ref3 = MMS://server2/virtualdir/movie.asf
Ref4 = HTTP://server2/virtualdir/movie.asf
BaseURL=HTTP://server/virtualdir

[Description]
Program Title=Title of Your Program
Program Description=The Description of Your Program
Program Author=Your Name Here
Program Copyright=Copyright Notice
```

Adding other locations where you can find your ASF file gives viewers a better chance of finding your file in case one server goes down, or if they are behind a firewall and can only use HTTP streaming. The description data is shown when users view the file properties.

Step 4: Creating HTML and ASF Links

Once you've finished creating your ASX files, you obviously need to create links to them on any web page. Use regular HTML linking to link the ASX files, such as:

```
<A HREF="movie.asx">Click here to watch the NetShow movie</A>
```

ASX files are handy because you can put them in many places besides HTML pages. You can put them in email messages so users can simply double-click and bring up the NetShow Player to view files. You don't even need to open up your browser. You can also put them in Microsoft Office files and send them to friends and colleagues. This is a great way of exchanging video files; for example, instead of sending the whole video through email, you just send the ASX file.

Step 5: Uploading Files to the Server

This is the easiest step. Just copy the files (HTML, ASX, and ASF) into your web server (if you're just using HTTP streaming) or to the NetShow Server location and you're ready to test it out.

While you're thinking about your web server, you should check it to make sure it can accept the ASF and ASX MIME types. Microsoft has a page that lists multiple server configurations (including WebStar, Apache, Netscape, Microsoft's IIS,

NCSA, etc.), so you can make sure that it accepts ASF and ASX file formats. See www.microsoft.com/netshow/mime.htm for more information on how to set the MIME types for your specific server.

Step 6: Playing NetShow Files

The NetShow player is the client program used to view ASF content. The NetShow Player is an ActiveX control for IE and a plug-in for Netscape Navigator. There are versions for Windows 3.1, 95/NT, UNIX, and Macintosh. NetShow is also integrated into Microsoft's Internet Explorer 4.0 suite, and will eventually take over as Microsoft's all-purpose multimedia player, capable of playing standard downloadable files as well as streaming files like ASF. The NetShow external player should still be made available to Internet Explorer 3.0 users.

You can watch NetShow movies in a variety of ways:

Use the standalone NetShow player. Simply load the NetShow player (in Windows95 it is usually under Start/Programs/Microsoft NetShow) and then choose File/Open File or File/Open Location. You can then type in a web address or choose a local file.

Launch from a link in a web page. Using a standard A HREF web link, you just click on that hyperlink to load the standalone player and play the NetShow file.

Embedded in a web page. Using the HTML EMBED command, you can place an ASF file inside a web page. The external player will not load, but will play embedded in the page. Files can be started using script applications, too.

NetShow Player

Like most audio and video players, NetShow has regular play controls, like Fast Forward, Rewind, Seek and Stop buttons (see Figure 10.4). Naturally, the Seek controls will be grayed out if you're transmitting live. You can also change other options, like choosing your default transmission protocol (to bypass company firewalls) and buffer size (for better, uninterrupted streaming). NetShow 2.0 supports Intel's MMX multimedia improvements so you get faster rendering of graphics.

When playing an ASF file, you can change viewing options or just see stream information. To look at the properties of a file that you are listening to, choose

Figure 10.4 The NetShow player has VCR-type controls and a navigational Seek bar.

File/Properties or right-click anywhere on the player and choose Properties. Some of the things you can do include checking details on the file like the title, author, copyright, window size, source of the file, and transport protocol. You can also see a pie graph that shows you the statistics on the incoming file, like how many packets you've received and how many you've lost. The Advanced tab allows you to change the buffer size, enable or disable network protocols, or set proxy addresses.

When compared to the RealPlayer, NetShow looks very plain. If you want to watch a movie or listen to files, you must open up your browser first and find some content. Unlike the RealPlayer, there are no preset buttons. Even a bookmarking feature would have been nice.

Step 7: Working with NetShow Server

In step 1, you should have already installed all NetShow components, including the NetShow Server. If you haven't done so yet, do it now. Remember, you need Microsoft Windows NT 4.0 Server to run the NetShow Server. If you're just running Windows95, you can still install other Server components so you can administer a remote server—it just won't let you install the actual server. If you select the default options, it installs the NetShow Server and other tools to help you manage and administer NetShow streams. They should be located under the Microsoft NetShow menu. All the installed components and administration tools are web-based, so you must have Internet Explorer 3.0 or later installed. Since everything can be controlled via the browser interface, you should find that things are easy. At any point, you can pull up a help file for more information on a particular server tool. There are many administration options and tools, and they can't all be covered here. Make sure to check out the help files and use the Wizards to guide you through some setups.

> **TIP**
>
> Even though there are no bookmarking features, you can still save locations of some of your favorite sites on your hard drive. Here's how: When you get to the ASX link that would normally launch the NetShow player, choose to save the ASX file to your hard drive instead. If using Windows95, you can put the ASX shortcuts on your desktop or in their own directory. Now, whenever you want to revisit those files (either live or on-demand files), you can just double-click on them to launch the NetShow player—you don't even need to open up your browser. You'll probably want to rename those ASX files so you'll know what they are, like "WHTZ Live Radio Station.ASX." You can also use this tip for any other programs in this book that use pointer files.

The server tools that are installed in your Microsoft NetShow directory are outlined here:

Welcome to NetShow Server. This is an introductory web file that should be the first thing you look at after installing the Server. It describes the Server and tells you how to set up a server and administer it. It is also the launching point for running the NetShow Administrator. The Administrator Documentation gives you in-depth information on how to use the Server and Administrator products. There are also links to Microsoft's website for more up-to-date information.

Microsoft NetShow Administrator. This will be your main interface or homepage for NetShow administration. From here, you can add, remove and set up Servers, either local or remote (see Figure 10.5). Once you add a server, you can use the Administrator to help you configure channels, manage streams, and monitor connections and ongoing events. You can also schedule events. It is also used to set up unicast or multicast sessions and can display the event monitors, described later in this section.

Figure 10.5 The NetShow Administrator is your starting point where you can add or delete servers and manage your NetShow content. This is the "Getting Started" pane.

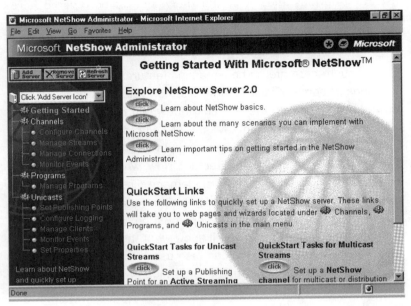

Microsoft NetShow Server. This is the actual program that delivers the ASF files to clients all over the network. It is installed as a service under NT.

NetShow Unicast Event Monitor. The Unicast Event Monitor is for monitoring or troubleshooting the NetShow Server. You can check for problems or irregular events by looking at the log in the middle of the screen. It can also log every server event (see Figure 10.6). You need to have administrative access to the server before you can use this.

NetShow Channel Event Monitor. This works like the Unicast Event Monitor except that it lets you observe channels that are set up for multicasting. All activity is displayed in the main text area in the middle of the window.

Microsoft Server Event Log. This is a program that logs events from the NetShow Server and saves them to a database. To enable logging,

Figure 10.6 The Unicast and Channel Event Monitors do exactly what they say they do: monitor and log multicast and unicast sessions so you see how many connections you have and what files are being served.

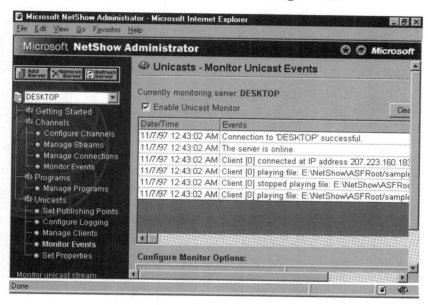

just open the program and check the Enable Logging box and type in the address of the NetShow Server you want to monitor. You can set filters to log only certain server actions or limit the length of the log.

Connecting the NetShow Server

Now that you've installed NetShow and added a server (either a local or remote server), you must now make some decisions. Will you use live or on-demand multimedia? If live, you must use the Real-Time Encoder to connect to the NetShow Server. For on-demand content, just drop files into the Server's directory. Also decide which protocols you will use, UDP, TCP/IP, HTTP, or RTP. Last, decide whether you want to use multicasting or unicasting for your event. If you want to use multicasting, you need to set up a channel so that users are notified that you are planning on transmitting a multicast event at a certain time. Users can then check in and ask to be let into the multicast stream when it is delivered. Unicasting doesn't need this since every stream is sent individually to every user who requests the stream.

Remember, unicasting is what is used most often. With unicasting, a separate copy of the data is sent from the server to the client for each person who requests it. This can easily flood your network. Multicasting sends a single copy from the server and it is distributed throughout the network using multicast-enabled routers. Obviously, this drastically decreases your network traffic load. Chances are you will use multicasting on your intranet more often than on the Internet, since the infrastructure isn't completely available yet.

The NetShow Server is very scaleable. Although much depends on network size and file size, you can usually transmit 52 concurrent 28.8Kbps streams on a T1 line (1.54Mbps). Using a T-3 connection (45Mbps) ups your simultaneous streams to 1,562. The NetShow Server can be installed on several computers, so that more simultaneous streams can be transmitted. Also, you can dedicate one server to handle just live content while using others for more distribution. See the Manage Clients window to see how many users are connected to your server at any time (see Figure 10.7).

Figure 10.7 This screen shows you all the clients connected to your server. Here, just one client is connected and watching a NetShow movie.

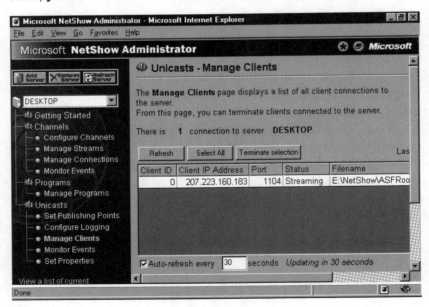

On the downside, using the server requires that you use a Windows NT 4.0 Server. It doesn't seem likely that many companies will want to buy NT machines or switch operating systems, but for those already using Windows and NT Server, this is a no-brainer. The NetShow Server can be used with Intel-based machines or those using Digital Equipment Corp.'s Alpha chip. The NetShow Server can be downloaded for free and it is also included in Microsoft's Site Server, an environment for enhancing, deploying, and managing websites.

Partners and Third-Party Tools

Microsoft is leveraging its power in the computer industry so that many third-party companies are releasing companion programs and showing their support for NetShow and the new ASF file format. Here are some of the major announcements and partnerships:

- Vivo Software (www.vivo.com) supports the ASF format in its new Producer 2.0 authoring tool. Just convert and then save the file as an ASF file. Vivo also makes a separate program called Producer for NetShow ($695) which only handles ASF creation and authoring. It is much easier to use than the command-line programs that Microsoft uses.

- Digital Evolution, Inc., (www.digev.com) is supporting ASF in its Media Conveyor program. It helps build interactive multimedia that feature animations, synchronized audio, hot spots, and even 32 frames-per-second video.

- Sonic Foundry's (www.sfoundry.com) Sound Forge, a Windows sound editor, also supports the ASF format.

- TAG 1.0. (www.digital-ren.com) is a time-based audio, video, and animation authoring tool that lets you easily create interactive ASF files. You can add hotspots, create illustrated audio, or convert any audio or video file to ASF format.

- Ephyx (www.ephyx.com) released V-Active, an authoring tool for creating interactive ASF files. It includes the ability to create video hotlinks.

- Intelligence At Large, Inc., (www.ialsoft.com) created Windows 3.1 and Mac versions of the NetShow 2.0 player. It will also release NetShow authoring tools for the Macintosh.

- AudioNet (www.audionet.com) is converting much of its content to ASF format. AudioNet, the largest Internet broadcast network, hosts and broadcasts many live and on-demand audio and video events like concerts, radio stations, speeches, sporting events, and other special events. Previously, AudioNet had almost all of its content in RealAudio format.

- RealNetworks (formerly Progressive Networks) and Microsoft entered into an agreement to fully support the new ASF format. Microsoft released a version of the NetShow Server that can stream RealAudio and RealVideo files. RealNetworks will also support ASF as well as its own RealMedia files.

- VDOnet (www.vdo.net) is adopting ASF into its VDOLive streaming product and will focus on developing applications for broadband networks. To further cement their relationship, Microsoft also bought a minority stake in the company and has a seat on its board. Sony is the first user of Microsoft's Professional Video Server that makes use of broadband networks for full-screen, interactive streaming. Sony is using it to create full-service, in-flight entertainment (IFE) systems for passengers, including full-screen, full-length feature films, music videos, music, shopping, games, travel information, and more.

- Numerous companies are creating and hosting NetShow content like live special events and on-demand content.

Should You Use NetShow?

Because Microsoft is making so many partnerships with other streaming vendors, you must get to know NetShow. Already, Microsoft has entered into agreements with AudioActive, Liquid Audio, VivoActive, VDOLive, and RealNetworks. All plan on supporting Microsoft and ASF in the future. The only companies that aren't in on this alliance are companies that use MPEG-based architecture, like Xing's StreamWorks. They are left out in the cold.

If all goes according to Microsoft's plan, NetShow will be the market leader in streaming multimedia, and their ASF files will be ubiquitous so that ASF becomes the standard streaming file format on the Internet. In fact, Microsoft's plan for ASF will be to eventually replace AVI (Video for Windows) and WAV file formats. Naturally, all of this won't happen overnight, but the seeds are being planted now, so it makes sense for you to learn and perhaps even test NetShow. Unless some drastic shakeups occur in the market, NetShow is sure to be a major player. Even if you choose not to implement NetShow, you should at least become familiar with its components and understand how they work together.

In short, if you're already a Microsoft shop, the decision to use NetShow may be an easy one. Other streaming vendors may have simpler software, but NetShow combines powerful features and file integration into one powerful and free package.

Pros and Cons

NetShow is a very good system, especially for those organizations using Microsoft Windows. This tight integration with Windows is also its major problem. It is *too* Windows-oriented; only real Windows jockeys can appreciate all of NetShow's features. Not every IS manager will want to switch from his or her own server (say UNIX or Macintosh) to use the NetShow Server, which requires the expensive Windows NT Server 4.0. Fortunately, NetShow also supports server-less or HTTP streaming, so you can keep your own server and keep your costs down.

Server-less streaming is good, but to get the real power of NetShow, you must use the NetShow Server. It gives you the flexibility to use multicast or unicasting, choose transport protocols, bandwidth management, transmit live events, and more. It also does not limit your streaming capacity like other programs—the number of users that you can serve is dependent on your network and the number of servers that you are using. In this regard, the NetShow Server is a very good, mature product that takes advantage of new features like RTP and multicasting. Using the Server also allows the viewers to seek anywhere within a file, something that can't usually be done with HTTP streaming. The Server comes with Wizards to help you set up and initiate multicast sessions and provides plenty of help resources.

Another big plus is that Microsoft is taking the lead in the streaming multimedia market. It is the one to watch and is at least trying to consolidate the industry, so there aren't so many proprietary streaming file formats. Whether it will succeed is not yet clear, but it's on the right track. Soon you will be able to use ASF files with almost any other major streaming vendor's production tools and server programs. ASF files are a big improvement over the existing streaming file formats because they can handle audio, video, and slide show in one file format; other vendors support only video or audio and use multiple file formats.

Perhaps the biggest shortcoming of NetShow is that it does not have a core authoring tool or converting program. The production tools are a motley collection of command-line programs and full-fledged programs that don't work together very well, and since there is no central program, you are left to your own devices when creating an ASF file. The Real-Time Encoder is great for live transmissions but is a bit confusing when you just need to do a simple AVI or WAV to

ASF conversion for on-demand files. The other option is to use the command-line programs, but learning to use them is tedious and tends to be so confusing that you'll be screaming for a nice friendly graphical interface. The only good side to those command-line programs it that they make it easier to use other operating systems (using emulators, perhaps) or older computers that don't support Windows95. Nevertheless, the lack of a cohesive, easy-to-use production tool is a big flaw that will hopefully be fixed with the next version of NetShow. Fortunately, there are some very good third-party ASF editors available that are much better than anything Microsoft has available.

About Microsoft Corp.

According to Microsoft, 11 million NetShow players have been distributed and over 100,000 servers have been downloaded since its NetShow 2.0 launch in mid-1997. Around the same time, Microsoft acquired VXtreme Inc., maker of another streaming program called WebTheater. In future versions of NetShow, WebTheater should be fully integrated into one program.

A higher-end version called NetShow Professional Video Server is also available for those who need a high-quality, full-screen video on their broadband network. It is available for on-demand movies and other applications like hotels, kiosks, and in-flight entertainment.

With its numerous business deals, acquisitions, and partnerships, Microsoft is taking the lead in the streaming multimedia market. Clearly, NetShow is one to watch.

Microsoft Corp.
One Microsoft Way
Redmond, WA 98052-6399
(206) 882-8080
www.microsoft.com

REALNETWORKS'
RealAudio and RealVideo

I n 1995, Progressive Networks created the first streaming Internet audio program called RealAudio, an amazing breakthrough for Internet multimedia. No longer did users have to download audio files; they could listen to live or stored files on the fly while they were downloading. Although the sound was tinny and barely equaled AM-radio quality, RealAudio was an unmitigated success. Two years later, Progressive Networks released a streaming video system called RealVideo and an advanced player called RealPlayer that played both audio and video files. Sound quality improved dramatically, and even video looked good. Later in 1997, Progressive Networks changed its named to RealNetworks and announced support for streaming animation, called RealFlash, based on Macromedia's Flash animations. This whole new streaming solution is called the RealSystem 5.0.

RealNetworks is clearly at the forefront of streaming technology. It has constantly improved its products and has the lion's share of the streaming audio and video market. RealNetworks boasts over 15 million downloads of its players.

The RealSystem is a three-part client/server system that also supports HTTP streaming. The components include:

RealPlayer. This is the free player that can play all types of RealMedia files (RealAudio, RealVideo, and RealFlash), and is the most popular streaming multimedia player on the Internet. The RealPlayer works as either a plug-in or a standalone player and is launched whenever a RealMedia file is encountered. The RealPlayer comes bundled with

Microsoft Internet Explorer 4.0 or is available for download at RealNetworks' website. It is available for multiple platforms like Windows 3.1, Windows 95/NT, Mac, and UNIX.

Encoder Tools. There is no one tool that handles all the encoding duties but three different programs. Two programs, RealPublisher and RealEncoder, are essentially the same except that RealPublisher has options that automate publishing and HTML creation. Both can be used to encode live or on-demand audio and video. The third program is an audio-only encoder called RealAudio Encoder that can encode live and on-demand audio. All programs except for RealPublisher are free.

RealServer. There are two servers available. RealNetworks' main product is the RealServer Basic Plus, which serves all RealMedia files and has plenty of reporting capabilities. Its other server, the RealServer Basic, lacks some of the more advanced features but is free. Both run on a variety of platforms like Windows NT, UNIX, and Mac. The RealServer Basic can even run on Windows95.

Free and low-cost servers are making it easy for many companies and individuals to try out and use streaming multimedia on their sites. RealNetworks announced plans to drop prices and make some servers completely free.

RealSystem 5.0

With the unveiling of the RealSystem 5.0, RealNetworks is securing its place at the top of the streaming market heap. It hopes to make the RealMedia file format the number-one streaming format on the Internet.

Some of the new features of the RealSystem 5.0 include:

- *Better audio and video compression.* Audio is now "near CD-quality" for 28.8Kbps users. There are also higher bit rates available (all the way to 300Kbps), making the RealSystem suitable for use over company intranets.

- *Support for Macromedia's Flash streaming animation called RealFlash.* These animations can be long form and can include a synchronized RealAudio track to provide a rich multimedia experience.

- *Support for 56Kbps modems like X2 and K56Flex.* If you have one of these faster analog modems, you can expect much better quality, or even stereo sound.

- *Full-screen video for ISDN and faster connections (100Kbps to 300Kbps).* RealNetworks uses Microsoft's DirectDraw system for full-screen rendering to Windows95 and NT users.

- *Better advertising ability.* Ad rotations to place advertisements in the beginning, middle, or end of a stream. More detailed demographics and statistics.

- *Pay-per-view support.* Broadcasts can be password-protected, so you can charge for certain shows like analyst briefings or live concerts.

- *RealVideo support of interactivity with video maps.* Video maps, which work like ordinary image maps, are hotspots on a video that are clickable; when you click on a certain section, it will launch an event (like a URL, or a new RealMedia file) or scan to a different location in the current file.

- *Buffered Play.* This is for when you want to view a clip that exceeds your current bandwidth. The file will be completely or partially downloaded (buffered) before playing. Although downloading a file can take a long time, it is good for when you want to see higher-quality video or listen to CD-quality audio and don't mind waiting for the download.

- *Support for IP multicasting, specifically on intranets to reduce bandwidth.*

- *Multimedia that is synchronized with web content via scripts or other animation.*

Essentially, the RealSystem is the name for the entire product line that Real-Networks sells. It is grouped into three major streaming solutions:

Internet Server. This system is best for ISPs, web broadcasters, multi-media developers, and sites that want to host lots of RealMedia content. It includes RealAudio, RealVideo, and RealFlash and supports commerce capabilities. Many use it to include video commercials between broadcasts, much like television broadcasting.

Intranet. The Intranet Solution includes a number of different packages to fit any size company intranet. Packages include client plug-ins, the Real-Server, and the RealPublisher for quick content creation and publishing. The Intranet Solution is also IP Multicast-enabled for reducing bandwidth on your network. You can also purchase a RealVideo training bundle for your intranet to provide on-demand video desktop training for popular software applications to all employees.

Commerce Solution. This Commerce RealServer is the newest addition to the RealSystem and is used for broadcasting secure transmissions over networks. For example, you can make certain events available to a small number of users or allow for password access to any event. This is good for distance-learning applications, briefings, and pay-per-view broadcasts. The Commerce RealServer works with existing external database programs and provides complete demographic tracking and reporting functions.

Prices for these systems start at around $5,000, but they should be available free on a trial basis. If you don't choose one of the systems just described, you can also mix and match components and build your own system.

The main components of the RealSystem are discussed next.

RealNetworks' Basic Server 5.0

The Basic Server 5.0 is the best way to start out using RealMedia. It is free and comes complete with everything you might need to host content. You can handle about 500 28.8Kbps modem users on one Pentium computer. If you need more capacity, you can use a dual- or triple-processor computer or a faster UNIX computer with the Alpha processor.

During installation, you must answer questions in order to set up the RealServer. First you're asked for your name and license number, the latter of which should come with your software or in an email message if you downloaded the program. Next, enter the port number for your server (you can choose the default) and your email address if you want to be notified when the RealServer encounters error messages. Once it is completely installed, the RealServer automatically plays a test message to make sure it is installed correctly. Once the server is running, things pretty much run themselves, so you won't have to bother with the server unless you want to shut it down. In Windows NT, the RealServer is installed as a service, so you can make it automatically run at startup. It also installs the Real-Server Control Center for testing your server and tweaking some options.

In order for your server to recognize your RealMedia files, you must copy them to the default server's directory, usually c:\real\server\content.

To monitor your server, use the RealServer System Manager that was installed alongside your server. The System Manager can tell you how many people are logged on to your server, what files are being served, client IP addresses, and much more.

RealNetworks' Basic Server 5.0 is available free for many popular UNIX systems, as well as Windows95 and NT platforms.

Basic Server Plus

The Basic Server Plus has all the features of the Basic Server plus a few more. It can support RealFlash streaming animations as well as RealAudio and RealVideo. It also comes with the RealPublisher content creation tool and graphical monitoring tools.

The Basic Server Plus costs $695 and includes the RealPublisher. If you want to add RealFlash support, the upgrade costs $295. The Basic Server Plus is available for a variety of UNIX machines and Windows 95/NT platforms.

Encoding Files to RealMedia Format

RealVideo is optimized for performance at 45Kbps. That means that users with 28.8Kbps won't see everything that RealVideo has to offer. Those with the new analog 56Kbps modems, however, can usually reach downstream rates that are high enough. There are marked improvements in audio quality and lip synchronization at those speeds, so it pays to upgrade to a 56Kbps modem. Unfortunately, 28.8Kbps modems will remain popular for a few years so, as a web developer, you should assume that users will still be using that speed. You should try to support a wide array of client connections, so you might want to include 28.8Kbps, 56Kbps, 128Kbps, and faster streams on your website.

Encoding files means knowing something about the codecs provided with the RealSystem. Most of the time your encoding options are descriptive, so if you are transmitting a talking-head video, you can choose a codec called Video 28.8Kbps Talking Head. A music video might use the configuration Audio 28.8 Music—Stereo. More advanced users can tweak the compression settings like frame rate, bit rates, and sampling rates and get better results. As with all encoders, it makes sense to test your output stream, so you can see what the audience will be seeing.

RealNetworks recommends keeping a maximum total bit rate of 19Kbps for 28.8Kbps users. At 56Kbps, you should keep the total under 44Kbps. That's because you want to leave room for errors in case there is too much network traffic.

There are three tools: the RealAudio Encoder, the RealEncoder, and Real-Publisher. We'll take a look at all three programs next.

RealAudio Encoder 3.1

RealAudio Encoder 3.1 is available for Windows 95/NT, Macintosh PowerPC, and many UNIX platforms. The RealAudio Encoder is used to create RealAudio files from live and stored content and includes a waveform analyzer and plenty of the newest RealAudio codecs.

The RealAudio Encoder can convert stored or live audio and output it as a RealAudio file (.RA) or to a RealServer. If using stored content, select the file and choose your compression settings. If using live input, you must enter a RealServer host address and port number in order to start encoding. You can choose from a number of different RealAudio preconfigured compression settings, like Real-Audio 3.0 Mono Voice, RealAudio 5.0 Music Stereo, and many more (see Figure 11.1).

When you are broadcasting live and want to save an archived file for later viewing, simply select both live and stored outputs. That way, anyone who missed your live broadcast can view it later. Both the RealEncoder and RealAudio Encoder support this feature.

Don't forget to enter the title, artist, and copyright information in the boxes on the lower left-side of the window. You can also choose to enable Perfect Play to let users with slow modems play faster bit rate files. The Selective Record option is for those users who can record content with the RealPlayer Plus. Unfortunately, the RealAudio Encoder can't perform batch encoding; it just handles one conversion at a time.

Figure 11.1 Select the file you want to encode and your compression. Press the Start Encoding button to finish the encoding process.

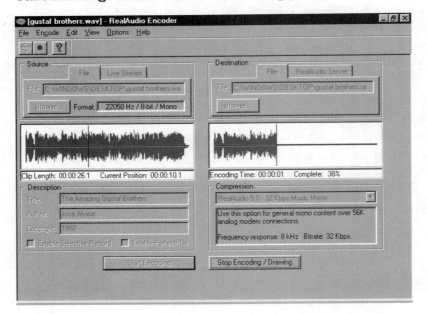

Since the RealAudio Encoder just handles audio, you probably won't use this program very often. This is best for those with older computers or those using platforms not supported by the RealEncoder 5.0. You can download the Real Audio Encoder free from the RealNetworks website at www.real.com.

RealEncoder 5.0

The RealEncoder is your all-purpose tool for converting audio and video (AVI, WAV, AU, and QuickTime) into RealAudio and RealVideo formats. It does not handle RealFlash content.

The RealEncoder is very versatile; it can be used with a RealServer or with standard HTTP servers so it can handle on-demand and live media. The destination can be stored as a file on your hard disk or sent to a RealServer for live broadcasts. It includes many RealAudio and RealVideo codecs, as well as numerous predefined templates for easy encoding. This newest version of the Encoder can handle many new bit rates, from 14.4Kbps Audio to High-Quality Video at 300Kbps.

Follow these steps to encode a file with RealEncoder:

1. *Open RealEncoder.* You'll see the main startup screen with two preview windows for use when converting video files (see Figure 11.2).

Figure 11.2 This is the opening screen of the RealEncoder. The left window is your input preview video and the right is the output.

2. *Choose File/Open Session.* At this screen, you must choose your input and output files (see Figure 11.3). You can choose to capture from a live source or from a file. Next choose the destination: either a RealMedia file or send it to a RealServer for live output. (If you choose to output to a RealServer, make sure you know your RealServer's IP address and port number.) The easiest way to get started is to choose an existing WAV or AVI file and save the output to your hard disk. Click on the Save As button to type in the output filename and press OK.

3. *You will be taken back to the main window.* If you've chosen an AVI or MOV file, the Source Input window will have the first frame of your movie. (If you chose to convert a sound file, that video window will be blank.) This is a good time to decide if you want to view your input and/or output videos during the encoding process. Select View/Show Source Input or View/Show Encoded Output to make your choices.

 The RealEncoder cannot handle batch encoding; it only encodes one file at a time.

Figure 11.3 Choose your input and destination sources. In this case, an AVI file is the source file and it will be saved to the hard disk.

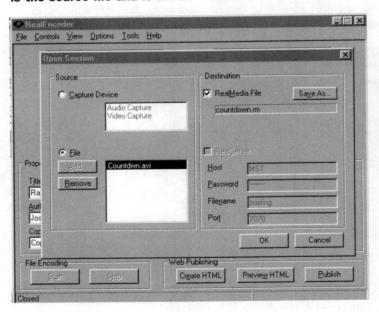

4. *Type in the properties of the RealMedia file.* Such properties can be Author, Copyright, and Title of the file.

5. *Next, select your coding from the Templates scrolling window.* The codecs are listed in plain English, so you know exactly what you're getting. For example, you can choose Audio 28.8 Music Stereo or Video 28.8 Talking Heads. New in this version of the Encoder are bit rates of 80, 100, and 300Kbps. At these speeds, users can see very high-quality video, or even full-screen video. If you're familiar with encoding files, choose the Advanced tab and adjust your own settings (see Figure 11.4) or even create your own customized template.

6. *Last, press the Start button to begin encoding (see Figure 11.5).* Encoding time depends on the length of your file and the speed of your computer. Compared to other encoders mentioned in this book, it is one of the fastest. Once it is finished encoding, a Statistics window appears so you can see the actual frame rate, bit rate, and other information on the file.

Figure 11.4 The Advanced button opens up a new screen where you can customize the encoding or create your own templates.

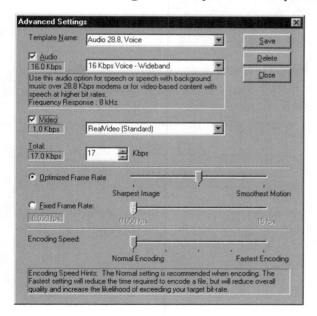

Figure 11.5 During the conversion process, you can watch the input and output preview windows to monitor it for quality. You can press the Stop button at any point.

NOTE The Web Publishing buttons in the RealEncoder (Publish, Create HTML, and Preview HTML) don't work. You have to buy the RealPublisher to get those options. See the section on Pointer and Metafiles for more on creating your own pointer and HTML pages.

Once the conversion is done, you are ready to copy the file to a regular web server or a RealServer. See the sections on creating pointer files for more on how to create a link.

To speed up the encoding process, the RealEncoder supports extensions for Intel's MMX processors. The RealEncoder is free and available for Windows 95/NT and Macintosh Power PC. You can download the latest version from RealNetworks' website.

RealPublisher

The RealPublisher is simply the more advanced and costlier version of Real-Encoder. It has all the features of RealEncoder, but it includes an HTML wizard for no-hassle creation of HTML web pages and pointer files. It also adds the Publish button, which allows you one-button publishing to a RealServer or web server.

> **NOTE** During installation, the RealPublisher automatically looks to see if you've installed the RealEncoder on your computer. If so, the RealPublisher will ask you to uninstall that program first before continuing installation. That's because the RealPublisher is the more advanced version of the free RealEncoder. Simply select Yes to uninstall the RealEncoder and finish the installation process.

To convert files, simply follow the steps outlined in the preceding section for the RealEncoder. The only things new to RealPublisher are three buttons: Create HTML, Preview HTML, and Publish:

Create HTML. Clicking on this button brings up a wizard that creates an HTML page for your RealMedia file. It will first ask you to choose your RealMedia file. Next, select the playback method: either Pop-up Player for launching the RealPlayer or Embedded Player for playback inside a browser page. Type the caption to identify the RealMedia file and the name of the HTML file you want to create. The HTML page is created as well as the pointer file. Press Preview HTML to open up your default browser and take a look at the page. Naturally, you can edit the newly created HTML to better suit your purposes.

Preview HTML. Once you've gone through the Create HTML button once, you can simply click on this button to open your browser with a local copy of the HTML page. Test it by clicking on the link and making sure that the RealMedia file starts playing. See Figure 11.6 for an example of an embedded player.

Publish. Once you're satisfied with the HTML page (and have made any changes or additions to it yourself), you can publish it with RealPublisher. Press the Publish button to start the wizard. Begin by choosing the HTML file that was created. Next, choose what server method you will use, HTTP or RealServer. If you've chosen a standard web server, enter the name and location of the server (usually in the form ftp.server.com), followed by the directory and password information. If you're using a RealServer, you'll also be prompted to enter the hostname for the server. If applicable, enter your username and password, too. You are then ready to upload the files. Press Finish to upload the RealMedia, pointer file, and HTML document to your server(s).

Figure 11.6 You can also embed a RealMedia file so it plays inside a browser window.

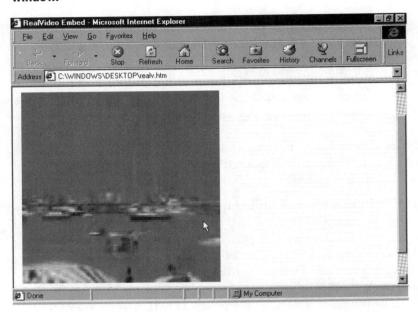

Once it's finished, don't forget to test everything. If the Publish wizard fails to transfer files successfully, you can always just upload files manually with any FTP program.

The RealPublisher costs $49.99 and is available for Windows95 and NT only. It can be purchased at their RealStore, www.realstore.com.

Creating RealFlash Animations

RealFlash animations mostly resemble cartoon-like movies, but they can be anything you want to author (see Figure 11.7). In order to create RealFlash streaming animations, you need to create them with Macromedia's Flash 2. You create them as you would any Flash file, but you need to export them and convert them with the encoders. For detailed instructions on creating RealFlash animations, read the "RealFlash and RealAudio Content Creation Guide" at RealNetworks' DevZone (www.real.com/devzone/index.html).

Also, go to Macromedia's website at www.macromedia.com for more information and to download a trial copy of Flash 2.

Figure 11.7 Here is a RealFlash movie (animation based on Macromedia Flash).

Pointer Files and Metafiles

The easiest way to create RealNetwork's pointer files is to use the RealPublisher program. If you're just using the RealEncoder or the RealAudio Encoder, however, don't fret. Creating pointer files is easy.

Like many streaming multimedia programs, RealNetworks uses text files that point to actual RealMedia content. RealNetworks calls them *metafiles* and they have a RAM extension (RealAudio Metafile). The RAM file is a text file that contains the address of the RealMedia file, using your choice of protocol. For example, when using HTTP streaming, the pointer file looks like the following:

```
www.server.com/content/video1.rm
www.server.com/content/video2.rm
```

In this example, the RAM pointer file includes two URLs, so users can play the two separate clips similar to moving between tracks on a CD. You can add as many or as few URLs to a RAM file, but just make sure that each is entered on its own line.

The other popular format is when you're using the RealServer to stream your files. Substitute the PNM protocol for HTTP, as shown here:

```
pnm://servername:port/path/filename.rm
```

The PNM simply means that you are using a RealServer. You can use your computer's name, IP address, or DNS name. Specifying the port is optional.

Creating a pointer for a live broadcast works the same way. It is a good idea to include an introductory audio or video clip (like an advertisement or plug for your website) before going on to the live event. Such a file would look like this:

```
pnm://www.server.com/intro.rm
pnm://216.26.33.32/liveshow
```

Finally, create your HTML page and the link to the RAM file you just created.

Pointer files are invisible to the typical user accessing your content. He or she can simply click on the link, and the RealPlayer opens up. Alternately, you can make a RealMedia file embed onto a browser window. For more on the HTML and EMBED commands you can add, see the RealNetworks page at www.real.com/create/plugtest/index.html. It has a working tutorial where you can play with different RealPlayer controls and layouts. The pointer files for the embedded player use the .RPM extension (RealPlayer Plug-in Metafile).

Using the RealPlayer 5.0

The RealPlayer 5.0 is one of the more advanced and user-friendly streaming multimedia players (see Figure 11.8). It has Stop, Play, and Pause buttons as well as a Seek bar for moving within a clip. There are also Forward and Rewind buttons for moving between different clips (if any).

Unique to the RealPlayer are preset buttons called Destination buttons. You can program the presets to play RealMedia files from a list of categories. Once you select your Destination programs, small logos appear on the buttons; just click on a button to begin playing the file. This is perfect for when you don't want to open your web browser.

The RealPlayer plays audio, video, and animation. When playing an audio file, the player can be compact and the video window doesn't pop up; it only appears when it encounters a video or animation file. Right-click on the window to resize it, choosing from normal, 2X, or full-screen (see Figure 11.9). Depending on your computer, software, and Internet connection, you may not be able to view full-screen video. The first time you try, the RealPlayer will let you know if it is not successful.

Another improvement from earlier versions is new player view modes. You can select from three different sizes: normal, compact, and auto-size. Normal is your

Figure 11.8 The RealPlayer 5.0 playing a video.

default view and yields the biggest window. To save screen real estate, choose compact or auto-size. It creates compact windows with just the necessary player controls.

 TIP Do you want to know what RealVideo and RealAudio content is available on the Web? The RealPlayer 5.0 can automatically take you to websites that have a wide range of RealMedia content. Just choose Sites/Real Content from the menu. Choose Timecast, LiveConcerts, MusicNet, and Film.com websites and your default browser will take you to those sites. Timecast is a great place to start because it keeps track of all audio and video content including live events, radio stations, and simulcasted TV feeds.

RealPlayer 5.0 adds a system tray icon to Windows95. You can double-click on the icon to open the RealPlayer or bring it to the top of all open windows. You can also right-click on the icon to bring up a small menu where you can play preset Destination buttons or open the RealPlayer.

The RealPlayer and the older RealAudio player are available for free for Windows 3.1, 95/NT, Macintosh, and many flavors of UNIX, like FreeBSD, Linux, Solaris, and IRIX.

Also available is an enhanced version of the RealPlayer, called the RealPlayer Plus. This program plays the same content, but adds more preset buttons and the

Figure 11.9 You can view a movie at twice the normal size, but you may notice too much pixelation, especially on slow modem connections.

ability to scan for live audio and video content, much like a car radio. You can also save some RealMedia clips to your hard drive, so you can play them back even when you're not connected to the Internet. The RealPlayer Plus is available for Windows95, NT, and Macintosh PowerPC computers for $29.99.

Broadcasting On-Demand and Live Events

Now that you know the basic features and have an overall feel for the RealSystem, you can put it all together and use all of the components to transmit on-demand or broadcast live events.

Transmitting on-demand events is easy, it works like any other system profiled in this book. The good thing about using the RealSystem is that you can choose between client/server or server-less (HTTP streaming). If you don't plan on having much content or many visitors, HTTP streaming should be good enough. For heavy-duty use, a RealServer is recommended. The Basic Server is simple to use and even comes available for Windows95 systems; however, you shouldn't use the

Windows95 version over the Internet because it lacks the security features of dedicated server systems like UNIX and Windows NT.

Here are the steps you should use for on-demand events:

1. Install the RealServer, encoders, and the RealPlayer on your system. The server and encoder can be on one machine. If you just want to use HTTP streaming, you can skip the server.

2. Encode content into RealMedia format using RealPublisher, RealEncoder, or RealAudio Encoder. At this point, you can add other multimedia elements or video maps. (See the next section on creating interactive video maps.)

 RealPublisher and RealEncoder support drag-and-drop encoding. Simply click on a video file and drag it onto an open encoder window. The path and filename will automatically be entered for you ready for conversion.

3. Create your RAM pointer files. (If you're using the RealPublisher, it will do this step and the next two steps for you with the push of a button.)

4. Create your HTML page and link to the RAM file.

5. Copy the RAM, HTML, and RealMedia files to the web server. If you're using a RealServer, copy the RealMedia file to the RealServer directory, usually c:\real\server\content.

6. Configure your web server MIME types to support RealMedia content. (Check the RealNetworks web site for specifics on setting up your web server to accept real content.)

7. Play the file.

Live broadcasting is just a bit more complex. Setup can be more difficult because you *must* use a server. Depending on the size of your broadcast, you can use a dedicated machine for your server or run it from the same computer handling the encoding duties. Your encoding machine should be physically at the live event. If you are using a remote server, you can connect to it via any network connection, but use a fast connection like ISDN or T1. You can use the Internet to connect them, but you may not get good results because you'll need much more bandwidth than the Internet can handle.

Here is the most basic method of transmitting a live event:

1. Attach the audio or video source to your computer's audio or video cards. (You can also broadcast stored files as live or "tape delayed" events.)

2. Install the RealServer and Encoder onto your computer(s). Make sure the server is up and running.

3. Open your Encoder and Choose File/Open Session. Choose your source: either live audio, or video capture, or a stored file from your hard disk. Then choose your destination; in this case, the RealServer. You must input the server's hostname, port number, and directory. Most important, enter the name of the live event under the filename box. This is the name of the link that you will use later. In the example in Figure 11.10, the name of the event is called "briefing." (If you want to keep an archived copy of this event, also check off RealMedia file and name the file as shown in Figure 11.10.)

4. Enter the properties, including name, title, and copyright information. Also check off the options to allow recording (Selective Record) of the event.

Figure 11.10 Here you must choose your source and destination for your live event. It is important that you enter the correct name, password, and port number for your RealServer and name your broadcast under the filename box.

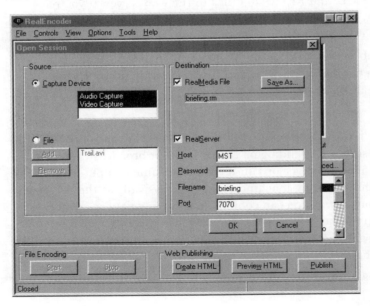

5. Select an existing template for the file you are transmitting. You can also adjust your own settings by pressing the Advanced button.

6. Click Start to begin the broadcast.

7. Create a RAM pointer file for this event. In this case, it will be something like: pnm://www.server.com:7070/briefing.

8. Save the RAM file and link it to your HTML document. Publish the RAM and HTML documents to your web server.

9. Now test the stream by clicking on the link. Your RealPlayer should open up and you should be tuning in to your live stream.

Creating Interactive Video Maps

RealVideo supports interactive video maps, but its command-line tool is too awkward to use and will probably be phased out. The next best thing to use is Ephyx's V-Active for RealVideo 1.0. With V-Active, you can encode your AVI or QuickTime video into RealVideo and then add interactive elements like going to a new URL or opening another RealVideo file(see Figure 11.11).

Figure 11.11 V-Active can be used to encode existing videos and to add interactive hotspots to your video.

Go to www.ephyx.com for more information or download a trial version on the enclosed CD-ROM.

Should You Use the RealSystem?

The RealSystem is so versatile that it can now be used by just about anyone. If you are a large company that hopes to handle large amounts of streaming multimedia, you should choose the client-server system in order to get the distribution power, reporting capability, and flexibility in a RealServer. On the other hand, if you have a smaller website and just want to stream a few multimedia files, you can use RealSystem's HTTP streaming instead. If you want streaming multimedia on your intranet for high-bandwidth applications, the RealSystem can handle that as well. Do you just need audio? Will you want to move to video later on? Want streaming animation? Do you need to use commerce and pay-per-view applications? The RealSystem does it all. You don't have to pay a lot of money either, especially with HTTP streaming.

The popularity of the RealPlayer is yet another reason to use it. Having a large installed Internet user base is key to getting your content seen.

No matter what your needs, you can't go wrong by choosing the RealSystem.

Pros and Cons

The RealSystem has many advantages, so it's no surprise that it's the most popular streaming solution available. Some highlights:

- Both HTTP streaming and client/server solutions.
- The powerful and ubiquitous RealPlayer is practically an Internet standard.
- Multiple platform support for both the client and server.
- Streaming audio and video is scaleable so both small and large networks can use it.
- The addition of pay-per-view and advertising models lets you add yet another revenue model.
- Free and easy-to-use encoding tools.

And the list goes on.

With so many advantages to the RealSystem, it is difficult to find something wrong with it. Just about the only bad thing is that is still uses proprietary file formats. Even though Microsoft is an investor in RealNetworks, there has been little collaboration or agreement on a universal file type so far; and compared to the completely free NetShow system, using a $5,000 RealServer is expensive. One way to avoid high start-up costs is to use the free starter Basic RealServer or HTTP streaming. So in the end, the choice for many mainstream web developers who want high-end streaming media comes down to two big heavyweights: NetShow and RealSystem.

About RealNetworks

RealNetworks (formerly Progressive Networks) invented RealAudio in 1995 and introduced the world to streaming audio. With the addition of RealVideo and RealFlash in 1997, RealNetworks has further strengthened its commanding market share in the streaming multimedia market. Its main competition is Microsoft's NetShow, but the two have been partners in the past. Microsoft announced support of RealMedia files in its NetShow product and is also a major investor in RealNetworks. With the release of RealSystem 5.0, Microsoft was strangely nowhere in sight. Both companies remain linked but still seem to be competing with each other. It will remain to be seen if the two companies can once again come together and try to set a standard file format for streaming multimedia or whether they will continue to release competing products.

RealNetworks has partnered with MCI to create a new service called the Real Broadcast Network. This network will allow mirrored RealMedia content for very large events. One event can handle about 50,000 simultaneous users, says RealNetworks. RealServers will be located in major nodes across the United States to take advantage of the network traffic; that way, one server won't be overwhelmed by heavy usage. The Real Broadcast Network is perfect for web developers who need to produce large live events or that want to completely outsource their entire streaming media operation. It's also a good way to test the streaming media waters. Prices range from about $1,500 a month for special events to just under $6,000 for a continuous 24-hour operation.

One of the more profound announcements was the opening of the RealStore on the Web (www.realstore.com). The website has a number of software packages for sale, like audio and video editing software, web tools, RealNetwork programs, and Macromedia products as well as promotional hats and shirts. The big breakthrough, however, is the availability of training videos for the RealSystem. The training videos are for Microsoft Word, Excel, and Windows95, and other popular office products. They are in RealVideo format and can be purchased online and then downloaded for immediate use on your network. The videos come with licenses for use on intranets, so workers can instantly access them whenever they want.

Now that the RealSystem is more robust and mature than ever, the company seems to be going away from the software side of the business and moving more toward content, distribution, and broadcasting services. During the fall of 1997, RealNetworks purchased Film.com (www.film.com), a major film review website. It plans to use its RealMedia technology to broadcast movie premieres, live reports from festivals, interviews, movie clips, and other move-related multimedia.

RealNetworks, Inc.
1111 3rd Ave, Suite 2900
Seattle, WA 98101
www.real.com
(206) 674-2700

STREAMWORKS:
MPEG Video

If you've ever seen video over the Internet, you've surely encountered MPEG video. MPEG is a very good compression method that yields impressive results. If you compress QuickTime and AVI movies into MPEG format, the resultant files will be rather small, and you won't lose much quality. Better yet, you can even have full-screen video with MPEG while still maintaining relatively small file sizes. The problem is that MPEG movies are so rare online. Chances are most video is either QuickTime or AVI format. Outside of the Internet, MPEG is a worldwide standard that is used in a variety of ways. MPEG-1 video is already the standard for transmitting video over satellites or cable television. MPEG-2 is even being used on DVD to compress feature films into this new format. So what's wrong with MPEG? Why aren't more computer users using it?

The main problem is that the two most popular personal computer systems, Apple and Wintel, already have their standards. Apple uses QuickTime—when you capture video on a Macintosh, it is saved as a QuickTime movie. Similarly for Windows/Intel computers, Video for Windows (AVI) is the standard. To use MPEG, you have to convert it with either a hardware encoder or, more popularly, a software MPEG encoder. The other problem is that MPEG came along too late in the game, so it is hard to topple these twin towers of Internet video. The tide is shifting, especially with the popularity of Internet video and with software MPEG encoders. Chances are multimedia authors are seeing the advantages of MPEG and will use it more. NetShow includes the newest form, MPEG-4 video compression, but it also uses many other types of video codecs.

Out of all the systems discussed in this book, StreamWorks is the most well-known user of MPEG video. Recently, other streaming systems (Vosaic is one example) have begun using MPEG, but its use is still limited.

Working with StreamWorks

StreamWorks is one of the oldest streaming multimedia programs available. It was released in 1995 by Xing Technology and was one of the first streaming audio and video systems on the Internet. Like many early programs, it uses a client/server architecture. While other products like RealSystem and VDOLive have expanded to include HTTP streaming, StreamWorks is still clinging to the client/server format.

StreamWorks comes in two parts: the client and the server. You can also purchase a third component for real-time transmissions of live content or an MPEG software encoder, which is ideal for use with StreamWorks.

StreamWorks Player. A cross-platform software player displays the audio and video. It works as a helper application. It is free and available for Windows 3.1, 95/NT, Macintosh, and UNIX platforms.

StreamWorks Server. This is the server software that works alongside existing web server software. It sends real-time transmission of MPEG audio and video. You can send live and on-demand multimedia, as a unicast or multicast transmission. It is available for UNIX workstations and Windows NT 4.0. It is also scaleable, so you can add more streams as your needs grow.

Another component, StreamWorks Transmitter, is an optional hardware MPEG encoder. It is used to encode incoming audio into MPEG format for live Stream-Works broadcasts. For on-demand video, you can use Xing's MPEG encoder program called the XingMPEG Encoder. It isn't really part of StreamWorks, but it can be used to easily convert files from AVI and WAV to the MPEG format, ready for streaming.

The price of the entire StreamWorks system depends on the number of streams you want to transmit. The optional components like the Transmitter and the Encoder are separate. For more on pricing, contact Xing or visit their website at www.xingtech.com.

Using the StreamWorks Server

The Server works like any other server. It sends MPEG audio and video files to users over the UDP protocol. It can handle audio-only or audio/video transmissions; the StreamWorks player plays both formats. On a fast network, StreamWorks can send full-screen, full-motion video, with CD-quality audio. Xing says that StreamWorks is also multicast-enabled, so make sure your enterprise network can handle multi-casting.

To use the Server, simply install it on your server computer. Next, run the Server to activate it. Then you're ready. The server will just sit there and work in the background as it accepts requests and sends out the audio and video files.

The StreamWorks server is available for Silicon Graphics' IRIX, Sun Solaris, Linux, and Windows NT 4.0. It can coexist with existing web server software so you don't need new hardware. You can also purchase add-on software called Plus Packs to add more capabilities to the Server. The three Plus Packs available so far include a bit-rate reduction module, a program to distribute streams across several servers, and another that simulates live feeds.

Using the StreamWorks Player

The StreamWorks Player is not very flashy, but it does a good job. It has a compact onscreen display and just a few player controls, like a combined Stop/Play button and a sliding Seek bar. There are no Forward or Rewind buttons. When you click on a StreamWorks HTML link, the StreamWorks player loads, buffers the file, and begins to play. If you've selected a StreamWorks video file, then the player also opens up a new separate window to display the video (see Figure 12.1). If you've just selected an audio-only file, the second window won't open.

Figure 12.1 The StreamWorks Player has few player controls. When you watch a movie, a second, separate window opens.

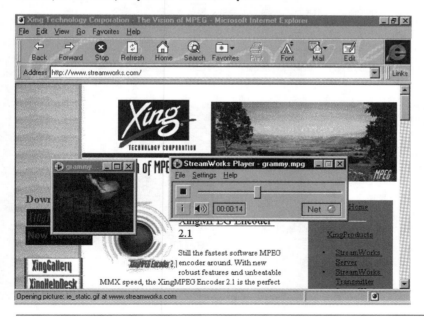

Another way to play StreamWorks files is to choose File/Open Stream and type in the URL for the stream. It is usually in the form: XDMA://204.62.160.178:1559/media/song1.mpx. This is telling the Player that the file song1.mpx is located at 204.62.160.178 and should be from a StreamWorks Server (represented by XDMA). If you've set up your server already and have a StreamWorks file ready to stream, just type your server's address as well as the directory and filename of your file. This is a quick way of making sure your server is sending out files properly. See the section, "Creating XDM Pointer Files," for creating links to HTML pages.

The StreamWorks Player can also give you detailed information about the file you are playing. Pressing the I button or choosing File/Stream Information opens a new window that gives you information on the file you are playing (see Figure 12.2). It shows the server address, stream name and length, video and audio attributes, and much more.

Before using the StreamWorks Player, you should ensure that it knows the size of your bandwidth. Choose Settings/Connection and make sure you've chosen your correct connection speed.

Figure 12.2 Check the Stream Information to see the stream name and other file attributes.

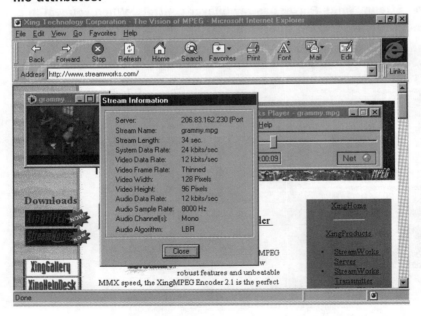

Always use a speed that most closely matches your own speed. If you choose a speed that is faster than what you're really using, StreamWorks will try to send the larger file and will overwhelm the player with data. As a result, your video and audio will be unwatchable. Perhaps the best way is to choose a custom speed, like 56Kbps. Simply choose Other and type in your connection speed.

The StreamWorks Player is a helper application and is compatible with all plug-in-enabled browsers, like Navigator and Internet Explorer. The Windows versions are MMX-enabled and also use Microsoft's DirectDraw technology to improve overall graphics quality. As mentioned earlier, StreamWorks can play full-screen, full-motion video (with CD-quality audio) on a high-bandwidth network. Over the Internet, StreamWorks' video quality is good, but isn't as fluid as VDOLive's or the RealPlayer's. The StreamWorks Player is free and available for Macintosh, UNIX, and Windows 3.1, 95/NT.

StreamWorks Transmitter

The StreamWorks Transmitter is a desk- or rack-mounted plug-and-play hardware MPEG encoder, adding live broadcasting to StreamWorks. Without it, StreamWorks can only stream on-demand audio and video. The Transmitter can also be used to speed up your encoding of stored StreamWorks videos so you can broadcast them later.

To use it, connect the Transmitter to your StreamWorks Server computer. Then simply connect the audio and video jacks to the Transmitter. Make sure the server software is ready and set your encoding options (bit rate, resolution, frame rates, etc.) for the output stream. That's it! The output file is encoded as an MPEG stream that can be sent to the Server or saved to disk for later broadcast. You have real-time encoding of live audio or video. The Transmitter comes in an audio-only version ($2,500) or audio/video ($6,500).

Encoding Movies with the XingMPEG Encoder

If you just want on-demand audio and video, you don't need the StreamWorks Transmitter; you can simply use stored content. If you already have your files in MPEG format, that's no big deal. But if you have lots of WAV and AVI files, you'll need a way to convert your existing multimedia into MPEG format. You'll also need to make your files compatible with StreamWorks format. That means the files must have certain filename extensions and be able to stream with the

StreamWorks player. Fortunately, Xing has covered all these angles; it makes the XingMPEG Encoder, a software MPEG encoder.

 NOTE You don't need to use the XingMPEG Encoder. There are many other MPEG software encoding programs. But for full compatibility, stick with Xing's program. It has preset options for encoding StreamWorks files so you can quickly get up and running.

The Encoder is just like any other software converter or encoder; it accepts AVI and WAV files and encodes them into MPEG format. It is good for making MPEG files just to save disk space, to create VideoCD movies, and, of course, to make StreamWorks files.

To begin encoding files for StreamWorks, first open up XingMPEG Encoder and you'll see the main window (see Figure 12.3). This screen shows you your Job Queue—all the files you have waiting to be encoded. If this is your first time using it, it will be empty.

1. Click on the New button to begin converting a new file.

Figure 12.3 The main screen of the XingMPEG Encoder shows all the files you have in your Job Queue.

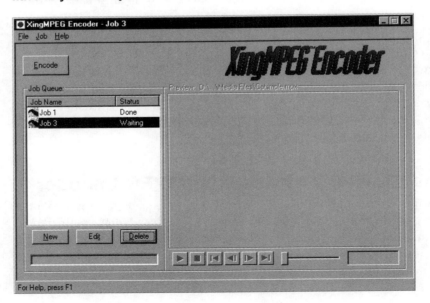

2. The Job Wizard window pops up. This is where you can select some preconfigured stream profiles. You'll see an MPEG-1 folder, a VideoCD folder, and a StreamWorks folder. Open the StreamWorks folder and you'll see an Audio/Video folder and an Audio Only folder. In this example, we'll convert an AVI movie with sound, so open the Audio/Video folder to see your options (see Figure 12.4).

3. The Audio/Video folder lists profiles that you can choose for your StreamWorks file. You'll notice that it sorts them by bandwidth—from 1.5MB to 128KB/14.4K modem speeds. Since we'll be transmitting this file over the Internet, we'll choose 128KB to 28.8K Modem selection. Click on it, and it will let you see the properties for this profile. You'll see frame rates, window sizes, and bit rates.

4. Press Next to continue. The next screen will let you enter the input file you want to convert. Either type in the full path or browse through your hard disk to select a valid file. Once it is entered, you'll see the Target path and filename. Make sure you remember where it is saving files. Make sure the options in the top of the screen reflect what you have: Audio Only, Video Only, or System. System simply means a file that has

Figure 12.4 Choose from among various audio and video compression profiles to encode a StreamWorks file.

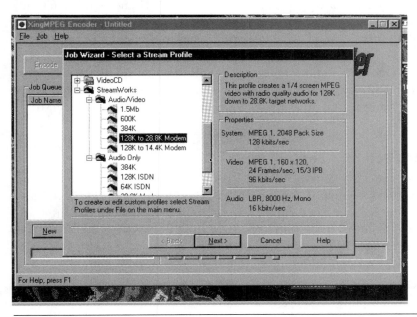

both audio and video. The filename extension on the target MPEG file will vary depending on which option you chose.

5. Then click Finish to return to the main screen that shows you the queue. You can press Encode now to begin encoding or choose more files and encode them all at once. The encoding process itself is very fast, but the actual speed may vary depending on your processor's speed.

6. When it's finished, the files in the queue will read "Done." You can leave completed encoding jobs in the Job Queue or you can delete them later. Now that your files are finished, you can test them on your server.

Since StreamWorks can handle a few different types of MPEG files, it uses different extensions. If you created an audio-only file, it will have an MPA extension; a movie-only file with have an MPV extension. If you chose a System file, it will have an MPX extension but may also have an MPG extension if you choose to compress it into a high-bandwidth MPEG-1 file. Last but not least, if you created a low-quality, audio-only StreamWorks file, it may have an LBR (Low Bit Rate) extension.

To test the files, play them. You can play MPV, MPA, and MPG files locally with any good MPEG player, like the XingMPEG Player. Unfortunately, you can't play LBR and MPX files locally; they must be played back with the StreamWorks Server and Player. Just set up the server and try them out to see how what they look like. See the next section on creating pointer files for more on linking them to HTML pages.

XingMPEG Encoder is a very good multipurpose MPEG encoder. It isn't only for StreamWorks files, you can use it to leisurely spend your day converting all your AVI files to MPEG format. You'll save lots of disk space. You can also create your own settings in case you don't like the ones that come preconfigured. The Encoder is available for Windows95 and NT and it takes advantage of Intel's MMX extension. It costs around $249 but it is also available for a 30-day, free trial period. There is also an Adobe Premiere plug-in available for those who purchase the XingMPEG Encoder.

Creating XDM Pointer Files

Once you have your StreamWorks files ready, you can put them on your StreamWorks Server's computer. You can place them anywhere, like in a folder called "videos." You then need to create a text pointer file with an XDM extension. This XDM file will point to the actual location of the StreamWorks media file. An XDM file can be created with any text editor and must be saved with the XDM extension, like TEST.XDM.

A typical XDM pointer file will look like the following:

```
stream=xdma://206.126.224.10:159/videos/vidtest.mpx
```

In the example, the XDMA simply means that the file is being served from a StreamWorks Server. We've also used the IP address and port number, but you can use the DNS address or leave out the port number. We're also telling it that the MPEG file is called VIDTEST.MPX and is located in the "video" subdirectory.

When you create your own XDM file, just change the subdirectory or filename of the StreamWorks file (MPA, MPG, MPV, etc.), and don't forget to add your server computer's IP address.

Updating the Web Server and HTML Page

Since you are adding a new file type to your web server you must add a new MIME type. Each web server uses a different method to add or change MIME types, so check with your server's documentation if you need help. The MIME type you need to add is:

```
application/x-xdma          xdm
```

This will enable your web server to accept the XDM MIME type to play StreamWorks files.

The next step is to update your HTML page that will contain the link to your StreamWorks file. Simply use the A HREF link to the XDM pointer file, as in:

```
<A HREF="http://www.server.com/home/test.xdm">Click here for the StreamWorks file</A>
```

Finally, don't forget to upload your StreamWorks files to the Server computer and the XDM files and updated HTML pages to your web server. Test everything one more time to make sure it is all running properly.

Should You Use StreamWorks?

StreamWorks should definitely be a top contender for anyone looking to implement streaming audio and video. It is a very good choice for use over intranets or other fast networks, because it can transmit full-screen, full-motion video very easily. StreamWorks is one of the few streaming video programs that already uses multicasting, so all that full-screen, TV-quality video won't be a drain on your network. It is also attractive to some companies because it supports MPEG, an internationally recognized standard for audio and video compression.

How about implementing it over the Internet? At low bit rates, StreamWorks doesn't do so well. That's just because of our slow 28.8Kbps Internet connections. If we all had ISDN or cable modems, StreamWorks videos would look great, but of course that isn't the case. You can get so-so video quality with a 28.8Kbps or

56Kbps modem, but it still ranks below programs like RealVideo, NetShow or VDOLive. Using StreamWorks as a live Internet audio broadcasting system is a good idea because audio quality is good and doesn't break up very often.

In terms of implementation and use, StreamWorks works well—there's nothing difficult about it. The only downside is the addition of the hardware MPEG encoder to capture and stream live audio or video. Most other systems just use a video capture card and software for live broadcasting. StreamWorks uses MPEG, so it needs the speed and power of the hardware encoder to achieve real-time encoding. Software MPEG encoding is quick but isn't fast enough to encode in real time. The hardware encoder costs more than your average video capture card, so take that into consideration, too.

Perhaps the biggest problem is that StreamWorks is being left out of Microsoft's plan for consolidation of the streaming multimedia market. While companies like Vivo, RealNetworks, VDOnet, and more have been backing Microsoft's NetShow product, StreamWorks has been completely ignored. This is a big deal because if these alliances become partnerships or acquisitions, and if NetShow's ASF file format becomes the new Internet standard, StreamWorks will be left on the outside. On the other hand, StreamWorks can choose another route by partnering itself with other MPEG video streaming vendors. Of course we won't know what will happen until it happens, but StreamWorks should be plenty worried about these developments.

Pros and Cons

StreamWorks has a lot of good things going for it. It can transmit full-screen, full-video at high bandwidths. It also handles unicast or multicast transmissions—that alone may be reason enough to use it on your intranet. StreamWorks wins major points because its client program supports all the major platforms. The StreamWorks player is available for many platforms like Windows 3.x, 95/NT, Macintosh, and UNIX computers. On the encoding end, the XingMPEG Encoder is perfect for Stream-Works files and other MPEG files. The Encoder even beats other software MPEG encoders in terms of price and features. It's just too bad it can't convert QuickTime movies or that there isn't a Macintosh version of the program.

Even with all this going for it, StreamWorks still falls short of the others of the Big Five streaming multimedia systems (VivoActive, VDOLive, RealSystem, and NetShow). StreamWorks doesn't have the player features, built-in live support, server options, or low bit-rate quality that other systems have. RealSystem has a much better and more sophisticated player interface. It also supports advertising and pay-per-view models—StreamWorks doesn't. StreamWorks also doesn't support HTTP streaming, unlike the other four systems. In fact, it only supports UDP, which can mean plenty of headaches for network managers. Lots of users trying to use StreamWorks behind a corporate firewall will be out of luck. Support for other protocols would be a good thing. In terms of cost, NetShow beats them all. It is unfortunate that Stream-Works doesn't have better video quality at 28.8Kbps speeds, but MPEG just wasn't made to support low bit rates. Other programs, like VDOLive, NetShow, and the RealPlayer, are better suited for the Internet.

The other disadvantage is that StreamWorks' Internet content is running dry and very stale. Although it has been around since the early days of streaming multimedia, many websites are no longer using it. It'll be hard to find sites using StreamWorks, and if you do find some content, you'll notice it hasn't been updated in a while. Your best bet for finding stuff to listen to or watch is to visit Stream-Works' Gallery page at www.streamworks.com/content.

About Xing Technology Corp.

Xing Technology's entire product line is focused around the MPEG audio and video format. Xing was one of the first companies to introduce streaming audio/video to the Internet but quickly saw competitors take the lead. Besides Stream-Works, Xing also makes MPEG players and encoders.

With the release of version 3.0 of StreamWorks, Xing has effectively rededicated itself to providing streaming audio and video solutions for the intranet and high-bandwidth markets. Support for low-bandwidth applications (under 128Kbps, for example) will continue, but Xing seems to be focusing on developing Stream-Works for use over intranets where audio and video quality can be excellent.

Xing Technology Corp.
810 Fiero Lane
San Luis Obispo, CA 93401
(805) 783-0400
www.streamworks.com
www.xingtech.com

TRUESTREAM:
Basic Video Streaming

Motorola released TrueStream in 1997, making it one of the newest streaming multimedia systems available. It streams video over any IP network and is scaleable, so it can be used at Internet speeds (28.8Kbps) or faster, like ISDN and LAN speeds. It doesn't handle audio-only or music applications at low bandwidths.

TrueStream is a client/server system with three components:

TrueStream Player. The player is a free plug-in for Netscape Navigator or a helper application for Internet Explorer. Its proprietary compression is good enough to be used on 28.8Kbps modems while maintaining a high frame rate and video quality. The player runs on Windows95, NT, and Macintosh computers.

TrueStream Producer. The producer is a free plug-in to Adobe's Premiere, a very popular video editing software. The Producer converts videos into the TrueStream format (with MOT extensions).

TrueStream Server. The server is the program that serves TrueStream files, and is available for UNIX and Windows NT systems.

TrueStream uses a per-stream pricing structure with prices as low as $495 to as high as $5,995 for an unrestricted server.

TrueStream Video Player

The TrueStream Player plays videos only; it doesn't support sound-only applications. Its sparse interface makes it different from the other players, because it just consists of the video window screen and a Play/Pause button. The player is a plug-in and helper application. To play files you just click on a link, and the player pops up and plays the file (see Figure 13.1).

You can also double-click on the TrueStream Player icon and play a local file; the File/Open window opens and you can select a TrueStream file (MOT extensions). When playing local files, you usually have to press the Play button to begin the movie. Another way to view movies is with the Netscape plug-in—movies appear inside a web page when used with the EMBED command.

Since there is just one button, you can't perform many functions. There are no Stop, Forward, Rewind, or Seek buttons. When watching a video, you can click anywhere on the video window to pause or play a file in progress or just use the Play/Pause button. To see a larger video window, use the zoom command to make the windows twice as big; choose Action/Stretch (2×) from the menu and then toggle it back to normal view.

The player has just a few more options. Under File/Options, you can choose the buffer size, network protocol (either UDP or TCP), and the notification method when the buffer is out of data. You can also see information on the file by choosing File/Properties, which shows you file size, name, and version number. Other options include customized views of the player like removing the menu bar and player controls so you have a very compact player (see Figure 13.2).

The player supports two industry-standard video window sizes called CIF and QCIF. CIF stands for Common Intermediate Format and is a pixel size of 352 × 288. QCIF (Quarter Common Intermediate Format) is smaller than CIF and is 176 × 144.

Figure 13.1 The TrueStream Player consists of just this one plain window and doesn't have many player controls.

Figure 13.2 Change the view of the player by getting rid of the player controls and/or the menu bar.

All TrueStream programs feature Smart Install, which automatically detects older versions. It also finds multiple browsers on your computer and installs the player into all of them, if you want. The TrueStream Player is available free for Windows95, NT 4.0, and Macintosh.

TrueStream Video Producer

The TrueStream Video Producer is an Adobe Premiere plug-in. Use Premiere as you normally would to create and edit your movie, and then use the plug-in to export QuickTime and AVI movies as Motorola TrueSpeech files (MOT). Using a popular and familiar editing program like Premiere is good, because you can edit and convert the file in one solid program. However, the unfortunate few who don't own Adobe Premiere are left out in the cold—without Premiere, it is impossible to convert movies, since Motorola hasn't released a standalone converter.

Before you use the producer plug-in, make sure your video file is of very good quality. This will translate well into the MOT file. Motorola recommends that you use a movie that has uncompressed 16-bit audio and uses uncompressed 30 frames per second video at a display of 200×150 or 400×300 for proper output to CIF and QCIF sizes.

To use the producer plug-in, use Adobe Premiere as you normally would. When you're ready to save the file as a MOT file, simply choose File/Export from the menu and select MOTFILE:

1. The MOTFILE window will open. Enter a filename then select the bit rate for the file.

2. Next select the size of the video window. The QCIF size (176×144) should be used for low-bandwidth connections. For faster speeds, use CIF (352×288).

3. Next select your audio compression. For 28.8Kbps connections, choose 5.3K for the audio.

4. Select Build to let Premiere save the MOT file. Compression time varies depending on your processor speed, file size, and frame size, but it can be slow. It can take roughly three to four minutes to compress a one-minute video.

5. Once it is saved, you can play the file by double-clicking on it or opening the TrueStream Player.

The TrueStream Producer automatically senses high-motion video and allocates greater bandwidth. It provides compression ratios in excess of 500:1, so high-quality video can be achieved even over 28.8Kbps modem lines. It uses Motorola's proprietary codecs. Audio compression is as low as 5.3Kbps while video compression goes to a low of 17Kbps. Compressed files for use over 28.8Kbps modems are about 200KB per minute. Files used over ISDN lines or larger are about double that size.

The TrueStream Producer is available free for Windows95, NT, or Macintosh PowerPC and works with Adobe Premiere version 4.2. In a strategic partnership with Adobe, Motorola announced that Adobe Premiere will eventually come pre-bundled with the TrueStream Producer plug-in.

TrueStream Video Server

The TrueStream Video Server is the program that controls the transmission of MOT files, including handling simultaneous streams. It uses the User Datagram Protocol (UDP) to send data. UDP is faster than TCP but is more error-prone. TrueStream can go around firewalls; when it encounters one, it prompts the user to switch from UDP to the firewall-friendly TCP protocol.

In Windows NT 4.0, you start the video server by executing the motvsd.exe file. You see the DOS window appear and a message telling you that the server is running (see Figure 13.3). To shut it down, just press the Close button.

The server also provides monitoring functions and usage statistics for use in website management. The log file is located in the server directory and is called motvsd.log. It keeps tabs on who is accessing your files and notifies you of any server errors.

Some other features of the server include video image correction and audio interpolation to correct video and audio gaps when there are lost packets, adaptive stream playback for adjusting the stream flow, and preconfigured CGI scripts to

Figure 13.3 Once you start the TrueStream Video Server, it brings up this screen. You can minimize it later so it won't get in the way of other applications.

embed video onto a web page. It also comes with sample MOT files so you can quickly get started using TrueStream.

The server supports 25, 50, or an unrestricted number of simultaneous video streams, depending on the version purchased. Prices start at $495 and reach all the way to $5,995 for the unlimited stream version. The free TrueStream Evaluation Server supports just two streams since it is just for testing purposes. The True-Stream Video Server runs on Sun Solaris, Windows NT, and Linux systems. You can download evaluation versions for no-risk testing before purchasing them.

TrueStream Pointer Files

TrueStream uses a few methods for linking MOT files to a web page. You can either embed movies onto a browser window or use the TrueStream external player. To accomplish this, you can use pointer files or CGI scripts.

 Since not everyone has access to a CGI script directory, this section will focus on pointer files. For more on CGI scripts, check out the sample HTML that comes with the server.

Pointer files are simple text files that call the actual MOT file. They can be created with any text editor and have an MTV extension. They contain three lines containing the server address, filename and port number. When you get the TrueStream Server, check out the sample MOT movies and MTV pointer files that are included, so you can get an idea of how they work.

Here is an example of an MTV pointer file:

```
server=170.0.0.1
port=1401
video=welcome_modem
```

As you can see, the server line just needs to have the IP address or the DNS address of the server. The port is preconfigured when you install the server, so that doesn't have to be changed. Last, the video line just needs to have the name of the TrueStream file, but be sure to leave off the MOT extension. Save this file and give it a name like welcome_modem.mtv, and then link that file to your web page. When a user clicks on that link, the TrueStream Player will launch and play the welcome_modem.mot file.

To embed a movie inside a browser window, you need to create a WMP pointer file. WMP files look exactly like MTV files, so use the example just shown. The only difference is that you need to include the EMBED tag instead of using the A HREF tag. For example:

```
<EMBED src="welcome_modem.wmp" height=146 width=178 VideoControls=off
ClickControl=yes>
```

Load your browser and test it. The video should appear in a small window in your browser. If you have problems using the plug-in with Navigator, make sure you're using the most recent plug-in available. Also make sure that the plug-in is located in the proper plug-in directory; otherwise, it won't work.

Steps for Using TrueStream

Now that you know about the three components to TrueStream and about pointer files, here is how they all work together. Follow these steps to use TrueStream:

1. Install the TrueStream Player, Producer, and Server onto your computer.

2. Load a movie with Adobe Premiere and use the Producer plug-in to save it as a MOT file. Alternatively, if you don't own Premiere, you can use the sample MOT movies that come with TrueStream.

3. Copy the MOT file to your TrueStream server directory. The default directory is c:\motorola\truestreamserver\movies. This is where you must put movies in order for TrueStream to serve them. If you're using the sample movies, there will already be four MOT movies in that directory.

4. Create the MTV pointer file. (See the previous section for specifics.)

5. Create an HTML page and make a link that points to the MTV file.

6. Post the MTV and HTML to your web server and everything should be ready for your test.

7. Start your TrueStream Server by executing the motvsd.exe file. (Once it is started, you can minimize the window since you can't do much with it.)

8. You can double-click on the MTV file or click on the HTML link to play the file.

9. The external player should load and play the MOT file.

The TrueStream Server can run alongside a regular web server with no problems. Remember to check your server log (motvsd.log) to see server activity and to check for errors.

Should You Use TrueStream?

Because of its scaleable bandwidth, TrueStream is good for use on both intranets or the Internet. The problem with using it on the Internet is the lack of content; most Internet users have never even heard of TrueStream. Nevertheless, it works well on intranets since you create your own videos and don't have to rely on other companies and sites.

Those who need audio or music applications should look elsewhere. Motorola admits that TrueStream's 28.8Kbps audio compression settings are too low for music applications—it is optimized for speech. This is evident because TrueStream doesn't have support for audio-only files. Also, TrueStream is not for broadcasting live video; it is strictly a video-on-demand system.

Pros and Cons

At its core, TrueStream is a very basic streaming program, perhaps because it is so new. It doesn't do anything exceptional and neither the server or client offer anything new. It works like the other client/server streaming video systems, but it doesn't offer enough features or controls like the "Big Five" video programs—it has a way to go to reach their level of sophistication.

Its main problem is its lack of live support. Since TrueStream uses Adobe Premiere to convert movies, there is no live encoder. All files must be stored on the server for on-demand broadcasts. This may be fine for some users, but with so many different programs supporting live broadcasting, this feature is proving more important to web developers.

Using the TrueStream Producer plug-in with Adobe Premiere can be a very good thing. Since most multimedia developers already use Adobe Premiere, having a plug-in makes the conversion process very easy—there is no need to learn a new video editing or conversion program. The problem is that not everyone owns Premiere. TrueStream should consider making a standalone converter (and live broadcasting option) for use when Premiere isn't an option. This will make it easier for non-professionals and beginners to get started making TrueStream videos.

Last, TrueStream's pricing structure is per-stream. Back when streaming multimedia was just beginning, per-stream pricing was the norm, but nowadays most programs are capable of transmitting unlimited streams. TrueStream's prices aren't very high considering other vendor's prices, but per-stream pricing is rather limiting.

In sum, TrueStream is at a disadvantage because it was released so late. While other streaming video vendors have already created version 4 or 5 releases, True-Stream is just getting out of the starting gate. So many other companies have already captured a significant share and it will be difficult for TrueStream to make a dent. Motorola is gambling that there is enough of a market for yet another streaming multimedia product.

About Motorola, Inc.

Motorola is one of the largest communications companies in the world. It provides wireless communications, cellular technology, modems, cable modems, semiconductors, and paging services to consumers and businesses.

TrueStream was released by Motorola's Information Systems Group, a supplier of network products and integrated network solutions. The TrueStream streaming multimedia system is Motorola's first all-software product. Some clients using TrueStream include Raptor Systems, Inc. and Bolomedia Inc.

Motorola Information Systems Group—Streaming Media Products
20 Cabot Boulevard
Mansfield, MA 02048-1193
www.mot.com/truestream

CVIDEONOW:
Video with a
CGI Script Server

14

CVideoNow is yet another recent entry into the streaming audio and video market. It was released in 1997 by Cubic VideoComm, a maker of defense systems that just recently entered the streaming multimedia arena. It is a client/server system, but it is unique in that the server is not a program—it works more as a CGI script. You simply install the server program into the host computer running any popular web server software. CVideoNow uses a proprietary video codec to compress the audio and video but also uses the Lernout & Hauspie audio codec for even better audio quality. Depending on your bandwidth, you can deliver video that approaches television quality, along with large-screen windows.

CVideoNow consists of three components:

CVideoNow Player. This is a free helper application that plays the files. It works with Netscape 2.0 or higher, Microsoft's Internet Explorer 3.0 or greater, and other browsers.

CVideoNow Producer. The producer compresses AVI files and converts them to CVideoNow files (CVC extension). It is available for Windows95 and NT.

CVideoNow Server. The server is a CGI script called CVCServer.DLL and streams the compressed video files. It can be used on any standard web server, including Sun Solaris, Netscape servers, NCSA, HTTPd, Apache, Free BSD, Windows NT, or O'Reilly's Web Site Pro server. It can even be used on Windows95 with its Personal Web Server software.

You need to have administrator access to the web server to install and start the server, so it may prevent some people from using CVideoNow. You also need access to the CGI scripts directory. So, it may be hard to use CVideoNow if you're running a remote server or if you're using a web provider to host your site.

Pricing for CVideoNow starts at $500 and goes to $1999 for a 100-stream version.

CVideoNow Player

The CVideoNow Player interface is rather simple and doesn't have many VCR-like controls. It has a toolbar at the bottom of the screen that has Mute, Stop, Pause, Statistics, Exit, Help, and Enlarge buttons (see Figure 14.1). A "Clip Meter" at the top of the window displays the running time of the file and the total time.

The player can play files locally or on the Internet. To play files locally, just double-click on any CVC file and the player will load and play it. To view files over the Internet, just click a link and the player will pop up. There is no File/Open menu, so you cannot select files from your hard drive or from the Internet. Also, when watching a local file, you can't rewind the movie to play it again; you have to close down the player and double-click on the file to watch it again.

 Right-click on the window area to see a shortcut menu of all the functions of the player. You can choose all the options from the menu and toolbar here, including showing or hiding the toolbar buttons.

Figure 14.1 This is the CVideoNow Player playing a file over the Internet.

Figure 14.2 This is the double-sized video. You can toggle back and forth between normal and double size at any time while watching the video.

You can enlarge the size of the video to double its normal size. Click on the Enlarge button in the toolbar to toggle between the regular and double sizes. The enlarged video looks very good, unlike other programs that look too blocky (see Figure 14.2). CVideoNow keeps the video sharper at enlarged sizes.

Choose Options/Statistics to view comprehensive statistics on the file you are watching. The screen shows you the frames per second rate, the packets that are being received (and lost), filename, total time, the data rate of the file, and much more (see Figure 14.3). Oddly, there is no way to close the Statistics window once it is opened; you have to close the player.

The CVideoNow Player is free and is available for Windows95 and Windows NT computers.

CVideoNow Producer

The CVideoNow Producer's job is to convert AVI movies into CVideoNow format (CVC extension). It does this in a very straightforward way. The main screen of

Figure 14.3 The Statistics screen shows you advanced data on the file and on the packets you are receiving from the server.

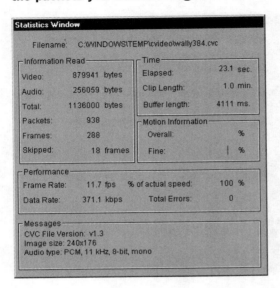

the producer allows you to enter the filename of the input AVI file, enter the name of the output CVC file, and press the Begin Encoding button (see Figure 14.4). Unlike some producer/converter programs, the CVideoNow Producer has no video preview window to show you the movie as it is being compressed. CVideoNow achieves compression ratios from 200:1 to as high as 500:1.

NOTE Your input AVI file must be of a certain type or the producer will not accept it. It can be anywhere from 32 × 32 to 320 × 240 and must be using the YVU9 format (Intel's codec) or YVU 4:2:2. Audio must be 8kHz or 11kHz and can be compressed with TrueSpeech or Lernout & Hauspie. If you're unsure of the format of an existing AVI file, right-click on the movie and select Properties. Then choose the Details tab to see the audio and video compression formats and other specifics. If the file doesn't match those parameters, use a video editor to compress the existing movie into the YVU9 format. The YVU9 codec can be downloaded from CVideoNow's website (www.cvideonow.com).

Figure 14.4 This the main screen of the CVideoNow Producer where you select the input and output files. Before compressing, press the Adjust Quality button to change compression options.

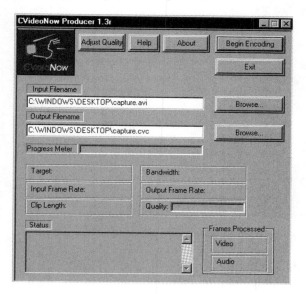

The main work is in selecting the compression method. You have lots to work with and it is all controlled from the Adjust Quality screen. Press the Adjust Quality button to bring up the Adjust Quality Settings screen (see Figure 14.5). Unfortunately, the compression settings and options are somewhat confusing, so you'll probably spend a lot of time using trial and error to find a good quality image. That also means you'll have to test the videos live on your server to see how they look under real-life conditions.

First, leave the Bandwidth Limited box checked off; when that option is on, the CVideoNow Producer controls the bandwidth of the movie. You can then change the Control Options and select either Auto Adjust Quality & Frame Rate, Fixed Frame Rate, or Fixed Image Quality.

Auto Adjust. The default is Auto Adjust. If you leave it there, you will only select the minimum frame rate and image quality settings. Select your new minimums by typing in the new number and using the slider knob. You can also leave these settings at their defaults.

Figure 14.5 The Adjust Quality Settings screen is where you select the compression options for the file. You can set frame rates, image quality, and more.

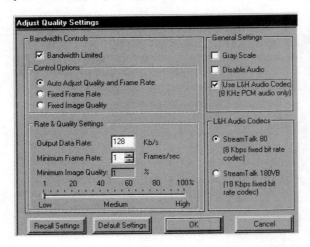

Fixed Frame Rate. To have a fixed frame rate, select the Fixed Frame Rate option and then type in the output frame rate that you want the clip to have. You should leave the frame rate at about 10 fps or less for 28.8Kbps connections; otherwise let CVideoNow adjust the bandwidth by checking the Auto Adjust box. For faster connections, you can even go full motion at 30 fps, but your file size will be very large.

Fixed Image Quality. If you want to increase the picture quality of the movie, select the Fixed Image Quality button. The Quality Setting slider bar now will read Fixed Quality Setting. Slide the knob along the bar, with 1 being the lowest-quality setting and 100 being the highest. You should use this option when you want to create a better-quality picture while sacrificing motion or frame rate.

Those are the main options to consider. You can also tinker with the audio settings. On the right side of the Adjust Quality Settings screen, you can choose to disable audio completely or select a new audio compression: L&H Audio Codec. The Lernout & Hauspie audio codec is very popular and very good for speech. If you select that codec, you can also choose between two bit rates: StreamTalk 80 (8Kbps) or StreamTalk 180VB (18Kbps). Leave it at 8Kbps for 28.8Kbps movies or switch it to 18Kbps for variable bandwidth.

Once you're satisfied with all your quality settings, press OK, and you will be asked if you want to save those settings. If you want to use these settings again, choose Yes; otherwise, you will lose your settings and will have to adjust them from scratch the next time.

TIP At any time in the Adjust Quality screen, you can recall your last saved settings by selecting the Recall Settings button. However, make sure you mean to do this, because it doesn't have a warning dialog box. You can also completely reset the options to their default selections by choosing the Default Settings button. Again, it doesn't ask you to make sure, so be careful where you click.

The conversion process goes by fairly quickly but it depends on the compression settings you choose. When you're ready to convert the file, press the Begin Encoding button, and it starts to encode. You'll see a progress meter along with a percentage. When it is finished, the Status bar provides information on the file, like image size, audio codec, and video type. Your output frame rate and bandwidth are also shown (see Figure 14.6).

Figure 14.6 After the conversion process, the producer tells you information about the newly compressed file, including output frame rate, bandwidth, and more.

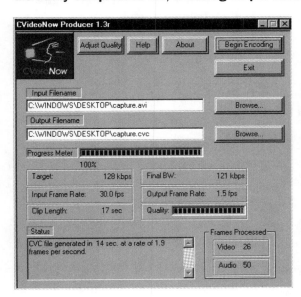

Since the producer isn't very clear about compression methods used and doesn't preview the file, it is up to you to check your output CVC file. Simply double-click on the CVC file and the CVideoNow Player should load and begin playing the file. You can see what the file will look like, but it won't be a good approximation of the conditions over the Internet. You'll have to post the files to your web server and test it that way to really see what it looks like.

The CVideoNow Producer is available for Windows95 and Windows NT 4.0 only. Check the website for the latest pricing information.

CVideoNow Server

As mentioned earlier, the CVideoNow Server works differently than most servers: It is actually a CGI script that must be installed in the script folder of your web server. This means you need local access to the web server to install the server software.

During installation, the CVideoNow server does everything for you. It automatically finds the CGI script directory on your hard drive or lets you specify one if you changed it. It installs the CVCSERVER.DLL file as well as a program called CVCEdit.

CVCEdit should be run before trying to run the server to ensure that everything starts correctly and that the right configuration file was created. When you load it, it will ask you for your customer key. Once that is generated, you can start serving files and using the server (see Figure 14.7).

Because you need access to the script directory, it may not be good for those users who don't have access to one. Some web hosting companies do not automatically give

Figure 14.7 This is the CVCEdit window. It shows you your IP address, server name, and number of streams you can serve.

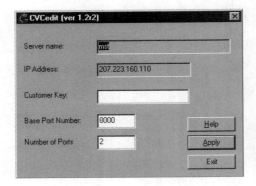

customers access to those directories because of security issues. That's why the CVideoNow Server is best run on a local machine where you have access to your directories. If you use a web hosting company or other presence provider, ask if you can use CGI scripts.

Pricing for the CVideoNow Server is based on the number of video streams that can be transmitted at the same time. For 20 concurrent streams, the price is $500; the 50-stream version is $999 while the 100-stream version costs $1,999. There doesn't seem to be a way to increase the number of concurrent users, nor is there a mirror option. It seems 100 is the highest number of users it can handle, but that may change in future versions. It also doesn't support IP multicasting to cut down on bandwidth.

To run the CVideoNow Server you need access to a web server like NCSA HTTPd, Apache 1.1, O'Reilly's Web Site Pro web server, Microsoft's IIS, or Netscape servers. It can run on many flavors of UNIX, Windows95, and Windows NT 4.0.

Creating Links with CVideoNow

Unlike most streaming multimedia programs, CVideoNow does not use pointer files; instead, it uses a more complex script call. In order to play a CVideoNow file, you must use an ordinary A HREF tag to link to the file. The example shown next is for use with the Windows95 Personal Web Server:

```
<A HREF="http://desktop/Scripts/CVCserver.dll?GetCVCFile?FileName=/Webshare/Wwwroot/
video.cvc">Click here for video</A>
```

The example is calling the CVideoNow file video.cvc from the default web directory. The server is called "desktop" and it is calling the CVCserver.dll program under the Scripts directory. When you create a link, you simply change it to your attributes, including your computer's name and the CVC filename and subdirectory.

It is similar for Windows NT and the Internet Information Server (IIS):

```
<A HREF="Scripts/cgi-bin/CVCServer.DLL?GetCVCFile?FileName=/InetPub/movies/video.cvc">
Click here for video</A>
```

The preceding example is assuming that you are using the defaults for your web server directory and are serving a file called video.cvc from the "movies" subdirectory. The scripts and CGI-BIN directories are also the default selections for IIS.

UNIX users use a similar method:

```
<A HREF="http://www.server.com/cgi-bin/CVCServer.cgi/usr/web/htdocs/cgi-bin/movies/
video.cvc">Click here for video</A>
```

The example just shown is using a full path link, but you can also do relative links or remove the server name.

CVideoNow supplies you with an HTML page with sample links for a few different web servers. Use this to help you get started creating links. Just start your server, open the page, and click on the appropriate link for your web server to watch a demo video (see Figure 14.8).

There is no plug-in, so you can't embed the clip into the web page.

CVideoNow Live and CVideoNow Conference

Cubic VideoComm recently released a live broadcasting system called CVideoNow Live for live video unicast transmissions. It also announced a two-way videoconferencing system for multipoint communications called CVideoNow Conference. You can find much more about these products at Cubic's website at www.cvideonow.com.

Should You Use CVideoNow?

Files created with the CVideoNow Producer can be used over the Internet or over faster networks. For intranet use, you can create large, good-quality files. Over

Figure 14.8 You get a demo HTML page so you can try out your server and use it on your own pages. It offers links for servers like O'Reilly's Web Site Pro, Microsoft PWS, and IIS and UNIX servers.

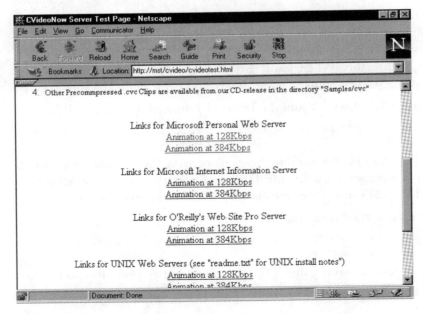

slower connections, like the Internet, you may have some unsynchronization between audio and video, which means a slow frame rate.

CVideoNow is good for those users who will use on-demand video and have no need for animation or audio-only applications; it is *not* for those who need live audio or video.

CVideoNow is also good for those who have direct and local access to a web server. Those using web hosting services may not be able to install to a CGI directory, so it is not for every user. CVideoNow is a good way to eliminate those bulky server programs that other streaming systems have. Using scripts is a leaner way to serve files, but it doesn't give you the network manageability that full server systems provide.

If you're looking for a large user base, CVideoNow is not for you. It is too new and hasn't fully penetrated the Internet market. Also, the player is only available on the Windows 95/NT platform, so many users can't use it at all. CVideoNow, like other programs, is in its infancy so we'll have to tune in to see how it matures.

Pros and Cons

CVideoNow is too new and untested to know how it will do against the other streaming systems. In terms of features and server options, it falls woefully short when compared to the RealSystem or NetShow. Because it uses a CGI script server, you won't have full server controls or manage streams like you can with the full-fledged client/server systems.

The player component is not very sophisticated and could use more controls and a better look. CVideoNow handles on-demand streaming very well and has very good resolution when viewing at double size. It doesn't lose detail like other programs do.

The disadvantages to CVideoNow is that its producer program is a bit complicated and therefore will take some time to understand the different compression settings. It doesn't use plain English descriptions, nor can you easily select the frame rates and quality like other programs. Also, it only accepts very specific AVI files, ones that have a certain compression or size. This is very limiting. It can be very annoying to convert files with a third-party program before converting it again with the CVideoNow Producer. It would be best if it could accept other video file formats.

The per-stream pricing systems it is somewhat limiting as well, especially when you consider that the maximum number of streams you can purchase is just

100 concurrent users. There is no option to buy unlimited streams, there are no mirroring options or multicast support, and you can't stream live events.

All in all, CVideoNow is a good starter system, but it lacks many features of the "Big Five" streaming video systems.

About Cubic VideoComm

Cubic VideoComm is a subsidiary of Cubic Corporation, a high-technology firm that makes a wide range of products, including ground combat training ranges for the military and automated fare collection systems for mass transit. Cubic Video-Comm's main product is the CVideoNow streaming video system. It has also released a video email program called CVideo-Mail.

Cubic VideoComm
9333 Balboa Avenue
San Diego, CA 92123
(619) 505-2030
info.cvc@cubic.com
www.cvideonow.com

GTS AND EMBLAZE:
No-Client Multimedia

15

Practically every streaming multimedia system uses a three part client/ server architecture consisting of a player, producer, and server. The two programs in this chapter, GTS (Graham Technology Solutions) and Emblaze, are unique. They are both client-less systems, meaning that they don't need any plug-ins or helper applications; instead, they use Java to play streaming files. This no-client approach comes close to having a universal player—anyone with a Java-enabled browser can play streaming files. This means you can increase your audience, giving you an advantage over programs that use plug-ins and external players.

The two systems are otherwise very different. GTS uses a completely server-based system to stream only live audio or video. Emblaze is both server-less and client-less, and can stream only on-demand audio, video, and animation files. GTS needs a UNIX server to send streams, while Emblaze files can be simply placed on any web server. GTS' entire line of products consists of servers, while Emblaze's products consist of producers or authoring tools to convert and create multimedia files.

Other streaming multimedia programs have been released that also use the "no plug-in" solution, but they stream just animation files. Vosaic (discussed on the CD) also released a Java-based player recently. It seems that this is becoming a very popular way to play streaming files.

Advantages to a No-Client System

Although they are called no-client systems, it is somewhat a misnomer. More accurately, these programs are "no plug-in" and "no external player" systems. In the case of Emblaze, the player is a small Java applet that is downloaded in the background, which then plays the streaming multimedia file. Similarly, GTS just needs a Java call to the server to begin sending the stream.

There are many disadvantages to using plug-ins or helper applications. If you've ever installed plug-ins and helper applications for your browser, you know what a hassle it can be. The main hassle is downloading. Perhaps this has happened to you: You visit a site and are enjoying yourself until the site notifies you that you need a certain plug-in to view a picture, listen to a song, or to watch a video. Right off the bat, that website will lose many visitors who may not have the time or inclination to download another plug-in. Chances are you already have lots of plug-ins installed and don't want to download and install yet another one.

If you do decide to download the plug-in, you have to make sure it's compatible with your hardware, operating system, and browser. Unfortunately, most of the plug-ins currently available are made for Windows95 and NT—Macintosh and UNIX users are often left out in the cold. Also, some plug-ins are specific to Netscape Navigator and don't have native support for Internet Explorer (ActiveX controls) or other popular browsers.

If you are fortunate enough to download the right plug-in or helper application, you may have to wait a long time. Most plug-ins are large files, so you lose valuable time waiting for the download to finish before you can continue visiting that cool website. After installation, you usually have to restart your browser or even your computer. There is always a chance that the new software may conflict with other programs.

Another problem is that plug-ins are updated often. Whenever there is a new version, you have to download that new program and install it on your system. This can happen every few months and, without the newer version, you're usually out of luck again since you can't access those files. What's worse, if you delete or uninstall your browser, you will lose all your installed plug-ins, and you'll have to download and reinstall every one.

The solution to this is to have a no-client system. Right now, the only way to have no-client systems is to use Java applets to download tiny players that play the incoming multimedia file. Watching videos or listening to live audio is as easy as visiting a website with a Java-enabled browser and clicking on a link. The file arrives, and the applet plays it immediately. Already, a few streaming multimedia programs use this approach, including GTS, Emblaze, and Enliven (for more see Chapter 19, "Enliven: Streaming Banner Advertising and Interactive Multimedia."

More vendors are looking to this as the way to play files, so this may be the future of multimedia players.

What about ActiveX? It's a somewhat elegant solution, but it still can't compare to the ease of use and universality of Java. ActiveX controls know when you need to download a new ActiveX control. When you come to a page that requires a new ActiveX control, it automatically downloads and installs itself. Downloading occurs in the background, and once it is installed, you can quickly continue browsing. The problem is that ActiveX only supports Microsoft Internet Explorer and Windows95.

With a completely no-client solution like Emblaze, everyone is a winner, not just users who don't have to download files but web developers as well. They benefit from having a much larger audience that can include users of any operating system, any platform, or any browser. Likewise, software developers won't have to waste time writing plug-in software for multiple platforms; with Java, it can be written once and read anywhere, on any platform. At least in theory...

A Few Exceptions

There are a few issues to be resolved before this really takes off. First, there needs to be a Java standard for all operating systems. Microsoft is already trying to use a specialized Java that is optimized to run better under a Windows virtual machine. If this happens, it will effectively split Java into two different camps.

Also more needs to be done about security with Java applets. Many users and even web developers are still afraid of the power of Java and may choose to turn it off. This needs to be addressed before Java really becomes a standard for playing files.

So far, it is unclear if this Java-client method will succeed and become popular. Perhaps what may end up happening is that there will be a combination of push, ActiveX, Java, and plug-ins that will help you take care of any plug-ins or special players you might need. With push technology, programs can be sent to you on a regular basis to update programs or add patches. ActiveX comes close, but it is still a Windows-only solution.

The more mundane solution is to have browsers come installed with a wide array of plug-ins. Already some popular plug-ins like Shockwave and RealPlayer come standard with Microsoft Internet Explorer and some Netscape Navigator browsers. This can certainly help with downloading and installing these plug-ins, but there are always new versions and new plug-ins being released all the time. Catching up with all of them is a full-time job, so chances are we'll probably still see messages like "Plug-in not installed" for a long time to come.

Working with GTS

Graham Technology Solutions (GTS) specializes in delivering live audio and video over IP networks. Aside from just plain audio and video, it can also do remote device control and surveillance by allowing control of camera angles, zooms, pans, and other actions. GTS sells audio and video servers that accept input from live sources and distributes the feed to clients with Java-enabled browsers. The GTS system consists of three products:

GTS Audio Server. This is a server program that runs on UNIX workstations. It accepts incoming analog audio and sends the digitized data back out to anyone who calls up the Java reference on a web page.

GTS Video Server. This works exactly like the Audio Server except this accepts audio and video input.

GTS Proxy Server. The Proxy Server is used to replicate broadcast feeds so that you can reach a larger audience. These servers can be linked together to create very large broadcasts. Generally, these are used on intranets. For replicating Internet broadcasts, GTS offers an Internet Broadcasting Service that allows you to use remote proxy servers located at different nodes on the Internet.

All of the GTS products require Sun or Silicon Graphics UNIX workstations with their respective operating systems. If you don't own a UNIX workstation, GTS can sell you the hardware as well as the server software.

Viewing GTS Broadcasts

Tuning in to GTS broadcasts is very simple: Just connect to the a website with a Java-enabled browser, choose your connection speed, then start viewing. The best way to find broadcasts is to check GTS' website at www.graham.com. There are some sample broadcasts, as well as a few sites actually using GTS.

When you select to watch a movie, for example, you are asked to select your connection speed to the Internet. Usually you have a choice of 28.8Kbps, ISDN, or T1. Once you click on your choice, you are taken to the actual page. Since there is no plug-in or external player, movies are embedded onto a browser page (see Figure 15.1). The movie loads very quickly with just a small wait time.

Web programmers and authors can build any kind of interface or player controls to the GTS broadcast using regular graphics and Java commands. Most movies let you change the frames-per-second rate so you can adjust picture quality.

Figure 15.1 This is a sample of a GTS video broadcast. Most of the time you are given the option to switch the frames-per-second rate as shown here.

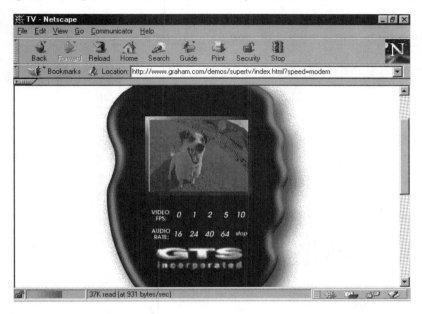

Listening to an audio broadcast works the same way. Choose your connection speed first, and it will then take you to the actual audio transmission. Depending on the interface that was programmed and created, you will see just a plain interface or a fancy radio-like graphic (see Figure 15.2).

That bad part is that video and audio quality can be very bad on 28.8Kbps connections. Video is very choppy; GTS says that a 28.8Kbps user can expect 1 frame-per-second video, which isn't very good, especially when compared to some other programs in this book that promise 10 to 15 frames per second over 28.8Kbps. Graham says that at ISDN speeds, you can see about 5 frames per second, while at T1 speeds you can see full motion (30 fps). Your actual frame rate will differ depending on network traffic. Audio quality suffers as well. It breaks up far too often, and since many broadcasts are live, you don't get a second chance to hear it. Most people can deal with shoddy video, but having bad audio is unacceptable. After all, when video breaks up it isn't that noticeable; not so with audio. Any little hiccup or pause can be extremely distracting.

One of the coolest aspects of GTS is that you can remotely operate cameras or other equipment over the Internet. GTS has some demos where you can move,

Figure 15.2 Audio broadcasts work the same way: Choose your bandwidth and the program appears. This is an interactive jukebox where you can listen to a few songs.

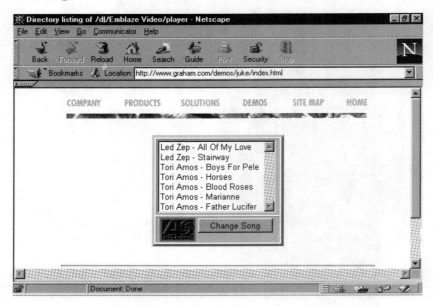

pan, and zoom the camera (see Figure 15.3). Although this is fun to show off to your friends, there are some real-life applications as well, like remote surveillance and monitoring applications.

Which browser should you use? GTS recommends using Navigator 2.0 or later for audio and video. Navigator is the only browser that support the "multipart/x-mixed-replace" MIME type needed to view video with GTS. Internet Explorer doesn't support this MIME type but it's possible that it may be fixed soon. You can still listen to GTS audio with Internet Explorer as well as Sun's HotJava browser.

GTS Audio Server

In order to broadcast audio, you need to use the GTS Audio Server. It can handle live or on-demand audio and sends it via HTTP, so it can bypass corporate firewalls. The server works by accepting input from any source and compressing it to an 8kHz and 16, 24, 40, or 64Kbps mono signal for rebroadcast to the Web. Since it mostly supports higher bit rates, only those clients with dual-channel ISDN or

Figure 15.3 This remotely controlled camera is pointed at Rockefeller Center in New York City. Note the zoom, pan, and preset buttons in the control bar.

faster connections will fully appreciate the quality of GTS. At 28.8Kbps, you can hear audio, but it will break up too often.

To use the audio server, follow these steps:

1. Install the GTS Audio Server onto your UNIX machine. Make sure it is near the audio source.

2. Connect the sound inputs to the GTS Audio Server.

3. Then, simply enter the Java applet code like the own shown here onto your web page:

```
<applet codebase="http://www.server.com" code="Audioapplet.class" width=3 height=3>
<param name=URL value=audio.au>
</applet>
```

4. Post your new web page to your server and test your signal. Anyone who uses a Java-enabled browser will then be able to hear audio.

There are two ways to increase your feed and allow more users: For intranet use, GTS' Proxy Server replicates your feed. If you are using it over the Internet and are expecting a very large audience, you can use GTS' Broadcasting Service, which allows you to use remote proxy servers to take the load of your own web server.

The GTS Audio Server runs on a Sun SPARCstation 5 or higher running at least Solaris 2.4 or an SGI running IRIX 6.2. Check out Graham's website for pricing and other platforms.

GTS Video Server

Transmitting video is accomplished with the GTS Video Server. Unlike other systems, GTS uses a new approach, JPEG video, to grab video frames. To make videos, GTS captures the frames and converts them into JPEG format. The image is then sent along to the web server where it is sent onto a web page and displayed. There is no disk access, so there is one less reason for slow-downs. Like audio, GTS recommends using an ISDN (128Kbps) or higher client connection for video. With 28.8Kbps, you can only expect a frame rate of about 1 frame per second.

The number of users that can tune in to a broadcast is limited by your bandwidth. To increase the number of users on your intranet and lower the use of your bandwidth, you can add Proxy Servers, described in the next section. If you're on the Internet, you must use GTS Internet Broadcasting Services to increase the number of users.

Videos are displayed inside web browser windows, so web designers can build customized pages around the video images. They can also create remote user controls like zoom, pans, and other movements if so desired.

Video window sizes vary depending on the video capture hardware and frame-grabbing software. Sizes can range from 160 × 120 all the way to 640 × 480. Although much depends on what size is being captured, you can also add HTML code that allows viewers to resize or zoom the video window.

The GTS Video Server works with Sun workstations running Solaris 2.4 or higher and Silicon Graphics running IRIX 5.3 or higher. To grab video, you need a video capture card like the Sun Video Card or a Parallax Xvideo Xtra card.

GTS Proxy Server

The proxy server is used to increase the number of users that can receive your broadcasts. It is made to be used on an intranet, so that your network won't be bogged down by all the heavy audio and video streams. It works by distributing GTS broadcasts throughout your intranet. (For Internet broadcasts, you must use GTS Event Broadcasting Services discussed in the next section.)

The proxy server replicates the outgoing data and sends it to its final destination. A single proxy server can serve up to hundreds of users depending on the size of your network, the frame rate, and size of the file. Better yet, you can connect multiple proxies to each other and increase your audience dramatically. The proxy server can also cache web pages to reduce access time. You can also control access to broadcasts by controlling IP addresses, domain names, or requiring usernames and passwords before tuning in.

The GTS Proxy Server works with Sun workstations running Solaris 2.4 or higher and Silicon Graphics running IRIX 5.3 or higher.

GTS Internet Event Broadcasting Services

For those who don't want to build or maintain their own broadcasting facilities GTS offers a live-event broadcasting service. It works by connecting to a series of proxy servers at major ISP network nodes. The incoming broadcast feed is sent to the proxy servers and the data is then sent to users everywhere. GTS can also help you acquire the audio or video feed; all you need to do is insert HTML code in your page that calls up the feed and gets the users to come to your website.

You can buy or rent the hardware and software from GTS. If you choose to rent the equipment, it comes complete with everything you will need; you just need to supply the information necessary during installation, like server location, IP address, and more. Then add the HTML code to the web page and post it to your site. The remote proxy server requests a single copy of the audio or video transmission from your site, then takes it and redistributes it to other proxy servers. From there, the event is ready; anyone with a Java-enabled browser can tune in. If you choose, you can even control access with a password so that only authorized users can tune in.

The broadcasting service is best for live events like meetings, conventions, training, or other one-time sessions. You work with GTS to set up the time for the actual broadcast. GTS will work with you to design, network, and customize the broadcast to your needs, the number of clients, and your bandwidth. GTS can even operate the equipment during the broadcast.

This is a good solution because you save on the actual costs and don't have to worry about everything that could go wrong if you were on your own; you can simply concentrate on the event itself, not the technology side of it. A similar solution is available for intranet use. It uses the same equipment, but you will have to purchase the audio or video server, as well as the proxy servers for better distribution.

For more information and for pricing of the GTS Broadcasting Services, see Graham's website at www.graham.com.

Other GTS Broadcasting Options

GTS also provides other options for those with special needs. It has a Satellite Rebroadcasting service that allows you to simulcast your satellite events onto the Internet. GTS acquires the satellite feed and then digitizes it to broadcast over their proxy servers all over the Internet. All you have to do is add a line of HTML code to your page to point to the proxy server, and users can quickly tune in to your satellite feed. Satellite rebroadcasting is good for when you want to take advantage of an existing satellite feed by distributing it over the Internet. You can then make it a pay-per-view event and charge users for tuning in. Fees and times must be handled with GTS, so contact them for more information.

Remote Device Control

For those wanting to control devices remotely, GTS offers a very smart solution: Their audio and video servers can be made to connect to a wide array of equipment. It can be used for surveillance, security, monitoring, and more. You can remotely control cameras, TVs, VCRs, microscopes, research equipment, and anything else that connects to the GTS server. Connections can be serial, parallel, or IEEE-488 interfaces. The hard part is up to you—writing the CGI scripts or Java commands to control the applications and user controls. One simple control as shown in Figure 15.4 is to use it to control a camera. You can zoom in, out, pan, or select preset camera positions.

Should You Use GTS?

GTS shines when it comes to live broadcasting over an intranet. It can be good over the Internet, but clients will need a very fast connection. At anything less than ISDN speeds, audio and video quality are unacceptable. If you're planning a live event and can control bandwidth, GTS is a good way to go. If you're just planning on using it on your intranet, it can also be useful.

For those who have a need for surveillance and remote-controlled applications, GTS is a good choice. It is the only program available that can intuitively connect to remote equipment for remote control.

GTS is also good for those developers who don't want to bother with installing and updating client software. It is perfect for those times when you have a wide range of platforms that need to tune in to a broadcast and you don't want to limit your audience.

However, because of its lack of support for low bandwidth, it will have a tough time getting mainstream attention. It may be that GTS is content to handle just high-bandwidth applications and intranet use, but this can seriously limit its market.

Figure 15.4 Here is another view of a remote control camera, this time of GTS' headquarters in California.

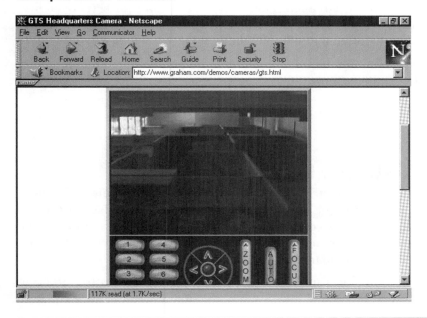

Pros and Cons

GTS shows lots of promise, but when used over the Internet with 28.8Kbps modems, its video and audio quality is dismal. GTS recommends that users connect via a dual-channel ISDN line (128Kbps) to get satisfactory performance. At T1 speeds, GTS looks very good—you can get full motion and very clear audio. Unfortunately, not everyone can connect at T1 speeds.

For intranet use, GTS can be very good because you can allocate more bandwidth to audio or video and because you can use GTS Proxy Servers to mirror the broadcasts to more users. It would be much better if GTS could support IP multicasting, but perhaps that's something that Graham can work on for a future release.

The Java client is great for increasing your audience. Since many applications are interactive in nature, it can be very fun to remotely control cameras or other equipment over the Internet. However, because there is no stable player or interface, it has a lack of player controls. There are usually no Stop or Play buttons—to stop playing a file you have to press the Back button on your browser or go to another page.

About Graham Technology Solutions

Graham Technology Solutions is a fairly new company that released the GTS system to provide no-client access to streaming audio and video. Its core markets are for live-event broadcasting, remote surveillance, and rebroadcast of satellite feeds. Its clients include Sun Microsystems, Silicon Graphics, and National Semiconductor.

Graham Technology Solutions
20823 Stevens Creek Blvd., Suite 300
Cupertino, CA 95014
(408) 366-8001
www.graham.com

Emblaze No-Client Multimedia

Emblaze is one of the newest streaming multimedia systems. It is unique because it does not need any plug-ins or servers—Emblaze uses a small 50KB Java player that is downloaded to a user's computer in the background, which then plays the audio, video, or interactive animations. You simply create or convert the files and then put everything on a standard web server.

There are three products in the Emblaze family, all encoders or authoring tools:

Emblaze Creator 2.5. Creator is a multimedia authoring tool that resembles Macromedia Director. It can create Shockwave-like interactive animations, but Emblaze files can also include audio and video. (For more on streaming animations see Chapter 20, "Streaming and Almost-Streaming Animation.") Emblaze Creator costs $995 and is available for Windows 95/NT and Macs.

Emblaze Audio. This program is used to compress audio files. It is available for Windows 95/NT and Macintosh computers for $295.

Emblaze Video. This program compresses AVI or QuickTime movies into the Emblaze format. Emblaze Video costs $295 and is available for Windows 95/NT and Macs.

No programming or Java knowledge is required; the software does all the work. All three products automatically create the required HTML page (and applet commands), so you can quickly use it or copy the commands to other HTML documents. You can then use third-party web authoring tools to continue creating the HTML page.

Emblaze audio, video, or animation files can be any size at all—there are no size restrictions. They accept a large number of standard file types like AVI, MOV, QuickTime, BMP, WAV, AIFF, SND, and JPEG. Once you've created Emblaze files, simply copy them to your web server and they are ready to be played. Any user with a Java-enabled browser, on any computer (Windows, Mac, or UNIX) can play Emblaze files. It is scaleable, for use over low- (as low as 14.4Kbps) or high-bandwidth networks.

Emblaze Creator 2.5

Emblaze Creator is a full-fledged multimedia authoring tool that can create interactive animations, and mostly resembles programs like Macromedia Director or Flash. All three programs have a timeline interface and plenty of tools for creating and editing objects, but Emblaze Creator can also include audio and video. There is no limit to the size of an Emblaze file, so you can create CD-ROM-length animations.

Emblaze Creator is good for graphic artists, web developers, and JavaScript programmers. Artists can use the Director-like drag-and-drop interface to get started with Emblaze quickly. Likewise, advanced users and JavaScript programmers can play with the script and source code to take full advantage of all the features of Emblaze Creator.

Like other multimedia authoring tools, Emblaze Creator has many options for drawing and importing files. Emblaze can import files like GIF, JPG, WAV, AIFF, SND, AVI, and QuickTime. You can have many windows open at once to best work with the file—windows include a drawing tool, preview window, and a text editor. You can also set compression rates for part of the file or for the entire Emblaze file. Creating an interactive Emblaze animation is a long process and can't be completely covered here; however, some highlights of the Emblaze Creator are presented.

You can use the Draw Window to draw your own images (see Figure 15.5), freehand or using predefined shapes, as well as different brushes and colors. Emblaze Creator doesn't have advanced drawing tools, so sometimes it makes sense to continue using your existing professional drawing tool, like Adobe Illustrator.

The MediaBank Window (see Figure 15.6) is where you store your media files when you're creating Emblaze files. You can organize all your Emblaze drawing objects, text, audio, video, or imported graphics that you want to use on the project.

Don't forget to run through the tutorial and play with the sample files it installed. Learning to use Emblaze Creator isn't terribly hard, but it does mean that you have to learn how to use a completely new authoring program. Die-hard Director users may not like to learn something new, but the Emblaze Creator

Figure 15.5 The Draw Window is a basic drawing tool to help you create graphics.

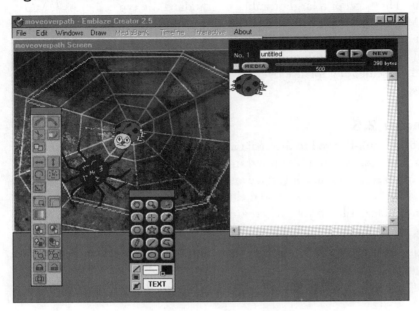

does create compelling files. Since no plug-ins are required, end users may like this best of all.

Saving and Playing Emblaze Files

Once you've successfully created an Emblaze file, you should save it so you can edit it later. Files are saved as Projects, but to use them on the Internet, you save them as Titles. Choose File/Create Title to produce all the required Emblaze files. They include:

BLZ. The actual Emblaze file.

HTML. It contains the required HTML code and applet that automatically calls the Emblaze file. You can later edit the page to suit your needs or simply copy this code to another page.

EV. If you included video, it creates this separate file.

EA. This contains the compressed audio track (if any).

EF. This contains compressed pictures (like GIF and JPEG) that you imported.

Figure 15.6 Use the MediaBank to organize all the elements in your Emblaze file.

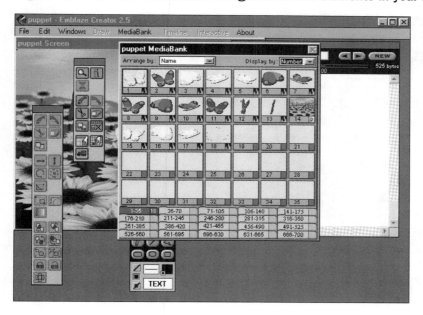

JPEG and GIF. These are the JPEG and GIF files you imported but that aren't compressed. Text will also appear as GIF files.

To play an Emblaze file, place all of the preceding files in one folder along with the Java Player components. The player components can be found in the Emblaze Player subdirectory and come in two flavors: Java-only or JavaScript. Java will be used for most browsers, while JavaScript is used on Netscape Navigator. The easiest way to play Emblaze files is to copy all the Emblaze files into this subdirectory, then double-click on the HTML file to play the file (see Figure 15.7).

Remember that you need to copy all these files (Java player files and all Emblaze files) to your web server; otherwise, visitors won't be able to play them.

Emblaze Creator is available for $995, but you can download trial versions from Emblaze's website at www.emblaze.com. It is available for Windows 95/NT and Macintosh.

Emblaze Audio

Emblaze Audio is for audio-only conversions. It accepts 16-bit WAV, SND, or AIFF sound files and exports them as Emblaze audio files. It also creates a corresponding

Figure 15.7 This is a sample Emblaze animation playing over the Internet.

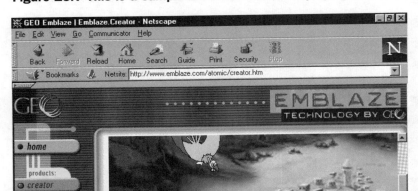

HTML page so you can quickly convert, copy, and publish the file onto your website. Emblaze Audio has just one screen that lets you perform all tasks. It has a user-friendly look, with large, well-labeled buttons (see Figure 15.8).

Unfortunately, there aren't many options. You can't select an output bit rate or change other file attributes like the sample rate or bit rates. You must create and edit the file using third-party audio editing tools first, then use Emblaze Audio as the final step to convert it. The output format of all Emblaze audio files is 16-bit, 8kHz. The output bandwidth is 13.3Kbps, so it can be streamed by 14.4Kbps modem users.

Follow these steps to use Emblaze Audio:

1. Open a sound file. If you're using Windows, you can only convert WAV sounds. Macintosh users can only compress SND and AIFF files. Press Open when you've selected the file and to return to the main screen.

2. The filename you selected will appear in the main screen.

3. Check the box if you want Emblaze Audio to create the HTML file for you. If you don't let it create the HTML file, you will have to do it yourself. (Hint: It's a good idea to always have it create the HTML file for you.)

Figure 15.8 The main window of Emblaze Audio has all the commands you will need. Making an Emblaze file is as easy as selecting an audio file and then pressing the Compress button.

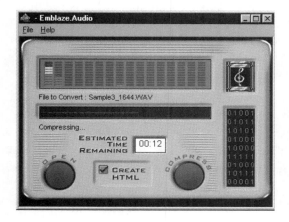

4. The last step is to convert the file. Press the large Compress button or choose File/Compress from the menu. It will ask you to select a filename. Press the Save button when you are finished.

5. As it compresses the file, you will see a progress bar and the estimated time remaining. You'll also see a waveform frequency display and an equalizer displaying the file's amplitude. (To abort the compression process, simply press the ESC key.)

6. Once it is completed, the output file will have an EA file extension. If you selected the option, the HTML file will also be created.

7. To listen to the file, copy both of the new files into a new directory, then copy the Emblaze Java player files into the same directory. The player files are located in the Player subdirectory. It includes four files with a CLASS extension. Once all the files are in one directory, open the HTML file to listen to the Emblaze file.

When publishing to the Internet, you must copy the EA, HTML, and all the CLASS files to your web server. Make sure to test it one more time to make sure it plays correctly over the Internet.

Audio Emblaze is available for Windows95, NT, and PowerPC Macintosh for $295.

Emblaze Video

Emblaze Video is a standalone program that compresses AVI and QuickTime movies into Emblaze format.

Before using Emblaze Video, you must make sure that your video is the best quality available. Your movie should be an AVI or QuickTime file that is 10 to 15 fps. The video size should be 128 × 96, 176 × 144, or 240 × 176. If you choose a video that is not one of those three sizes, the program will stop and will not let you convert the file. Go back to your video editing program and change the video size and frame size first.

Now that you have the proper file, you are ready to compress it with Emblaze Video. Open the program and you'll see the one and only program screen. Everything you need to do can be done here (see Figure 15.9).

Follow these steps to compress an Emblaze video.

1. Click on the Open button to select a file. You can also choose File/Open to bring up the open window. Select the AVI or MOV file that you want to convert and press the Open button.

2. You'll be taken back to the main screen. The name and path of the file you are converting appears on the screen.

Figure 15.9 The main window of Emblaze Video is user friendly. It is as easy as selecting the file, then pressing the Compress button.

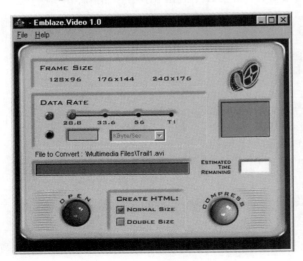

3. Select your data rate: Click on the 28.8, 33.6, 56, or T1 slide buttons to choose the output speed that you want to create. Alternatively, you can use a custom bit rate by typing in the new data rate. Don't forget to choose the units you will use, either KByte/Sec or Kbit/Sec.

4. Next, decide whether you want to create an HTML file. The Create HTML box has checkbox options for Normal Size and Double Size. If you just check the Normal Size box, Emblaze will automatically create a standard HTML file for you that you can make changes to. You can also choose the Double Size option; this will create an HTML file that makes your video appear twice its size. You can choose one, both, or none of the options. It is recommended to choose at least one option; otherwise, you will have to type in the required HTML on your own.

 The HTML that Emblaze creates is a plain blank page—not very exciting. You can either enter more HTML in the same document or move the HTML Java applet code onto an existing HTML page. Just make sure you copy everything between the <APPLET> and </APPLET> codes.

5. Finally, you're ready to compress the file. Just press the large Compress button and it will prompt you to name the Emblaze file. Once you've typed in the name, the conversion process will begin.

6. During compression, the preview window will display the video as it is compressed, and the progress bar will show you how much has been converted and show a percentage rate (see Figure 15.10). The Estimated Time Remaining box will also let you know when the file conversion will end. (To abort the compression process, simply press the ESC key.)

7. Once it's converted, it will create a number of files. You'll see a .EV file (for compressed video), an .EA file (for compressed audio, if the file had an audio track), and the HTML file (the default is the name of the origi-nal video file with the HTML extension). If you selected the double-size HTML file, it will have the same name as the normal HTML file, but it will have a D in front of it, like Dvideo.html.

8. To test your video, copy all the files into a new directory. Also copy the Java player files located in the Player subdirectory of the Emblaze Video direc-tory. The subdirectory contains the files necessary to play Emblaze files. They include several files with a CLASS extension and one EV.BIN file.

Figure 15.10 During the conversion process, Emblaze Video shows you a preview and tells you how much time is remaining.

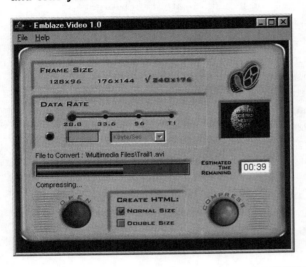

9. Once everything is in one directory, open your Java-enabled browser and open the HTML file(s). The video should start playing after a short buffer time (see Figure 15.11).

If you chose a double-size video, you can load that HTML file as well. It will be double your normal video window, up to a maximum of 480 × 342; however, the video will probably be highly pixelated.

When publishing the Emblaze video to your Internet website, you must copy all the files, including all CLASS files, the EA, EV, and HTML files, to the same web server directory. Make sure to test it one more time to make sure you copied all the files correctly.

> **NOTE** Emblaze Video is made for easy conversions, so even beginners can use it; unfortunately, that means that you won't have many options. For example, you can't change the video's frame rate or window size; you must change these parameters before compression. Advanced web developers may be frustrated by Emblaze Video's lack of features that are usually found in other encoder programs.

Figure 15.11 Open your browser and open the HTML file to view the newly created Emblaze video file. You can later make changes to the HTML and reposition the video within the window.

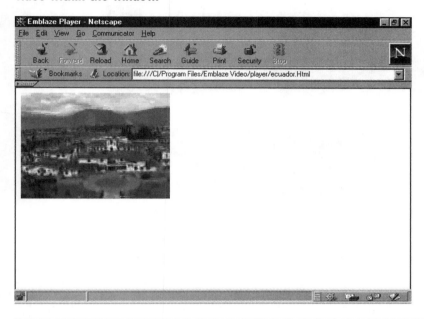

As shown in Figure 15.12, you can place Emblaze videos anywhere in a web page, just like any other web element.

Emblaze Video is available for Windows 95/NT and Macintosh computers for $295.

Should You Use Emblaze?

Emblaze is best for sites that don't plan on having extremely heavy traffic or are prepared for the traffic. That's because the no-server technology doesn't let you manage streams. Those who want to broadcast live audio or video will have to look elsewhere; this just handles on-demand content.

It is best for Internet use, since it supports many users and multiple platforms. Emblaze is not very scaleable; when used on an intranet it doesn't take advantage of all the available bandwidth. Audio especially can't be improved or modified and

Figure 15.12 This is a demo video from the Emblaze Website.

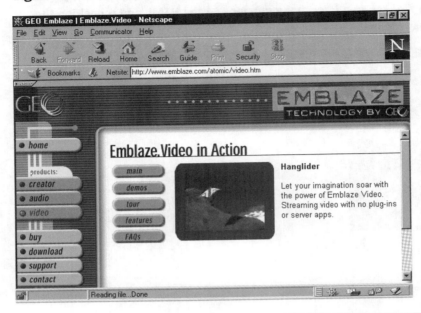

there are occasions when sound quality can be much better. This seems like an Internet-only product.

Emblaze Audio and Video are easy to use so practically anyone can put streaming multimedia on his or her website. Beginners will feel at ease with the big, bright, easy interface, but professionals may grumble at the lack of advanced features. Emblaze Creator follows the feel of Macromedia Director, so using it won't be difficult for long-time Director users. However, those new to animations and web multimedia may find Emblaze Creator to be difficult to learn.

All in all, Emblaze is a powerful yet easy-to-use solution that is already a very solid performer.

Pros and Cons

Emblaze has a lot going for it. Its server-less and no plug-in approach is revolutionary. No other product on the market can stream audio, video, and multimedia and do it this easily. The downside to the server-less approach is that you are severely limiting the size of your audience, depending on your available bandwidth. Since you don't have a server, you can't have any stream management or know who is playing your files. Perhaps more important to some developers, Emblaze only handles on-demand audio or video—without a server, you can't have live multimedia. On the plus side, this also means no high server or per-stream costs.

The no plug-in interface also has some drawbacks. The main problem is that there are no player controls—no Stop, Pause, or Play buttons. A file begins to play when you visit a web page with an Emblaze file embedded into it. There is no way to stop playback; pressing the Stop button on the browser doesn't work. Also, there are no visual cues, so you don't know if a file has stopped playing because it is finished or because of an error. The lack of file information like author, filename, or copyright means that you have to enter that information onto the web page manually. It would also be nice to have an external player pop up when playing a file, especially sound. That way, you'd be able to surf and listen in the background instead of having to open a new browser window or sit on one page for a long time.

On the creation side, it will be very hard to penetrate into Director and Flash markets with Emblaze's authoring tool. Director is a very popular and very sophisticated program, and many Director users may balk at having to learn yet another program. Fortunately, the programs are somewhat similar. Nevertheless, Emblaze's products have put other vendors on call. Can it get any easier to add streaming audio, video, and animation to your website without the use of plug-ins?

About Geo Publishing Inc.

Founded in 1994, Geo Publishing is a software publisher that makes authoring tools for streaming audio, video, and animation. Their three products, Emblaze Audio, Emblaze Video, and Emblaze Creator all can create streaming multimedia that doesn't need plug-in players or servers.

Geo Publishing is a U.S. subsidiary of Geo Interactive Media Group Ltd., an Israeli Internet software company.

Geo Publishing
21110 Oxnard Street
Woodland Hills, CA 91367
(818) 703-8436
(888) GEO-4WWW
www.emblaze.com

Summary

The no-client area will certainly grow—it is just *so* new. Video and audio players may not be very good for Java players, because good players should have lots of functions like, Stop, Seek controls, and preset buttons, which are too complicated to accomplish with Java. Also, Java can be a bit processor intensive and slow to respond. Nevertheless, the no-client approach is a very attractive solution and works best with animation programs. A good number of streaming animation programs like Shockwave, Flash, and Enliven already support Java playback. For more on these programs see Chapters 19, "Enliven: Streaming Banner Advertising and Interactive Multimedia," and 20, "Streaming and Almost-Streaming Animation."

IP MULTICASTING
over Intranets

I n the beginning of the streaming multimedia boom, most early streaming
programs catered to Internet and other low bit-rate solutions, because most
users had 14.4Kbps or 28.8Kbps modems. There wasn't much need for faster
streaming systems since they were usually not scaleable for use on faster networks. As analog modem speeds have now increased to around 56Kbps, and with the
growing popularity of ISDN, streaming multimedia responded by scaling higher and
delivering better quality.

At the same time, the number of corporate intranets skyrocketed; likewise, the
demand for high-quality audio and video networks also increased. On an intranet,
speeds range from 10Mbps to 100Mbps and more, so full-screen, full-motion video
and CD-quality audio are possible. There weren't many broadband streaming
programs to take advantage of these very fast networks; just a few start-up companies
responded by releasing streaming video systems used for intranets.

Slowly, other companies realized the potential of this new market, but there are
still few dedicated high-bandwidth streaming programs. More common are Internet
systems (like NetShow or RealMedia) that have been improved in recent years to
accept both low- and high-bandwidth applications. This poses a problem because the
needs for high-bandwidth audio and especially video are rather different from low
bandwidth needs. First, video should be very high quality, preferably full-screen and
full motion (30 frames per second); anything less would be sorely disappointing. In
a corporate environment, you don't want to settle for matchbook-sized video screens
or herky-jerky video. Of greater importance, the streaming data being sent over the
network should not interfere with the rest of the network applications; it should run
alongside all the other regular traffic without slowing it down. That meant that
unicasting was not a very good solution. The answer was IP multicasting.

The four programs in this chapter, StarWorks, StarCast, Spotlight, and IP/TV all are intranet-ready systems that promise high-quality audio and video. They all support IP multicasting, which is key to reducing bandwidth. One outgoing video stream can serve hundreds or even thousands of users. This chapter focuses on systems that use IP multicasting, but there are some other programs like NetShow that also use it.

However, before focusing on the four systems, you should ask yourself: Why do I need to put a video network on my intranet?

The Need for Video Networks

More and more companies are realizing how important intracompany communications are, and with the popularity of intranets, companies are communicating like never before. Things that used to be done on paper, like purchase orders or requisitions, can now be done over an intranet. Likewise, scheduling and email have transformed the corporate workplace.

The newest intranet revolution is video networks. They can be used in a wide variety of applications. Can you use audio or video on your intranet? Here are some examples of these applications for a video network, most of which are already in use by companies:

Video training. Employee training is one of the fastest growing applications on a streaming video network. You can capture analog training videos to a hard disk so employees can have on-demand training videos. That way, employees can look up specific sections where they need more help and get answers on policies or procedures at any time. Also, training videos can be replayed later for better understanding and retention. Video training is also helpful for those companies that have scattered offices in a large campus or spread out across the country. Employees no longer have to travel to a centralized training location, they can remain at their desks. Just imagine the savings in travel and lost work time. Live training and seminars are also possible. Fortunately, interaction is not lost—some training programs allow easy integration of slide show presentations and allow real-time feedback from the audience.

Video greetings. New hires can sit at their desks, turn on their computers, and view a greeting from the CEO or the president of the company. Also, human resources policies, history, and other company background information can be stored for viewing at any time.

Live broadcasts. Any live broadcast that you want to send to employees from news shows or live events can be sent via video networks. Smith Barney uses StarWorks to send out full-screen news programs, briefings, and stock reports to every analyst's desktop. This can be called *video push*, since broadcasts are sent to desktops for everyone to watch.

Company communications and announcements. Much like live broadcasts or on-demand training, these videos or audio messages can be transmitted to the entire company. They can also include recordings of meetings or conferences, stock reports, and any other corporate communications.

There are so many other applications. Any company, large or small, can benefit from a video network. Analyze your company's needs and see what applications are centered around audio and video that can better be presented on employees' desktops. Or, if you have many live meetings or face-to-face training sessions, computer-delivered video is the next best thing to being there. Already many entertainment companies, manufacturing plants, educational institutions, and financial companies are using video on their intranets. The need for business multimedia is becoming very important and *is* the way of the future.

What Should You Look for in a Video Network?

Combined, the three programs in this chapter have all the ingredients necessary for a good video network. They are all complete systems, from clients to servers, and some even include hardware like MPEG encoders. What should you look for when deciding to implement video on your intranet? The most important things to consider are:

IP multicasting. This should be the first thing to look for in an intranet streaming video network. It will save you bandwidth and won't disturb your other crucial network traffic. Remember, just one video stream can serve thousands of clients with no effect on your network.

Support for live and on-demand audio and video. Live broadcasting gives you the option to show events, meetings, and speeches and send them to every connected desktop computer. This can save travel time, lessen the loss of productivity, and ensure that your messages get seen and heard. For on-demand media, you can have training videos, welcome messages, or other information you need to impart on a regular basis. If the system supports unicasting, a searchable database of on-demand movies would help users find what they are looking for.

Full-screen and full motion video. These should be supported by your video network; anything less is disappointing to clients. With multicasting, you can use the savings in bandwidth to increase the quality of your video so you get 30 frames per second and very high-quality audio.

Cross-platform support. Most networks are a hodgepodge of different computers, from Macintosh to Windows of varying types. Unfortunately, only StarWorks has a client program for Mac users. The most popular client is still Windows95 and NT.

Network manageability. It is also crucial to make sure your network is running smoothly and isn't bogged down by the streaming data. Naturally, this is handled by IP multicasting, but using new protocols like RSVP and RTP gives you speedier delivery and guaranteed delivery of data.

Your existing network and technology. The system should be compatible. That way you won't have to purchase new computers or hardware encoders. If you feel that your network needs the extra power, talk with your vendor to make sure your network doesn't fall short.

No-client or Java-playing systems. These are best for intranets. That way, system administrators don't have to go to every client computer and install and update client software—it can take many hours to manually install software on 100 to 200 computers. Unfortunately, none of the programs mentioned in this chapter support Java playing or no-plug-in players. This may change as more vendors realize the importance of having a universal client.

Bandwidth. Always consider the current number of users on your network. Some systems have a maximum number of concurrent unicast streams that can be transmitted. Always have a plan to quickly increase the number of simultaneous users so you won't be caught short. With multicasting, that won't matter much since your network bandwidth shouldn't be affected. Nevertheless, you may need to increase your network to a 100BaseT Ethernet network, perhaps to give you more bandwidth.

Support for UNIX and Windows NT computers. These are the most popular servers on a LAN. If you have a Windows network, you may not want to buy a UNIX computer for your video network.

Satellite reception and distribution. These should be considered for reach over WANs and other remote networks. If you already use satellites to broadcast information, or if you need to spread your message to remote locations, this is a very good option.

Tech support. The whole process of installing and testing your network isn't easy and will take some time. For times when you need help, make sure you can call the vendor and get assistance. Your vendor should also help when your network needs to be upgraded for more users or greater bandwidth.

Working with StarWorks

StarWorks is a video streaming system primarily for use over intranets, created by Starlight Networks. It can broadcast live and on-demand unicast streams. In order to ensure quality and delivery, StarWorks uses something it calls StarStream to handle bandwidth reservation and traffic-shaping. This technology ensures peaceful coexistence with other network applications.

The system consists of the StarWorks Server and Client programs. The StarWorks Server streams the data to clients, which is sent over the faster but less reliable UDP protocol. You can choose low or high compression and high or low bandwidth, depending on the application and the network you are using. StarWorks comes with diagnostic tools so you can see what's going on in the video network. It also comes with a bandwidth reservation system so that StarWorks won't interfere with other network applications. Each StarWorks Server handles 300 streams. For more simultaneous streams, you can use multiple servers or multiprocessor computers.

StarWorks Requirements

The StarWorks Client player is available for Windows 3.x, 95, NT, and Macintosh computers. It is configured as a plug-in or as a helper application for Microsoft Internet Explorer and Netscape Navigator. Figure 16.1 shows a custom view created for General Electric.

StarWorks runs on Windows NT and UNIX-based platforms like Sun Solaris. The NT version costs $6,495. Pricing is based on streaming capacity; for example, the StarWorks 100M system means that it supports a total of 100Mbps of streaming data. The number of users will vary, depending on your data.

Working with StarCast

The StarCast system is Starlight's multicasting solution. This is best used for live, time-critical delivery of multimedia but can also be used for stored content. It can multicast full-screen and full-frame, TV-quality MPEG-1 video over any standard IP network like Ethernet (10BaseT) and Fast Ethernet (100BaseT). It is also possible to use StarCast with the on-demand servers of StarWorks.

Figure 16.1 Starlight created this custom browser page showing StarWorks movies for General Electric.

> **NOTE** Although StarCast and StarWorks work together, they can also be used separately. Starlight seems to be trying to meld the two systems. It released a beta client program called the Starlight Client that can be used with both StarWorks and StarCast.

StarCast consists of two components:

StarCast Multicaster. This captures and multicasts live or stored media. It accepts any analog source like a video camera, cable, VCR, TV, and others. Starlight says it can send out 10,000 streams from one server, although much depends on your network's bandwidth. The Multicaster is available for Windows95 and costs $1,495.

StarCast Viewer. This is the client program for viewing multicast events. It costs $149 per seat and is available for Windows95 and NT (see Figure 16.2).

Hardware encoding is optional, but you'll get better results using an MPEG-1 video encoder on the Multicaster and an MPEG-1 decoder on the client's computer.

Figure 16.2 This is a sample video displayed on the StarCast Viewer. A new client program that plays both StarCast and StarWorks videos should be out by the time you read this.

Also available is the StarCast Recaster, which is used for satellite multicasting. The Recaster is great for those companies with many different locations or that use WANs. One satellite feed can be sent to any Recaster receiver, no matter where they are. Once it reaches the Recaster, it can send the multicast stream directly to clients in that network. That way, two different locations can receive the same broadcast even if they are on separate networks and are geographically distant. The Recaster works with the Hughes Network DirecPC (www.direcpc.com) satellite to receive the data. The Recaster costs $995 and is available for Windows95 only.

About Starlight

Starlight Networks was founded in 1992, and its primary business is video networking, including the StarWorks and StarCast systems. Already in the works is an integrated viewer for viewing both StarWorks and StarCast to be called the Starlight Viewer. This may lead to a more integrated product line. Starlight has about 400 clients, including Smith Barney, Bloomberg, and CSX.

Integration with other streaming products is also forthcoming. Starlight recently partnered with RealNetworks (formerly Progressive Networks) to market and resell each other's products. Starlight will focus on intranet applications, while

RealNetworks will tend to the Internet market. At the same time, future versions of Starlight's products will support Microsoft's ASF file format.

Starlight Networks
205 Ravendale Drive
Mountain View, CA 94043
(415) 967-2774
www.starlight.com

Working with the Spotlight Network VideoServer System

Tektronix Inc., best known to computer users for its Phaser line of color laser printers, recently entered the video streaming market with the Spotlight Network VideoServer system. Spotlight is an expensive, high-end system that streams MPEG-1 video over intranets and other private, broadband networks. Like Starlight, it also handles multi-casting and is best used over Ethernet networks (like 10BaseT or 100BaseT) or faster.

The Spotlight Network VideoServer System is a client/server system consisting of three parts:

VideoServer. This is a hardware/software solution that streams the on-demand files. It is also a video database.

VideoEncoder. The VideoEncoder is also a hardware/software package. It accepts incoming analog or digital video and converts it into an MPEG-1 video stream. The output stream can multicast to clients or be sent to the VideoServer.

VideoBrowser plug-in. This is the client plug-in program that decodes and displays the MPEG-1 streams.

Like many of the systems discussed in this chapter, pricing for the Spotlight system is rather high. A 30-stream version costs $45,000. The VideoEncoder itself costs $19,995. The Spotlight Network can send streams as regular unicast data or as multicast. It can achieve full-screen, full-motion MPEG-1 video over a 400Kbps connection.

VideoEncoder

The VideoEncoder is a real-time video compression and transmission program. It is hardware based to quickly encode the incoming NTSC or PAL video source into an MPEG-1 output video stream. The output stream can be sent directly to users' client computers via multicasting or it can be stored in the VideoServer for later retransmission.

Administration and access are handled via a browser interface. That way, administrators can access the encoder via any computer connected to the network.

VideoServer

For on-demand video delivery, the VideoServer must be used. The VideoServer is a hardware/software solution that stores the MPEG-1 video streams as files that can later be delivered to clients. It can support just a maximum of 100 simultaneous unicast streams, so if you have more users, try multicasting.

The VideoServer also has a browser-based interface to monitor the video network and your video files. The database can be used to catalog the videos. Users can type in keywords and search for movies to quickly find and play on-demand videos.

VideoBrowser Plug-In

The client system is a browser plug-in. It can be used on regular PCs running Navigator or Tektronix's own network computers. It can receive live multicast shows from the VideoEncoder or on-demand unicast movies from the VideoServer. Files are sent through the regular HTTP protocol.

For best results, a hardware MPEG-1 decoder should be used. That frees the client computer and lets the hardware handle the processor-intensive decoding duties. With a hardware addition, full-screen, full motion video can be achieved; otherwise, you can expect somewhat smaller video screen sizes.

About Tektronix, Inc.

Tektronix, Inc., was founded in 1946 and is a maker of measurement products (including oscilloscopes, analyzers, and other test equipment) and color network laser printers. It is also well known in the TV and film production industry for its production equipment, editing systems, and video networks. For more on Spotlight, visit www.tektronix.com/Network_Computers/Products/system.html.

Tektronix, Inc.
Tektronix Video and Networking Division
26600 Southwest Parkway
P.O. Box 1000
Wilsonville, OR 97070-1000
(503) 685-4005
www.tektronix.com

Working with IP/TV

An early adopter of IP Multicasting is Precept Software, Inc. In 1996, it released FlashWare, a program for viewing multicast shows on the Internet Multicast Backbone, or MBone. The MBone is part of the Internet that can send high-speed, high-quality multicast data, usually audio and video. Now with IP/TV, Precept has stepped up and delivered a live and on-demand multicasting system for use on Windows95 and NT computers. It is codec-independent so it can use any industry standard, even MPEG video, for full-screen video.

IP/TV is a client/server system with three components:

IP/TV Server. This is the server component that sends out the multicast streams. It is used on Windows95 and NT.

IP/TV Program Guide. This works like the "TV Guide" of IP/TV. All broadcasts are listed here. It works with the server to send out streams at scheduled times. It is compatible with Windows NT or UNIX.

IP/TV Viewer. This is the Windows 95/NT client used to view schedules shown in the program guide and to view the multicast movies.

IP/TV uses a few industry-standard protocols like RTP (Real-Time Transport Protocol) and RSVP (Resource Reservation Protocol). RTP is a now-ratified standard for sending real-time data like video broadcasting and videoconferencing. RSVP is used to reserve a certain amount of bandwidth for sending time-critical data, usually for video. Unlike RTP, RSVP isn't an international standard yet. It is hoped that these two protocols will be used to decrease bandwidth and deliver better-quality audio and video.

For demographics and for checking users on your network, you can use Precept's StreamWatch software. It can monitor all events, tell you the number of viewers, list email addresses, tell you starting times of programming, program reception quality, and much more. StreamWatch works on Windows95 and NT.

IP/TV Video Server

The IP/TV Video Server is the workhorse of the system. It sends out the multicast streams as a single stream to all clients according to the schedule set with the Program Guide. The video server can capture live video or accept stored content. When capturing live video, you can select practically any codec for audio and video, and choose the bandwidth, frame rate, and window size.

It can even carry multicast content over WANs and slower, non-multicast networks. The IP/TV Video Server runs on Windows95 or NT and costs $2,995.

IP/TV Program Guide

The IP/TV Program Guide acts essentially like a TV guide for IP/TV broadcasts. The program guide helps administrators schedule and manage events. It also manages the number of audio/video streams allowed on the network. The program guide doesn't actually serve the files, it is just the intermediary between the server and the viewer. It shows program name, description of event, total time, repeat time, bandwidth and frame rate, window size, and more (see Figure 16.3).

A particular event can be password-protected so that only certain users can tune in to a program. IP/TV is also compliant with the MBone broadcasts, which means that viewers can tune in to intranet or MBone broadcasts. There are plenty of MBone applications, including videoconferencing and video broadcasting from educational institutions and other companies. You can find more information about how to receive broadcasts and how to join the MBone by visiting www.mbone.com.

IP/TV is the first system that most resembles TV on your desktop computer. You can scroll through program listings or channel surf by tuning in to broadcasts in progress. The program guide runs on Windows NT or UNIX web servers and costs $995.

IP/TV Viewer

The IP/TV Viewer is a standalone client program for checking program listings and viewing movies. Every time you start IP/TV Viewer, a new copy of the network's

---

Figure 16.3 The program guide is for managing videos. You can add programs, channels, and see a listing of your shows, including time, date, and name of file.

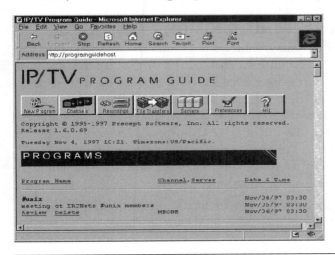

program listings is downloaded from the program guide. It can also update the listings periodically while connected. You can schedule programs or view one that is currently playing. You can also channel surf.

There are full controls, so you can adjust the look of the viewer, stop the movie, raise the volume, change frame size, or even increase the window size to full-screen without increasing bandwidth. There is also a statistics display so you can see if there are any network problems. It features a unique feature called Slide-Cast, which allows you to watch two videos simultaneously: one shows the presenter, and another shows the presentation or slide show. You can also press the Question button to launch your browser and ask the moderator a question in real time.

IP/TV Viewer is available as a plug-in and standalone application for Windows 95 and NT and costs $149.

About Precept Software, Inc.

Precept was founded in 1995 and created IP/TV to bring high-quality, multicast video to LAN and WAN desktops. Cisco Systems, Inc., maker of networking equipment, took an equity stake in Precept and is planning to use its IP multicast-enabled routers with IP/TV.

Precept Software, Inc.
1072 Arastradero Road
Palo Alto, CA 94304
(415) 845-5200
info@precept.com
www.precept.com

Pros and Cons of IP Multicasting

Implementing IP multicasting on your intranet is a no-brainer. On an existing network, upgrading your routers to be multicast-enabled is a simple, inexpensive task. Most new routers already are multicast-enabled. To get it to work on your network, you might need to upgrade your network memory or install new software. Perhaps the only downside to multicasting is trying to get it to work with non-multicast networks like the Internet. Unfortunately, many ISPs and backbone providers haven't upgraded to multicasting. It seems that they are all waiting for each other to commit. The IP Multicast Initiative (www.ipmulticast.com) was formed by Internet companies to spread the word, demystify multicasting, and promote its use.

On a cost basis, it makes lots of sense to switch to multicasting. The savings in bandwidth and a better network will more than make up for the cost of upgrading your routers or buying new ones.

On an intranet, multicasting has so many advantages it's a wonder more companies don't use it. You can save precious bandwidth and prevent your network from being saturated by the audio and video data. IP multicasting takes up just one stream, no matter how many clients are tuning in. The advantages are obvious and cost effective.

Summary

The four programs mentioned in this chapter aren't the only solutions that you should consider on your network. Microsoft's NetShow also uses multicasting and it is free. StreamWorks also uses multicasting. Graham (GTS) provides very good quality video over high-speed LANs and it doesn't need a plug-in, just Java. Other programs like Oracle's Video Server and WebFORCE Mediabase by Silicon Graphics are also pretty sophisticated and can be useful on any large network that needs high-quality video. You should consider programs that scale well to fast networks or that are made for high-quality audio and video. Other Internet-only systems may not scale high enough or deliver full-screen, full-motion video like the intranet-ready systems.

Talk to any IS administrator who is thinking of implementing streaming video and he or she will tell you that the most important consideration is bandwidth. Network bottlenecks occur because of CPU overload and disk I/O lag, but the most common problem is too much traffic. With unicasting, networks are often saturated and slowed by the huge amounts of video and audio. Multicasting solves all this. It is the key to having a fast, happy network and a happy administrator. Multicasting is the way of the future and so are video-enabled intranets.

STREAMING
VRML and 3-D

Although we live in a three-dimensional (3-D) world, everything in our computers is limited to two dimensions. We can see word processor applications, QuickTime movies, and high-resolution still images, but they are all limited to two dimensions. As the processing power and graphics capabilities of personal computers improved, we saw some 3-D graphics, but they were always limiting. The area of computer gaming is where the best advances have come from. Games like Doom, Quake, or Tomb Raider really show off what 3-D can do, and the influx of new 3-D graphics cards is making 3-D computing a very hot topic. Generally, only games are benefiting from the advances in 3-D; other fields have failed to use it well.

In 1994, 3-D was formally introduced to the Internet, but it was very crude. It was dubbed VRML (pronounced VER-muhl) for Virtual Reality Modeling Language. VRML is to 3-D what HTML is to the Web; it is the official language for creating 3-D worlds. It consists of text commands like HTML that construct VRML graphics and worlds. Since its introduction, VRML has slowly matured into a very competitive field, but it has not achieved mainstream success; it is still a niche market. Nevertheless, dedicated groups of VRML enthusiasts, 3-D companies, and graphic artists have continued creating and developing VRML so that it is now ready for prime time.

Okay, so what's the catch? It's a big one: Most VRML files don't stream. VRML files need to be downloaded completely before the user can view them. Even worse, most VRML files tend to be very large, ranging from as small as 90KB to over 400KB. That's the bad news. The good news is that there are new technologies that are making streaming VRML a possibility. Already one can progressively download VRML files so you can start using it while it is downloading.

Unfortunately, streaming VRML is so new that only one or two programs can do it. There is still no industry-wide streaming solution. Nevertheless, the few programs that do allow streaming VRML show how promising it is and what lies in the future.

The next section explains more about VRML and how it works, and then we get right into some of the leading VRML programs. This chapter also shows you what programs can help you get started in creating 3-D images and worlds. Beware, because 3-D creation is a complex and processor-intensive work.

A smaller section in this chapter deals with panoramic programs that allow you to see 360-degree views of a photographed scene. The effect is similar to VRML, but the photos usually aren't 3-D, just flat, two-dimensional photos or graphics. You can zoom in and out and pan in any direction with panoramic images, but you can't actually see three dimensions.

What Is VRML?

The term *VRML* is thrown around often, so it is best to clear things up right away. VRML means nothing more than being able to see 3-D images and movies on your computer. More specifically, it is the standard for viewing 3-D images on the Internet. VRML is not really virtual reality as in headsets and power gloves—you don't need any special hardware to see VRML on the Internet. You don't even need a 3-D graphics card. Practically anyone with a good multimedia system and graphics card can enjoy VRML. As always, it helps to have a fast processor because VRML can be very processor-intensive.

VRML was "invented" in 1994 by Mark Pesce and Tony Parisi. Together, they built a 3-D web browser and coined the term *VRML*. Later that year, a standard for creating 3-D was desperately needed, so the specifications for VRML 1.0 were released. By 1995, VRML 1.0 caught on and there were many people creating VRML objects; however, VRML 1.0 was static. You could move around and interact with objects (like being taken to another URL or opening a MIME type), but that was it.

The most used standard is VRML 2.0, although the newer VRML97 was recently passed as an international standard in December 1997. VRML 2.0 is more interactive than version 1.0 because it can include animation, sounds, scripting, Java, sensors that trip when you move to a certain area, and collision detection. If you've ever played first-person, 3-D games like Doom or Quake, you already know how VRML works. In order to see VRML images, you need a VRML 2.0 or VRML97 compliant viewer, of which there are many available.

Unfortunately, VRML is not the only type of 3-D available. Some companies have released competing proprietary systems that are quite similar but not compatible with VRML. You can view these other 3-D programs with each company's proprietary viewers.

To see VRML images, you'll need to get one of the many VRML 2.0 or VRML97 compatible viewers. They come as plug-ins or ActiveX controls for either Navigator or Internet Explorer. When you access a VRML file (WRL or compressed WRL.GZ files), your browser opens up the viewer and displays the program inside the web page. You can also get standalone VRML browsers. Choosing a good VRML viewer can be tough, since they are all a bit different with slightly different interfaces. This chapter introduces you to the most popular VRML viewers and some other proprietary browsers. As you use the viewers, you'll see which ones you're most comfortable with and develop favorites.

Using VRML

So the big question is, what can you do with VRML? Plenty. The most basic thing is being able to see objects in three dimensions. You can rotate, zoom in and out, pan objects, and see them from any angle. You can also walk around or fly. VRML can let you see how lighting affects the object, shading, textures, and any number of other effects like fog, smoke, and haze. More advanced VRML creations allow you to use multiuser worlds where you can move and interact in a world by opening doors, ordering cyberdrinks, or chatting with other live people (see Figure 17.1).

A 3-D programmer creates and invents interaction in any 3-D world. There are now many 3-D worlds and communities on the Internet that resemble real-life communities. People can pick an image to represent themselves in that world (called an *avatar*) and interact with others and walk around. You'll see some examples later in the chapter.

How do you create VRML files? It's a bit complex. If you were to open a VRML file (WRL or WRL.GZ extensions) with a text editor, you'd see that VRML is just a series of hierarchical text commands, much like HTML. A VRML viewer takes those commands and interprets them into the graphical output that you see. VRML developers could technically create a VRML file by hand, but that would be incredibly difficult and time consuming. The most common way to create a VRML world is to use one of the many graphical programs where you can drag and drop images and quickly create VRML files. You can even create links to other websites, other VRML pages, RealAudio, video programs, Java, or anything else that is handled by your browser and plug-ins. Like HTML, VRML accepts any MIME type that your browser can handle.

Unfortunately for Macintosh users, VRML is very Windows centered. There are just a few Macintosh VRML viewers; most are Windows 95/NT. Even Mac

Figure 17.1 Here is a sample of a VRML world. You can move around and manipulate objects.

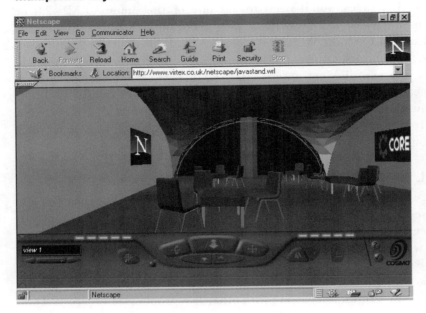

VRML editors are scarce. This is a shame since the Mac has always been popular with graphic artists and designers. Windows NT is frequently the platform of choice for serious VRML creation.

Applications for VRML

VRML is lots of fun, but what about some applications for it? What can you do to justify VRML to your boss? Practically anything on a regular web page can be used with VRML. Here are some current applications:

Science and space. The most recent and most visible example of VRML was on the Pathfinder Mars Mission. Many companies created sample VRML files of animated sequences of the entire mission. Some even patched together actual color images returned from the probe to create a VRML file. You could look around the Mars landscape and move the rover anywhere in the VRML world (see Figure 17.2). The engineers at JPL who launched and controlled Pathfinder used VRML that could be seen with 3-D glasses.

Figure 17.2 With VRML, you can see and explore faraway places like this Mars landscape.

Education. Learning about a topic is enhanced when you can actually see it in action, control it, or view it from any angle. You can view an ancient city, view biological models, the structure of DNA, and see some scientific principles and laws in action.

Simulations. Like education, you can run simulations on a variety of equipment, like driving a car, piloting a helicopter, and learning to operate other expensive equipment. That way, if you crash a plane it won't cost billions of dollars. The Mars mission is a good example of a successful and compelling simulation. Already there are tutorials that show you how to install SVGA cards or how to clean your mouse.

Business. Yes, there are even business applications. You can have presentations, marketing materials, and your whole product line in VRML form.

Travel. One use for travel is to display your new resort space and other new facilities you have available. You can show the complete interior and exterior spaces, like the pool, golf course, or hotel lobby. This is a great way to showcase a new building, too. VRML puts the traveler directly in the space, albeit in a VRML world.

Shopping. Already there are a few merchants setting up shop in a VRML world. VRML is great because you can really look at merchandise from any angle, see colors, textures, and more. One shop in Florida set up a Corvette dealership to sell cars (see Figure 17.3). Just click on any car and an HTML page will load to continue your shopping experience.

Medicine. Virtual Reality, especially when used with VR goggles, is great for medical applications. Already, some therapists have begun using it as a way to help people conquer their phobias like spiders, heights, planes, or anything else. It can also be used in other medical uses like virtual surgery or showing complex medical procedures.

Architecture, engineering, construction, or interior design. This is one of the most common applications. Some companies have set up sites to showcase some unique buildings and interior spaces (see Figure 17.4). VRML can be used to simulate the construction or manufacturing processes, too. You can check the lighting, exposure, the view outside of

Figure 17.3 Shop for a Corvette virtually, and then pay in real money.

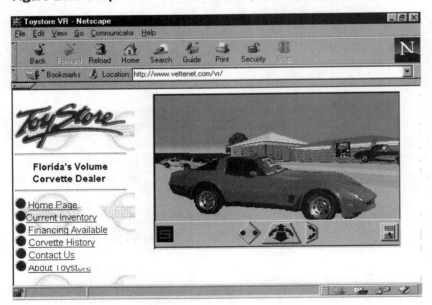

windows, and lots more. On the design and engineering side, you can create virtual prototypes and show them to employees or clients.

Real estate. Already there are some real-estate companies that have put up VRML sites. People looking to purchase homes and property can take a virtual look at the place. Visitors can travel up and down stairs, look out windows, and open doors. Developers can add an interactive talking tour or text script to guide buyers through the home. It is also handy for seeing the whole outside of the house so you can see every angle. When VRML achieves more photorealistic graphics, this will become even more important.

Entertainment. VRML and entertainment really go well together. There are plenty of games available. You can play pinball games, a 3-D blocks game, card games, chess, bowling, and more. Also, you have interactive animations, film previews, sound clips, and music.

Building Internet communities. The big buzz right now with VRML is multiuser worlds. This is where large numbers of people can log in to one server and interact with each other. You can type in your name

Figure 17.4 Want to see the home of tomorrow? Check out some models virtually.

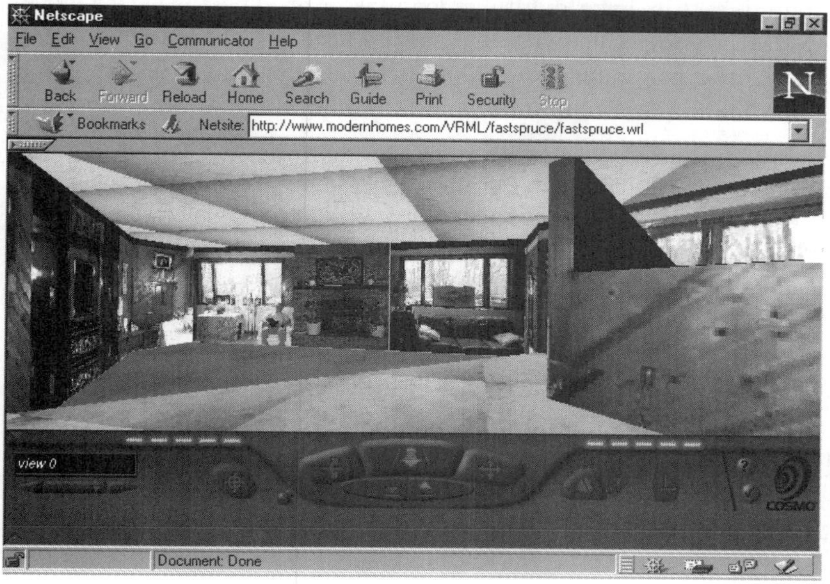

and choose an avatar to represent you in this 3-D world. Browsers like Sony's Community Place can even support live audio chat. More and more communities and virtual worlds are popping up all over the world.

Advertising and sales. Internet commerce gets a facelift with VRML; now you can show off your product in three dimensions. Another opportunity for revenue is accepting advertising within a VRML world. Some virtual billboards and other ads have already appeared inside some VRML worlds and more are on the way. If you can sell it, you can show it off with VRML. Then insert an HTML link to your site.

These are just some examples. The use of headgear and other VR equipment greatly enhances the 3-D experience, but isn't necessary. You can experience all these examples right now, with a good computer and a VRML viewer for your browser.

VRML 2.0 Viewers

To view a VRML (file with a WRL or WRL.GZ extension), you need a viewer. When you come across a VRML file, the plug-in takes over and displays the file inside the web page.

VRML viewers come in all shapes and sizes. Some have different interfaces to move around and interact in a world. Others load faster or allow for better movement within a VRML world. Which viewer is best? There are about three or four top viewers, with the rest being niche or seldom-used viewers. You should try a few of them to see which ones you like best.

 When testing them out, make sure you only have one VRML 2.0 viewer installed at any one time. Installing more than one at a time just won't work and may cause some headaches. Remember, only the last VRML plug-in you installed will be used for viewing WRL files.

The best thing to do is to download a few of them and install just one and see how it works. Then you should uninstall the last viewer and install a new one. Keep doing this until you finally find a good viewer that you can live with. That means saving the setup programs for each program you are testing.

Of course, you can also download one good, popular viewer and stick with it. Chances are you won't go wrong by installing any of the first two or three viewers mentioned next.

Cosmo Player 2.0 by Cosmo Software

The Cosmo Player is a VRML plug-in by Cosmo Software (a division of Silicon Graphics), and it is part of the Netscape Communicator 4.0 suite. You can get it as part of Communicator or download it from Netscape's software update page. Netscape had its own VRML viewer called Live3D bundled with Navigator 3.0, but that was discontinued. Cosmo is now its official VRML viewer, but you can use any VRML 2.0 viewer with Navigator.

Once you install the plug-in, you are ready to start visiting VRML worlds. When you first come to a web page with a VRML file (WRL), you will see your browser loading the WRL file. Cosmo Player 2.0 can stream VRML files, so you can start interacting in the world within a few seconds of it beginning to download. Full streaming isn't here yet, but Cosmo is already ahead of most viewers. WRL file sizes can be as small as 60KB, but an average size is around 140KB for a complex world. Some sites will be much larger. When the viewer finishes downloading, the image will appear in the browser window. The Cosmo Player control panel will be displayed at the bottom of the image (see Figure 17.5). Every VRML browser will have similar movement controls.

Figure 17.5 Cosmo Player loads the image and puts you at the starting point. You can use the control panel to change your controls and move around.

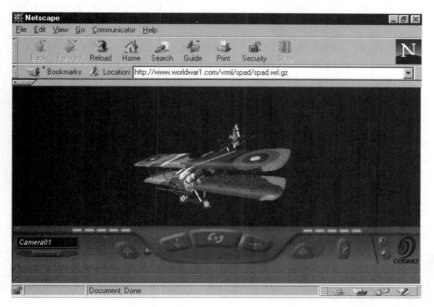

You start out at the home or starting point, but you can move anywhere in the world. To move, you must click and drag the mouse in any direction. For example, to move forward, you click once and drag the mouse forward. To turn left, you simply click and drag your mouse left, and so on for any direction in which you'd like to turn. The speed at which you turn your mouse determines the speed you move in a particular direction. If you ever get disoriented or want to start over, you can click on the Home button and come back to the starting location.

Moving around in a VRML world can be disorienting. That's because you can quickly spin yourself around to a new direction and not know where you are. Also, each viewer has its own controls for moving and viewing objects. The Cosmo Player lets you move and manipulate objects in a number of ways. You choose what you want to do from the dashboard panel at the bottom of the VRML window. It has two sets of controls that change at the flip of a switch on the dashboard: The first is for movements and the other is for object manipulation.

Movement Controls

You can move through worlds by the dashboard and mouse, keyboard controls, or a combination of both. The dashboard can be switched from the navigation controls to the manipulation control by switching a lever on the dashboard. The default selection is the navigation controls (see Figure 17.6).

The various buttons on the dashboard are lit, unlit, or completely deactivated for a particular file. You can click on any button (if active) to control your movements:

Go. This is the default control and the most common way to travel. It is the way you walk or move around in any world. Simply select this button and click and drag your mouse to move in any direction. You can also use the arrow keys to move in any direction.

Slide. Slide means that you move in a straight direction, like going straight up or straight down. You can also choose to move left or right for sidestepping without turning from your vantage point. As with Go, you simply select this button and click and drag to slide. Use Slide with the

Figure 17.6 The dashboard has all the controls you need to move around. Simply click and drag your mouse to move in any direction.

Float control. You can also choose the ALT key or the right-click button on the mouse to select Slide.

Tilt. Tilt can be compared to turning your head. You can tilt your head in any direction but you won't move anywhere. Simply select this button and then click and drag to tilt. You can also choose Tilt by pressing and holding the CTRL button while moving the mouse. When you let go of the CTRL key, the control will return to the Go control.

Gravity. Push the Gravity button when you want to stay on the ground. If it is selected, you won't be able to move far off the ground, but you can still use the movement controls to travel up or down or in any direction.

Float. Use Float for when you want to fly. Float works with the Slide control for going up and down. You move forward or back by using the Go button.

Undo Move. Pressing this button will take you to the last place you stopped. This is useful for when you get into a weird spot or don't know where you are.

Redo Move. Once you've pressed the Undo button, the Redo Move button becomes active. Press Redo to jump through the Undo selections.

Straighten. In case you get disoriented and want to level out, press the Straighten button. This will make you level out horizontally.

Seek. Seek means that you will travel to any item that you click on. Press the Seek button, then click on anything in the world. You will quickly be taken directly to that spot.

 There are various keyboard shortcuts, too. This is helpful because clicking and dragging the mouse a lot can wear out your mouse hand and your clicking finger. It's a good idea to look through the Help file for more on the keyboard controls.

Manipulation and Interaction

The manipulation controls work best when looking at a solitary object floating in space. Sometimes the movement controls won't even be active, so you'll have no choice but to just manipulate objects. These controls allow you to inspect objects, rotate them, or zoom in for a closer look. The three manipulation buttons are:

Rotate. Like the movement controls, you simply select this button and then click and drag in any direction to rotate the object.

Zoom. Push this button, then click and drag forward or backward to zoom in or out. This is good for moving straight to a selected object or location.

Pan. Selecting Pan moves the object left, right, up, or down, but without turning it.

Viewpoints

The quickest way to move around or change viewpoints is to use the Viewpoint controls. On the left side of the dashboard, the Viewpoint controls consist of a left and right arrow and a dropdown menu where you can select a new viewpoint. Viewpoints are programmed by the VRML author, so there may be no viewpoints or just a few. Select the dropdown menu to see what's available for a particular VRML file. When you select a new viewpoint, you will move quickly to that new spot. Similarly, the left and right arrows take you back and forth through the list of viewpoints.

Animations

VRML 2.0 is great because you can see animations and hear synchronized sounds or voices. You probably won't know if an image has animation or another corresponding effect unless you try it. Simply glide your mouse pointer around the image. When the pointer turns into a starburst (or a hand or something else in your VRML browser), it means there is an event associated with that object or area when you click on it. To help you, the status bar on your browser or the dashboard should give a description of the event. Sometimes it will take you to another VRML file, or to a new URL; it can really be any MIME type that your browser can handle. Simply click on the object to see what happens. If nothing happens when you click on it, try dragging the object.

 When there is audio in a VRML file, you are usually notified. That's because you shouldn't click on the object until it has finished downloading; otherwise, you won't hear the audio track. Simply wait until the VRML download stops and then click on the corresponding object to begin the animation and listen to the audio.

If there is animation, the sequence should start playing and there may even be audio. Other times, you'll just hear a sound or voice. It all depends on what the

VRML author programmed the file to do upon clicking on it. If the event was another WRL file or any other HTML page, that page will be loaded and displayed.

Changing the Dashboard and Other Options

You can change the look of the Cosmo dashboard to make more room for the VRML file. You can minimize or maximize the dashboard and the descriptive text line by pressing the Up or Down buttons on the extreme left side. You can have a compact display or even remove the dashboard completely (see Figure 17.7).

On the right side of the dashboard, you can choose other options like Help and the Preferences menu. Click on the Preferences button to change a number of options like speed, collision detection, headlights, image quality, mouse and keyboard controls, audio options, and other advanced controls. Last, you can also go to Silicon Graphics' Cosmo page by clicking on the Cosmo logo. From there, you can download new software or find new VRML worlds to explore.

About Cosmo Software

Cosmo Software is a division of Silicon Graphics, a huge player in the 3-D computing field. Silicon Graphics makes workstations, servers, and software, too. Cosmo Software makes a VRML authoring program called Cosmo Worlds for creating VRML graphics and worlds. Cosmo Worlds is available for UNIX and Windows NT. The Cosmo VRML Player is available for Windows95, NT, and some UNIX systems. To download the player, go to cosmo.sgi.com. You can also visit the

Figure 17.7 VRML authors can custom design a view, like creating a separate window or with no dashboard.

VRML Gallery at vrml.sgi.com to see some cool VRML objects, animations, and worlds.

WorldView 2.5 by Intervista Software

The next popular VRML 2.0 viewer is WorldView by Intervista. It is similar to Cosmo but has different controls and options. A version of WorldView is being bundled with Internet Explorer 4.0, and it can be downloaded as a separate component from the Help/Product Updates menu selection.

After you install WorldView, reboot your computer and go view some VRML files. The basic controls don't differ much from Cosmo, but it is good to know what they can do. There is a vertical control panel on the left side of the screen and another on the bottom (see Figure 17.8).

All the controls in WorldView are reviewed next. In all cases, once you press one of the buttons, you can control movement by using the mouse. As with Cosmo, you simply click and drag the mouse in any direction to move around. The distance that you drag the mouse will determine how fast you will move. When you stop dragging the mouse, you will stop moving. The mouse cursor will change to the

Figure 17.8 WorldView by Intervista is another popular player. It has similar controls to Cosmo but puts them on vertical and horizontal control bars.

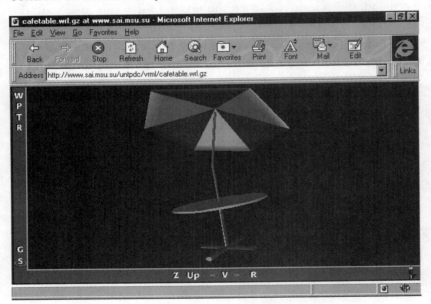

corresponding button graphic so you know what mode you are in. Alternatively, you can also use the arrows keys to control movement.

Walk. Allows you to move around. You simply click and drag the mouse in any direction.

Pan. Select this button to move in any direction on a vertical plane. This makes it easy to move an object around and center it on your window.

Turn. Turn changes the angle of your view. You can view it from any direction.

Roll. Use this button to rotate the object along a point in the center of the window. It will turn clockwise or counterclockwise, depending on which way you drag your mouse. Moving the mouse up and down will have no effect with Roll.

Goto. Click on this button and then click on any object to quickly zoom in for a closer look. Sometimes this won't always work correctly; it depends on what the VRML author programmed the file to do.

Study. This allows you to rotate an object in any direction. Click on Study and click and drag the mouse to any direction.

The bottom of the window has more controls:

Zoom Out. Click this once to move away from the image so everything is in view.

Straighten Up. If you get turned upside down and need to level yourself horizontally, press this button.

Viewpoints. This is the quickest way to travel around a scene. Use the left and right arrows to go to predefined views as programmed by the author. If there are no views programmed, the arrows will be inactive and grayed out. You can also click on the View button to look at all the viewpoints and choose any one.

Restore. Restore takes you back to the starting position or your original viewpoint when the file first loaded.

At any point, you can right-click on the window and bring up a small menu to change viewpoints or other program options. You can change graphics, textures, headlight, speed, and more.

Like Cosmo, WorldView can play animations, sounds, or jump to other locations. When you come across an activated object, your cursor will change into a hand. Just click on the object to see what happens.

WorldView is available for Windows and Macintosh users as a plug-in for Netscape Navigator or Microsoft Internet Explorer. It is available free of charge from Intervista Software's site (www.intervista.com).

Microsoft VRML 2.0 Viewer

Microsoft has its own VRML viewer that can be downloaded as a component of Internet Explorer 4.0. It is based on Intervista's WorldView 2.0.

If you are using Internet Explorer 4.0, you shouldn't download the plug-in from Intervista's site. Instead, download the viewer as a component of Internet Explorer by selecting Product Updates from the Help menu, then select to download the VRML 2.0 viewer.

Internet Explorer 3.x users can use this viewer as well, but they'll need to download and install Microsoft Java, DirectX, and ActiveMovie first. You can download the player from Microsoft's VRML site at www.microsoft.com/vrml. To create VRML files, Microsoft also has a VRML 2.0 Tools CD available for Windows95 and NT users.

Community Place Browser by Sony

Sony created a site called Community Place as a place to go to visit VRML worlds and meet people in a multiuser environment. You can also download Sony's VRML 2.0 viewer, called the Community Place Browser. It is available as a Navigator plug-in and a standalone browser for Windows95 and NT. The standalone browser is very handy when using non-Navigator browsers.

The standalone browser works like any other VRML viewer. When you click on a WRL file, the external Community Place browser will open. It then loads the WRL file and displays it after it has finished downloading. The controls are similar to most 3-D viewers. On the right side of the window are the main controls: Walk, Turn, Float, Home, Back, Forward, and Stop. There are also arrow selections at the bottom of the window, so you can click and move with those buttons as well. The Community Place Browser really looks and feels like a brand new browser. You can load new VRML pages or type in a location for a local file. Another cool feature is that you can bookmark VRML files. Like other programs you can also change lighting, textures, sounds, and the general look of the browser (see Figure 17.9).

Figure 17.9 The Community Place Browser is a good standalone browser for viewing VRML 2.0 files. There are plenty of multiuser worlds you can explore, too.

When you install the Community Place world, you can visit the Community Place Bureau and visit multiuser worlds. You need to choose your 3-D persona, or avatar, that will represent you and then enter the world to meet new people. In a multiuser world, the browser connects to a server where many people can log in, chat, and interact with each other. You see the avatars that they choose to represent themselves and you can chat in private groups or one on one or just walk around and explore. You can also get a voice-enabled plug-in so you can actually speak to other people.

Visit Sony's Community Place at vs.spiw.com for more information and to download the browser software.

Liquid Reality by DimensionX/Microsoft

Microsoft is yet again in the VRML world with a VRML viewer called Liquid Reality. DimensionX, the company that makes Liquid Reality, was acquired by Microsoft in May 1997, so it was unknown what the status or name of the new VRML viewer would be.

Liquid Reality was still available for download as of this writing, but it may be absorbed into a new product by the time you read this. The VRML viewer was written in Java and is similar to other VRML 2.0 viewers.

Liquid Reality is available for Windows 95/NT and some UNIX systems (Solaris and Linux). DimensionX was known as the industry's first Java startup and made the Liquid Reality VRML plug-in and 3-D authoring tools. For more on Liquid Reality and the DimensionX software line, go to www.microsoft.com/dimensionx or see Microsoft's VRML site at www.microsoft.com/vrml.

Other VRML Viewers

There's not enough space to show all the VRML viewers available; however, the following sections give you some options.

VR Scout by Chaco

The VR Scout VRML viewer was created by a company called Chaco Communications, but it merged with a company called LikeMinds (www.likeminds.com). VR Scout is available as a plug-in or ActiveX control that works with Windows95 and NT. It also comes as an external viewer for those browsers that can't handle plug-ins. For more information, visit Chaco's site (www.chaco.com).

Community Client 3D by blaxxun

The Community Client 3D is a VRML viewer from blaxxun Interactive, formerly Black Sun Interactive. It only comes as an ActiveX control for Internet Explorer on Windows 95/NT and they even have a scaled-down Java client. blaxxun also makes passports for multiuser worlds, so come here when you need to enter a multiuser world. Check out blaxxun's website at www.blaxxun.com.

Platinum WIRL by Platinum

Platinum's WIRL was originally made by VREAM and is still a popular VRML viewer. WIRL is available for Windows95 and is an ActiveX control for Internet Explorer 3.x and higher. Download it at www.platinum.com.

Zeus by Virtek International

Zeus is a VRML plug-in for Navigator and Internet Explorer, and claims to be one of the fastest viewers. See for yourself by visiting Virtek (www.zeus.virtek.com) and downloading the Windows95 and NT software.

Non-VRML 2.0 Viewers

For a complete 3-D experience, you shouldn't miss out on other viewers and 3-D viewers—there aren't that many. The biggest and most important one is Superscape's Viscape viewer. It is very similar to VRML. Fortunately, it is possible to run these non-VRML viewers alongside VRML 2.0 viewers since they accept different file types.

Try them out and see what other 3-D worlds are available besides VRML.

Viscape

Viscape is a very popular 3-D viewer, but it is not usable with VRML 2.0. That means you won't be able to use it for most worlds since they are almost all VRML 2.0. Viscape uses its own proprietary authoring tool called VRT to create 3-D worlds.

The viewer itself looks like any other HTML browser, with simple point-and-click options. You can control the resolution and texture detail as well as many other options. Viscape is used for exploring worlds, not so much for viewing and manipulating still objects like VRML.

Simply install Viscape and go to the Virtual World Wide Web (vwww.com) to explore this new world. The VWWW is really a world in every sense of the word—the first 3-D scene you see is your default world called SuperCity. In SuperCity, you can walk around, click on objects, and visit many different locations. It's your jumping-off point to the more than 400 different places to explore. There are games, shopping, entertainment, simulations, and multiuser worlds. The multiuser worlds are lots of fun since you can walk around, interact with objects, and talk to other real-life people. And SuperCity isn't the only city out there; a few companies have created their own cities that you can explore (see Figure 17.10).

The Viscape interface is similar to VRML browsers. You can walk, look around, and zoom in on objects. You can click on an object and it may take you to another virtual world, make a sound, or open up an HTML page. There are only three movement buttons. To walk around, you must first click on the Walk control button and then drag your mouse in any direction. You can sidestep left or right by pressing another button showing left and right arrows. The last button is for looking up and down. You can also press the Level button to make yourself horizontal or press Reset to go back to the starting point in the world. If you're exploring a far-off world, just press the Home button to take yourself back to the SuperCity.

The Viscape viewer can play just Superscape VRT files and their compressed files, SVR. It is available as an ActiveX control and Navigator plug-in for Windows

Figure 17.10 This is Cy-Berlin, a 3-D representation of Berlin. This is just one of 400 3-D sites that you can visit through the Virtual World Wide Web.

3.x, 95, and NT. It supports Microsoft Direct3D and is free for download at www.superscape.com. For more on creating virtual worlds, visit Superscape and check out its VRT, 3D Webmaster, and DO 3D authoring tools.

Quick3D by Plastic Thought

Quick3D is a viewer plug-in that lets you see Quick3D files (3DMF and QD3) from inside your browser. Since it is not a VRML viewer, it just displays files made by Quick3D. Like VRML, you can move around, view the object from any angle, and zoom in and out, but you are mostly limited to static objects and not whole worlds like VRML or Viscape (see Figure 17.11). Before watching Q3D files, you must go to quickdraw3d.apple.com and install QuickDraw 3D.

The free Quick3D plug-in is available for Navigator and Internet Explorer for both Macintosh and Windows computers. Plastic Thought also has many clip art 3-D images that you can try out or purchase for use on your website. Visit Plastic Thought's website (www.plasticthought.com) for more information and to create some Quick3D files yourself.

Figure 17.11 The Quick3D plug-in lets you quickly see 3-D images in your browser window.

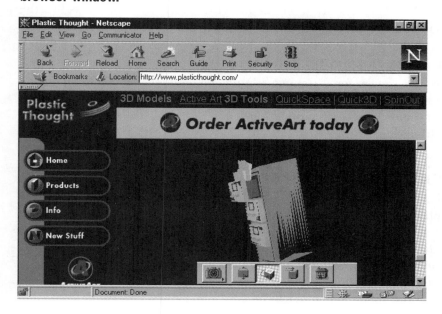

RealSpace Viewer by LivePicture

The RealSpace Viewer is a VRML viewer but it primarily plays LivePicture's RealSpace Image Worlds (IVR) files. It is available as a plug-in or a helper application for Windows 95/NT and Macintosh computers. Unfortunately, RealSpace Viewer is not completely compliant with VRML 2.0, so it is darn near impossible to view any VRML 2.0 worlds. Best stick with the VRML 2.0 viewers mentioned previously.

OLiVR by OLiVR/LivePicture

OLiVR was the first streaming 3-D player, but it was bought by LivePicture, Inc. LivePicture is known for its 360-degree panoramic, photorealistic images that could be seen with a browser plug-in (see next section for more). OLiVR (Online Interactive Virtual Reality) was a breakthrough program because it allowed streaming of 3-D objects. Although it was not VRML compatible, its results were very good and very quick. After just a few seconds of loading, the image appeared. It would download and display the rest of the image progressively.

For more on OLiVR, try www.olivr.com to see if that site is still available. If not, check out LivePicture's website (www.livepicture.com) to see what they're doing with OLiVR. Chances are it will be integrated into other products like the RealSpace Viewer.

RealiView 3D by Datapath Limited

RealiView is the viewer for watching 3-D images created by the RealiMation Space Time Editor. It works on Windows 95/NT for both Navigator and Internet Explorer. For more on creating RealiMation or to download software, go to www.realimation.com

Panoramic and Photorealistic 3-D

Yet another subset of 3-D are panoramic photos that can simulate 3-D. These panoramic photos offer 360-degree views of any scene, like a skyline, a room, or the set of a TV show. These images are actual photos (so-called photorealistic) as opposed to the completely computer-generated graphics of VRML and other 3-D programs. Pictures are stitched together to form a complete, 360-degree view. You can view anything by panning left or right, then zooming in or out. There are also hotspots so you can travel to another location or open a new web page.

Is this really 3-D? Not really. You can't walk through any location like you can with VRML, nor can you manipulate objects or see animations.

There are no file standards for panoramic images; all are proprietary and need their own respective viewers and plug-ins to view them over the Internet. The most popular program is Apple's QuickTime VR. Some of the 3-D panoramic programs available are discussed next.

QuickTime VR (QTVR) by Apple

No matter what Apple calls it, QuickTime VR is not a virtual reality program, but a 360-degree panoramic viewer for photorealistic images. You need the QTVR plug-in to see QTVR files, but there are lots already available. You can zoom in and out and pan left or right to see any part of the picture. It also includes hyperlinks or hotspots that can take you to another location (see Figure 17.12).

The QTVR plug-in is available for Macs and Windows 3.x, 95/NT. You can also download QTVR files and view them off line with the QuickTime player. Apple also makes the QuickTime VR Authoring Studio for creating QTVR images. For more on QTVR, visit Apple's site at quicktimevr.apple.com.

Figure 17.12 QuickTime VR is the most popular panoramic program. This is one striking example of a 360-degree view of the Grand Canyon.

LivePicture by LivePicture

LivePicture revolutionized 360-degree panoramic pictures on the Web and it is one of the most popular panoramic picture formats on the Internet. Like QTVR, you can pan or zoom to any location, and there are hotspots, too. The big difference with LivePicture is that it now supports Java playback. That means you can see LivePicture images without a plug-in; just use a Java-enabled browser (see Figure 17.13).

LivePicture makes a full line of picture editing software and Internet viewers. It also makes PhotoVista (for creating panoramic images) as well as RealSpace (a 3-D program similar to VRML). For more, visit LivePicture's homepage at www.livepicture.com.

Jutvision by Visdyn Software Corp.

Like LivePicture, Jutvision doesn't use plug-ins to view its panoramic pictures; it uses Java playback so practically any browser can view them. Download times are kept small as well; images appear very quickly. Like other programs, you can zoom

Figure 17.13 LivePicture is another popular format. It has a Java viewer for no-plug-in viewing of its panoramic images.

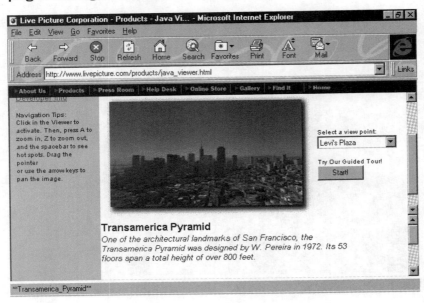

in and out or pan left and right (360 degrees). It also supports hotspots. Visit Visdyn Software at www.jutvision.com.

Surround Video by Black Diamond

Surround Video gets its name because it can use any still picture camera or even video camera to get 360-degree panoramic photos. It uses LivePicture's PhotoVista image stitching tool to patch the still images together to create a full panoramic image. You can also add hotspots, text, and sound. Surround Video needs an ActiveX control to view pictures on the Web. For more information, visit Black Diamond at www.bdiamond.com.

Creating VRML Worlds

You don't need to be a god to create a VRML world, nor do you need six days. You just need a computer, mouse, a little creativity, and a VRML creator. VRML authoring programs range from easy drag-and-drop tools to more complex Java and script-oriented programs. Although you can create VRML files by text coding, you'd have to be a mathematical genius to do it. It's clearly better to use the graphical programs that do it all for you. Creating VRML worlds has a steep learning curve, so don't expect to become a master overnight. Always remember the end user and try to keep your file size low for transmission over the Internet.

Check out the following list and visit each company's website for more information and to download trial versions.

Sony	Community Place Conductor	vs.spiw.com
Cosmo Software	Cosmo Worlds	cosmo.sgi.com
Cosmo Software	HomeSpace	cosmo.sgi.com
Microsoft	VRML Tools	www.microsoft.com/vrml
Platinum Technology	PlatinumVR Creator	www.platinum.com
3D Web	Spinner	www.3dweb.com
Radiance Software	Ez3D	www.radiance.com
Rapid Imaging Software	Landform	www.landform.com
Caligari	TrueSpace	www.caligari.com
Electric Café	ModelShop	www.eleccafe
Virtus	3-D Website Builder	www.virtus.com
Kinetix	3D Studio Max	www.ktx.com
Macromedia	Extreme 3D	www.macromedia.com
Ligos Technology	V-Realm Builder	www.ligos.com

VRML97 and Streaming VRML

One of the main reasons for VRML's success is that it is an international standard. In order to create standards, the VRML Consortium (www.vrml.org) was founded by a handful of companies. The VRML 2.0 specification was formally released in 1996, but work on the next version called VRML97 was already in full swing. In December 1997, VRML97 was ratified as an international standard by the ISO (International Standards Organization) and IEC (the International Electrotechnical Commission).

The VRML Consortium is also working on something called the VRML Streaming Channel Protocol, or VSCP. This new protocol would allow streaming of VRML (.WRL) files over IP networks. Although it was somewhat in the formative stages, VSCP was moving forward. Already, two companies, Cosmo and Intervista, have some type of competing streaming VRML capabilities. It is hoped that VSCP will also unify this new streaming format. You can read all the VRML specifications and get more information at the VRML Consortium homepage.

A Summary View of VRML

In terms of technology, VRML is just in its infancy. Although graphics have become more sophisticated and more realistic, there is still room for improvement with VRML; it is by no means perfect. Fortunately, advances in VRML are happening all the time. Here are some things that can improve VRML:

Streaming. Another way to make VRML more enjoyable is to use streaming VRML. Some vendors have already released some streaming, but standards and better compression are needed.

More adherence to standards. Speaking of standards, VRML needs better support from all 3-D developers—there are too many competing 3-D standards. Imagine if there was a competing standard for HTML? How fast would web growth have been? VRML needs these standards to grow just as fast.

Java playback. Will we ever see a Java applet that can play VRML files? It's possible. A no-plug-in solution would be great, but we're not even close to this yet. There are just too many VRML viewers available.

More intuitive controls. There are many different viewers, and each has its own movement and manipulation controls. Walking around in a VRML world can be tough, but it can be even worse if you have to figure out different controls for every program. There should be an easier way to move around. Think joysticks or keyboard controls. At the very least, let users choose which controls they want, much like you can change your movement controls in a 3-D game like Quake or Doom.

A killer app. So far, there are lots of applications for VRML, but nothing so impressive that there is a great overwhelming need for it. Entertainment is the best reason for VRML right now, but there is no killer app for VRML yet.

More support for VR hardware. Wouldn't it be great fun to have a VR headset and gloves to manipulate VRML objects? I think so, too. Unfortunately, there isn't much hardware available. Of course, this new hardware would be expensive, but boy would it be fun.

Multiuser worlds. Walking and interacting in a multiuser world is a lot of fun; it is also a great way to build a community on the Internet. Unfortunately, the novelty dies off after a while, especially when you go to a world with a population of zero and you're just walking around by yourself. Nevertheless, multiuser worlds will be a big deal one day.

How can VRML achieve more popularity? It needs native support from the two major browsers. Now that version 4.0 of Navigator and Internet Explorer have been released and 5.0 is just around the corner, VRML needs to play a bigger role. A built-in VRML viewer would go a long way. It would also help if America Online would somehow introduce VRML to its users.

As more people learn about VRML, it will gain in popularity. Why keep VRML a secret? The sky is the limit for VRML. Who knows what 3-D technology will enable us to do in a few years? After all, who could have imagined that we'd be where we are today with computers? Years from now, 3-D may be so popular that we may even be able to trash our keyboards and monitors and work with our computers in a 3-D world.

STREAMING
Email

18

Streaming email does not constitute a large portion of the streaming multimedia market. As such, this chapter only has one program, Video Express Email, that streams audio and video files. The other program, VideoLink Mail, makes self-playing files that must be downloaded completely before playing. VideoLink Mail is included here because it is such an easy-to-use program and because its compression is so good that a two-minute video message takes up only 1MB. With that ratio, it almost seems like streaming.

Both programs are targeted mostly to the consumer market. Consumers can make better use of them because they usually don't have access to web server space to dump their streaming files. Also, both work with capture cards and multimedia computers, something that corporate workers often lack. Both programs allow you record audio or video messages, but only VideoLink Mail lets you add existing multimedia files like AVI, WAV, and QuickTime movies.

Before starting on these two programs, however, let's revisit the world of streaming files and pointer files for a minute, so we can learn how the streaming email program works.

Streaming Email with Other Systems

As you've probably seen elsewhere in this book, the concept of using redirector or pointer files with streaming multimedia programs is almost universal. That's because the pointer file actually contains the location and information that your browser needs to stream it. Without one, your browser simply tries to download the file.

To the typical user trying to watch streaming multimedia, pointer files are invisible—users don't really know about them. All they know is that they have to click on a particular link to watch the movie. Then when the browser gets the file, it should automatically load the correct application, like the RealPlayer or the NetShow Player. To the web developer, creating these pointer files is crucial.

Pointer files are good because they are small and can be used practically anywhere. Although we've mostly been using them on web pages, they can also be inserted into email messages, put on your hard drive, inserted into Word documents, or carried around on a floppy disk. You can create a directory that just has pointer files and use them like a bookmark (see Figure 18.1). This is especially useful for programs that don't have a favorites or bookmark feature.

You can save pointer files to your hard disk in a number of ways:

• When using the Windows version of Navigator, right-click on the link and choose Save Link As. Mac users have a Save option by holding down the mouse button until the context-sensitive menu pops up.

Figure 18.1 Save your redirector or pointer files to your hard drive and organize them any way you want. Here, I've changed filenames and made a subdirectory so I can quickly access my favorite Internet broadcasts.

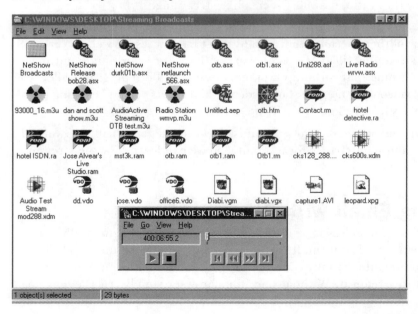

- If you're using Netscape, hold down the Shift key while clicking on the link. The Save As window appears, and you can select where you want to save the file. This is a shortcut for using the Save As for when you want to download a link. You can do this with any file type, like EXE, ZIP, or AVI and QuickTime files.

- Also in Netscape, right-click on a link and then select the Create Shortcut option in the menu. A small window will pop up displaying the URL and description of the link. Just press OK to close the window and save the shortcut to your desktop. From there, you can copy it to any sub-directory and rename it to something that you understand.

- In both Internet Explorer and Navigator, you can just click and drag a link anywhere and create Internet shortcuts. This is performed by clicking on the link, holding it, and then dragging it anywhere you want. Just let go of the mouse button to drop it somewhere. Many choose to place them on the Windows desktop for easy access. Since these are just shortcuts, you can move or delete them as you normally would.

- Another way of using pointer files is to save them as bookmarks or favorites. In Internet Explorer, simply right-click on the link and choose the Add to Favorites option. The pointer files will appear in the Favorites menu and then you can move them to folders to better organize them. Navigator works the same way except its menu options reads Add Bookmark.

Once you have the pointer files on your hard disk, you can then send them via email to a friend or colleague; just attach them to your email using your favorite email program. The pointer files are very small text files, usually no more than 1K, so they transfer quickly. When the recipient receives the message with the attachment, he or she can just double-click on it or save it to his or her hard disk. Double-clicking the file will automatically launch the appropriate player and play the file—as long as they stay connected to the Internet. The main problem with this way of sending streaming email is that sometimes the recipient doesn't have the proper player installed.

How can we overcome this problem? The streaming email program described in this chapter overcomes this dilemma in two ways: by providing a built-in player that is included in the file or attaching a small player that must be installed (just once) before playing files. VideoExpress Email even uses a pointer-file type solution.

VideoLink Mail

VideoLink Mail by Smith Micro Software is not a streaming player, but it is a very good system for sending and receiving video emails. To send video emails, you need to have a video camera attached to your computer and record the video live; VideoLink Mail does not accept pre-recorded audio or video messages. Receiving messages is where VideoLink Mail really shines—you can send video or audio emails in EXE format so all a person has to do is execute the file to watch the video—no player is needed because it is built into the EXE file. Since VideoLink Mail doesn't stream, it must be attached to email messages and downloaded completely before viewing.

The output EXE file compresses the audio and video very well. That's because VideoLink Mail uses compression technology from Smith Micro's videoconferencing software, Audiovision. A one-minute message can be as small as 500KB. As you can imagine, shorter clips take up very little disk space and more importantly, take less time to download.

VideoLink Mail messages are the next best thing to face-to-face communications. It really is videoconferencing over email—like sending a video voice mail. It is best used for personal communications and talking-head videos. It is not well suited for large broadcasts since you'll be sending out large files to everyone on your recipient list.

Sending VideoLink Mail Messages

Sending messages with VideoLink Mail is easy but is limited to those people with an input video source. You can use a parallel-port camera or a camera that connects to a video capture board. If you don't have video support at your desktop, you can still record audio if you have multimedia and audio capabilities. VideoLink Mail comes bundled with Smith Micro's videoconferencing program, which is sometimes included in videoconferencing kits.

When you start VideoLink Mail, you see all the controls that you need. There are Stop, Play, and Record buttons, a few other control buttons, a small video window, and not much else (see Figure 18.2). Before recording your message, you should type your name or email address at the Setup/User Name option from the menu.

To record, turn on your video source—you should see yourself smiling back at the camera. Then it is as simple as pressing the Record button to record yourself. To add audio, just click on the Talk button and begin speaking. When you're finished, just press the Stop button. You can then play back the file by pressing the Play button. Basically, that's all there is to it. Select the Tuning button to select some video options like brightness, color, and video screen size. You can only choose from among three video sizes: large (176×144), medium (144×112), and small (112×80). Not much of a range, but it's necessary for keeping the file sizes down.

Figure 18.2 VideoLink Mail opens to a blank video screen. Turn on your video and press the REC button to record your message.

To send a VideoLink Mail file, you can press the Mail button. Your default email program should then load and will attach the EXE file to a new outgoing mail message. If you select the Save button, you can save the EXE file anywhere on your hard drive.

Receiving VideoLink Mail Messages

When you receive a VideoLink Mail from someone, it arrives as an attachment. Simply save the message to your hard drive or double-click on the attachment to launch it. Immediately, the video will launch and begin to play. You can also load VideoLink Mail messages from your hard disk in the same way—just double-click to play them.

In the beginning of the video, you will see the name of the person who created the video. When the video ends, you get a self-promotional message from Smith Micro and it then closes by itself.

Should You Use VideoLink Mail?

Perhaps the only downside to VideoLink Mail is that it is for use with people using Windows computers only; Macintosh users are again left by the wayside. Since the

Internet community has a variety of operating systems and platforms, VideoLink Mail ignores a big chunk of the population. The only other problem is that you need to have a camera installed on your computer, so that rules out a large segment of business computers. In many ways, VideoLink Mail is a more of a consumer program than a business tool.

VideoLink Mail is best for people who own videoconferencing cameras or those with video capture cards who can connect video cameras to their computers. As such, it is best for talking-head videos. However, VideoLink Mail can also just record audio as an EXE file. This is useful for sending quick files out to friends or colleagues when you haven't time to get ready for the camera or are camera-shy. VideoLink Mail comes bundled with some cameras and videoconferencing systems. It also works with Smith Micro's videoconferencing program, Audiovision. VideoLink Mail is available for $29.95 for Windows95.

Smith Micro Software, Inc.
51 Columbia
Aliso Viejo, CA 92656
(714) 362-5800
www.smithmicro.com

Video Express Email

Video Express Email is a streaming email system that allows you to send streaming multimedia to anyone, whether he or she has the Video Express Email player installed or not. The player can be sent along with the multimedia message and installed. Video Express Email works differently than VideoLink Mail, however. First, when you send a message, you're just sending out the text pointer (or redirector) file. That means a very quick, no-download email delivery for the recipient. To play the file, the recipient just needs to double-click on that link and it begins streaming. Naturally, the person must stay connected to the Internet when receiving and playing Video Express Email messages.

Another difference is that sending streaming multimedia mail with Video Express Email means installing a (large) program to send out messages. (Any email client program like Eudora, America Online, or Netscape Mail can actually receive messages.) At first glance, the program looks like any regular email program except that there are other options for recording and creating multimedia files (see Figure 18.3). You can attach stored files or record brand new audio or video programs from within Video Express Email and then send them out. Like VideoLink Mail, that means you need to have audio and, optionally, video input installed on your computer.

Figure 18.3 With the Video Express Email program you can load or record your own streaming audio and video messages. It has an interface that resembles an email program.

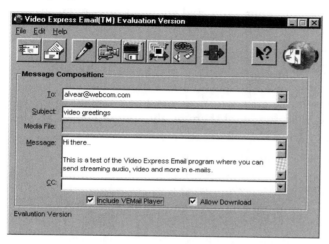

Perhaps the best way to experience Video Express Email is to view files that are sent to you. Visit ImageMind's website to send yourself some mail; you can choose from audio, video, or slide shows. Just enter your name, email address, and Internet connection speed and you will be sent a file via email. If this is your first time using Video Express Email, check the option to receive the player, too. In a few minutes, you will receive the test email. Simply use any email program to open it, install the player, and then view the audio or video message.

Video Express Email can use ASF, WAV, AVI, and QuickTime files. You can also choose to stream a PowerPoint presentation.

Video Express Email is available for Windows95 and NT only. (Macintosh versions are forthcoming, says the company.) Pricing is rather peculiar; it is based on a subscription basis that starts at $5 a month for unlimited messages. Purchasing the Video Express Email program to create files costs an additional $59.99. Image Mind also keeps a directory of Video Express Email users so you can exchange messages with other users.

Sending Messages with Video Express Email

Working with Video Express Email is like using a regular email program. Just enter the recipient's email address, any text message, and then select the multimedia file to use—that's it. Follow these steps for a more in-depth, step-by-step procedure.

1. First, when you first start Video Express Email, you have to go through some routine setup questions like your name and email address and your Internet connection speed. Then you're sent to the main screen, which looks like a blank email message.

2. To send a Video Express Email message, simply enter in the recipient's email address and type in your message and subject like you normally would. Next comes the multimedia portion. You can choose to send an audio, video, or slide show. You can record them on the spot or choose an existing file from your hard drive.

3. If want to record and send video, press the Video button, and a new capture window will appear. Select your video compression (Video Express Email recommends you pick Full Frames, Uncompressed format for best quality), then wait for your local window to appear (see Figure 18.4). From there, you can start recording by pressing the red Record button, or change your options under the Options menu selection, like your window size or color controls.

4. After you record your message, select File/Exit and you will jump back to the main Video Express Email screen. The video you just recorded should

Figure 18.4 The capture window appears, and the local video window is shown so you can begin recording your video greeting.

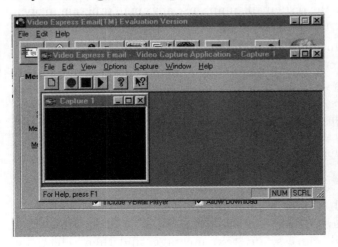

appear in the Media File section, along with its path and filename. Remember, you can also send audio or existing multimedia images in the same way. You can also send slide shows created for NetShow.

5. If this is the first Video Express Email message that your recipient will receive, he or she will need to download and install the Video Express Email Player. Check the box that reads "Include VEMail Player" to attach a copy of the player along with the rest of the message. Optionally, your recipient can visit Image Mind's website to download the player, which will need to be installed once per computer.

6. It is a good idea to preview the multimedia file before sending it. After you've finished recording or selecting your outgoing multimedia file, preview it by pressing the Preview Message button. You will be asked to choose a bandwidth speed that you want to compress it to. Then press OK to begin watching the preview for that bandwidth. You can always change your compression and bandwidth selection before sending the message. To change your codec options, go back to the main menu and choose File/Preferences. From there, open up the Audio Transport Rate Preferences screen to change codecs and audio options, like lowering the sample rate, switching to mono or stereo, and so forth.

7. Once you've previewed the file, you can press the Send button to send your message. You will be asked if you want to change your compression and bandwidth settings before you continue. If you are happy with the existing configuration that you chose during preview, leave it as is and continue sending the file; otherwise, select a new bandwidth. You can choose from 14.4Kbps all the way to T1 speeds. Once you choose a speed, the program will encode the multimedia file.

 You must be sure to convert your file to a bandwidth that is less than your recipient's Internet connection speed. If you convert it to a higher speed, the clip won't play. You can choose from 14.4 to 28.8, 33.6, ISDN, and T1 speeds, so try to match them as best as possible.

8. Your next option is to select your transport protocol. Choose from Video Express Email Transport or regular Internet protocol. The Video Express Email Protocol is supposed to be more reliable, but your results will vary.

9. Finally, press the Send button and the message will be sent. Make sure you're connected to the Internet at this point; otherwise, transmission

will stop. As the message is being sent, you'll see a scrolling message saying "Transport in Progress" running across the window. You'll receive notification when the message transmission is completed.

Some options to consider before sending a message include attaching the player to the message in case the recipient doesn't have it. Just check off the corresponding box at the bottom of the window. Next to that is the Allow Download checkbox. Enabling that option means that the recipient can also download the actual message as well as stream it. That is a good option for when the recipient would like to have a better quality, perhaps uncompressed, video file.

 To send messages faster, don't send the Video Express Email player or the actual downloadable multimedia file. These seriously slow down your transmission, especially with large files. Only send downloadable files if your recipient absolutely needs a copy for offline viewing.

Choosing the Create Multimedia Slide Show button opens up Microsoft's ASF Editor program. This program allows you to create your own multimedia slide shows that include audio, still pictures, and script commands. (For more on NetShow and the ASF Editor, see Chapter 10, "Microsoft NetShow: The Future of Streaming Media.")

Receiving Video Express Email Messages

When you receive Video Express Email, you get your message the same way as you receive your other emails. Use your regular email program to check your messages. You will get the Video Express Email along with the small text file attachment. Unless you chose to send the player and/or allow downloading, email retrieval from your host will be very fast.

Your email message may look something like Figure 18.5. It includes the Video Express Email player that will allow you to view and stream the file.

If you haven't already done so, click on the file called SETUP.EXE to install the Video Express Email player. Once that's done, it is installed for good and you need not install it again unless you uninstall it later.

The last step is the easiest. Most email programs like Netscape Mail and Eudora allow you to double-click on the message to launch it with its specified player. Double-click on it and the Video Express Email miniplayer should launch and play the message (see Figure 18.6). If you're having trouble receiving the

Figure 18.5 Your email program should display the attached file pointer and the file player called SETUP.EXE. In Eudora Pro, you can just double-click on the VGX pointer file to launch and view the Video Express Email message.

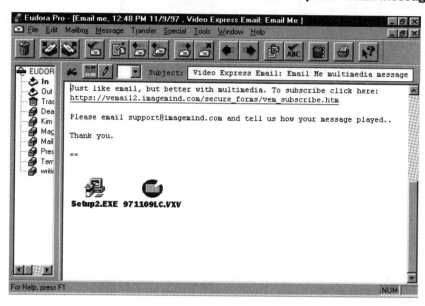

message, it probably means that the multimedia message was encoded for a speed greater than you can handle. Just email the sender and ask him or her to re-encode it to your bandwidth.

If you want to reply with your own Video Express Email message, press the Reply button on the player. If you have Video Express Email installed, it will load and bring up a reply message so you can send back your own multimedia message. When you've finished viewing the file, you will be asked if you want to save it for 30 days or delete it completely. Make sure you want to delete the file because you can't get it back once it's gone.

Should You Use Video Express Email?

The main problem with Video Express Email is its whole underlying framework. Basically, what you send via email is just a pointer file. Once the recipient clicks on it, it loads the player and begins to stream the file. As described earlier, other streaming Windows programs can already do this and they don't need to use an

Figure 18.6 The miniplayer launches and plays the movie back for you. If you receive an audio image, you just see an animated speaker graphic.

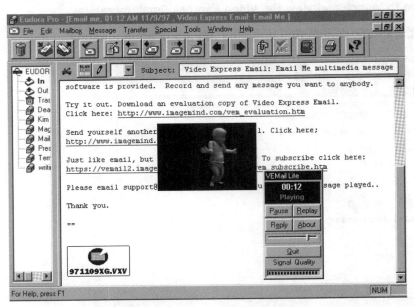

external email program to send streaming messages; you can send any pointer file via your regular email program. For example, with NetShow you simply create your file, upload it to the server, then create the ASX pointer file and attach it to your email. For those who don't have NetShow installed, you can include a link to Microsoft's site to download the player. So, in effect, NetShow and Video Express Email work the same way. The main difference is that with Video Express Email, you don't need to have your own server to upload files.

The other problem is that you don't have much control over the stream. There is no volume control, no Seek bar and, worst of all, you can't save the multimedia files to your hard disk after you finish watching the stream. The sender must attach the actual compressed file to the email message instead. In this case, you already lose out on the benefits of streaming mail if you attach the file.

The main advantage Video Express Email has over the other programs in this chapter is that it does do honest-to-goodness streaming of AVI, QuickTime, ASF, and WAV files. This means you can send very large files without worrying about download times. You also don't need to open your browser to view streaming files, although it can be used as a helper application. You can also send stored media and not just record audio or video like Smith Micro's VideoLink Mail.

Bottom line, Video Express Email is a product for consumers—business users will not want to play with such a clumsy interface, nor will they have time to learn how to send messages with the Video Express Email. Last, the pricing scheme for Video Express Email is just plain awful. After all, who will bother to pay a subscription fee for something that can be accomplished better with other programs? The whole subscription policy seems very misguided in a world of many options for streaming multimedia.

Imagemind Software, Inc.
5 Triad Center, Suite 600
Salt Lake City, UT 84180
801-350-9461
800-321-5933
www.imagemind.com

PureVoice

Qualcomm, makers of the popular Eudora email program, released PureVoice, a program that allows users to send and receive voice email messages. PureVoice isn't a streaming program, but it uses a powerful compression scheme so that the voice files are very small. A 30-second voice message takes up just 40KB. It works with Eudora as a plug-in, but can also be made to work with many other mail programs. You can only record messages, and you can't attach other sound files, so you need a microphone and multimedia computer. Also, both the sender and receiver need to have the program installed (see Figure 18.7).

PureVoice is free and is available for Windows 95/NT computers. Check out Qualcomm at www.qualcomm.com or go directly to Eudora's homepage at www.eudora.com.

CVideo-Mail

Cubic Videocomm, maker of CVideoNow, released an audio and video email program in mid-1997 called CVideo-Mail. CVideo-Mail allows users to record and send video email to anyone. It has a preview option to test files before they are sent. You simply record a video or audio message and attach it to your email message. With just a click of the mouse, the recipient can load the CVideo-Mail program and begin viewing files.

Figure 18.7 PureVoice is for sending voice email messages to other users. It doesn't stream, but its files are very small.

The CVideo-Mail software will be bundled with a video capture board and will cost under $200. Since it doesn't come with a camera, you can use any popular desktop video camera or your camcorder. CVideo-Mail was released for use with the Eudora email programs from Qualcomm but should be able to handle other programs.

Cubic Videocomm
(619) 505-2030
www.cvideonow.com.

Summary

With your options limited to just one streaming email program, things don't look that good yet. It's possible that more vendors may add support for streaming video mail messages, but chances are that it won't happen any time soon; there just doesn't seem to be an adequate market for it—yet. Yes, there are some viable business applications (think of streaming slide shows, video greetings, audio email), but not many business computer users have multimedia capabilities at the office. That's not likely to change for some time. The advances in usage and market share must come from the consumer market. After all, consumers are more likely to have videoconferencing cameras or video capture cards installed on their home computers.

While Video Express Email is not a bad system, it is still somewhat cumbersome to use on a daily basis. Email isn't likely to change much for the time being, but in the not too distant future, we will probably all use some form of video and audio email system—streaming or not. The option to record audio or video (like

PureVoice) will probably be standard on some email programs soon because no matter how small the current market, sending video or audio email messages is still very compelling and downright cool. Imagine finally getting to see a faraway relative or a colleague in another state. As is often said, you can't convey much with just text and cutesy ASCII characters. Facial expressions, speaking tone, gestures, and eye contact are sorely missed in the current online environment. Sometimes a video email message is the quickest and best way to talk to someone without actually being face to face. This is almost the same field as desktop videoconferencing, which is slowly becoming more popular

In the mean time, we will at least have telephones. There is no software or bandwidth to worry about with phones, and it is always so much easier to pick up a phone and call someone than it is to send an audio or video email message. Chances are, that won't change much any time soon.

ENLIVEN:
Streaming Banner Advertising and Interactive Multimedia

19

ultimedia on the Internet was fully realized with Macromedia's Shockwave program. Shockwave is a program that allows CD-ROM-style animation and interaction over the Internet. Developers can create Shockwave games, animate menu and toolbars, or create other fun, colorful, and interactive sites. Shockwave movies are created with a program called Director, also made by Macromedia, and is the leading program used by many CD-ROM developers. Director's easy portability from CD-ROM to Internet and its multiplatform approach make it a very popular developer's tool.

Shockwave's only problem was that files tended to be rather large, and they had to be downloaded completely before being played. A new multimedia program, Enliven by Narrative Communications, was created to eliminate long downloads. Enliven is a streaming multimedia system that streams Director movies. Version 2.0 of Enliven doesn't even need a client plug-in to view Enliven files; a miniplayer is sent along with the data. This way, anyone with a Java-capable browser can view Enliven files.

When Enliven 1.0 was first released, it was marketed as an animation player that competed with Shockwave. Now that Shockwave also streams data, this has become a moot point. Files created with Director 6.0 can be streamed just like Enliven. Version 2.0 is now being marketed as a banner advertising system. Enliven ads appear almost at once and have plenty of interactive ability along with animation and sound. Since no client program needs to be installed, this means a much wider audience.

Enliven is a three-part client/server system:

Enliven Client. No plug-in is required to play Enliven files. The player is sent along with the rest of the Enliven data and is less than 20K in length. Everything happens in the background, so animations play quickly.

Enliven Xtra. This is a plug-in for Director 5.0 that is used to create Enliven files. Converting Director movies to Enliven format is as easy as using the Save As option.

Enliven Server. The server is available for Windows NT and Solaris UNIX computers and handles all the streaming of Enliven files. It also provides ad tracking and record-keeping information. Since Enliven is very ad oriented, much of the information can be analyzed by third-party ad servers like NetGravity and Accipiter. You get full results like click-through rates, mouse overs, and much more.

Steps for Implementing Enliven

Installing and setting up Enliven can be a laborious process. That's because Narrative recommends that you use a dedicated Windows NT Server machine as your Enliven Server, meaning you'll need at least two servers. In addition, you can always use more than one Enliven Server to accommodate more simultaneous streams. For a full description of common setups and configuration processes, see the documentation that comes with the Enliven Server.

To begin using Enliven, you need to do the following:

1. *Install and set up the Enliven Server and Xtra programs*. (For more on installing the Server and configuring server options, see the Enliven Server section later in the chapter.)

2. *Create Enliven ads*. Use Director 5.0 (or later) and the Enliven 2.0 Director Xtra to create your Enliven files. For more on authoring Enliven files, see the Enliven 2.0 Authoring Guide that comes with your system. Save the files as Enliven format by choosing Xtras/Enliven/Save As Enliven. The Director movie will be saved as an NCB (Narrative "cab") file.

3. *Create the web page*. Insert the proper HTML into your web page so that users can stream Enliven ads. The HTML is surrounded by the APPLET tag. Here is the HTML code for a typical ad called FILE.NCB:

```
<applet code=file.class
codebase=www.yourserver.com/dir/file.ncb
archive=file.zip
name=file
width=464
height=60>
<param name=cabbase value=file.cab>
<paran name=url value="file.njs">
</applet>
```

(For the latest HTML codes, see the authoring guide on Narrative's website.)

4. *Post Files to the Enliven Server*. Copy the NCB file to the Enliven data directory, usually c:\enliven\data directory. Also make sure to post HTML files to your regular web server.

5. *Play Enliven*. Now that everything is up and running, test it by loading the web page and viewing the Enliven file.

Enliven Client

The Enliven Client is built with 100% Pure Java, so it is compatible with all Java-enabled browsers like Internet Explorer and Netscape Navigator. It only needs to load once and can later play any subsequent Enliven files you encounter. The player itself is just under 20K long, so ads will begin to load very quickly, and since it uses Java, Enliven allows extensive, cross-platform access.

Think back. When was the last time you clicked on a traditional banner ad? If you're like most web surfers, chances are you hardly ever click on them. Clickthrough rates are notoriously low for most banner ads. Enliven give your ads an edge so they will stand out from the crowd (see Figure 19.1). They'll have animation, interaction, and even sound, so they don't even seem like ads. You may feel compelled to begin clicking and interacting with the ads without even thinking.

Previously, advertisers mostly used animated GIFs (also known as GIF89a animations) to create eye-catching banner ads. Animated GIFs are just a series of small GIF images that are rendered quickly so that they look like animation. It is a crude yet inexpensive way to animate objects. The only problem with animated GIFs is that they aren't interactive. For those looking for more interactivity and control over animations, Java was the next choice. Java is popular with web advertisers, but because of its complexity, not many use it to its full potential.

Enliven combines the best of both animated GIFs and interactive Java applets so you have highly animated and interactive files that load up almost instantly.

Figure 19.1 Enliven ads can be very interactive. This ad actually incorporates a game into a banner ad.

Also, Enliven was created to be a full-fledged advertising system with full reporting and tracking abilities. It can tell you who's watching the ads and what they're doing with them. The Enliven Client keeps track of ad hover time, clickthrough rate, display time, and even keyboard input. It sends this information back to the server where it is recorded.

Enliven Xtra

Enliven Xtra is the plug-in for Macromedia Director 5.0 and above. Using it is as easy as creating Director movies as you normally would and choosing Save as Enliven from the Xtra menu. Once saved, you can test the ad on your local drive. Files are saved as NCB files and contain all the elements of an Enliven file, including the Narrative Java stream file, browser information, and the Java viewer.

Since this book doesn't deal with creating multimedia movies, we won't get into how to use Director. Suffice it to say that Director can be a difficult program to master—newcomers to multimedia authoring will have an especially rough time.

Use the included tutorial with Director 6.0 to get a firm grasp of the basics and to create your first Director file. Not every client computer will have a state-of-the-art system, so Enliven also allows designers to substitute GIF animations instead of Director movies.

For more help on creating Enliven files with Director, see the documentation that comes with Enliven Xtra.

Enliven Server

The Enliven Server is the workhorse of the system. It handles all the requests for Enliven files and sends them out to the recipients. Enliven data is sent through the HTTP protocol to allow playback through corporate firewalls. It also uses its own proprietary protocol called NMSP (Narrative Media Stream Protocol). Both work very well, but you should use HTTP when you must bypass corporate firewalls.

Enliven only sends unicast transmissions, not multicast, because of its extensive reporting abilities. The Enliven Client takes information received from each user and sends it back to the Server, where it compiles statistics. The Enliven Server keeps these user logs and various data and exports them into third-party databases and ad servers.

The Enliven Server installation process is described here:

1. Install Enliven Server on your Windows NT Server 4.0 computer. During installation, you are asked for the web address of the Enliven Server and web server. Narrative recommends that you not install the Enliven Server and your web server on the same computer, because Enliven uses port 80, just like most web servers. If you must use them on the same machine, change the port number on your web server.

2. Enliven then asks you what type of log files you want to use, either NetGravity or Accipiter type. You also need to enter your server's port number and CGI-BIN directory location.

3. Once installed, an icon called Enliven Server is placed on the Control Panel. To access Enliven Server services and change options, just double-click on the icon. At this time, you should enter your license number. Click on the License tab and enter the license you were given (see Figure 19.2).

This completes installation. The program defaults to installing files in the c:\enliven directory. It also creates three subdirectories: one houses the Enliven ads, the second holds the log files, and the third contains the Help files.

Figure 19.2 The Enliven Server has options for configuring Enliven. At the License tab, type in the license number provided by Enliven.

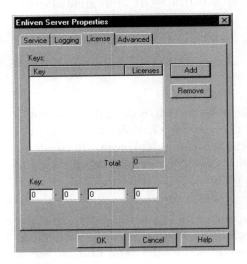

Configuring Enliven Server Options

You can change Enliven Server's options by going into the Control Panel window and double-clicking on the Enliven Server icon. You can add licenses, enable or disable logging, change transport protocols, and set the directory that will house Enliven files. The Advanced tab sets maximum simultaneous threads, seconds to time-out, and minimum idle time. You can also switch log formats from plain ASCII text to either NCSA or Microsoft IIS format (see Figure 19.3).

 Whenever you make changes, you must restart the Enliven server for them to take effect.

Monitoring Enliven Server

To monitor what's going on with Enliven Server, select Programs/Administrative Tools/Performance Monitor from the Start menu. Performance Monitor is a program in Windows NT that monitors connections and allows you to get statistics. For example, you can get information on the bytes received, number of connection attempts, streams sent, errors, and much more.

Enliven Server 2.0 is compatible with Windows NT 4.0 Server and Sun Solaris. The unlimited CPU license version costs $39,995, but you may be able to

Figure 19.3 Change Enliven's options in the Control Panel in Windows NT. Here you can set the logging for the Enliven server.

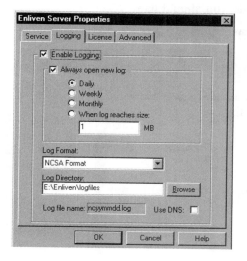

purchase less-expensive licenses. Check Narrative's website for more information on pricing.

 Enliven can also play long, Shockwave-type files. If you plan on using Enliven for these longer files, you must set your server's MIME types for Enliven Content. See the documentation that comes with the Enliven Server and Xtra for more information on setting MIME types. Remember, this is optional for when you want to enable viewing besides the Java client.

How Many Streams Can Enliven Deliver?

The number of streams you can have depends on a number of things. First, if you are using a trial or beta version of the program, you may be limited to only 20 simultaneous streams. More important, the number of streams depends on things like your server's connection speed to the Internet, size of the Enliven file, speed and type of the server's computer, and number of Enliven Servers used. To help you calculate how many simultaneous streams you can handle, use Narrative's Server Requirement Calculator at www.narrative.com/support/calculator.htm (see Figure 19.4).

Figure 19.4 Narrative's Server Requirement Calculator can help you find out the maximum number of concurrent streams. It can even recommend what speed your computer should be and how much RAM you should use.

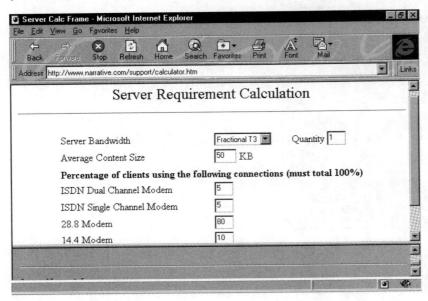

Keep in mind that the calculator is not an exact tool; it is just a rough estimate so you can figure out how much load your server will be handling. The best way to use the calculator is to use a "What If?" model and try a number of different calculations. Use the results to find out if you need bigger bandwidth or need to add more Enliven Servers to your system.

Enliven Hosting Services

If you don't have the money or time to put up your own Enliven Server, Narrative can help you. It has hosting services where you can keep your Enliven content on outside servers and simply send it out to client computers when files are requested. This arrangement keeps your initial costs very low and makes ad-tracking and administration painless tasks. Consequently, this allows practically anyone to use Enliven, not just the big websites that can afford the high price of the Enliven Server.

Using hosting services is also the fastest way to get up and running with Enliven and is a good idea for first-time banner advertisers. Once you've created your Enliven file, you can quickly think about your next ad campaign instead of worrying about administration or other server headaches. It also makes it much easier to expand your advertising—as your advertising needs grow, so can Enliven.

Another reason to use outside hosting services is when you have a large volume of ads. It is perfect if you don't want to bog down your web server with simultaneous requests or when you don't want to use up your company's precious bandwidth.

Hosting services are available in 25-, 75-, and 250-stream packages, and start at $1,500 a month. Other high-volume packages are available, too. There is also an option to pay per impression, with a one-time setup fee of $3,995 plus $.01 per impression served. You get everything included in your program: support, maintenance, and ad reporting.

If you already have a dynamic ad campaign or plan to implement one, it may make sense to convert to Enliven. If you're an ad agency, chances are you've seen it in action already and have already considered using it.

Should You Use Enliven?

In its latest incarnation, Enliven 2.0 has been completely redesigned as a web advertising system. If you're at all involved in creating compelling and interesting ads for your company, you should at least try Enliven on your site. It offers some compelling advantages over traditional banner ads. If you're already using Java or animated GIFs to create ads, using Enliven and Director is more user friendly.

Aside from banner advertising, you can have many other practical applications for Enliven. You can play and distribute CD-ROM titles, create marketing materials, make interactive web games, preview new books and movies, have product demonstrations, or make children's activities like interactive storybooks and educational games. Additionally, Enliven supports pay-per-view models or subscription models to give you yet another revenue stream.

If you can say yes to the following, you should consider using Enliven:

- Do you want to create engaging, interactive advertising that is results oriented?

- Do you want to deliver CD-length Shockwave movies and animations to clients over the Internet?

- Do you want to reach the broadest cross-platform audience, especially those using Java-capable browsers?

- Do you already work with Director movies or want to create Director movies for your site?
- Are you an Internet advertising company that works with banner ads?

Pros and Cons

For those interested in banner advertising and streaming animations over the Web, Enliven is a very good choice. The best thing about Enliven is that it uses the Director industry-standard multimedia authoring program so that developers don't have to learn to use a new software product. Enliven's main competition is Shockwave, but they are rather similar, just differing in their general purpose and audience. Now that Shockwave movies are capable of being streamed, there is little difference between the two. Shockwave movies even use a Java player like Enliven and share the same authoring program, Director, so developers can use either, depending on their preference. The only problem with Director is that it can be a rather difficult program to master. If you've never used Director before, be prepared to take extensive notes and to try the tutorials.

Enliven's no-client solution is rather elegant and many other animation programs are using this approach as well (see Chapter 20, "Streaming and Almost-Streaming Animation"). With other programs, you have to install plug-in viewers; Enliven gives you instant play with no plug-in required. On the downside, using Java to play Enliven files isn't always a good idea. Those who have older computers and browsers, which aren't Java compatible, won't see the Enliven ads, just normal replacement ads. Also, Java tends to be slow, especially on older computers.

Another major benefit is the extensive logging and tracking ability of Enliven. The Enliven Server works in the background to handle streams and capture important marketing information. Unfortunately, the server software is very expensive. That's why Enliven offers hosting services. Instead of spending all that time and money working with the server, you can easily get started creating your ads.

Since Enliven works in the background, most users won't even know about Enliven. They'll just see your animated, interactive banner ad that now features sound. Your ad now becomes your new front door, drawing new customers to your site. The best reason to use Enliven is because your ads will stand out from the usual banner ads. That means higher clickthrough rates and more traffic to your website, increasing your bottom line.

Because Enliven is so new, it is hard to tell what will happen. Will Enliven be successful in the long term? Right now, Enliven has no direct competition.

Microsoft is developing a Java drag-and-drop advertising system called Liquid Promotion. It works similar to Enliven, but just uses a friendly Java authoring system, not Director. Unfortunately, Liquid Promotion wasn't released at the time of writing, so you'll have to check with Microsoft for more information. Will other products be released that directly compete with these? Chances are that the answer will be "yes." Web advertising hasn't fully realized its potential, so there is room for some newcomers.

If you've been on the Web in the last few months, chances are you've already seen an Enliven ad and probably not even known about it. So if you're not already using Enliven, perhaps your competitor is.

About Narrative Communications Corp.

With the release of Enliven 2.0, Narrative Communications is trying to reinvent web advertising. Enliven allows ad agencies and advertisers to have interactive, streaming ads that keep in-depth statistics and reports. With Enliven, advertisers can quickly see what response their ads are getting.

When Enliven 2.0 was released in mid-1997, Enliven had the support of over 20 companies, including web advertising companies (Poppe Tyson, Accipiter, and DoubleClick), major websites (CBS SportsLine, EOnline, Wired, and Lycos), and multimedia design companies (Circumstance Design, ImaginEngine, and W3-design). As word spreads, more companies are expected to switch to Enliven.

Of all the products featured in this book, Enliven found a way to make its own niche in the streaming market. It created a real product that makes creative use of streaming multimedia.

Narrative Communications Corp.
1601 Trapelo Road
Waltham, MA 02154
(800) 978-8670
(617) 590-5300
www.narrative.com
info@narrative.com

STREAMING AND
Almost-Streaming Animation

20

Much of this book has focused on audio and video, but there is a growing number of streaming animation systems available on the Internet. Some don't even require plug-ins, instead opting for Java players that are downloaded in the background. This chapter focuses on some of the best and most promising animation programs.

Some of the systems may not be "streaming" per se. Some require a short time to download the entire animation first. Thankfully, download times aren't that long, ranging from 15 to 20 seconds to a minute or more. Such programs are included here because of their promise; it will only be a matter of time before they add streaming capabilities.

This chapter doesn't tell you how to create animations—each program is different and authoring can be a long, creative process. Rather, this chapter focuses on showing you what programs are currently available and how they work. To create multimedia and animation, you'll have to download and try the respective authoring tools for each individual program reviewed here. Some programs are best used to create short special effects like animated logos or menu bars. Others are full-fledged multimedia tools that allow you to create interactive movies, games, and other interfaces with sound or music. Unfortunately, there is no standard for web animation so all the programs use proprietary authoring tools. Nevertheless, you can really create some very compelling and yes, *cool* sites with these programs. Have fun trying them out, and more importantly, have fun playing with the authoring programs so you can add some animation to your site.

What Are Some Applications of Streaming Animation?

What can you do with streaming animation? Plenty. As you'll see, animation programs range from small animated icons to large, interactive games. The next sections discuss some of the more fun and compelling uses of streaming animation, using programs like Shockwave, Flash, and mBED. Also included here is Enliven, the streaming animation program used for banner advertising.

Games

Shockwave has always been used for interactive entertainment and extremely well done games. It may shock you to play these fully interactive games over the Internet. In Figure 20.1, you can see an example of a game from the Sports Illustrated for Kids website. You can use the mouse to move a character, hear sounds, get scores, and try to break your high score.

Who uses games on their sites? Companies like movie studios, TV networks, publishing companies, software companies, or anyone else who wants to entertain

---

Figure 20.1 A popular use of streaming animation on the Web is for games and other entertainment-oriented pages.

---

the audience. Adding fun games and animation is a sure way to attract more web traffic and get more return visits, too.

Audio

For audio, Shockwave is perhaps the best animation program. This versatility in animation, games, and audio makes Shockwave a very popular and powerful program. It also has the ability to stream audio (see Figure 20.2). Already, there are plenty of Shockwave audio sites.

Emblaze, covered in depth in Chapter 15 "GTS and Emblaze: No-Client Multimedia," can also create streaming audio. It can also stream animations and on-demand video. Both Shockwave and Emblaze are great for adding high-quality audio to your website.

Banner Advertising and Marketing

The best advertising and marketing program, Enliven, is covered in depth in Chapter 19, "Enliven: Streaming Banner Advertising and Interactive Multimedia." Enliven is a streaming animation program that uses Java to display banner ads.

Figure 20.2 Aside from games, Shockwave can also stream audio. This program lets you be your own Web DJ.

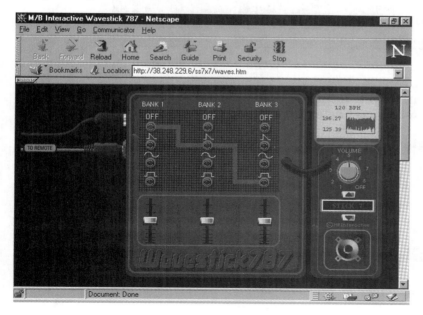

That way, almost anyone with a Java-enabled browser can see the ads. Ads aren't limited to being banner-sized; you can create long, full-screen interactive ads that also include sound. The combination of a strong advertising tool and easy creation of Enliven ads makes this a very powerful program.

Of course, any animation program can be used for marketing or other business purposes. You can create a Shockwave movie for your company to showcase your product line. You can make it look like an animated, interactive presentation (see Figure 20.3). If you use Shockwave for your presentations or slide shows, you can also add a synchronized audio track for voice-over or music.

Customized and Interactive Interfaces

Like the presentations and slide shows shown earlier, creating interactive sites and interfaces is possible with powerful programs like Shockwave and mBED. Using mBED, you can create games and screens that look like PointCast (www.point-cast.com) where you can check news, sports, and weather (see Figure 20.4).

Figure 20.3 Macromedia uses Shockwave and Flash to show marketing animations like this one at Intel.

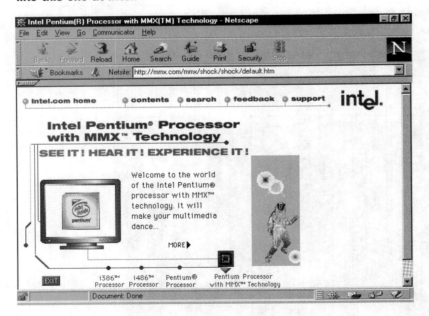

Figure 20.4 mBED is versatile because you can create simple animations for very complex interactive pages like this one.

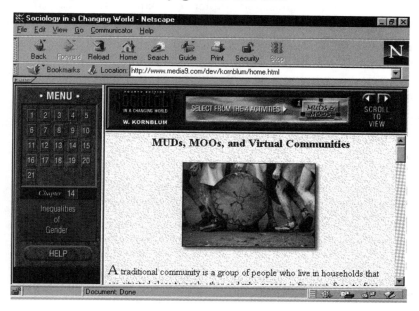

Dancing Logos: Snazzing Up Your Site

For short animations like dancing logos, bouncing balls, dancing monkeys, shooting stars, and other small tasks, programs like Flash and Sizzler are best. These tiny animations mostly resemble animated GIFs but are better than animated GIFs, because they can be longer and can even include audio.

Exploring Shockwave

The most popular streaming animation program is Shockwave by Macromedia. It essentially invented Internet animations by allowing CD-ROM multimedia to be used on the Internet. The latest version of Shockwave has improved so much that it can now handle highly interactive, feature-length streaming animations with streaming audio. The ability to stream is rather new to Shockwave; previously, a Shockwave file had to be completely downloaded before playing could start. Now Shockwave is even used for audio-only applications.

Shockwave files are good for many types of applications. You can create interactive games, advertising, marketing presentations, and audio-only playback. Many record companies, film studios, TV sites, and graphics companies use Shockwave to enhance their sites with fun and interesting animations.

The authoring tool behind Shockwave is Macromedia Director 6.0. Director is perhaps the most popular CD-ROM authoring program available. It has a timeline-based interface where you can drag and drop objects like files, graphics, and sounds to create rich animated movies (see Figure 20.5).

Since Director was first just a CD-ROM authoring tool, Shockwave movies tended to be large with no streaming ability. Now Director 6.0 allows for streaming playback over the Internet via Shockwave plug-ins; in fact, Director will even support a Java player so that plug-ins won't be necessary. Director will then be able to export movies in three formats: as standalone executables, Shockwave plug-ins, and for use with Java players. The addition of Java gives Shockwave an almost unlimited audience, since anyone with a Java-enabled browser can get "Shocked."

The Shockwave plug-in or ActiveX control is available for Windows 3.x, Windows 95/NT, and Macintosh systems. It also comes preinstalled with some versions of

Figure 20.5 You create Shockwave files with Director, an advanced multimedia authoring tool.

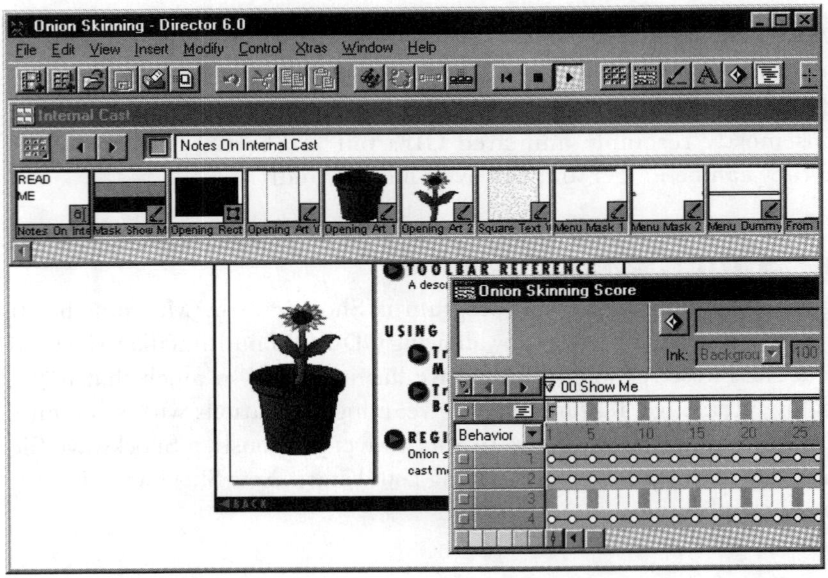

Navigator and Internet Explorer. Macromedia's Director authoring program is available for Macintosh and Windows 95/NT.

Exploring Flash 2

Macromedia also makes Flash, a vector-based animation format similar to Shockwave. The main difference is that Flash is best for playing short, quick animations like animated icons, logos, banners, and menu bars (see Figure 20.6). Flash movies can even include sound.

To watch Flash movies, you need to install the free Flash plug-in player or ActiveX control. Alternatively, you can also use any Java-enabled browser like Internet Explorer or Navigator. Macromedia announced support for Java playback of Flash and Shockwave movies in October 1997.

Like Shockwave, you can create Flash movies with Macromedia Director or with the Flash authoring program. Macromedia announced a new authoring utility called Aftershock for Flash. Aftershock helps designers by creating the HTML and Java applets for all browsers and platforms. It embeds the Flash movie in an

Figure 20.6 You can use Flash animations to spice up your website with cool animated logos or short movies, as shown here in Audioactive's website.

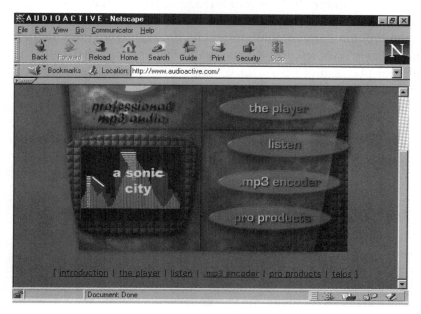

HTML page, which can automatically detect a user's browser to see what playback option it can use. That way, Flash movies can be played back with the Flash plug-in, Java, or with an animated GIF. Essentially, this guarantees that users will be able to see your Flash movies no matter what.

Another development of Flash is that it is now included with the RealSystem. The RealPlayer from RealNetworks can play RealAudio, RealVideo, and now, RealFlash. The advantage to using RealFlash is that you can create long, cartoon-like animations with synchronized audio.

Flash plug-ins are available for Windows 3.1, Windows 95/NT, and Macintosh. Of course you can also choose to use your Java-enabled browser so you don't need to install a plug-in. You can get the Macromedia Flash authoring program and Aftershock for Windows 95/NT and Macintosh platforms.

For more on Flash and Shockwave, visit Macromedia's website (www.macromedia.com). Macromedia is a maker of software authoring tools for use over the Internet, CD-ROMs, and other applications. It also makes graphics programs, tools, sound editors, and other multimedia software for use by developers on Mac and Windows platforms.

Exploring Enliven

Enliven was covered in Chapter 19, "Enliven: Streaming Banner Advertising and Interactive Multimedia," but it deserves some mention in this chapter. Enliven is a Shockwave-like animation program that streams long animations. It can include sound and plenty of user interaction. What makes Enliven good is that it uses a small Java applet to play Enliven files. That way, anyone with a Java-enabled browser can view the animations after just a very short download and buffer time. Like Flash and Shockwave, Enliven files are created with Director, using a plug-in or Xtra.

Enliven is now being marketed as a banner advertising system. Already, many advertising agencies and companies have begun using Enliven. If you've seen or heard a banner ad lately, chances are you've seen an Enliven ad (see Figure 20.7).

Although banner ads are the norm, a new type of web advertising is large-screen ads displayed in between web pages or when playing online games. These ads are called *interstitial* ads, because they are shown between pages of web content, like when traveling from page to page. They are already a big deal with advertisers who see this as the next wave in web advertising. Bigger ads means more time and more room to send the message, which means more interaction, more animation, and more sound. That's good news for programs like Enliven.

Figure 20.7 Unlike Java and animated GIF ads, Enliven can track user actions and file activity to give you a good idea of how your ads are being received. Here all the monitoring of the user's actions is being done behind the scenes. The ad server tracks all the movement, mouse overs, clicks, etc., from the user.

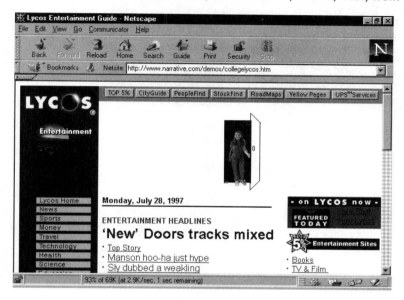

Enliven uses a client/server animation system; Shockwave and Flash just use an authoring program and can be served from any web server. The Enliven Server is available for Windows NT and UNIX systems. For more information and to see sample ads, go to Narrative's site at www.narrative.com.

Exploring Emblaze

For sheer flexibility, nothing beats Emblaze by Geo Software. It streams on-demand audio, video, and animation. Better yet, Emblaze doesn't need a plug-in player because it uses Java for playback. See Chapter 15, "GTS and Emblaze: No-Client Multimedia," for more specifics on Emblaze.

The Emblaze authoring tools consist of audio and video encoding programs and a multimedia authoring tool called Emblaze Creator. Creator is an animation authoring program that resembles Macromedia Director. You can add graphics, audio, or video to an animation file (see Figure 20.8). To view Emblaze files, you just need to go to the page with a Java-enabled browser and the files start playing after a short buffer time.

Figure 20.8 Emblaze streams audio, video, and animation on any Java-enabled browser. No plug-ins are needed.

Emblaze Creator is available for Windows 95/NT and Macintosh for around $995. For more on Emblaze and its audio and video encoders, visit Geo Publishing's website at www.emblaze.com.

Exploring Sizzler

Sizzler, by Totally Hip Software, is a streaming animation program that mostly streams small graphics like animated icons, titles, and menus. It can also play sound (WAV files). Sizzler mostly resembles animated GIFs since they don't usually have a long playing time like Flash. Sizzler files are usually compressed to as low as 20K, but you can make larger files. Keep in mind that you should keep file sizes low so they can be streamed better.

To create Sizzler files, you need to use the Sizzler editor/converter. It is simply a converter that takes your existing animations and converts them into the Sizzler format (see Figure 20.9). That means you already need to have animated files created; Sizzler won't help you do it. You can use PIC or QuickTime movies in the Macintosh version of the editor. For Windows, you can import AVI movies or DIB files, which are sequences of files that make up the animation.

Figure 20.9 The Sizzler Editor can import graphics and movies and convert them into the Sizzler format for Internet streaming.

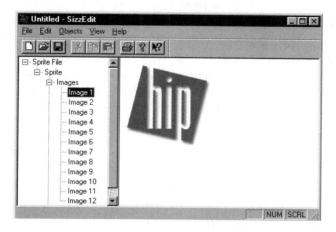

Once you've imported everything, you can add a sound file (WAV format) or a URL so that you can go to a different location when the animation is clicked. The editor then creates the EMBED tags for the HTML page and puts it on the clipboard. From there you can paste it on any web page.

Sizzler has been around for a while, but there aren't very many sites using it. Also, not many users actually have the required plug-in to watch Sizzler animations. The Sizzler Editor is available for Macs and Windows 95/NT. The plug-in is available for Windows 3.1, Windows 95/NT, and Macintosh. You can download the plug-in and editor from the Totally Hip Software website (www.totallyhip.com).

Exploring WebMotion

WebMotion by Astound, Inc., is a full multimedia authoring program that creates files that can be played with any Java-enabled browser. The player is a small, 20K Java applet that plays WebMotion's animation files.

Creating WebMotion files requires the WebMotion authoring program. It has a timeline interface where you can click and drag objects into the active area. You can import a wide range of pictures like BMP, DIB, TIF, GIF, JPEG, and PCX (see Figure 20.10). The objects can be moved, rotated, or set in motion in any direction or speed. You can also add sound and interactivity, so that clicking on the animation can take visitors to a different URL or another animation.

WebMotion also comes with a library of clip art images and other graphics. When you're finished creating your masterpiece, it can upload the file to your web server. WebMotion also creates a sample HTML page so you can copy and paste the code to your own HTML page. In case there some users out there who don't have a Java-enabled browser, WebMotion can also create an animated GIF file.

The WebMotion authoring program is available for Windows 3.1, Windows95, and Macintosh for $69.95. Astound, Inc., is a Canadian software company that makes multimedia programs, including sounds and graphics editors and other creation tools. Visit Astound's website at www.golddisk.com to download a trial version or to purchase the program.

Exploring mBED

mBED by mBED Software is rather different from other streaming animation systems. mBED animations can be small icons and animated buttons, but mBED can also be used to create and play longer files, like games, interactive menus, and other interfaces (see Figure 20.11). mBED can also handle sounds, including Real-Audio files.

To watch mBED movies, you need to install a plug-in or ActiveX control for your browser. The data is sent through the regular HTTP protocol so there is almost no wait time. Loading takes as much time as any large JPEG or GIF image.

Figure 20.10 The Astound WebMotion program uses a timeline interface so you can create a wide range of animated buttons, logos, banners, and more.

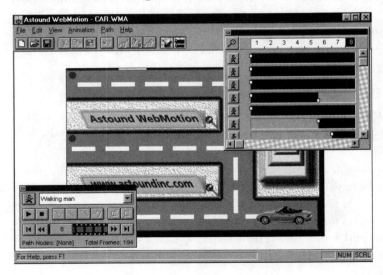

mBED can best be compared to a fully functioning language, similar to Java. Its files are simply text files saved with the MBD extension. These *mbedlets* as they are known, are simply interactive applications embedded in a web page, so an mbedlet can be practically anything you want it to be, depending on what you program it to do. The MBD file is saved on your regular web server along with your other HTML files. It can include JPEG, GIF, WAV, and AU files. The mBED player simply reads the MBD text file and builds the structure of the mbedlet.

Creating the mbedlets is as complex as an HTML file because commands consist of text commands and tags. Learning all the features and commands, however, can be complex, but you can create a simple animation rather quickly since it is a lot like learning a new programming language. The mBED website has complete documentation so you can create text MBD files through the online tutorial.

For nonprogrammers, mBED released the mBED Interactor 1.1, a graphical authoring program. Instead of learning complex text commands and tags, you can use a graphical interface (see Figure 20.12). You can import graphics and sounds and add interactivity without losing the richness of the text commands. mBED can also work with Dynamic HTML, so you can have extra-rich web pages. When you've finished creating your files, Interactor makes the MBD and HTML files for you, so you can quickly post them to your server.

Figure 20.11 At You.com, mBED created this customized, fully interactive mBED file that displays news stories and responds to users' clicks and commands.

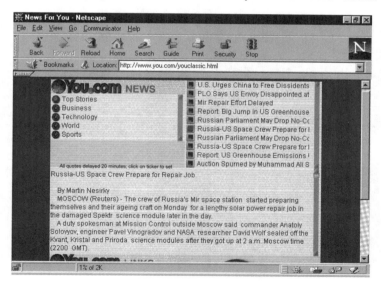

mBED Interactor is available for $249 for Windows 95/NT and Macs with a 30-day trial version. mBED Software's (www.mbed.com) main competitor is Shockwave, which can handle long files and play highly interactive movies.

Exploring WebAnimator

WebAnimator by DeltaPoint, Inc., is a less-popular program and hasn't received much notice. Like other programs, it requires a plug-in to play interactive, animated files that can include sound. WebAnimator doesn't stream files, but uses compression to send files; a small animated text title takes up around 12K, so playback time is usually quick.

Creating files requires the WebAnimator authoring program. You can use it to create animated buttons, headers, and menus. It uses a storyboard so you can quickly see what you are creating. It accepts standard graphics files like BMP, JPEG, PCX, GIF, and more. For sound, it can accept SND, AIFF, and WAV files. WebAnimator comes complete with plenty of templates so you can quickly begin creating files.

The WebAnimator plug-in and authoring tool is available for Windows95 and Mac platforms. Visit DeltaPoint's website at www.deltapoint.com or www.sitetech.com for more information.

Figure 20.12 The easiest way to create mbedlets is to use the mBED Interactor, a full-fledged, multimedia authoring system.

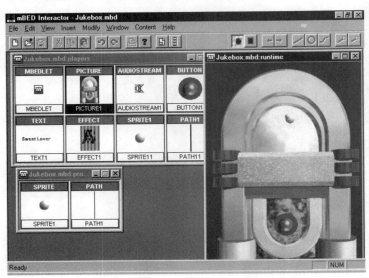

Figure 20.13 The WebAnimator authoring program lets you import graphics and sounds.

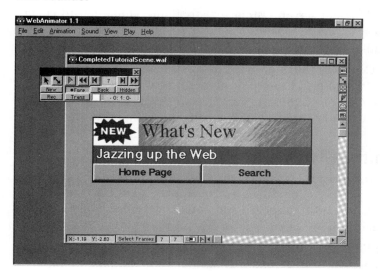

Exploring Scream

Scream by Saved By Technology is a little-known animation program (no streaming) that differentiates itself because it can synchronize animations with MIDI songs. Scream animations are mostly colorful, text images that tend to have a quick redraw time (hence "scream," as in screaming-fast animations). To view Scream animation, you need to use a plug-in for Navigator or Internet Explorer for Windows 3.1 and 95.

Before viewing a Scream file, you should set your monitor for 800 × 600 with 256 colors for best viewing, and maximize your browser window to see the full effect. You can stop the animation at any point by pressing the ESC key. You also need to change your browser's cache file to be at least 4000KB.

The Scream Editor (for Windows95) is used to create Scream animations. It comes with fonts, demo animations, and the ability to import WAV and MIDI files. You can program a Scream file to respond to certain cue points in the music file. The Editor costs $99, and trial versions can be downloaded from Saved By Technology's website (www.savedbytech.com).

Exploring Media Conveyor

Media Conveyor by Digital Evolution is yet another little-known program. Like Enliven, it consists of a client-server system for streaming animation to clients. Files can also contains synchronized sounds and hotspots. To watch Media Conveyor files, you need to install a player in the form of a plug-in or ActiveX control.

To create Media Conveyor files, you need to use the Media Conveyor Studio available for Windows95 and NT. The server program is available for UNIX and Windows NT systems. Currently, there is no Mac support at all. For more information, go to Digital Evolution's Media Conveyor site at www.mediaconveyor.com.

Exploring AnimaFlex

AnimaFlex gets its name because it specializes in creating animations consisting of warping and other rubbery animations. It can display 2-D or 3-D effects. To watch these animations, you need to use the AnimaFlex player available as a plug-in for Windows or Macintosh browsers.

You create AnimaFlex files with the RubberWeb Composer program available for Macs only. For more on AnimaFlex, visit RubberFlex Software's website at www.rubberflex.com.

Exploring Liquid Motion Pro

A roundup of streaming animation programs wouldn't be complete without Microsoft and its Liquid Motion Pro program. Liquid Motion Pro is a drag-and-drop authoring program that creates Java animations. It can have animation, sound, and plenty of interactivity. Basically, it gives you all the power of Java, but with an easy-to-use interface.

Unfortunately, not much is known about the status of Liquid Motion Pro since it was recently purchased by Microsoft from Dimension X, a company at the forefront of Java deployment. Microsoft was said to be releasing the next upgrade, Liquid Motion Pro 2.0, and making it their own, so it may even have a new name by the time it is officially released. Also of note was a product called Liquid Promotion, that would make it easy to create interactive Java advertisements, like banner ads. For more on Liquid Motion Pro, visit Microsoft's site at www.microsoft .com/dimensionx.

What Should You Look for in a Streaming Animation Program?

Streaming animation can be fun and very interactive, but before deciding on a system, consider some of the features that you should look for:

- If your goal is to have the most number of people watching your creation, choose one that uses a Java player. If you use an unknown animation tool that needs a plug-in, chances are that many people won't be able to see your animation. This is especially true if you choose more obscure animation programs like Scream or WebAnimator. Also, the more advanced programs can create animated GIFs for those systems that don't support Java.

- Another important consideration is streaming. As you've seen, not all programs can stream data. If this is important to you, look into Shockwave, Flash, Emblaze, or Enliven, since they all support streaming (and Java playback). Don't forget to keep an eye on other promising programs that may later decide to support streaming or that aren't quite released yet, like Liquid Motion Pro.

- Ask yourself what you need on your site. Do you just need animation? Do you need sound? Is MIDI good or do you prefer WAV sound? Will you need video? Do you need small, animated logos and menus or do you need a complete authoring tool that can give you full-length movies, CD-quality audio and interactive interfaces? Look closely at these programs to see if they can deliver what you want.

- Also take a look at all the authoring tools to see which one works best for you. Some can't import many file graphics or sound files or don't have good tools. Others are too simple and simply work as converters, not authoring programs. On the other hand, a program like Director can be rather complex. And don't forget about price—if cost is a major consideration, you may want to consider something less expensive.

- Test some of the more interesting programs out for yourself. Practically all the authoring tools in this chapter have fully functioning trial software available so you can test them out before purchasing. Take advantage of these offers and see how they work and if they can fulfill your needs.

Pros and Cons

Streaming multimedia on the Internet is a definite plus. The newest trend of using Java playback is a great use of Java. Plug-ins are just too much of a hassle, especially when viewing short animations or animated pictures. Having Java playback is the first step to creating a universal and ubiquitous multimedia player.

Is there a downside to streaming animation? Nothing major so far. There are problems with the capabilities of each individual program, since some can't send sound or need plug-ins to play files. You can do plenty with animation. Perhaps the main problem is that some programs still don't have streaming capability;

however, that should change in the not too distant future. Practically any way you look at it, using streaming animation is a plus. It shows off your creativity, attracts new users, and livens up a normally dull Internet.

The Future of Streaming Animation

There is little doubt that the leaders of streaming animation are Shockwave and Flash. They command the largest market share and can be seen at many websites. Is there room for competition? Certainly. Newcomers like Emblaze, Enliven, and mBED are powerful and versatile animation programs that can give Shockwave and Flash a run for their money. The great thing is that some newer animation programs are beginning to serve a particular niche. Enliven, for example, is concentrating on banner advertising, and Flash is used for smaller animations.

So what will the future bring? The first thing that can change the face of animation is Java playback. If more of these programs begin to support Java playback, users would see lively animated sites without worrying about which plug-in they need to download. Simply put, Java playback (or some other no-client method) is a must for the smaller companies to compete with the giants.

The future will also bring more interactivity. There will be a greater emphasis on interacting with the user and there may even be new things added like live chatting so multiple users can play a Shockwave game, for example.

Another way to bring animation to the next level is with more sophisticated yet easier-to-use authoring programs. Programs like Macromedia Director are very powerful programs but are not for the artistically challenged. Would an industry-standard multimedia file format help the industry? Possibly, but that may limit competition. Besides having different authoring programs, it won't make a difference if Java playback becomes more widespread.

In short, the Web will be a more graphical and dynamic place than it is now, in ways that we find hard to imagine. Animations will be more commonplace, more people will be able to see them (from user of high-end workstations to WebTV users), and they will stream to get to everyone faster. There will be more audio, better animation, and more programs using video, too. In the future, there may be a mixed multimedia file type that handles audio, video, animation, still pictures, and 3-D or VRML (Virtual Reality Modeling Language).

But alas, "streaming" VRML programs are already here, and you can learn more about that in Chapter 17, "Streaming VRML and 3-D."

PSEUDO-STREAMING
and Streaming MPEG

Most of this book focuses on streaming proprietary audio and video formats. With most of these programs, you must convert standards-based files into a vendor's proprietary file type. This chapter focuses on how you can view AVI, QuickTime, and MPEG movies while they are downloading. This process is sometimes called *pseudo-streaming* or *progressive downloading* since it is not real streaming. You are still downloading the video, but at least you can watch whatever has been downloaded.

This chapter is split in two parts: The first deals with creating and watching AVI, MPEG, and QuickTime "fast-start" movies so you can watch files as they are being downloaded. The second half deals with a program called Net TOOB Stream that actually streams MPEG movies.

Fast-start movies are files that are optimized by a proprietary compressor, so that you can download them progressively and watch them as they are being downloaded. To watch fast-start movies, you need the proper players and plug-ins. There are two programs: CineWeb, which streams MPEG movies, and ClearFusion, which pseudo-streams AVI movies. QuickTime movies can be converted into fast-start movies with a program called MovieScreamer. You can view fast-start QuickTime movies with Apple's QuickTime MoviePlayer or with any other compatible player.

The second section of this chapter focuses on a true server-less system that streams MPEG movies. To make streaming MPEG movies, you just need to buy a hardware MPEG encoder to properly encode the video files. You can then place the files on any web server and view the movies with a player called Net TOOB Stream. The player does all the work in decoding the movie, so it plays in real time.

Another way of watching movies on the fly is to use Microsoft's ActiveMovie program that comes with Internet Explorer 3.0. It is able to progressively download almost any type of multimedia file from WAVs, AVI, and QuickTime movies. Unfortunately, this program doesn't exist anymore—it has been integrated into Internet Explorer 4.0 and is called DirectShow. However, if you're still using IE 3.0 with 32-bit Windows operating system, this is a very good way to go.

What Are Fast-Start Movies?

As just described, fast-start movies simply let users view a movie while it is still downloading. This isn't like the streaming we've seen in the rest of this book. The file is downloaded normally, so a 10MB AVI movie will still take around 20 to 30 minutes to download. The advantage is that you can view whatever portion of the file that has been downloaded. These programs give you the liberty of previewing files so that you can interrupt the download if you don't want to wait for the whole thing.

To make fast-start movies, you must convert them using a proprietary compression scheme. That means downloading the software codec driver, installing it on your computer and then compressing your movie using your favorite video editor. In the case of MovieScreamer, it is a complete compression program, not just a driver.

Converting a file into a fast-start movie doesn't affect it and usually doesn't even change its file size. What it does do is add some header information that makes it easier to download and view it at the same time. Watching fast-start movies is easy as long as you download the proper players and plug-ins from each vendor. You can't use one player to view another vendor's fast-start optimized file. The only exceptions are fast-start QuickTime movies, which can be viewed with practically any QuickTime player.

Why aren't all MPEG, AVI, and QuickTime movies made into fast-start movies? Mostly because fast-start movies are so new and not many multimedia authors know about them. Also, some aren't willing to use these new and usually proprietary codecs on all their multimedia files. Another problem is that not every client program can handle these movies. Since you have to download so many programs, it doesn't make it practical for many users. The only thing that can help this is if the industry accepts and recognizes these new codecs. So far, this isn't happening, but perhaps you will soon see improved multimedia players working with fast-start movies.

Another major problem is that these programs don't work with many platforms. Windows95 and NT are the ones supported most, although Macs are also represented with QuickTime movies. Nevertheless, most of these programs don't work on other operating systems.

In the sections following, there are three solutions that have fast-start solutions. The first is Digigami Inc.'s CineWeb, a browser plug-in that lets you view streaming MPEG movies as well as progressively download other file types. The second solution is called MovieScreamer, a program that makes fast-start QuickTime movies for viewing with most any QuickTime player. Last is ClearFusion by Iterated Systems, which pseudo-streams AVI movies.

Pseudo-Streaming with CineWeb

CineWeb is a multimedia player that plays a wide range of multimedia files, including AVI, ASF, MPEG, QuickTime, and many audio formats. It is a plug-in for Netscape Navigator 2.0 and above. (It does not currently work with Internet Explorer, but there may be support in the future). Once you install CineWeb, it takes over practically all of your multimedia playback needs. This can be a boon, but you may not always want CineWeb intercepting and playing every file format you find on the Web.

CineWeb plays movies right within a web page; there is no external player involved. Once you select a file, CineWeb takes over and begins to play it. A progress bar at the top right of the window also shows you the size of the file and the progress of the download (see Figure 21.1).

 CineWeb works with Windows95 and NT only; it does not support Windows 3.x. Make sure that you're using the 32-bit version of Navigator, or CineWeb will not work properly.

What about streaming? CineWeb streams only MPEG movies. It can also play "fast-start" QuickTime movies that have been optimized with its MovieScreamer compression scheme. CineWeb can play other files like AVI and Microsoft's ASF movies, but it cannot stream or fast-start them. In development is CineWeb Pro, which will reportedly "stream" AVI movies. (ClearFusion, discussed later, can create and play "streaming" AVI movies.) If you're not watching a fast-start or other "streaming" movie, then the whole file must download completely before you can watch any of it.

MPEG and QuickTime movies can be viewed after only 15 percent of the movie has been downloaded. You can change this option by right-clicking anywhere in the movie window and selecting CineWeb Options. From there, you can change

Figure 21.1 CineWeb plays files from within a customized web page. Notice the progress bar and file size that tells you how long until the download is finished.

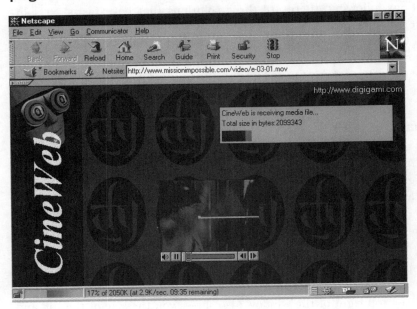

many different settings like connection speed, percent needed to be downloaded, and cache size (see Figure 21.2).

Viewing movies with CineWeb is easy; just click on a movie or go to a web page that has a movie embedded in it and CineWeb will begin playing it. This is great for web developers because you don't have to do anything different in order for people to use CineWeb. With this approach, the burden falls on the client to use the right player.

Perhaps the biggest problem with CineWeb is that it plays and hijacks many types of multimedia files. Once you install CineWeb, you're basically letting it take over playing duties for AVI, MOV, MPEG, AU, WAV, and MIDI files. Even worse, it doesn't have a good uninstall program; remnants of the program are sometimes left over so you have to delete files manually.

Getting ready to download and install CineWeb can be a chore. You are directed to download and install a whole host of compression drivers, Microsoft's ActiveMovie player, and QuickTime players before you install CineWeb. While this may be the best way of getting CineWeb to work, it is much too tedious and

Figure 21.2 CineWeb can also play files inside a regular web page. Here the Options window is open so you can customize options and playback.

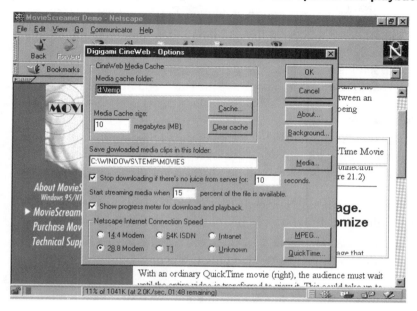

confusing, especially for a casual web user. This can stop a novice from downloading and using CineWeb.

 To temporarily disable CineWeb, you must rename its plug-in DLL file located in Netscape's directory: Depending on your system, find NPCINE16.DLL (16-bit) or NPCINE32.DLL (32-bit version) in Netscape's plug-in directory and rename it to something like NPCINE32.BAK. The next time you load Navigator, it will ignore that DLL file so it will appear as if CineWeb is not installed. Don't forget to rename it back to its original name when you want to use CineWeb again.

Another downside is that CineWeb is not a free plug-in. After a 30-day evaluation period, you must pay $29.95 if you want to continue using it. Lastly, CineWeb doesn't support Internet Explorer or other operating systems.

Whether you use CineWeb is up to you; it has its pluses and minuses, so use the 30-day trial period to see if you like it enough to keep using it.

TIP Digigami also makes Plugsy, a program that helps administrators handle MIME conflicts or change file associations for Netscape plug-ins. After a trial period, it costs $29.95. You can change, add, or remove plug-ins from various types of files. This program is mostly for advanced users, since there are no meaningful instructions. Also, it can be difficult to know what program or plug-in is being used since you just see filenames.

Converting Files to MPEG

The makers of CineWeb also make other products that essentially can be used together to make streaming movies. Since CineWeb users need to use the MPEG file format, you can use a converter called MegaPEG that converts AVI and QuickTime movies into MPEG (see Figure 21.3). You can download a trial version that has all its features available, but it displays a visible and distracting watermark in the output file. MegaPEG works with Windows 95/NT and costs $495.

MegaPEG is a very good program and it is easy to use. Just select the files that you want to convert and add them to the batch list. Once you choose options like

Figure 21.3 MegaPEG converts AVI and QuickTime movies into MPEG format.

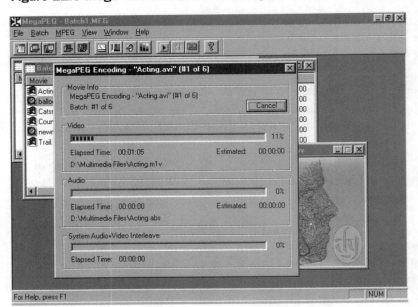

output data rate, bit rate, and compression rate, you just press the Make MPEG button and it begins.

Compression is very good. It converted a 13MB AVI file into a 5MB MPEG file at a 28.8Kbps data rate, and the output MPEG video looked just as good as the original high-quality video. The problem is that converting files takes a very long time, even on a Pentium or Pentium II computer. Make use of the batch list for long unattended or overnight conversions. Some professionals even use a dedicated computer to handle all their MPEG conversions; however, if you only do occasional converting, you probably won't need this.

There are other MPEG conversion programs on the market, of course. MegaPEG is just very handy since you'll probably be visiting Digigami's website to download the latest CineWeb plug-in.

Fast-Start QuickTime Movies with MovieScreamer

MovieScreamer is Digigami's program that makes QuickTime movies into fast-start QuickTime movies. You can play fast-start movies with CineWeb or even with Apple's QuickTime plug-in player (see Figure 21.4). Both programs recognize fast-start movies and begin to play them after just a few minutes of loading. Again, this is not real streaming but more of a preview of the file. Typically, you will be able to play the first few seconds of the file after just a few minutes of downloading. As the download continues, you will continue to be able to play more. A slider bar tells you the position of your movie and tells you how much of the download you have left.

Using MovieScreamer to create QuickTime movies seems like a very good idea, and web developers can convert large batches of files at once with it. If you're using the Netscape Navigator plug-in (Windows only), you can drag any QuickTime file into the browser window to instantly convert it to fast-start format. MovieScreamer does not affect video playback, so even if you use another QuickTime player, things should be the same. MovieScreamer is available for Windows and UNIX platforms. Prices range from $199 for Windows and $199 to $995 for the many flavors of UNIX.

About Digigami, Inc.

Digigami specializes in Internet multimedia products. All four of its products, CineWeb, MovieScreamer, MegaPEG, and Plugsy, are aimed at making it easier to view and play movies over the Internet.

Figure 21.4 You can play fast-start enabled MovieScreamer movies with any QuickTime viewer.

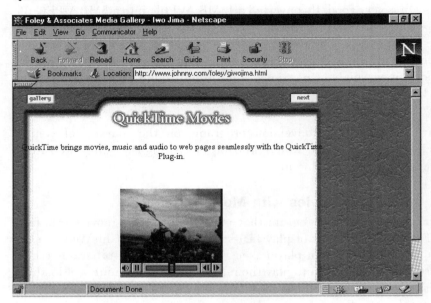

Digigami, Inc.
624 Broadway, Suite 200
San Diego, CA 92101 USA
(619) 231-2600
www.digigami.com

Apple's QuickTime MoviePlayer and Plug-Ins

Apple doesn't necessarily have a streaming player, but its QuickTime plug-in for Macs and Windows can play fast-start QuickTime movies (see Figure 21.5). To download Apple's QuickTime player, go to the website at quicktime.apple.com. There you can get the proper plug-ins for your platform as well as the QuickTime VR player add-on.

Perhaps of more importance is QuickTime 3.0 due to be released in early 1998. Here are some of the new features:

- New QuickTime 3.0 plug-ins for Windows and Macs. They will work with both Internet Explorer and Netscape Navigator.

Figure 21.5 Apple's QuickTime plug-in can play MovieScreamer fast-start movies. The downloaded portion of the file can be played while it continues downloading. Notice the progress bar, which tells you how much you have left to retrieve.

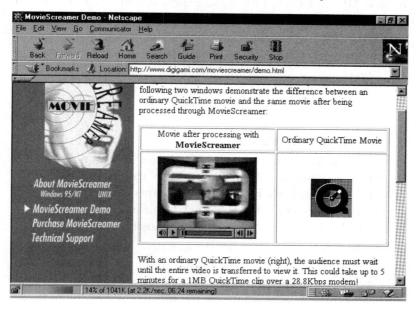

- Support for more file types besides QuickTime, like AVI, MPEG, WAV, MIDI, AIFF, AU, and MPEG Layer 2 files.

- A new QuickTime VR 2.0 player. See quicktimevr.apple.com for more information on QTVR or see Chapter 17, "Streaming VRML and 3-D."

- The ability to include multiple tracks so that developers can add different language tracks or make QuickTime movies with variable data rates and compression formats. This enables viewers to see the best movie possible over their Internet connection.

As with all products in development, some of these features may change by the time they are released. Go to the website (quicktime.apple.com) for more information.

About Apple Computer, Inc.

Apple was one of the leaders in the personal computer industry in the 1980s. Not only is it known for its Macintosh computers, but Apple also make peripherals, software, and PDAs (the Newton). Its QuickTime movie format is a cross-platform solution that handles audio, video, and other data to create one of the leading multimedia formats on the Web. QuickTime was recently selected by ISO to be the framework for the new MPEG-4 video format, so expect lots of renewed interest in streaming QuickTime movies.

Apple Computer, Inc.
1 Infinite Loop
Cupertino, CA 95014-2084
(408) 996-1010
www.apple.com

Fast-Start AVI Files with ClearFusion

One of the best players is Iterated Systems' ClearFusion, a plug-in and ActiveX control that plays Video for Windows (AVI) movies while they are downloading. Once you select an AVI file, playback is almost instantaneous (although downloading files on the Internet can seem to take forever). ClearFusion works very well by allowing you to watch the downloaded portion of the movie.

Depending on how you link the AVI movie on the web page, ClearFusion displays it in two ways: inline inside the web page or in a separate miniwindow. If you use the EMBED tag, the movie loads and plays within the web page. If you don't see player controls, you can right-click anywhere on the movie window to get menu options (see Figure 21.6). From there, you can use the Play, Rewind, and Stop buttons. Once it has finished downloading, you can also save the file to your hard drive.

If you insert the AVI file as a regular HREF link, ClearFusion opens up a new window (see Figure 21.7). The window isn't really a new application, but resides and floats within the browser window. In this view, you can use the player controls to play, stop, or seek a new position. Also, like any other window, you can move it around and resize it. The Option button located right next to the Play/Stop button allows you to do a number of things, like controlling the playback speed or resizing the window. To save the file to your hard disk, right-click on the movie window and choose the Save File As command.

The quality of a ClearFusion movie depends on your Internet connection speed and the type of compression used in the AVI movie. On slow connections, movies tend to look somewhat jerky, and there isn't very good audio synchronization. The best thing to do is to allow the whole movie to download completely, so it will be cached to your hard drive. Then you can rewind it and watch the movie from the beginning, and the quality should improve dramatically.

To improve "streaming" performance, Iterated says that you should compress movies using its compressor/decompressor called ClearVideo. Movies without ClearVideo compression may not look very good or you won't be able to hear the audio portion. ClearVideo is a video codec that lets you create and compress QuickTime, RealVideo, ActiveMovie, and AVI files. Movies are smaller in size and are more stream friendly. Once you've installed the codec on your computer, it can be used with any popular video editing program, like Adobe Premiere. The codec is a software driver available for Windows 95/NT and Macs for $395.

> **NOTE** Having trouble making ClearFusion work? It may be because another program is taking over your AVI files. The best way to make ClearFusion work is to reinstall it and then try to view an AVI file again. Also try to disable other multimedia viewers that may be associated with AVI files. Then ensure that you have at least 10MB free on your hard drive to cache movies. If you're using Windows95, you must use the 32-bit version of Netscape. Last, remember that ClearFusion only works with AVI files; other plug-ins or programs will display QuickTime and MPEG movies.

Figure 21.6 ClearFusion can load and play AVI movies from inside a web page. Also shown is ClearFusion's context-sensitive menu.

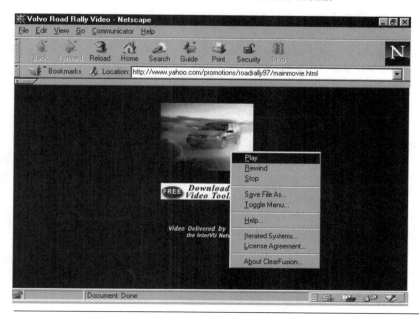

Figure 21.7 Another option is to link an AVI movie directly and let ClearFusion display a floating window over your browser window.

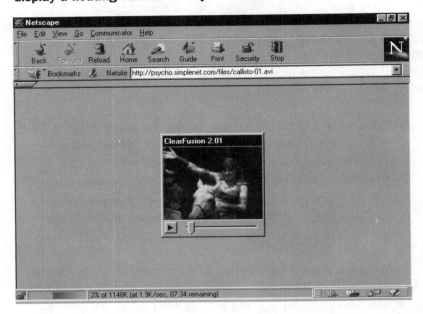

Putting AVI Movies on Your Site

There's no special way to put a video on a web page; just drop the AVI files onto your web browser and edit your web page. You can either use the EMBED tag or the HREF command. No matter what method you use, the important thing is that your audience must be using ClearFusion to view the AVI movie while downloading. If they have another plug-in or helper application handling AVI movies, Clear-Fusion will not load.

If you want to have the AVI file displayed inside a web page, use the EMBED HTML code:

```
<EMBED SRC="example.avi" height=176 width=144">
```

By using the height and width commands, you can resize the video into any window size you want. You should, however, try to keep the same height and width as the original file. If you make it too large, the pixels become large and blocky, and you lose much of the detail.

The second way is the old-fashioned way:

```
<A HREF="example.avi">click here</A>
```

Users must click on the "click here" link in order to begin watching the video. Once it's clicked, ClearFusion takes over and loads the video in a floating window where you can watch playback while it downloads.

About Iterated Systems, Inc.

Iterated Systems is mostly involved with video compression, like its ClearVideo product. ClearVideo has gained popularity with a number of vendors and multimedia authors. It works so well that ClearVideo is being used by Progressive Networks' (now called RealNetworks) RealVideo for streaming video.

Iterated released ClearFusion because there was no program on the market that made AVI files stream or play on the fly.

Iterated Systems, Inc.
7 Piedmont Center, Suite 600
3525 Piedmont Road
Atlanta, GA 30305-1530
(404) 264-8000
(800) 437-2285
www.iterated.com

Progressive Downloading with ActiveMovie

The easiest way to experience fast-start movies and audio files is to use Microsoft's ActiveMovie, an ActiveX control that was made available with Internet Explorer 3.0. ActiveMovie enables you to listen to or view files as they are downloading much like the other players mentioned earlier. A sliding bar shows you what has been downloaded already and what is left (see Figure 21.8). Unfortunately, Active-Movie only works with Internet Explorer running on Windows 95/NT computers. It also doesn't speed up downloads—files still take the same amount of time to download.

What is ActiveMovie? It is an ActiveX component built to handle all the standards-based multimedia files including AVI, MOV, MPEG, AIFF, AU, and WAV files. The only major file types ActiveMovie doesn't support are MIDI (MID, RMI) or MPEG Layer 3 (MP3) sound files. When used with Internet Explorer, Active-Movie automatically opens and starts to download the file when you click on a multimedia file.

You can use ActiveMovie to play files on your hard disk; just double-click on any supported file type and ActiveMovie will load and play the file. Another way to

Figure 21.8 Microsoft's ActiveMovie can progressively download a multimedia file and let you view or listen to it while it is downloading.

load ActiveMovie is to run it through the Start menu. Choose Start/Accessories/Multimedia menu, and click on the item called ActiveMovie Control. From there, a menu appears where you are prompted to load a file. Since ActiveMovie hijacks so many file associations, you may want to take some back and use them with other programs. To change files associations, choose ActiveMovie File Types from the Start/Accessories/Multimedia menu. Then pick and choose which file types it should handle.

 Sometimes you just want to download the file and watch it later. To download the file, right-click on the link and choose Save As from the menu. On Macs, you just need to hold down your mouse button for a second until the shortcut menu pops up, then choose Save As. Alternatively, if you're using Netscape Navigator you can quickly save files by holding down Shift as you click on a file.

ActiveMovie can play a file embedded on a web page or in a separate window (see Figure 21.9). You can show or hide the player controls or the running time display by right-clicking on the window. It has all the normal player functions, like play, stop, start, rewind, and forward functions. It also has a slide Seek control to jump to other locations in the file. Right-clicking can also bring you to more options like auto rewind, auto repeat, volume, balance, and even finding out which codecs are being used.

ActiveMovie consolidates your multimedia players into one handy player. After all, why have so many players for different multimedia types? Perhaps the only problem with ActiveMovie is that it sometimes has trouble playing back

Figure 21.9 ActiveMovie can run inside a web page if used with the EMBED tag, as shown here.

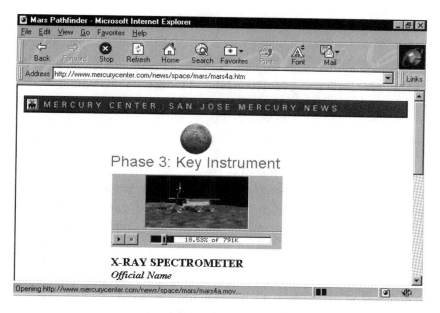

some QuickTime movies. For that reason, you should always have a copy of Apple's QuickTime Movie Player on hand.

With the introduction of Internet Explorer 4.0, ActiveMovie has been integrated with the browser and it works less like an external program. You can still use it to view multimedia on the Internet or locally on your hard drive, but Windows98 will likely do away with ActiveMovie as we know it. Eventually, it may be combined with the NetShow player. You can always continue using Internet Explorer 3.0 so take advantage of the many benefits of ActiveMovie.

About Microsoft Corp.

Microsoft is the world's leading software company and has been in the computing business since 1975. Microsoft is perhaps best known for its Windows operating system and its web browser, Internet Explorer. It is also involved in many other facets of the computer industry: hardware, games, networking, multimedia, and Internet products. With the upcoming releases of Windows98, Windows NT 5.0, and Internet Explorer 5.0, Microsoft hopes to solidify its lead in the Internet arena.

Microsoft Corporation
One Microsoft Way
Redmond, WA 98052
(425) 882-8080
www.microsoft.com

Net TOOB Stream: Streaming MPEG Movies

Net TOOB Stream from Duplexx Software is a standalone multimedia player available for Windows 3.1 and Windows 95/NT. Net TOOB is also one part of a streaming solution that can stream MPEG movies. It doesn't use proprietary file types or codecs, just a hardware addition that captures and compresses movies in real time. Net TOOB Stream is comparable to TrueSpeech, covered in Chapter 6, "TrueSpeech: Streaming Speech." Like TrueSpeech, it is server-less and uses a standards-based file type.

Net TOOB Stream can play an MPEG movie in three ways: streaming, buffered streaming, and downloaded. Streaming means that the file is coming in real time (see Figure 21.10). Buffered means that the video must be buffered and downloaded before playing. This is good for detailed videos or very short files where

Figure 21.10 Net TOOB Stream can stream MPEG movies. Depending on your bandwidth, you can view low- to very good-quality MPEG files.

streaming isn't important. Downloaded video means just that: The video must be downloaded completely. This is best for long files or for higher-resolution and high-quality movies.

Net TOOB is also a multimedia file viewer that can play many downloaded multimedia file types like AVI, QuickTime, MPEG, WAV, MIDI, and more. As a multimedia viewer, Net TOOB does an adequate job, although its interface can be awkward and confusing. Nevertheless, it is good for Windows users who want an all-in-one multimedia player.

Getting Ready to Stream MPEG Movies

Duplexx Software makes a complete MPEG streaming package. There are two parts: the client and the hardware MPEG encoder:

Net TOOB Stream. The client program that plays streaming MPEG movies. As described earlier, it can also play downloaded files like AVI and QuickTime movies as well as audio files. Net TOOB Stream costs $19.95 but can be evaluated for free for 30 days.

ShowSite. This is a hardware addition, an MPEG encoder card, that you can use to encode your movies into MPEG format. It is a real-time encoder, and it encodes audio and video at the same time, so there is almost no waiting. It makes it easy to create low frame-rate MPEG movies. It is available for Windows95 and NT and costs $1,395.

Creating streaming MPEG movies is a five-step process:

1. Capture and encode the movie with ShowSite.
2. Configure MIME types on your web server.
3. Create the pointer or XPG text file.
4. Edit the web page and create the links to the movie.
5. Copy all files to a web server.

After that, you're ready to go out and play them. Make sure you test your files thoroughly to ensure that they work properly.

Step 1: Encode MPEG Movies with ShowSite

Net TOOB requires that you encode movies to MPEG format for them to be streaming movies. Its solution is ShowSite ($1,395), a hardware encoder that you add to Windows95 or NT computers. ShowSite comes with software that makes it easy to capture and encode files in real time. All you have to do is install the board, connect your video input (camera, VCR, etc.), and press Record on your computer. ShowSite captures the file so it is small enough to be streamed at whatever data rate you want, from 28.8Kbps to LAN speeds.

ShowSite works because it creates MPEG movies at low frame rates. They won't be very good quality, so they should generally be used as preview files. It makes good sense to create higher-quality downloadable videos for anyone who wants to take the time to download them.

Duplexx recommends making MPEG movies that are 7.5 fps or 15 fps. Once they are created, files should have filename extensions of M15 or M75, depending on the frame rate you choose (M75 for 7.5 and M15 for 15 fps). You can put files of both frame rates on your site so that users with faster connections can view the better-quality files. Slower users will probably use the files at 7.5 fps, since they will stream better. By way of comparison, a one-minute video clip encoded at 15 fps will yield a file of approximately 1.5MB. That same video at 7.5 fps will yield a file of approximately 750KB. Use 7.5 fps for movies that are short or for talking-head videos. For movies with a lot of motion and action, choose 15 fps. You can also have movies with 30 fps, but they won't be streamed, they'll just be downloaded.

Step 2: Configure MIME Types for Web Servers

You must change and configure new MIME types for the web server that you are using. This only needs to be done once per server. Depending on what web server you are using, adding and changing MIME types is different. The basic information is as follows:

For the MIME types video/mpeg, add the file types M15 and M75.

Create a new MIME type, video/mpeg-realtime, with the file type .xpg.

 NOTE MPEG files that can be used with Net TOOB have the M75 and M15 extensions. The XPG file is the text file that points to the actual MPEG file. See the next section for more on the XPG file.

Because there are so many types of web servers available, we can't include instructions for adding the MIME type for every web server. Instructions vary from server to server. You should see your web server's manual or Help file for more on configuring a new MIME type. Alternatively, you can visit Net TOOB's web page at www.duplexx.com/mime.html. If your web server is handled by a third party or is hosted off site, you should email the webmaster and ask him or her to configure this new MIME type.

Step 3: Create the XPG Text File

Like other server-less systems, Net TOOB Stream needs to have a corresponding XPG text file that points to the real MPEG file. That XPG pointer file contains information about the file, including server location, size, window size and location, and data rates. The XPG file can be created with any ASCII text editor, and you can name it anything you desire, as long as you keep the XPG extension.

Following is a sample XPG file. The file shows you the correct format and then shows you the options for each command. Each command will be separated by the word "or." Keep in mind that only one option is supported for each command. An explanation of the command will appear in parentheses. Remember that when you create your own XPG files, do not include the parenthetical information and use only one command option.

```
[Info]
Title=Title of Clip
Artist=Your Name
Copyright=Copyright 1996
Window=INTERNAL or EXTERNAL (the movie will be displayed inside a WEB page or with
the standalone Net TOOB Stream player)
HAlign=WINDOW or LEFT or CENTER or RIGHT (Configures placement on a page when using
the Internal command above)
VAlign=WINDOW or TOP or CENTER or BOTTOM (Places the video on a web page)
X=240 (The X coordinate to place a movie on a page. Not used for WINDOW)
Y=450 (The Y coordinate for placing a movie. Not used for WINDOW)
Code=(site registration code)
CodeDate=(expiration date of code)

[28.8K]
URL=www.website.com/directory/28_clip.m75 (This must point to the actual filename)
UserName=anonymous (Anonymous is the only option now. This command is reserved for
future version of NET TOOB)
password=(reserved for future version of NET TOOB)
FileSize=60000 (insert the size of the file in bytes)
FileDate=160702 (for caching purposes)
MediaType=A/V or VIDEO ONLY or AUDIO ONLY (Choose what type of MPEG file you are using)
```

As you can see, the first part of the file with the [Info] header contains general information on the movie itself, like copyright, title, artist, and page alignment. Next comes the Data Rate section, which is separated by the data rates that you will be using for your file. You can create MPEG files that span any number of data rates as long as they are separated by the appropriate header, as in [28.8K] and [56K]. In our example, there was only one data rate option, 28.8K. The Net TOOB Stream player automatically recognizes the client's transfer rate and selects the right file to play.

If you find creating XPG files to be too difficult, Duplexx has an XPG Wizard program that helps you create them. It also comes bundled when you purchase ShowSite. See the Duplexx website for more information on ordering the software.

Step 4: Create the Link on Your Web Page

The link on your web page must point to the XPG file, not to the MPEG file. Use standard A HREF linking, as in:

```
<A HREF="mpegvid.xpg">Click here</A>
```

If you forget and link to the actual MPEG file, it won't work with Net TOOB; it will simply try to download and open the file like any other MPEG file.

Step 5: Copy Files to the Server

The last step is to copy all files, the web page, XPG file, and MPEG file to the web server. If you're on a remote server, upload all files to the proper directories.

Don't forget to test everything before putting it up live.

Playing the Streaming MPEG Movie

Once Net TOOB Stream is installed on a client computer, users can begin to view streaming MPEG movies. There are no firewall restrictions, since the MPEG movie is streamed along with other web data.

Typically, movies should be clearly marked as being Net TOOB Stream-capable MPEG files, since no other player on the market can stream them. Also, try to use a number of different data rates like 28.8K, 56K, and higher so that you cater to a number of different users and connection speeds. (Remember that if you try to play a file with a data rate higher than your own, the video will be buffered, not streamed.) You should always try to give users as many options as possible so that they can choose the frame rate and data rate.

Should You Use Net TOOB Stream?

Is Duplexx's solution any good? It is a somewhat clunky, inelegant solution. It is no where near as good as the client/server programs in the rest of this book. A better idea may be to use an easier approach like VivoActive, since it is server-less and requires no hardware encoder. Also, it doesn't use those long, complex, XPG pointer files.

One big issue is video quality. Watching Net TOOB MPEG movies on the Internet with a 28.8Kbps connection leaves much to be desired. Frame rate is usually around

7.5 frames per second, and the image tends to be a bit fuzzy and unclear. At higher speeds, the video does get better, but you must reach LAN speeds to get really good quality.

Pros and Cons

While using Net TOOB and ShowSite is not a terribly expensive or complex solution, it does have its difficulties. The first problem is the MPEG encoder. Duplexx is rather pushy about using its own card, ShowSite. Duplexx says that using other hardware or software solutions will probably not work with Net TOOB, since it requires very low data rates and bandwidth to stream files. Some developers may balk at installing an MPEG encoder card that may not be used very often or whose function can be accomplished with software. Another minus is that ShowSite is made only for on-demand videos; there is no support for live video. In the future, Duplexx plans on releasing a live solution. Also, ShowSite is just an encoder and is not used as a decoder. Net TOOB Stream uses software to decode the incoming stream.

Perhaps the biggest problem is the small user base. Not many people on the Internet use Net TOOB Stream to stream MPEG movies. Just remember one of the cardinal rules for making streaming multimedia: Just because you build it, doesn't mean that they will come. Net TOOB users must download, install, and eventually purchase Net TOOB Stream to get much use out of it. Perhaps using Net TOOB Stream and ShowSite on an intranet makes better sense, since you can make higher-quality videos and can control the bandwidth better.

In any event, Net TOOB is doable, but if you're looking for server-less systems, you can find better solutions elsewhere in this book.

About Duplexx Software, Inc.

Duplexx Software provides a whole solution for creating and playing streaming MPEG movies. Net TOOB Stream player is a popular multimedia player for playing downloaded files, but there isn't much content for streaming MPEG files. So far, companies like Ford, Nortel, and Putnam are using it on their intranets for announcements, training, and executive messages.

Duplexx Software, Inc.
35 Congress Street
Salem, MA 01970 USA
(508) 745-7144
info@duplexx.com
www.duplexx.com

Summary

As you can see there are plenty of ways to get downloadable movies and sound files to your computer. The problem is that there are too many solutions. Realistically, no end user will ever want to download so many programs (Net TOOB Stream, ClearFusion, CineWeb, QuickTime, ActiveMovie) to listen to files or watch movies. Many users balk at downloading any new or unknown plug-in. They want a simple way to experience multimedia without having to download drivers, plug-ins, and codecs first.

The other problem is that these programs sometimes unceremoniously crash into each other. When you install a program, many file types are hijacked without your permission. Sometimes, you may be surprised by which program tries to play a file. The best way to get everything straightened out is to reinstall the programs you are comfortable with and want to continue using. You can also change file associations manually, but that can be tedious. Clearly, there should be a better way.

Will there ever be a cross-platform solution for transmitting standards-based multimedia to your desktop? ActiveMovie is a no-brainer for Windows 95/NT users, but since it only supports one platform, it doesn't go far enough. It certainly seems possible, but so far, there are just lots of disparate solutions that aren't quite there. That's why using streaming file formats will be so important in the future. Perhaps someday, downloadable files will go the way of the dodo and we'll just have one standard streaming multimedia format on the Internet that everyone can play on any platform, browser, or player. Until that day, we'll still have to deal with downloadable AVI, MPEG, and QuickTime movies.

PART THREE

FUTURE DIRECTIONS

THE FUTURE OF
Streaming Multimedia

22

Like anything happening in this fast-developing world of computers and the Internet, the future of streaming multimedia is hard to predict. It's possible to see the *near* future, anywhere from six months to one year, but anything farther off is anyone's guess. Change in the streaming multimedia industry will come, but it won't happen overnight—it will be a slow evolution. Companies will fold, and startups will be created; other companies will merge, and some companies will split up; partnerships will be broken, and new alliances will be brokered; technologies will evolve, and old ones will fade away; new programs will appear, and others will never be seen again.

The beginning of streaming multimedia by RealAudio in 1994 was the beginning of the end for traditional multimedia. However, traditional multimedia isn't dead, and it will cling to life for some time to come. Like other old-fashioned technology (think 3-1/2 inch disks), downloadable multimedia will still exist, but it will diminish in importance. It's just a part of the overall evolution of computers.

This chapter focuses on highlighting new and emerging technologies that will change the face of streaming multimedia. Come and look into the "crystal ball" to see how streaming multimedia might evolve.

Ten Things That Will Revolutionize Streaming Multimedia

As you've no doubt concluded, streaming multimedia is not a perfect technology, but it is still in the formative stages. After all, it's been less than three years since it was introduced. What will change? What events will occur? What technologies are key to continuing the growth of streaming multimedia? What companies or people are important? What hardware will be important? What will be the killer app of streaming media?

Let's look at some of the hottest technologies and advances that will revolutionize streaming multimedia. The points mentioned next may not be as important on their own, but taken together, they will have a profound impact on the streaming multimedia industry, the Internet, and computers in general.

Bandwidth

First and foremost, bandwidth is extremely critical to streaming multimedia; it is responsible for the quality of the audio and video that is delivered. With the right amount of bandwidth, you can see *full-screen*, *TV-quality* video from your computer. Unfortunately, most users are lingering at speeds of 28.8, 33.6, or 56Kbps. The bandwidth problem isn't with the Internet—data travels quickly over the Internet backbone. It is the last leg of the trip from the ISP to your desktop where things slow down. Modems of 28.8Kbps are just too slow to ever allow large screen, good-quality video.

Several new technologies, however, promise to speed Net access to home users and even office users. Following are seven emerging technologies that will one day change the way we access the Internet.

ISDN

Because of its easy availability and relative low cost, ISDN is perhaps your best value if you want high speed. It is four times faster than a 33.6Kbps modem, and ISDN adapters cost around the same as an analog modem. Installation fees and per-minute fees, however, make this impractical for home or leisurely use—your phone bill can rack up high charges in no time flat. Likewise, ISPs tend to charge more per month for ISDN connections than for regular dial-up connections.

In the beginning, many phone companies were slow in providing ISDN access, but things have been steadily improving. Another downside is that depending on where you live, installing your ISDN line and getting it to work with your computer can be a real headache. However, ISDN lines are becoming more readily available from most regional phone companies, though, so it may be your best bet if you need high-speed access now.

Cable

Why install new wires when you can use a wire that's already coming into your home? Of all the promised techniques, cable seems to be the most promising for home users. That's because a very large percentage of homes already subscribe to cable TV or are in an area that allows cable hook-up. Businesses, on the other hand, don't usually have cable lines running to office buildings, so they may choose to use other technologies like T1 or ATM. A number of U.S. cities already have cable access—prices are low, generally about $40 a month including $70 to $199 for initial hook-up and equipment.

How fast is it? One cable provider, @Home (www.home.net) (see Figure 22.1), says speeds can range from 256Kbps to a high of 3Mbps. Speeds depend on what cable company you have and what type of connection it uses. The catch is that bandwidth is shared by everyone on the line, so you won't always get your promised bandwidth. (Fortunately, TV images won't be affected by these slowdowns.)

Is cable access available in your area? The best way to check is to visit your cable company's website or give them a call and ask. Some cable companies that have started access include Comcast, Cox, Rogers, Shaw, TCI, and Cablevision. The downside to cable is that if you're a frequent laptop traveler, you'll need to keep your ISP dial-up access since cable doesn't provide phone access. Nevertheless, as cable access becomes available in more areas, you'll probably see many people giving up analog modems and moving to cable.

Figure 22.1 @Home provides high-speed cable Internet access to home and office users.

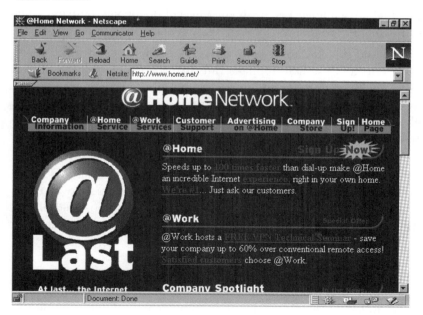

Satellite

Another option is to connect a small satellite dish and mount it on your rooftop or exterior wall. Vendors like Hughes Network DirecPC (www.direcpc.com) are the most popular. With satellite systems, Web data is delivered via satellite at speeds of 200 to 400Kbps. These speeds are for downloading only; uploading is handled by regular analog modems and your normal ISP account. These systems tend to be better for those in remote locations where copper wires and other high-speed systems aren't available.

Satellite can be expensive, too. There are setup costs, dish cost, and a monthly fee of about $19.95 on top of that. Since upload speeds are limited to your analog modem, it's a steep price for one-way speed. Hopefully, prices will come down, and upload speeds can be increased in the future.

ADSL

ADSL stands for Asynchronous Digital Subscriber Line, the most common type of DSL. There are other types of DSL, so you might see the acronyms xDSL or DSL used to represent the various types of digital subscriber lines. DSL works over regular copper phone lines like ISDN. ADSL is much faster, though, and it isn't complicated to set up like ISDN. Speeds for DSL can reach from 2Mbps to about 52Mbps, but upload speeds will be somewhat slower. Whereas cable modem users can experience a decline in speed as more users simultaneously connect, DSL avoids this problem by using individual telephone lines. DSL is the province of the phone companies, but they are already missing the boat on ISDN, so it doesn't look very promising for DSL.

To use DSL, you and your ISP must both have DSL connections with the phone company; however, you can't use DSL to make calls like you can with ISDN. So far, DSL service is severely limited, so it will be hard to find phone companies that are offering it. Only one regional Bell company, US West, is selling ADSL subscriptions, and the monthly costs are very high. This may limit its audience to small businesses and other professionals willing to pay the big bucks. Chances are, prices will fall as DSL becomes more popular.

American Information Systems (www.ais.net) has begun offering ADSL for home use by running lines to luxury apartments in Chicago. Tenants pay an extra $100 per month for downstream speeds of 1.5Mbps and upstream speed of just 64Kbps. So expect to see your phone company making this technology available in your area in the future.

Wireless Internet Access

The great thing about wireless isn't so much its promised bandwidth as its portability. With a wireless connection, you're free to roam around. You can connect to the Internet from your car, on a plane, on the beach, or anywhere else you have the urge. Some companies are already opening up this market. There are microwave systems being tested in cities like New York, Las Vegas, and Washington, D.C. A company called CAI Wireless Systems (www.caiwireless.net) announced wireless Internet service in a few eastern cities. It has a bandwidth of 27Mbps, but in a real-world situation, you can expect downstream rates of about 400 to 800Kbps. Unfortunately, you'll need to keep your modem to handle upstream data transfers.

Just a pipe dream? It's mostly speculation so far. Using part of the television broadcast signal is another choice. Companies like WaveTop (www.wavetop.net) and Intel are using the VBI (vertical blanking interval), which is the space between the television pictures to send web information to PCs with TV tuners. Of all the systems, wireless looks the most enticing but the most difficult to implement. It requires many antennae strung around cities, especially around remote locations.

High-Speed Analog Modems

Although not a digital solution, high-speed analog modems like 33.6 and 56Kbps modems are a very good alternative. They are less of a hassle than ISDN connections and cost much less. You also don't have to wait for the phone company to come and install your line; you can buy a modem almost anywhere and install it yourself. One downside is that connections almost never reach the promised speed: Many 56Kbps modems can only connect at around 40Kbps to 44Kbps, for example. Perhaps the main problem with high-speed modems is that they have competing standards (X2 and K56Flex), so the modem you buy needs to be the same type as that being used at your ISP. Fortunately, this incompatibility will soon disappear now that the International Telecommunications Union (ITU) has decided on a standard for 56Kbps modems.

T1 Line

A T1 connection is the high-speed digital connection of choice for many businesses and even some hard-core home users, but these lines are still very expensive. T1 prices can go as high as thousands of dollars a month, but prices are slowly dropping. Leasing a T1 line may cost as low as $300 per month, although that doesn't count startup equipment and setup time. They carry 1.5Mbps upstream (leaving your computer) and downstream (arriving). Only the most hardened Net nerds should attempt to lease their own T1 lines. There are too many complexities and costs are too prohibitive for the casual home user who wants more bandwidth. T1 lines (and faster T2 and T3 lines) remain a fixture in corporate offices, but they aren't practical for mainstream use. One good idea is to find a way to share the costs of a T1 line with others, like people in an office building, community, or home complex.

Keep an eye out for these technologies. Eventually, everyone will be able to access the Net at 1Mbps or so, but it won't be for a few years at least. In fact, many aren't even available right now. So don't ditch your 28.8Kbps modem just yet. Besides, it may one day be a collector's item.

Compression

Another way of reducing our reliance on high-bandwidth networks is to use better compression. The key is not to just compress multimedia into a small size; the key is to make it small and *watchable*. Just look at the MPEG Layer 3 audio codec. MPEG-3 is so good that there is no noticeable difference between the original and the compressed file.

The problem is that video has much more information. Consider the following: To send a raw movie at 30 fps at 640 × 480, you need over 27Mbps. One minute of this movie will need 1.7Gbps. Without compression, not even a T1 line can help you see this movie. With compression, you eliminate redundant data, thereby dramatically lowering the data rate needed. Some programs discussed in this book compress the video so well that they can provide full-screen (640 × 480), full-motion (30 fps) video over 10Mbps or 100Mbps LANs. At 28.8Kbps, users simply can't ever hope for TV-quality video over the Internet. You can lower your data requirements with smaller windows sizes and lower frame rates, but 28.8Kbps still won't be fast enough.

MPEG video compression is very good. MPEG video is being used on TV, in satellite broadcasting, and on DVD to compress movies onto the disc. Already the newest version of MPEG video compression, MPEG-4, has been announced and Apple's QuickTime format will be its foundation. How much better can MPEG compression be? For streaming multimedia to achieve breakthrough success, compression must continue to improve. But have we hit a brick wall? Will there be better compression down the road? Again, we can only wait and see.

IP Multicasting

Another important technology is IP multicasting. For most applications, it works beautifully; just one stream from the server can be transmitted to hundreds or thousands of users at a time. This is perfect for information that is needed regularly, like office news or for scheduled live video training sessions. It works best for closed networks where you can actually set up an IP multicast network. So far, multicasting is just beginning to be implemented on some LANs, but over time, you can expect this to be the preferred delivery method for most broadcasts.

IP multicasting over the Internet may take some time, but many streaming programs already support it; it's just a matter of setting up the equipment all over the Internet. What's needed is support from ISPs and web hosting companies. One company is doing something about it already. UUNet (www.uu.net) introduced UUCast, a multicast service for ISPs and websites. It placed multicast routers on its Internet backbone, so companies just send UUNet one video stream and UUNet replicates it to anyone on their network. Already ISPs like Earthlink, CompuServe, MSN, WebTV, and America Online have joined. This sounds like a very good beginning.

Of course, the rise of multicasting doesn't mean that unicasting will disappear. Unicasting is necessary to serve individual streams so users can use true on-demand video at any time. Both can work together on one system and complement each other. For streaming video to be really useful on an intranet, it needs multi-casting. It can save you so much bandwidth, you may look for new applications to use up the rest.

A Universal Multimedia File Type

AVI, MOV, RAM, TSP, LQT, WRL, MPA, WAV, ASF, MPEG. Does this read like an eye chart? These are just some of the file extensions used in multimedia files. Every streaming system in this book with the exception of those using MPEG video, a worldwide standard, is a proprietary system. Proprietary file types can only be used with one software and use their own codec. Proprietary files may be good for the respective companies, but they are bad for end users. Want to view a RealVideo file? Download and install the RealPlayer. Want to watch a VDOLive movie? Download and install the VDOLive Player. You get the idea. This is no way to be user friendly or grow an industry. Every company is working on its own ideas and file formats instead of coming together to create an industry-wide format.

It would be great if there was one file format, so all you had to do was click on a link to play it. It would be great if you could play a RealAudio file with StreamWorks, and if all these proprietary systems would be interoperable. It would be great if there was just one multimedia file format on the Internet, and you could use any player to play it. Finally, it would be great if more programs used Java as a player to send video and audio, thereby entirely eliminating the need for plug-ins and proprietary players.

The first solution would be interoperability, but interoperability would mean we would still have 20 different file formats floating around. That's 20 file formats that one universal player would have to keep track of. The other solution would be to use just one universal streaming file format. Alas, how likely is this? To its credit, Microsoft is trying; however, Microsoft's motive may be controlling a standard rather than trying to be humanitarian. Microsoft is trying to make its ASF file format the standard file type for streaming multimedia. While it is true that ASF is not codec dependent like the rest, it cannot be called an open standard yet. Microsoft has made agreements with Vivo, VDOLive, and RealNetworks. The first baby steps have come to pass: NetShow can now play RealAudio and RealVideo files. Is this the beginning of the end for multiple file formats?

Microsoft

Microsoft deserves its own mention, because no matter what you think of Bill Gates & Co., they have done some good. Windows98 promises many features that will make Internet use and access easier. It also will bring the TV and Windows closer together.

Without Microsoft, all the consolidations and agreements in the streaming industry might not have happened. As mentioned in the previous section, Microsoft made agreements with the other major streaming vendors to support its NetShow product. Plus, Microsoft is a 10-percent minority stockholder in RealNetworks and also has an investment in VDOnet. Furthermore, the acquisition of VXtreme in 1997 solidified Microsoft's future in the streaming market. The most important part of this was not the actual software but the engineering behind the program. Many VXtreme folks were heavily into Java, and now Microsoft has gained this important knowledge base.

Microsoft is taking the Internet and multimedia very seriously and has a vision for the future. Its purchase of WebTV, the maker of Internet set-top boxes that connect to television sets, sends a clear signal that it wants to get into this convergent area of TV and computers. Yet another clue is Microsoft's investment in the cable company, Comcast.

Where is Microsoft headed with all these deals and acquisitions? What other companies will Microsoft swallow? What is Bill Gates' master plan? Just think about Microsoft and the areas that it is involved in. In the Internet area, it already has an online service (MSN), a real estate site, a car purchasing site, a banking/investment site, browsers, multimedia, email, city guides, and lots more. Mix that with its dominance in operating systems, office productivity software, and networking, and don't forget about cable news network, MSNBC, and its other cable investments. Microsoft currently is and will continue to be in almost every facet of our daily lives.

Convergence: Web, TV, and Computers

Making the transition from Microsoft to convergence is very apt. As we've seen, Microsoft already has its hand in almost everything.

In reality, the big deal is with Internet multimedia and streaming. Want proof? Consider all the companies that are developing or have already released streaming multimedia systems. Some of them include Microsoft, Motorola, IBM, Intel, Silicon Graphics, Netscape, and RealNetworks. The list reads like a Who's Who in the computer industry. There are plenty of not-so-big companies also trying to stake a claim. These companies know that streaming video over the Internet is just the beginning. The winner in the streaming video market can take a huge lead in the Internet/TV arena when convergence finally happens. They're all trying to cash in and make a dent in the market, so they won't be left out when bigger things start happening.

What will happen with convergence and how long before it starts happening? It's too early to predict anything for sure, but it will be big. Will we eventually see NetShow video appearing on our TV sets? RealAudio and RealVideo support for WebTV users is coming soon. Will the networks and broadcasting industry sit back while Internet companies move in on their territory? Already, chipmaker Intel rolled out Intercast (www.intercast.com), a technology that blends TV and the Internet. With Intercast, you can watch TV and surf the Web right from your computer. You can surf the Internet as you usually do, but you get a much more integrated interface for accessing information and watching TV (see Figure 22.2). To see the future of TV, you just need to make sure your cable or satellite company uses Intercast, buy a TV tuner card, and then hook up your cable or satellite dish to your computer.

Wink Communications (www.wink.com) is slightly different because it moves the interactivity from the computer to the TV set. Wink can add interactive elements to anything, from TV shows to commercials. Users can order products, get more information on a movie or sports team, or answer trivia questions. Channels and networks must add Wink hardware so that users can access Wink content. Already, channels like The Weather Channel, Court TV, and NBC offer Wink TV.

This is just a glimpse at what may happen. Can Microsoft's WebTV be far behind in combining television and the Internet? Will this convergence finally bring us that long sought-after technology of movies-on-demand? Will it mean more interactive TV like Intercast or Wink? What other unknown applications can we expect to come from this convergence? Stay tuned.

Figure 22.2 This Shockwave demonstration at Intel's Intercast site shows you what the screen will look like.

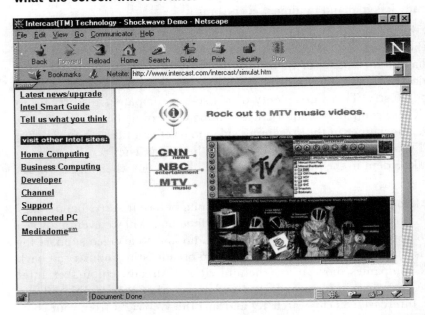

Desktop Video and Editing

With the arrival of better computers and better multimedia, computer owners are seeing more audio and video, meaning more Internet audio and video, too. Many new computers are arriving with digital video cameras preinstalled for use in videoconferencing, and some even include video capture cards.

Digital cameras are becoming popular for videoconferencing, but they can also be used for video capture. Those with capture cards, even inexpensive ones like a TV tuner card, can be used to capture video.

The biggest area of growth will probably be desktop video, specifically the low-end video capture and editing market. The most popular products are external video capture devices that connect to a parallel port and capture video from any video source, like VCRs, TV, and camcorders. Makers from Iomega, Alaris, Intel, and many others have already entered this market, and many other manufacturers are releasing similar products. They all hope to replicate the success of Play Inc.'s Snappy, a still-image capturing system that sold like hotcakes. Companies are hoping that consumers (home users mostly) will flock to these devices to capture video for use over the Internet or for putting their home movies on their computers.

If these consumer-oriented capture devices sell well, a large number of people will be introduced to computer video. They will also need to learn about compression, editing, and storing files. More video is being used on the Internet, and more video is everywhere. Users may even want to try out hosting and playing some streaming video.

Multimedia Advertising

Advertising could be the application that really makes video popular. It is also another revenue stream for people using streaming multimedia. For example, some web sites using RealAudio and RealVideo have had ads appearing in programming since at least 1996. Usually, the ad appears first, followed by the requested program, although some prefer to include the ad at the end. One of the more ubiquitous ads was a 30-second video for MCI. It was basically a television commercial for long distance, with audio and video that was displayed in RealVideo format. Now there is much more advertising (see Figure 22.3).

If you are using RealAudio or RealVideo on your site, you too can start accepting real advertising. Or, you can make a RealVideo ad automatically pop up when you visit a certain page on your site. Some Internet-only radio broadcasts feature

Figure 22.3 Here's another ad appearing in RealVideo. It has a clickable video screen so you can be taken directly to the advertiser's web page.

commercials just like any other traditional radio broadcast. Sound interesting? Sometime in the future, we can expect it to more closely resemble TV. You might see a 5-minute clip, followed by a 30-second ad, then another clip, and so on. Like banner ads, video and audio advertising will be everywhere.

Video banner advertising, like the V-Banner by InterVU (www.intervu.net), will also become more popular. A picture is worth a thousand words, but an effective video can mean a thousand customers. Imagine being able to show off your product to hundreds or thousands of web surfers. You can make quick streaming clips or make longer videos integrated into your web page.

Another method is those interactive, animated Enliven banner ads. Enliven offers advertisements with sound, streaming capability, Java playback, interactivity, and plenty of usage data. This is a great example of what can be done with streaming multimedia today and what it will be like in the future, too.

Killer Application

Despite all the hubbub about streaming multimedia, there are few true "killer" or must-have applications. Streaming video over the Internet is really just for entertainment right now. Many sites use video to make cool videos or audio, like a clip of a music video from a new band. Other companies like CNN or ESPN use it for news and sports where video really informs and enhances the image. Still, most of the sites using streaming audio or video are big corporations, like movie studios, TV stations, news organizations, and so forth. What are some possible killer applications in the future? Let's look in the crystal ball again.

Internet Broadcasts

The age of 500-channel "television" is here already, except it is on the Web. Perhaps the number should be raised to 1,000 or 5,000 channels; there are many sites and users with video-on-demand. With today's streaming technology and some hardware, almost anyone can create his or her own video show and broadcast it over the Web. (Ted Turner, watch out!) The question is: Do people want to see it? You can record anything on video and slap it on the Internet, but there needs to be really compelling reasons to use it first.

Pay-Per-View

With so many videos available on the Net, will there soon be pay-per-view movies? It seems like a great way to get more revenue. You can have training videos that companies can buy or rent from you or you can offer music videos (or songs) for rental. If you are sponsoring a trade show, you can charge money to simulcast the training sessions or other industry talks. You can even have interactive training sessions where users can see presentations and hear audio and video. For VRML, you can charge users to play games or to use multiuser worlds. Much like the Internet was mostly free, most audio and video content is free, but this will surely change. As the Internet moved to a more commercial-oriented medium, so will multimedia like audio and video

Training

So far, the killer app for enterprise video is training. Many intranets are putting their networks to work by using live or on-demand video training. There are so many advantages: save time, save travel costs, fewer travel headaches, and better learning and interaction. Employee training is one of the biggest expenses of any company—why not use a mix of on-demand videos and live multicast training sessions instead? On-demand videos can be self-paced, so employees can go over a certain topic again for better comprehension. Video is better than those stacks of manuals for learning retention. At the RealStore (www.realstore.com), you can even buy training videos (like help on using Windows95, Word, Excel, and other programs) that are broadcast with RealVideo.

| NOTE | Training is a great application, but before going headlong into it, there are some drawbacks or things to consider. To save money, you should convert existing course materials into streaming video materials. After all, why reinvent the wheel? That may mean hours of converting video or hiring an outside bureau to help you create training videos from your manuals. Another consideration is time. If you're planning live training sessions to be broadcast in different time zones, you need to do some time shifting, especially if you have locations in other countries. You may need to broadcast multiple training sessions to better suit some locations. Another important consideration is to make sure all your client computers have audio and video capability. So many corporate workers have older computers or don't have multimedia, that you'll need to do some upgrading if you're serious about intranet audio and video. Look especially at those users with laptops, since their multimedia capabilities vary widely. Lastly, using video instead of face-to-face training can seem impersonal to some employees; having a combination of live, on-demand manuals and in-person training seems like the best solution.

Commerce

Commerce is a big application and will lead the growth of the Internet. You can see some commerce examples with streaming multimedia at sites like CDNow, an online music store. CDNow (www.cdnow.com) lets you listen to 30-second clips of artists to hear samples before you buy music, and LiquidAudio and its music partners are bringing that to the next level by allowing purchasing and downloading of music. Animation and VRML also bring new commerce ability. You can have interactive animated shopping sites with synchronized audio, or you can show off your item in three dimensions using VRML. Soon, we'll use virtual money, visit virtual worlds, and see virtual merchandise.

New Protocols: RTSP, RTP, RTCP, RSVP

The new wave of networking protocols is somewhat confusing. This can all be technical gobbledygook to you, but others really enjoy this stuff. In any event, it helps to know what's coming with these new protocols, so let's clear it up with definitions:

> **RTSP**. Real-Time Streaming Protocol. This protocol will be used to initiate and direct delivery of streaming media. RTSP can work with RTP and HTTP to control and deliver Internet media. You have full stream control, security, and you can even use IP multicasting with it. It was submitted to the IETF for ratification and may be ratified by sometime in 1998. Major proponents of RTSP are RealNetworks and Netscape who have been joined by several other companies.

> **RTP**. Real-Time Transport Protocol. This is a current standard already ratified by the ITU and IETF as a lower-transport protocol. Some streaming programs already use RTP, and it can be used with RTSP or work independently.

> **RTCP**. Real-Time Control Protocol. This is part of RTP and is used for time-critical Quality of Service applications.

> **RSVP**. Resource Reservation Protocol. This is a type of guaranteed service, that asks for a certain amount of bandwidth to be used for an application. This provides an end-to-end guaranteed service, which may be better suited for applications that need high upstream and downstream throughput.

> These protocols will enable better, faster, and even guaranteed delivery of data, so there'll be no more dropped packets. For more information, head to RealNetworks'

RTSP page (www6.real.com/rtsp/) or visit the ITU (www.itu.ch) or IETF (www.ietf.org) to see if they have been ratified yet.

Ten Technologies to Watch

Anything that benefits streaming multimedia will benefit the Internet as well. All the items discussed earlier will be important to us all. But there are so many other advances and new products being released all the time that it can be hard to keep track of them all. What should you keep an eye on? What is emerging? They can't all be covered here, but the next sections list some up-and-coming technologies that we'll be seeing a lot more of in the future.

Videoconferencing

Internet videoconferencing is a distant cousin of streaming audio and video. It is two-way communication as opposed to one-way. You can connect one on one to another user or with a group of people, like a video chat room. Right now, there are dozens of Internet videoconferencing systems available for Windows95 and Macintosh users, but there is no real market leader. Microsoft has gotten into the game by giving away its NetMeeting program with Internet Explorer 4.0, but other programs have held onto market share.

The great thing about the videoconferencing industry is that it has agreed on a standard that makes all programs interoperable. (At least in theory—this is pretty new, so it may take some tweaking for software to work together.) For example, someone using NetMeeting can communicate with someone using White Pine's CU-SeeMe (www.cu-seeme.com). Interoperability is just the improvement streaming multimedia needs.

Internet Telephony

Along with videoconferencing, voice over the Internet will continue to improve. You can presently use your computer and the Internet to call other web users, but more importantly you can now even reach a telephone on the other end, not just a computer user. You can actually dial a telephone and talk to someone in another country at considerable savings over normal long-distance costs. Voice over the Internet doesn't have pin-drop quality yet, but there have been many advances in compression and quality recently.

Many companies are now experimenting with using Internet telephony to send faxes and make long distance phone calls. As you can imagine, this will spell trouble to the long-distance carriers, who make much of their money from businesses, fax transmissions, and international calls. So far, they aren't too concerned but that's just because IP telephony is so new. Once more people (and companies) start using IP telephony, competition will really heat up. Someday soon, you may get a call from a telemarketer asking you to switch your long-distance company to Microsoft.

Java

As this book has shown, Java plays an very important part in streaming multimedia. Many companies are using Java to play audio, video, and animation files, so that no plug-in is required. This is a great use for Java, something that its maker, Sun Microsystems, is probably gleeful about. Java must continue to be a "write once, run anywhere" language; otherwise, it will splinter off into many divergent paths. Unfortunately, Microsoft is using a slightly different version of Java that runs optimized on 32-bit Windows computers. That means you need to write Java for Microsoft Windows 95/98/NT users and another version for everyone else.

Push

In late 1996 through early 1997, push was the darling of the Internet. Companies flocked to provide push news, sports, and weather to computer desktops. Now that the buzz has calmed somewhat, it makes sense to take another look at it. Both Internet Explorer 4.0 and Communicator 4.0 include some type of push to send web pages to your desktop. However, these work best for people who are always connected to the Internet. New versions and products have been using push to make life easier for you. Some companies are making push that can deliver data as well as audio and video to desktops. Since push technology can be bandwidth intensive, some companies are looking to IP multicasting for sending out push data. As more people use high-speed Internet access and are always connected to the Internet, you can expect push to become popular once again.

Animation and VRML

Animation and VRML are key to the development of multimedia. Animation has come a long way since the early days of Shockwave. Programs like Flash, mBED, Emblaze, and Enliven are leading the way to a highly interactive, animated Web. This interaction will change dramatically so that one day we won't need plug-ins at all, and we'll all be accustomed to highly animated sites.

VRML, too, has seen a dramatic improvement. You can now watch animations within a VRML world, hear sound, and even see video. With the VRML97 specification and new streaming players, VRML will continue to improve and be better received by mass computer users.

FireWire

For professional video capture, FireWire is very good news. FireWire, or the IEEE 1394 connection system, is nothing more than a very high-speed (400Mbps) digital connection to your computer somewhat like parallel or serial ports on steroids. So far, FireWire doesn't have many applications beside video capture from digital camcorders to computers. To use FireWire, you'll need a FireWire PCI card installed on your computer and a compatible DV camcorder (Sony or Panasonic make them). FireWire is perfect for video capture because it uses a fast digital connection, so there is practically no loss of audio or video quality—the data stays in digital form through the whole capture process. So far, there are few FireWire cards available, but miro, Truevision, and Fast have some available. FireWire is not for the video-meek or the amateurs—it is for high-end, video professionals who can afford the high price and need high quality digital capture.

Metered Bandwidth

Metered or tiered bandwidth means that intranet managers and ISPs can control the bandwidth used on a network. New software allows you to distribute just a certain amount of bandwidth to certain tasks. It is called *metered* because theoretically you can charge extra for high-bandwidth applications like streaming video or videoconferencing. You can charge by the megabyte or by the actual bandwidth used. Check for companies and products like Xedia (www.xedia.com), Packetshaper (www.packeteer.com), Ipath (www.thestructure.com), Fore Systems (www.fore.com), and Ipsilon (www.ipsilon.com). They sometimes use hardware, software, or a combination of the two to control bandwidth.

DVD-ROM

DVD is an important step for computing. Although the first-generation DVD-ROM drives weren't that great, new upgrades being released now are better in terms of price, compatibility, and storage. DVD-ROM disks can hold 4.7GB of data on a single side, or 9.8GB double-sided. There will also be recordable DVDs as well as rewriteable DVDs. DVD movies being sold now use the MPEG-2 video codec and the Dolby Digital codec for audio, also known as AC-3. This is important because DVD-ROM will eventually replace CD-ROM, and that means more room to hold longer movies, games, software titles, and, of course, multimedia.

USB

If you bought a new Windows-compatible computer in the last year or so, you probably have USB ports but have never used them. USB (Universal Serial Bus) is a new way to connect devices like mice, keyboards, monitors, joysticks, drives, printers, or other peripherals to your computer. The difference is that USB is much faster (12Mbps) than your old serial or parallel connections and it is true plug and play, so you can disconnect or connect devices on the fly. It can even support 127 devices at once. USB will eventually replace the slow, serial and parallel ports we use now since Windows98 will finally take full advantage of these connections. We will be able to daisy-chain a lot of equipment together, so we'll probably never run out of devices to hook up to our computers. There are only a few USB products on the market so far, (the first was a USB digital video camera) but plenty more will be on the way. Although USB and FireWire may seem similar and perform similar functions, both serve different markets and will most likely work together. So keep an eye out for new USB devices and get on the bus.

Internet 2

A new, bigger, better, faster Internet is being developed right now by over 100 universities and many high-tech companies. It will be called *Internet 2*, (www.internet2.edu). The Internet we use now was originally intended to be used by academics, scholars, and scientists. The Internet has evolved such that it is now used by marketers, advertisers, shoppers, teenagers, and everyone else. Internet 2 will be for research and educational use only and is promised to be 100 to 1,000 times faster than the first Internet. Development is slow going, so details are sketchy. Companies involved include Digital Equipment, IBM, MCI, and Sun Microsystems. Can you imagine what can be done with that speed? Videoconferencing, streaming data, push, data collaboration, and more. Eventually, Internet 2 is expected to be turned over to the public after a few years, making way perhaps for Internet 3.

Which Vendors Will Succeed?

There are many programs to choose from and they all have their plusses and minuses—you shouldn't leap into streaming multimedia too quickly. Weigh your options and make sure that you actually need it and that there are practical applications that you actually use.

Which companies will succeed out of all the ones mentioned in this book? Which ones will fold and pack it in? The successful companies will:

- Be cross-platform. This will enable you to send targeted media to desktops no matter what the operating system.

- Have video-on-demand.

- Support IP multicasting.

- Support its products and have good customer support.

- Make applications that make your daily work easier and solve problems.

- Have some type of commerce angle, like advertising or sales.

- Save you money in the long run with a good return on your investment in hardware and software.

- Conform to industry-wide standards to ensure long-term growth.

- Support HTTP streaming as well as client/server.

- Have a large client base.

- Forge key alliances with other important companies or nab important clients.

- Be one of the first to come out with a good, high-quality, innovative product. Historically, those that blaze the trail on the Internet are winners. Think of Yahoo!, Netscape, RealAudio, etc.

- Support Java or some other way to eliminate plug-ins.

What other qualities are important to you and your company?

Summary

So far, streaming multimedia is in the formative stage. New deals are being announced all the time. Existing products are constantly being updated. By the time you read this book, many things will have changed. There will be new products, a market leader, and perhaps the end of proprietary streaming formats. When the dust settles, you can bet Microsoft will be at or near the top.

The future of streaming multimedia means no less than the future of the Internet and the future of computing. Where it will ultimately take us is anyone's guess.

Streaming multimedia will finally be successful when we no longer talk about it as something separate and distinct from regular multimedia. Streaming multimedia will have finally arrived when we can remove the word "streaming" from the title of this book.

A COLLECTION OF
Miscellaneous Streaming Multimedia Systems

Unfortunately, this book can't cover all the streaming multimedia programs. So far, we have covered the major programs that you should be familiar with and other unique technologies. The problem is that there are so many streaming audio and video programs continually released; it is difficult to keep up with all the new products. This chapter contains a potpourri of additional streaming audio and video systems that couldn't be covered in depth in this book. It gives you some details about the programs and how they work, so you get a glimpse of the range and number of systems available to you.

Don't think that the programs listed in this chapter are any worse than the other systems mentioned in this book. On the contrary, many are actually very good. One has received much praise from the computer press (WebFORCE MediaBase), while another has Java-playback ability (Vosaic). Another system is a network of mirrors that can host your video and deliver it to clients in a timely manner (InterVU). There are many large companies whose products are covered in this chapter, like Intel, Silicon Graphics, Netscape, and IBM. There are streaming video systems and even a client/server streaming 3-D system. There are also many audio programs here like a streaming MIDI system (Crescendo), streaming speech, and interactive music (Beatnik).

Some of these programs are older and not used very often. Others were either too new to test or were unreleased. Either way, they still deserve mention in this book. I hope to present the whole spectrum of streaming multimedia so that ultimately, you will seek out more information and decide for yourself which programs suit your needs.

More Streaming Video Systems

There are so many streaming video systems it can make your head spin. Earlier in the book, you've already seen at least 12 video systems. This chapter adds another five or six to the bunch. As you'll see, some big-name companies like IBM and Intel are getting into the act, as are unknown companies that are just jumping into this field. This section focuses on some new and not-so-new video systems that are available. Some are so new that you may find that product names have changed. Simply check the manufacturer's homepage and then do a search on "streaming" to see if you can find the software.

Vosaic

Vosaic by Vosaic LLC has a number of products that can stream audio and video. It includes a client-server system and a Java-playback system for no-plug-in, live or on-demand audio or video. The following list sums up Vosaic's repertoire:

Vosaic TV Station for Java. This is Vosaic's live video solution that allows Java playback, so you don't need any plug-ins. You can send data to a large number of clients over the Internet, including 28.8Kbps and 56Kbps modem users. TV Station has been used to transmit the Mars Pathfinder Mission and other high-profile events.

Vosaic Radio Studio for Java. This is an audio streaming program with Java playback. It uses HTTP streaming to send data from regular web servers. The program comes with a converter that converts WAV, AVI, AIFF, AU, and MPEG sound to GSM format. GSM sound can play back audio even at speeds as low at 14.4Kbps. Radio Studio runs on Windows95 or NT and comes with the Java RadioApplet for playback. All you do is add a button on a web page for playback. Just press the button, and after a short buffer time, the audio starts to play.

Vosaic RadioStation. This is similar to RadioStudio, but is its more advanced cousin.

Vosaic's client server system is called the MediaSuite. It has three components: the client, server, and encoder.

MediaClient 1.02. The MediaClient is the client program where users view incoming Vosaic streams. It has full VCR-type controls (see Figure A.1). Data that is sent from the server can dynamically adapt to the current bandwidth, so video looks stable no matter what the traffic. The

Figure A.1 Vosaic has two systems for streaming: one that uses Java and another that uses a plug-in. Here is the plug-in program showing video from the Mars Pathfinder mission.

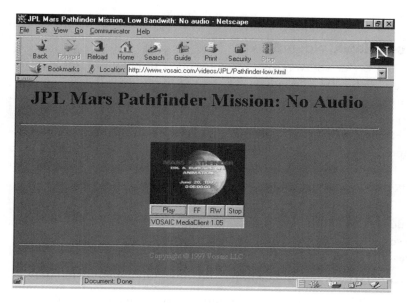

MediaClient is available for Windows 95/NT, Mac, and UNIX (SPARC Solaris 5.5 and IRIX 5.3).

MediaStudio 1.06. The MediaStudio is used to convert audio and video files from MPEG, AVI, and WAV source files into Vosaic format. It comes with a software MPEG encoder, but you can use hardware, too. The MediaStudio comes free with the MediaServer and is available for Windows95 and Windows NT.

Vosaic MediaServer 1.04. The MediaServer is the server component. It works with any regular web server and is available for Windows95, NT, Linux, SGI IRIX, and Sun Solaris. It can control how many people can log on at once and offers sophisticated logging capabilities to get accurate demographics.

Vosaic's technology was created by The Department of Computer Science at the University of Illinois in 1994. They dubbed it "video mosaic," or Vosaic. In 1996, the company Vosaic LLC was formed to bring this technology to market.

Vosaic LLC
1524 Cloverfield, Suite F
Santa Monica, CA 90404
(310) 315-9211
www.vosaic.com

Concurrent MediaHawk Video Server

Concurrent MediaHawk Video Servers are unlike any other programs in this book in that they are for very high-end use. MediaHawk is a full-hardware/software solution featuring computers with multiple processors, RAID (Redundant Array of Independent Disk) disk arrays, along with redundant power supplies for constant, no-failure use. MediaHawk supports 50 to 1,000 simultaneous video streams and can provide up to 8,000 terabytes of storage capacity. Quality remains high, no matter how many streams are being served. Every MediaHawk system comes with a Concurrent multiprocessor, high-performance computer with the PowerMAX OS operating system. As you can see, this isn't just your ordinary streaming video solution.

MediaHawk doesn't use multicasting; it delivers independent streams to every user. That way, every video can be custom delivered depending on network speed and quality requested. There is no single encoding of streams.

Concurrent's MediaHawk line of hardware/software systems are listed here:

MediaHawk-SX. This is a mini-tower computer that supports up to 50 digital video streams. It costs $29,900.

MediaHawk-MX. This is a rack-mount or tabletop computer with multiple processors (PowerPC chips) that can stream up to 225 video streams. Its starting price is $55,900.

MediaHawk-LX. The LX is Concurrent's high-end system. It can use five processors to serve 375 streams but can be custom-configured to handle over 1,000. Its base price is $77,900.

MediaHawk serves TV-quality video to clients that can completely control the movie with VCR-like controls including pause, fast forward, and rewind. The clients are generally noncomputer equipment like television sets, information kiosks, and computer monitors. MediaHawk is not for use with personal computers like Windows or Mac, although it does support UNIX for intranet use. MediaHawk is best used for in-flight entertainment, interactive gambling, intranets, hotels, cable entertainment, pay-per-view videos, kiosks, shopping, weather information, and any other video-on-demand use.

MediaHawk is included in this book because the future of computer video is with applications like these. With the arrival of high-speed connections like ADSL, cable, and ATM, we'll be seeing video-on-demand everywhere.

Concurrent sells computer systems and real-time and video-on-demand systems. MediaHawk's customers include Mitsubishi, SAAB, Volvo, and B.F. Goodrich.

Concurrent Computer Corp.
2101 West Cypress Creek Road
Fort Lauderdale, FL 33309
(800) 666-4544
(954) 974-1700
www.ccur.com

Silicon Graphics' WebFORCE MediaBase

MediaBase from Silicon Graphics is a complete UNIX system. It comes as a hardware (the WebFORCE workstation) and software (MediaBase) solution that can be quickly implemented and scaled for use on the Internet or for high-quality applications like intranets and film studio needs. MediaBase supports streaming over 28.8Kbps connections or over very fast networks like Fast Ethernet (100-BaseT) or ATM. It can send live or on-demand audio and video to a large number of clients. On-demand unicast streams are supported, but it also uses multicasting. It can stream to hundreds of on-demand users or thousands of multicast users depending on available bandwidth.

The hardware part of this system is Silicon Graphics' UNIX workstation called WebFORCE. If you don't own its workstation, you can most likely use MediaBase on your UNIX computer on your intranet. The server software is browser-based, so you can monitor operations, check network usage and server logs, and much more. MediaBase also comes with content management software for generating a video catalog to keep track of your growing video library. You can also allow full searching of all videos as well let users browse through the titles.

On the client side, viewers need to use a plug-in or helper applications available for Windows95, NT, Macintosh, and UNIX computers. They can see full-motion video and have full VCR controls. For better video quality and decoding, you can use MPEG decoders at client stations.

MediaBase is meant for high-end usage like entertainment on demand, multimedia, education, and kiosks, but it can also be used on an intranet with very good results. If you're a UNIX shop, MediaBase is a very good choice. MediaBase can be purchased in 10, 20, 50, 100, 250, and 500 user versions, and it comes with Silicon Graphics' hardware servers like O2, Challenge, and Origin.

Silicon Graphics sells workstations and makes software for a variety of applications. Partners of MediaBase include companies like Xing Technology, Vosaic, and RealNetworks. You can find out more about the MediaBase systems and WebFORCE workstations at www.sgi.com/Products/WebFORCE/Mediabase/.

Silicon Graphics, Inc.
2011 N. Shoreline Blvd.
Mountain View, CA 94043
(650) 960-1980
www.sgi.com

Galacticomm WebCast

WebCast specializes in live audio and video broadcasting that doesn't need a plug-in; it uses server push technology to push video frames to the browser. The best way to describe how WebCast works is to think of those spy cameras that have proliferated on the Internet. They show live camera views of street corners or beaches around the world. Unfortunately, WebCast doesn't support on-demand video, just live broadcasting.

WebCast supports just Windows95 and NT computers. It comes in three flavors:

WebCast Lite. This is the free trial version of WebCast. This version only supports one stream so it's good for one-on-one use, but it doesn't support audio—just video. To use it, sign up at Galacticomm's website, download the software, and set up your equipment. You can be up and running in just a few minutes.

WebCast Personal. This is best for personal use. It can handle four simultaneous streams and support audio *and* video. It has advanced features like call waiting, password access, an address book, caller ID, and call blocking. WebCast Personal costs $29.95 if you purchase via download, or $49.95 retail.

WebCast ProServer. The ProServer is for business use. You can add merchant ability and all the other advanced features mentioned in the Personal system. It can handle up to 26 simultaneous streams and has all the advanced features of the two smaller systems, including email ability, polling and accounting, and management. The ProServer costs $995. You can use the WebCast Video Broadcaster Add-on to give your ProServer an additional five video streams. The Add-on is an additional $495.

WebCast works best if you have a constant connection to the Internet, because WebCast sends the captured camera frames from your local computer to WebCast's website. From there, viewers can visit the WebCast users' page at webcast.gcomm

.com and select a user from the list. The video should appear in just a few seconds. If the video is down, it may mean that you've chosen someone showing video with dial-up access and that they aren't connected now. Window size is usually 320×200 and your frame rate depends on your modem speed. At 28.8Kbps, you can expect no more than approximately 5 frames per second. You need to use Netscape Navigator to view WebCast video since only Netscape fully supports it. Internet Explorer users can now use WebCast, but it uses Java to show video.

WebCast is a great product for beginners who want to experiment with live broadcasting. Anyone with a parallel-port web camera like those used for video-conferencing can use it to broadcast to a small number of people like friends or family. It supports high-end capture board/camera combinations, which will yield better frame rates and quality. The WebCast ProServer is meant for business use, but the low number of simultaneous streams may limit its usefulness. It may be better suited for home office companies.

Galacticomm makes a wide range of Internet software, including online games, chat, BBS, and web server software.

Galacticomm, Inc.
4101 SW 47th Ave., Suite 101
Fort Lauderdale, FL 33314
(954) 583-5990
www.gcomm.com/webcast

InterVU Network by InterVU

The InterVU Network is technically not a software streaming system like the others in this book. It is a combination of an advertising system, a video hosting company, and a network delivery system. InterVU is a proprietary network that will also host your Internet video on a network of mirror sites, then deliver it to clients. It has mirror sites or delivery centers at different locations in the Internet backbone so that video is automatically delivered from sites that are closest to the recipient's location. This way, bottlenecks can be avoided. Ultimately, the InterVU network was created to facilitate the job of delivering Internet video to the largest number of users in a timely manner.

To help viewers get the right players, InterVU has a service called EyeQ. It allows users to download a series of free multimedia players so that they can see a wide range of Internet video. Included in EyeQ are MPEG, AVI, and QuickTime players. It also includes the VivoActive player. After downloading each of the players for you, it automatically installs them onto your computer. EyeQ can even alert you when software is out of date, a big plus in quickly changing "Internet time." Although downloading all these programs will take a very long time, it may end up saving you time in the long run. The main purpose of EyeQ is to prepare users to view all types of industry-standard video formats, making it easy to deliver the videos. The EyeQ package is available for Windows 95/NT users only, but software for Macintosh is coming.

EyeQ works well with the InterVU Network because it delivers video to a large number of clients. The InterVU Network also has a feature called All Eyes, which automatically detects and delivers video in the appropriate format for each user. For example, if a user doesn't have the VivoActive player installed, it will automatically deliver the video in another format, like AVI. If there is no AVI player installed, it will send it as an MPEG video, and so on. Basically, you can prioritize the order of the video format you want to deliver. Do you want VivoActive video to be the first choice of video that your viewers can view, or do you want to send it as an AVI file? If a person viewing your movie doesn't have any of the players installed, All Eyes will simply display a JPEG image.

The InterVU Network and All Eyes also make possible the V-Banner, a web banner ad that includes streaming video. Practically all users can see the video banner ads because it automatically changes the video to whatever player users have installed on their computers. Video ads are very compelling and fun. Clickthrough rates for V-Banner ads are purportedly two to three times the rates of ordinary banner ads. There have already been video ads from Goldwin Golf, Major League Baseball, Hewlett-Packard, Budweiser, and a preview of the movie Air Force One appearing on websites like Yahoo! and Lycos. They are banner ads that include a short repeating video clip (see Figure A.2).

Click on the banner ad to be taken to another page where you see the larger commercial (see Figure A.3). This one has sound, better quality video, and it streams. InterVU automatically detects the player best suited for you. If you don't have any multimedia player installed, it simply displays a JPEG image.

Is InterVU a good idea? It's hard to say because, so far, there aren't that many companies using it. There are some advantages, however, to this arrangement. If you are a small website and need to support more simultaneous viewers, InterVU is a good choice since it hosts and delivers video from its network. You're free to deliver web data, not video streams. Also, you won't need to invest in new software, hardware, bandwidth, or training when using video; just let InterVU worry about all that. On the client side, InterVU offers a good range of video players and even promises to deliver faster videos. The V-Banner system seems to be the best thing about InterVU. It is a fun and practical use for streaming video since, after all, a video ad is a great way to introduce users to your product.

Figure A.2 You can see V-Banner video ads at Lycos and Yahoo!. First watch the small clip in the banner ad, then click on the ad.

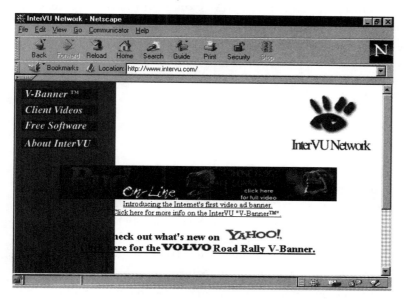

InterVU's main business is the InterVU Network and V-Banner. Support is coming for V-Banner in the way of ad monitoring from Accipiter and NetGravity, two leading advertising tracking companies.

InterVU Inc.
201 Lomas Santa Fe Drive
San Diego, CA 92075
(619) 350-1600
www.intervu.net

Intel Streaming Media Viewer

Another recent entry into the streaming multimedia market is Intel. It released the Streaming Media Viewer as a plug-in for Windows95 users. It is a streaming audio/video system for use over 28.8Kbps connections, and it can also handle still images with an audio track. It can be used on LANs, but the system is made for transmission of 28.8Kbps, so the quality will remain at that low data rate even on high-speed networks.

The Streaming Media Viewer is meant to be used in conjunction with Intel's Video Capture and Share Application and is available for Windows95 users only;

no support is planned for Windows 3.1 or NT. Intel also recently released the new Indeo 5.0 codec which delivers progressive downloading of non-streaming video files with improved performance on Pentium MMX and Pentium II computers. For more information on the Streaming Media Viewer go to connectedpc.com/iaweb/ streaming/index.htm.

Intel Corporation
2200 Mission College Blvd., P.O. Box 58119
Santa Clara, CA 95052-8119
(408) 765-8080
www.intel.com

IBM Bamba

Bamba is a new audio and video streaming system from IBM's laboratory website called AlphaWorks (www.alphaworks.ibm.com). Bamba was just finishing beta testing as this book was being written, but don't expect a big roll-out; most AlphaWorks projects are quietly available to any web developers who want to try them out. Bamba can stream using HTTP or its own LiveBamba protocol. It can also handle live or on-demand audio and video. The stream adjusts to the client's bandwidth, so it is scaleable for use at 10 to 300Kbps.

Bamba consists of three plug-ins, and an audio and video encoder. You need to install the Bamba Audio, Live Audio, and Video plug-ins to play Bamba audio and

Figure A.3 Once you click on a V-Banner ad, the main video commercial plays for you.

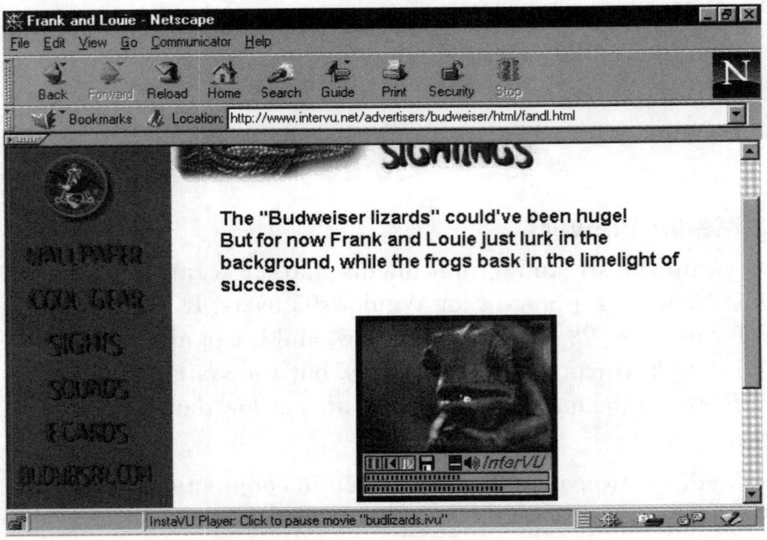

video. To convert files to Bamba format (ABA and VBA), you need to use the Bamba Audio and Video Encoders.

Bamba is available for Windows95, Windows NT, Macintosh and IBM's OS/2 Warp 4.0, which makes this program the only streaming multimedia program available for the OS/2 operating system. There is also an all-Java player available. So far, there aren't many places to see Bamba video or hear Bamba audio. You need to connect to the AlphaWorks site to learn more and experiment with it (see Figure A.4).

AlphaWorks is IBM's research center that is showcasing new products in development and other raw technologies. IBM was at the forefront of the personal computing revolution and still remains a major force in the computer market. It makes computer systems, storage devices, peripherals, networking systems, and software for businesses and home users.

International Business Machines (IBM)
One Old Orchard Road
Armonk, NY 10504
(914) 499-1900
www.alphaworks.ibm.com
www.ibm.com

Figure A.4 Bamba is IBM's audio/video system. This is the Bamba Encoder for converting files.

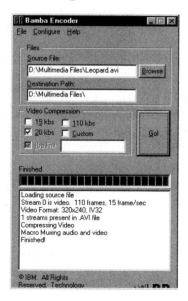

Envision Enterprise by Adaptive Media

Another new system is Envision Enterprise, so named because it is for use over Enterprise networks. It provides streaming on-demand audio and video, and is narrowly targeted to the corporate arena, so you probably won't find anyone using it over the Internet. Envision supports streams as low as 56Kbps to as high as 1.5Mbps.

Envision is an MPEG-based, client-server system. It optimizes delivery to clients so that video will look good on low-end computers or high-end Pentium computers. The three components of Envision are:

Envision MediaManager. This is the server software. It has tools to help manage and deploy the system. It works on Windows NT.

Envision Desktop. Desktop is the client component. It is available for Windows95 and NT and is a plug-in and ActiveX control.

Envision Studio. Studio converts audio and video MPEG files into Envision format. It is available for Windows95 and NT.

Adaptive Media also makes Envision 3D, a non-VRML, streaming 3-D system for use over corporate intranets. It is also a client-server system. Envision can accept and convert VRML 2.0 files, but is best used with professional CAD/CAM files. Mostly companies like engineering firms, construction companies, aerospace, CAD/CAM, and architectural firms can benefit from using it.

Adaptive Media Inc.
477 Potrero Ave.
Sunnyvale, CA 94086
(408) 481-1700
www.adaptivemedia.com

WebCRE by Sandalwood

One of the newest video systems is called WebCRE by Sandalwood Software. WebCRE was released in November 1997.

WebCRE is a server-less streaming audio/video system for Windows 95/NT. Sandalwood promises 10 fps video over 14.4Kbps, which is impressive, but the video window size is under 100×100 pixels. WebCRE has two video codecs and five audio codecs. Upon conversion with its codecs, the file can be compressed at a 600:1 compression rate. Unfortunately, when I tested WebCRE, there was a long wait time to view the movie, (too much buffering) plus the audio and video paused too often making the video unwatchable.

There are plug-ins for Windows 95/NT, plus you can use a Java-enabled browser for when you don't have the plug-in installed. Version 2.0 of WebCRE was slated to be released soon, so look for more at Sandalwood's website.

Sandalwood Software, Inc.
555 South State Street
Orem, UT 84058
(801) 379-0789
www.sandalwood.com
www.webcre.com

Oracle Video Server

Oracle, a top maker of database management software, is also a player in video networking. The Video Server is a high-end intranet system that can achieve full-screen, full-motion video along with CD-quality audio. Video streams can be in MPEG1 or AVI format, and MPEG2 streams are also supported with the proper hardware and bandwidth.

Oracle Video Server is a client/server system; the client software runs on Windows95 and NT, while the server runs on Windows NT and UNIX (including Sun's Solaris, SGI's IRIX, and Hewlett-Packards' HP-UX 10 operating systems). Its best performance is on Ethernet or Fast Ethernet networks or other faster networks.

Oracle is the second largest software company in the world. Although its main product line mostly deals with databases, Oracle has a wide range of enterprise products, tools and services. For more information on Oracle Video Server visit www.oracle.com/products/asd/video/video.html.

Oracle Corp.
500 Oracle Parkway
Redwood Shores, CA 94065
(650) 506-7000
www.oracle.com

More Streaming Audio Systems

Now that RealAudio has taken over the Web, it is tough for other streaming audio products to make much of a dent. Other vendors won't have much luck trying to compete against RealAudio. This section mostly has low-end streaming audio solutions. Some are free, while others are very low-cost and, with the exception of Netscape's LiveAudio, are not meant for business use. Most are aimed at the personal, home user who want to add streaming audio to their site at a low cost.

The coolest program is Beatnik, a non-streaming system that allows you to interact and control music on a web page.

Without further ado, take a look at some other streaming audio programs.

Netscape LiveAudio

Throughout this book, Netscape has been rather conspicuous by its absence in the streaming multimedia field. When Netscape released Navigator 3.0, it released a streaming audio program called LiveAudio. It was to be part of its LiveMedia architecture, which also included a VRML viewer called Live3D. Since then, Live3D has been dropped in favor of Cosmo Software's VRML viewer. LiveAudio still exists, but it hasn't been improved since its introduction. Netscape has been very slow in developing LiveMedia and in releasing new streaming multimedia programs. LiveAudio is stagnating while other vendors like Microsoft and RealNetworks have advanced their media products tremendously and even moved into the video streaming arena. It is possible that Netscape is working on a better audio or video streaming program, but they refuse to divulge their plans and no rumors have been circulating.

Nevertheless, LiveAudio still exists and can be found more on intranets than on the Internet. LiveAudio is a client/server system that can handle live and on-demand streaming audio, and it can stream AU, WAV, or LiveAudio files. The LiveMedia system has three parts:

Media Converter. This program converts AU or WAV files into the LiveMedia format. It is available for Windows95 and NT.

Media Player. This is the client plug-in that is used to listen to LiveAudio content. It is a plug-in, not an external player, so audio is embedded into web pages, and it offers good cross-platform support. The player is available for Macintosh, Windows 95/NT, and a variety of UNIX systems like Sun Solaris, SGI IRIX, and AIX.

Media Server. Netscape's Media Server is available separately or with the Netscape Enterprise Server. The Media Server is available for Windows NT and UNIX (Sun Solaris and SGI IRIX) for about $1,995 when included with the Enterprise Server.

For being a few years old, LiveAudio has some good features. LiveAudio uses a wide range of protocols like TCP/IP, RTP, and UDP to stream data. It also led the way to RTSP, a new streaming protocol, and IP multicast. Audio content can also be integrated with HTML, Java, JavaScript, or other multimedia.

As part of the LiveMedia architecture, Netscape has several partners, including Macromedia and RealNetworks. For more on LiveMedia, check out Netscape's site at home.netscape.com/eng/media.

Netscape Communications
501 East Middlefield Road
Mountain View, CA 94043
(650) 254-1900
home.netscape.com
home.netscape.com/comprod/server_central/product/media/index.html
info@netscape.com

Vocaltec's Internet Wave

Internet Wave is a free, server-less streaming audio system. It works with existing web servers to send good-quality speech and music to anyone using the Internet Wave plug-in. Since it uses the TCP/IP protocol, it can bypass firewalls. Internet Wave is available for Windows 3.1, Windows95, and NT.

Internet Wave comes in two pieces: the plug-in that plays the audio and the Internet Wave Encoder for converting files. You also get a CGI utility that you can install on your web server to allow clients to seek, forward, and rewind an IWave file. You can choose not to install the CGI utility, but users won't be able to seek.

The Internet Wave Encoder is fairly straightforward; you simply choose the WAV files you want to convert, enter the name and title of the file, then choose your compression method. You have four different choices:

Compression	Best Used for	Output Sample Rate
VSC77	Low-quality, speech-only files	5kHz
VSC112	Mid-quality audio, still best for speech	8kHz
VSC154	Very good speech and so-so music quality	11kHz
VSC224	Highest-quality audio, for 28.8Kbps users	16kHz

Follow the instructions on Internet Wave's site for more on using the CGI utility and linking it to your HTML file.

In order to make your browser play Internet Wave files, you have to assign that MIME type to the Internet Wave player. The first time you try to listen to a file, you will be prompted for the application to use; simply choose the program called IWAVE.EXE and associate it with all VMF files. The player can open local WAV files as well as Internet Wave files (see Figure A.5).

Figure A.5 Internet Wave is a free, audio-only streaming player.

The good news is that Internet Wave is completely free. To get the server utility and encoder, you just need to register and download them to begin hosting some Internet Wave files. Vocaltec makes Internet Wave and Internet Phone, software that can be used to talk with other people over the Web.

Vocaltec
35 Industrial Parkway
Northvale, NJ 07647
(201) 768-9400
info@vocaltec.com
www.vocaltec.com/iwave.htm

Headspace's Beatnik

Beatnik is an audio system that can play a wide variety of files. Describing Beatnik as just another audio system doesn't do it justice, however, because it's really an interactive music format. Users can actually interact with the music by changing pitch, tone, speed, playing instruments, starting new tracks, and much more. Alas, Beatnik doesn't really stream, but it doesn't have to because its files are small and play back very quickly.

You play Beatnik files with a plug-in for Macintosh, Windows95, and NT. It can play MIDI, MOD, AIFF, WAV, and AU files. The real fun is with Beatnik's own Rich Music Format (RMF). These files allow you to interact with them. For example, you can click on a picture to play a track, then start a drum track or play a short sound effect. Another effect, as shown in Figure A.6, is to glide your mouse over a picture to change the pitch of a note and much more. Basically, the Beatnik author can program the RMF files to do almost anything. The best way to learn about Beatnik is to experience it yourself. Once you install the plug-in, you can try out a series of cool sample pages that show off what Beatnik can do.

Creating RMF files can be complex, since there are so many things you can do with them. You need to use the Beatnik Editor, which is currently only available for Macintosh users. The Editor allows you to import music from MIDI, WAV, AIFF, and AU and convert them into RMF format. It also has watermarking ability to add copyright information with a 40-bit encryption algorithm. The Beatnik Editor for Windows 95/NT *should* be available by the time you read this.

Headspace was formed in 1993 to deliver rich music to the Internet. Besides the Beatnik player and Editor, Headspace also licenses RMF music to users for use on their web pages.

Headspace, Inc.
217 South B Street
San Mateo, CA 94401
(650) 696-9400
www.headspace.com

Crescendo by LiveUpdate

Crescendo is a streaming MIDI system; but realistically, MIDI files are usually small enough to be downloaded. Streaming MIDI files is almost like streaming a small JPEG image. Four- or five-minute MIDI files (average length for a song) tend to be around 40 to 50KB. That's why Crescendo is best for larger MIDI files.

Figure A.6 Check out the sample pages to interact and play some Beatnik music.

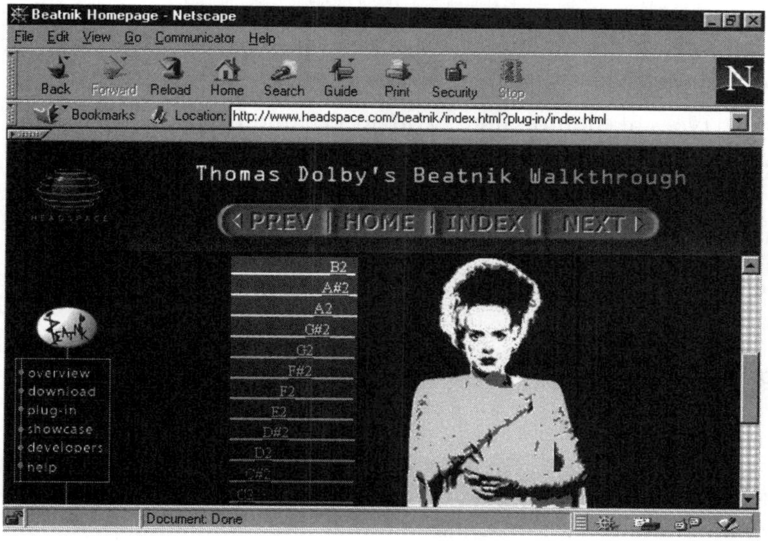

Crescendo works in one of two ways: Web developers can make their sites MIDI stream-enabled (with its StreamSite software) or users can purchase Crescendo Plus to stream any MIDI file. So, the burden of listening to streaming MIDI files lies with both users and webmasters.

To allow streaming MIDI on your site, you need to purchase StreamSite. Once it is installed, anyone with the Crescendo plug-in can listen to streaming MIDI. StreamSite comes in a personal version ($49.95), educational ($195), small commercial ($395), and for large commercial/ISPs (custom pricing).

Crescendo has a very compact player that is displayed on the web page with Stop and Play buttons as well as volume control. You can save MIDI files, unless the webmaster disabled the feature for a particular file. The regular Crescendo player can only stream at StreamSites; otherwise, you need to use the Crescendo Plus player, which can stream anywhere.

You can download the Crescendo player free, but Crescendo Plus costs $19.95. The plug-in is available for Macintosh, Windows 3.1, and Windows 95/NT.

LiveUpdate division of LABTECH
400 Research Drive
Wilmington, MA 01887
(978) 657-5400
www.liveupdate.com

EchoCast by EchoSpeech

EchoCast is a streaming audio program that handles both voice and music applications and generally has a pretty decent quality. It's possible for 14.4Kbps modem users to listen to EchoCast, but 28.8Kbps is best.

EchoCast uses two types of compression: Echo Speech and DolbyNet. The Echo Speech compression is good for speech-only applications, while DolbyNet is good for music. DolbyNet compresses at a 18:1 ratio, so sound can be as small as 7Kbps.

EchoCast comes in three versions:

EchoCast Lite. This low-cost version is just for on-demand audio at a maximum sampling rate of 8kHz. It costs $49.

EchoCast Pro. This professional version ups the sampling rates to include 8, 11, 16, or 22kHz; however, it cannot broadcast live audio. EchoCast Pro costs $249.

EchoCast Live!. For live EchoCast audio, this is what you need. There is no limit to the number of streams you can serve; it just depends on your bandwidth. EchoCast will automatically archive the event for later rebroadcast. It is available for Windows 95/NT and requires FTP access. You can also buy this in an intranet version. EchoCast Live! costs $399.

You only need the EchoCast plug-in to listen to files, which is available for Windows 3.1, 95/NT, and Macintosh for both Internet Explorer and Navigator. When you encounter an EchoCast sound, the plug-in will load and play the sound. The EchoCast player looks like a generic audio player, with volume control, Pause/Play button, and a Stop button. It also tells you the author, title, copyright information, and running time.

EchoCast is by Echo Speech, a company that does audio research and develops compression. EchoCast is its flagship product. EchoSpeech compression is also available for licensing.

Echo Speech Corporation
6460 Via Real
Carpinteria, CA 93013
(805) 684-4593
www.echospeech.com

ToolVox by Voxware

ToolVox is a streaming audio system. More accurately, it specializes in speech applications, like TrueSpeech by DSP Group. ToolVox works with your existing web server and, like all server-less systems, the number of simultaneous users depends on your bandwidth.

You play files with the ToolVox player 2.0. It has a sliding Seek bar to rewind or forward through a clip and regular buttons like Play and Pause. You can also change playback speed without changing the pitch of the original sound (see Figure A.7).

To create ToolVox files you need to use the ToolVox Gold Encoder or ToolVox Basic. The Gold Encoder has advanced options like batch encoding, recording support, and VoiceFonts, which allow you to change voices into cartoon-like voices. The Basic version doesn't have all that or an advanced codec, but it is free. ToolVox uses its own codec to compress speech so that one minute of speech takes up only 18KB.

The player is available free for Windows 3.1, Windows95, Macintosh, and UNIX. ToolVox is priced at $179 for a single site license and $999 for an unlimited site license.

Voxware, Inc.
305 College Road East
Princeton, NJ 08540
(609) 514-4100
www.voxware.com
www.toolvox.com

Figure A.7 ToolVox can play sounds embedded into a web page or by using this external player.

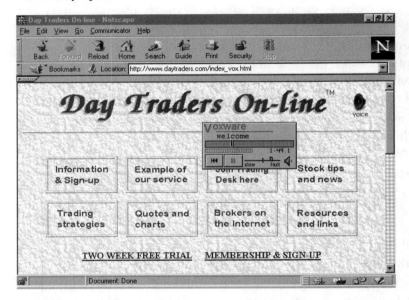

Summary

This appendix has shown a few things. First, there are too many streaming multimedia systems to cover in depth in just one book. Second, there is a wide range of products available, allowing you to stream MIDI, audio, video banner ads, interactive music, or use high-end video servers. Third, this means that we've included all the major streaming multimedia programs that are currently available—the rest are smaller, lesser-known programs.

WHAT'S ON
the CD-ROM?

The CD-ROM contains:

- Demo versions of popular streaming client programs and client/server systems
- Audio and video editing software so you can capture, edit, and compress audio and video files
- Sample versions of popular animation software
- Sample video files
- A glossary of terms used in streaming multimedia and computer video
- A supplement to Chapter 4 containing information on video capture cards and devices
- Full manufacturer's contact information including web links that take you to their websites

What is Freeware/Shareware?

Freeware is software that is free and distributed by disk, through BBS systems and the Internet. There is no charge for freeware, so it can be distributed freely as long as the user follows the software's license agreement.

Shareware (also known as user supported software) is a revolutionary means of distributing software created by individuals or companies too small to make inroads into the more conventional retail distribution networks . The authors of Shareware retain all rights to the software under the copyright laws while still allowing free distribution. This gives the user the chance to freely obtain and try out software to see if it fits their needs. Shareware should not be confused with Public Domain software even though they are often obtained from the same sources.

If you continue to use Shareware after trying it out, you are expected to register your use with the author and pay a registration fee. What you get in return depends on the author, but may include a printed manual, free updates, telephone support, etc.

Hardware Requirements

Since the CD-ROM contains many different types of programs, it's best to read each program's READ.ME file for more on hardware requirements. However, there are some general requirements. You should have audio and video capabilities and a CD-ROM drive (naturally). Also, you should have a fast Internet connection (preferably 56Kbps) for viewing streaming video.

For Windows 95/NT

The minimum requirement for many programs is a 486 66MHz computer with 8MB RAM, and at least 10MB of hard disk space. However, for video editing and capture, you should use a Pentium computer (Pentium II or other MMX computer is best) with over 16MB RAM, and more than 40 MB of hard disk space.

For Macintosh:

Generally the lowest requirement is a Macintosh with a 68020 processor, but you get better results with a Power Mac running System 7.0 or greater, a minimum of 8MB of RAM and at least 10MB of hard disk space.

Installing the Software

1. Insert the CD-ROM into your CD-ROM drive.

2. Each program is contained in its own folder on the CD-ROM. Open the folder containing the software you would like to install and either double click the install program (e.g., SETUP.EXE in the MGI folder) or decompress the file archive to your hard drive using the appropriate decompression utility. Windows files are in .ZIP format, Macintosh files are in .SIT format, and UNIX files are in the .TAR format.

Using the Software

The software is separated into the following categories:

Streaming Media Players

Audioactive Player version 1.2 for Windows 3.1, version 1.3 for Windows 95/NT and version 1.2A for Macintosh. Streaming audio player that can also be used as a MPEG Layer 3 player.

NET TOOB Stream version 3.5a for Windows 3.1, 95 and NT and Macintosh. All purpose-video player that can also play streaming MPEG movies.

StreamWorks Player version 3.01 for Windows NT 4.0 and UNIX. Player that allows you to experience streaming audio and video StreamWorks files.

The DJ player version 3.02 for Windows 95/NT. Listen to streaming music in various caterogies via a customized RealAudio-interface.

Complete Streaming Media Systems

TrueSpeech Internet Players and Converters, player versions 3.1b for Windows 3.x, version 3.2b for Windows 95/NT, version 1.04 for Macintosh 68K and version 1.04 for Power Macintosh. Also converters, version 1.0 for Windows 3.x, 95/NT and encoder version 1.0b for Macintosh. Includes a Batch Conversion Utility 1.0. Completely free streaming audio system.

VDOLive Player and VDOLive Debut Server and Tools version 3.0 for Windows95 and NT. A trial version of VDOLive complete with client, server and encoder tools.

TrueStream Video Server, Player, and Producer (Server version 1.2 for Linux, Windows NT, and Solaris, Player version 1.2 for Windows 95/NT, and Producer version 1.2 for Windows 95/NT and Mac OS). Demo version of this video streaming system that has servers for multiple platforms, client software, as well as the Adobe Premiere plug-in.

Audio Editors

CoolEdit 96 for Windows95 and NT. Shareware version of an easy to use audio editor for Windows.

CoolEdit Pro for Windows95 and NT. Demo version of a more advanced version of CoolEdit.

GoldWave version 3.24 for Windows NT. Windows audio editor.

Sound Forge version 4.0 for Windows 3.1, 95, and NT. Audio editor for Widows.

Macromedia SoundEdit 16. Sound editor for Macintosh.

Video Editors

MGI VideoWave for Windows95 and NT 4.0 . 30-day trial version of this video editing program for Windows.

Ulead MediaStudio Pro version 5.0 for Windows95 and NT. Trial version of a Windows video editor.

Animation Editors

mBED Interactor version 1.1 for Mac, and Windows 95/NT. Creates interactive HTML pages.

Macromedia Director 6.0 for Macintosh and Windows 95/NT. Creates interactive Shockwave movies.

Macromedia Flash 2 for Macintosh and Windows 95/NT. Creates vector animations with Flash.

Miscellaneous Streaming Software

EyeQ, the Multimedia Manager, January 1998 version for Windows95, and NT 4.01. Multimedia manager that installs a wide range of players.

iQ version 1.16 for Windows95. Demo software that enhances your streaming audio experience with 3-D audio.

V-Active for NetShow version 1.0 for Windows 95/NT. Creates interactive NetShow movies.

V-Active for RealVideo version 2.0 for Windows 95/NT. Creates interactive RealVideo 5.0 movies.

Video Express Mail version 2.3.27 for Windows 95/NT. Evaluation software that creates and sends streaming e-mail to other users.

Video Express Viewer version 2.2.10 for Windows 95/NT. Evaluation software that plays NetShow and other file formats.

Sample Videos: MPEG, AVI, and QuickTime

Four Palms Royalty Free Digital Video. Sample videos in MPEG, AVI and QuickTime format.

More Information You Can Use

Additional information on external capture devices, video capture cards, and video editing equipment

List of manufacturers

Glossary

User Assistance and Information

The software accompanying this book is being provided as is without warranty or support of any kind. Should you require basic installation assistance, or if your media is defective, please call our product support number at (212) 850-6194 weekdays between 9 am and 4 pm Eastern Standard Time. Or, we can be reached via e-mail at: **wprtusw@wiley.com**. To reach the author, e-mail jose@alvear.com.

To place additional orders or to request information about other Wiley products, please call (800) 879-4539.

INDEX

hotlinks, 7–8, 32
HTML
    creating links, 172
    and the Internet, 48
HTTP (HyperText Transfer
    Protocol), 48
    and bandwidth, 56–57
    HTTP streaming, 49, 51,
        52
    and Audioactive,
        117–120
    and server-less system, 51,
        52
    and VivoActive, 33–34, 127,
        138
H.263, 73, 162
HyperText Transfer Protocol.
    See HTTP

I

Imagemind Software, Inc., 41,
    315. *See also* Video
    Express Mail, Video
    Express Email
    address, 315
implementing streaming
    multimedia, 46–48
Indeo Video Raw YVU9C, 73
Intel H.263 and Vivo
    H.263, 162
Intelligence At Large, Inc., 179
Internet
    and bandwidth, 57
    bottlenecks, 16
    broadcasts, 18, 384
    building communities,
        281–282
    busiest times, 23
    history of multimedia, 3–4
    how it works, 48–49
    Internet 2, 390
    and I/P multicasting, 59
    protocols, 48–49
    telephony, 387–388
    vs. intranet, 60
    wireless access, 376–377
Internet 2, 390
Internet Phone, 30
Internet Service Providers.
    See ISPs

Internet Wave, 29–30
    cost, 29
    company, 29
    website, 29
Internet World, 18
Intervista Software, 290. *See
    also* WorldView 2.5
InterVU, 14
intranet. *See also* IP
    multicasting
    adding bandwidth, 56
    for high-quality
        audio/video, 16
    vs. Internet, 60
IP multicasting, 261–262. *See
    also* video networks
    benefits of, 57–58
    the future, 378–379
    implementing, 58–59
    pros and cons, 272–273
    website, 59
IP Multicast Initiative, 59,
    139
IP/TV, 270272
    a client/server system, 270
    company, 272
    IP/TV Program Guide,
        270, 271
    IP/TV Server, 270
    IP/TV Viewer, 270,
        271–272
ISDN, 374
    and quality, 16
ISPs (Internet Service
    Providers)
    and IP multicasting, 59
Iterated Systems, Inc., 361

J

Java
    description, 10
    and Flash, 37
    and the future, 388
    and LivePicture, 40
    and no-client systems, 51,
        238–239
    and ShockWave, 37
    and streaming video, 31
Jutvision, 297–298

K

Kinetix, 299

L

Landform, 299
Lernout & Hauspie. *See*
    CELP
Ligos Technology, 299
Liquid Audio, 8, 26–28, 89–90
    a client/server system, 89
    company, 26, 102
    cost, 27
    future of online music
        commerce, 100–101
    growing market, 101
    hosting services, 98
    Liquid MusicPlayer CD, 90,
        93–96
        Buy CD button, 95–96
        Buy Download button,
            95
        to download, 96
        Free Sample button, 95
        and URLs, 93
    Liquid MusicServer, 90, 93
        cost, 98
    Liquid Passport, 96–98
        to view, 98
    Liquid Track, 90
        to buy and download, 96
        creating, 90–93
    Liquifier Pro, 89–90
        cost, 93
        using to convert
            clips, 90–93
    music-only streaming
        play, 8, 27
    and piracy, 116
    pros and cons, 99
    use of Liquid Audio, 99
    website, 26
Liquid Audio, Inc., 26, 102
    address, 102
Liquid Motion Pro, 346
Liquid MusicPlayer CD, 27,
    90, 93–96
    Buy CD button, 95–96
    Buy Download button, 95
    to download, 96

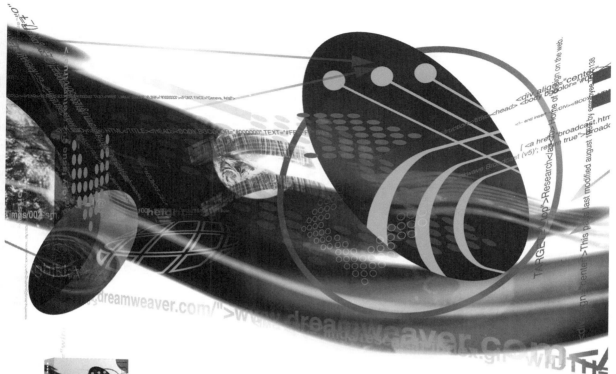

Discover the Design Tool of Your Dreams!

macromedia
DREAMWEAVER™
The Visual Tool for Professional Web Site Design

For the first time, you can take advantage of the productivity offered by a visual HTML development environment without giving up any control over source code.

Dreamweaver™ features error-free Roundtrip HTML™ between visual mode and source editors, absolute positioning, cascading style sheets, a Dynamic HTML animation timeline, an extensible JavaScript

behavior library, drag-and-drop table and frame design, and a repeating elements library for managing sitewide changes.

Dreamweaver integrates with your favorite HTML editor, assuring code integrity, flexibility, and access. Only Dreamweaver provides simultaneous WYSIWYG and HTML source editing.

Now you can use HTML layers, an animation timeline, and a library of multimedia JavaScript behaviors to create multimedia content without scripting. You can even extend the

user interface with your own JavaScript behaviors.

Site management features include style sheets, FTP for remote sites, file locking for collaborative development, and browser targeting reports.

Get all this in one professional package with Macromedia Dreamweaver!

For more information, visit
http://www.macromedia.com/ software/dreamweaver
or call **800 457 1774.**

macromedia®

Now the **best tools** for Windows and Macintosh multimedia also happen to be the **best for JAVA!**

The Director of Your Dreams

Create interactive applications for delivery over the Web and on CD-ROM, hybrid CD, and DVD-ROM using the popular and powerful **DIRECTOR®6 MULTIMEDIA STUDIO™** and Macromedia® Shockwave™.

Develop interactive, animated sales and marketing presentations, informational kiosks, educational and entertainment titles, training tutorials, and promotional web games that keep your audience coming back for more.

Now the most powerful cross-platform multimedia tool is also the most powerful Java multimedia tool. Play back your Director files as Java applets with the new Director Export Xtra for Java.

Web Multimedia in a Flash

If you want to create winning animations or integrate existing graphics into your HTML web pages, you can do it all with Macromedia **FLASH™2**

Use Flash to create animated, interactive advertising banners, navigation buttons, logos, technical illustrations, cartoons, and more. The compact Shockwave Flash player makes it a snap for everyone on the Web to view your creations. Flash files stream (play as they download), so your content immediately appears in Web browsers, even over slower modem connections.

Flash has always been the easiest way to create fast web animations for Windows and Macintosh. Now it's the easiest for Java, too, with the new Flash Player for Java.

For more information, visit **http://www.macromedia.com/software/director** or **http://www.macromedia.com/software/flash.**

To purchase, visit **http://www.macromall.com** or your favorite reseller or call **800 457 1774.**

macromedia®

John Wiley & Sons, Inc. is not responsible for orders placed with Macromedia.

What's on the CD-ROM?

Streaming media players
- Audioactive Player
- NetTOOB Stream
- StreamWorks Player
- The DJ Player

Complete streaming media systems
- TrueSpeech Internet Players and Converters
- VDOLive Player and VDOLive [...] Server and Tools
- TrueStream Video Server, TrueS[...] Video Player, and TrueStream Vi[...] Producer

Audio editors
- CoolEdit 96 and CoolEdit Pro
- Goldwave
- Sound Forge
- Macromedia SoundEdit 16

Video editors
- MGI VideoWave
- Ulead MediaStudio Pro

Animation creation tools and editors
- mBED Interactor
- Macromedia Director
- Macromedia Flash 2

Miscellaneous software
- EyeQ, The Multimedia Manager
- iQ

[handwritten note: June 28 (Wed) Test / June 29 (Thur) 7-9pm / Test.]

[...] w
[...] eo
[...] r
[...] G, AVI
[...] ree Digital Video

[...] can use
- [...] n on external [...] o devices, video capture cards, and video editing equipment
- List of Manufacturers
- Glossary

CUSTOMER NOTE: IF THIS BOOK IS ACCOMPANIED BY SOFTWARE, PLEASE READ THE FOLLOWING BEFORE OPENING THE PACKAGE.

To use this CD-ROM, your system must meet the following requirements:
- **Platform/Processor/Operating System.** Windows 3.x, 95 or NT (Minimum 486, but Pentium or Pentium II preferred). Macintosh or Power Macintosh System 7.x or above. UNIX operating systems (Linux, Solaris).
- **RAM.** Minimum 8MB, but most programs require 16MB or more.
- **Hard Drive Space.** 10MB for most files.
- **Peripherals.** None required, but you should have a sound card and speakers. For video capture, you need a video capture device.